UNPROFITABLE SCHOOLING

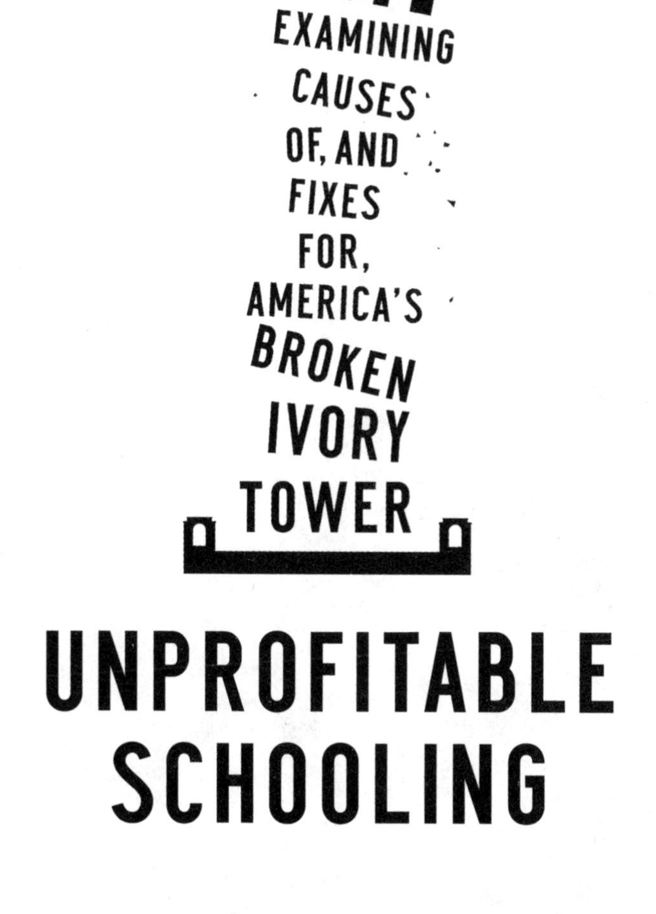

TODD J. ZYWICKI and NEAL P. McCLUSKEY, Eds.

ISBN: 978-1-948647-04-5
eISBN: 978-1-948647-05-2

Jacket design: Spencer Fuller, Faceout Studio.
Printed in the United States of America.

Library of Congress Cataloging-in-Publication Data

Zywicki, Todd J., editor. | McCluskey, Neal P., 1972- editor.
Unprofitable schooling : examining causes of, and fixes for, America's broken ivory tower / Todd J. Zywicki and Neal P. Mccluskey, eds.
page cm
Washington, D.C.: Cato Institute, 2019.
Includes bibliographical references.
ISBN 9781948647052 (ebook) | ISBN 9781948647045 (alk. paper)
1. Higher education and state--United States. 2. Federal aid to higher education--United States. 3. College costs--United States.
4. Education, Higher--Economic aspects--United States. 5. For-profit universities and colleges--United States.

LC173

378.73--dc23 2018053178

To Claire: May your life be as enriched by your professors as mine has been.
—Todd J. Zywicki

To Iona and Nat: You have taught me more about what matters in education than any book ever could.
—Neal McCluskey

CONTENTS

LIST OF ILLUSTRATIONS

Figures

Tables

ABBREVIATIONS AND ACRONYMS

AACSB–Association to Advance Collegiate Schools of Business
AAU–Association of American Universities
AAUP–American Association of University Professors
APSCU–Association of Private Sector Colleges and Universities
CFPB–Consumer Financial Protection Bureau
CHEA–Council for Higher Education Accreditation
ED–United States Department of Education
EDMC–Education Management Corporation
FAFSA–Free Application for Federal Student Assistance
FTE–full-time equivalent
GDP–gross domestic product
GE–gainful employment
HEA–Higher Education Act
HELP–Senate Committee on Health, Education, Labor and Pensions
HMO–health maintenance organization
IPEDS–Integrated Postsecondary Education Data System
IRB–institutional review board
MCO–managed care organization
NCA–North Central Association
PEI–prestige, excellence, and influence
PPACA–Patient Protection and Affordable Care Act

Introduction

Todd J. Zywicki and Neal P. McCluskey

Let's start with some basic facts:

- Inflation-adjusted undergraduate tuition and fees at public four-year colleges have roughly tripled over the past 30 years.[1] At some of the priciest private institutions they now exceed $50,000 a year.[2] That does not include room and board.
- For students who entered college in 2010, the six-year completion rate for four- and two-year programs was only 54.8 percent.[3]
- The percentage of undergraduate students ages 18 to 24 in their fourth (senior) year or above who ever received student loans rose from 50.5 percent in the 1989–90 school year to 67.7 percent in 2011–12. The average, inflation-adjusted cumulative loan amount ballooned from $15,400 to $26,600. That excludes Parent PLUS loans, which parents take out on their children's behalf, which grew even faster and higher.[4]
- As of January 1, 2016, 43 percent of federal student loan borrowers were either behind on their repayments or in a program allowing postponement of payments.[5]
- The National Assessment of Adult Literacy, conducted in 1992 and 2003, showed that the percentage of adults with educational attainment topping out at a bachelor's degree that were proficient

prose readers—able to read and comprehend writings such as news articles or brochures—dropped from 40 to 31. For "document" literacy—the ability to read and use a tax form or food label—the proficiency rate fell from 37 to 25. For people holding advanced degrees, the percentage scoring proficient fell from 51 to 41 in prose and from 45 to 31 percent in document literacy.[6] The Program for the International Assessment of Adult Competencies is a more recent analysis that is not fully equivalent to the National Assessment of Adult Literacy, but in 2014 it found that only 27 percent of Americans ages 16 to 65 topping out a bachelor's degree were in the top two of six levels of reading proficiency, and only 36 percent with advanced degrees were.[7]

- Time spent studying by full-time students dropped from about 25 hours per week in 1961 to 20 hours in 1980, to 13 hours in 2003.[8]
- National Center for Education Statistics data show that the inflation-adjusted earnings of full-time year-round workers ages 25 to 34 with degrees fell between 2000 and 2015. The annual earnings for the median such person whose top attainment was a bachelor's degree was $55,640 in 2000, dropping to $50,630 in 2015. For someone with a postgraduate degree, earnings dipped from $66,910 to $60,760.[9]

Collectively, these figures paint a bleak, frustrating picture of ballooning costs and declining returns in higher education. Coupled with major psychological milestones passed in recent years—in 2010, total student debt surpassed total credit card debt for the first time, and in 2012 total student debt broke the $1 trillion barrier—a lot of people have been asking, increasingly aloud: What is wrong with higher education? Is college worth all it costs? How can I know if I'm getting ripped off?

Whatever answers Americans are coming up with, they apparently are not on the side of academia. In September 1985, an already low 39 percent of survey respondents agreed with the statement, "College costs in general are such that most people are able to afford to pay for a college education." By 2011 that had dropped to 22 percent.[10] Meanwhile, the survey research organization Public Agenda found that between 2008 and 2016 the percentage of Americans who said yes to the question "do you think that a college education is necessary for a person to be successful in today's work world" plunged from 55 to 42 percent, after having risen steadily between 2000 and 2008.[11] Finally, while a 2014 survey of college chief academic officers found 96 percent thinking that their schools were "somewhat" or "very effective" at preparing students for the workplace, only 34 percent of business leaders in a separate poll strongly or moderately agreed that graduates had the necessary "skills and competencies" to be successful employees.[12]

Over the past several years, members of the public have been offered many answers to their pressing questions about what is happening in higher education. There have been those who have said that, yes, there are some troubles, but on the whole everything is functioning pretty much as it should. As economist Sandy Baum has written, college "does not always pay off immediately and does not pay off for everyone. The visibility of the minority of students for whom the decision to go to college (or at least go to their particular college) turned out to be questionable creates an exaggerated impression of the risks."[13]

Others have acknowledged big problems in higher education, especially affordability, and have identified who they think are the primary culprits: states that do not subsidize their public colleges and universities enough, forcing prices higher. In 2015, Terry Hartle, senior vice president at the American Council on Education, testified to a congressional committee, "The biggest factor driving price increases for most American families is the steep cuts by states in operating support for public higher education. In the last 25 years, states have systematically reduced spending in higher education, resulting in increased tuition at public institutions to offset reduced state revenue."[14] Although this assertion may seem to make intuitive sense, whether this actually has been the case is disputed.[15] Most obviously, prices have rapidly increased at private nonprofit institutions as well as at public ones, although the price increases at public colleges have been faster.[16]

Yet others recognize academia's troubles, especially its costs, but argue that they are, essentially, inevitable. Some higher education analysts believe that the cost of college must rise because it is an industry reliant on labor—human beings—and highly educated ones at that. Like the performing arts, examined by economist William Baumol, higher education may suffer from a "cost disease" at certain margins. Because these human beings, let's call them "professors," cannot be replaced by technology without a potentially significant change to the student learning environment, unlike, say, replacing assembly line workers with machines, higher education cannot become more efficient and realize big gains in productivity. So while makers of cars or smartphones can earn more by virtue of greater productivity, the people of academia cannot. But they must receive increasing compensation to keep up with the rising earnings of all those people making cars, computers, and other items in which technology can easily be substituted for labor. For this reason, economists Robert Archibald and David Feldman posit that when it comes to academia's cost problem, "the villain, as much as there is one, is economic growth itself. Economic growth has a wide variety of effects on the economy, but in the case of higher education . . . these effects all seem to conspire to make costs rise faster than the general inflation rate."[17]

Whereas Archibald and Feldman question the existence of a higher education "villain," many others think they have caught one red-handed: for-profit colleges. Enrollment in these institutions grew dramatically between 2004 and 2010, ballooning from about 880,000 to more than 2 million students.[18] Since that time, however, an unprecedented regulatory assault led by the Obama administration crushed the industry, leading to an overall shrinkage of the sector and the high-profile collapse of several industry leaders. These schools, often found in strip malls or online rather than on multi-acre, leafy campuses, respond quickly to changing student demands and enable working people to take the classes they want and move on. But they have also produced some questionable outcomes, including (a) just 42 percent eight-year completion rates at four-year institutions for students who started school in 2008 and (b) higher three-year loan default rates than the public and private nonprofit sectors.[19] For people entering repayment in 2013, proprietary schools had a cohort default rate of 15 percent, public institutions 11 percent, and private nonprofit institutions 7 percent.[20] At the same time, these are open-enrollment institutions that serve the most marginal students in the higher education sector—lower-income, less-qualified students with weaker academic backgrounds. When compared with the more relevant benchmark of community colleges, which still cater to more traditional, better-off students,[21] the outcomes of for-profit colleges are as good as or better, at least as measured by program completion rates.[22] That is not a particularly high bar to clear: for students who started community college in 2008, only 55 percent had completed any school by 2016.

Finally, there is the explanation that seems to best fit higher education's "misery index" of skyrocketing costs, declining learning, and increasing demand for degrees in jobs previously not requiring them. Most consistent with the available evidence is that the system has been fundamentally corrupted by massive subsidies coupled with stifled competition. The reality is that the people who control and are employed by colleges are as self-interested as anyone else—they can always think of something they could do with more money, so they take it from whatever source they can, including tuition-paying students via higher prices. Meanwhile, again from normal motivations, traditional colleges lobby to keep innovative, lower-cost alternatives out of the market, lest they face competition and have to give up many of the things they like—maybe tenure, luxurious facilities, or reduced teaching loads—to compete. Couple this with aid and direct subsidies to public institutions subverting students' natural incentives to get the best education at the lowest cost, and the recipe for higher education problems is firmly in place.

This volume looks beneath these contemporary political disputes to examine the question, "How did we get here, and where should we go?" Such an investigation requires an approach that looks at the issues from the perspective of both economics and history to understand the incentive and governance structures that have contributed to the peculiar combination of rising costs and declining quality in higher education. That combination is anomalous in the modern economy. Most economies advance in the opposite fashion—simultaneously declining costs and increasing quality. Through the dynamic process of competition, consumer choice, and creative destruction, other sectors innovate and respond to consumer demand to improve their product. Yet most higher education today (with the notable exception of for-profit colleges) appears to lack clear incentives to meet customer demand or to improve quality and reduce price. When traditional colleges do compete, they typically do so on margins unrelated to education quality, such as more elaborate dormitories, more successful football teams, or better-tasting cafeteria food.

In this volume, we ask whether the lessons learned from market competition in other sectors of the economy can be applied to higher education to bring about similar results: innovation, improved quality, and lower costs. Indeed, higher education seems ripe for shakeup. Yet innovation in that market is stifled by a dense network of third-party government financing, severe barriers to entry in accreditation, and maybe governance structures that put employees (faculty members and senior administrators) in a de facto ownership role.

We organized this volume into three—we hope logical—sections to take readers deep into America's ivory tower, and each section consists of several chapters penned by contributors with great experience and insights into postsecondary education. We commence with a focus on the historical development of and rationales behind American higher education. Next, we move into the current state of things. Finally, we feature chapters laying out the argument for unleashing competition in higher education.

In the first section, Jane Shaw Stroup, former president of the John W. Pope Center for Higher Education Policy (now the James G. Martin Center for Academic Renewal) kicks things off with a history of for-profit education in the days before the Morrill Act, the federal legislation that funded land-grant universities such as the University of Illinois and Purdue University. In it, she details (a) the crucial but unglamorous role that for-profit education had in training people like farmers and engineers and (b) how elites—not the people typically involved in the day-to-day work of agriculture and building stuff—pushed for "free" colleges to instruct people in a seemingly more dignified way.

Richard Vedder picks up the Morrill Act ball in the next chapter, examining how reasonable it is to conclude that this law (actually two laws, one passed in 1862 and one in 1890) essentially jump-started the American economy, as many academics, economists, and policymakers have proclaimed. Vedder—a professor emeritus of economics at Ohio University and founder of the Center for College Affordability and Productivity—determines that this view is mythological. The nation's great economic leap began well before the Morrill Act had had any significant effect.

Rounding out part one, West Virginia University economics professor Joshua Hall explores the development of federal student aid—all those grants, loans, work study, and so on—and how it elevated accreditation from a friendly measure to a towering wall barring new options from entering the market. Accreditation used to be a way for colleges to agree on certain measures of quality and have a membership organization—an accreditor—take a friendly look at a school and point out things to improve, and if a school proved impossibly recalcitrant, withhold the seal. Now, having that seal is the gateway to more than $100 billion in federal student aid, and not having it essentially means death. The gateway has proven a huge problem both for anyone who wants to bring a new school to life—you've got to live for a while to be accredited, but you've got to be accredited to live—and for any school that is different from what the big, old-fashioned accreditors demand.

The middle section of the book looks at things as they are today, starting with a chapter by George Mason University Law School dean emeritus Daniel Polsby. Calling on his decades of experience residing in the ivory tower and his own expeditions into the finance and functioning of George Mason, Polsby tries to get at what exactly is driving up college prices. He considers all the major explanations, and only one seems to ultimately ring true: it's the subsidies, dammit.

Next, Roger Meiners, the Goolsby-Rosenthal Endowed Chair in Law and Economics at the University of Texas at Arlington, takes on tenure, a favorite punching bag of people on the political right, especially, who think it protects taxpayer-funded employment for a (very much) left-wing professoriate and subsidizes laziness to boot. Meiners defends tenure as originally conceived, takes more issue with what it has become, and discusses what is to be done with this unusual academic institution.

How about administrative bloat? Todd Zywicki from George Mason University and Chris Koopman from the Center for Growth and Opportunity at Utah State University try to get their arms around this phenomenon. Essentially, they report, administration—and administrators—have expanded much faster than schools' academic functions and the professoriate that executes them. But how can that be if it is the professors who supposedly control academic institutions? Zywicki and Koopman suggest that (a) the increasing demand for lots of services and amenities by heavily subsidized students, (b) bureaucratic requirements from the governments that furnish those subsides, and (c) professorial acquiescence may all be to blame.

Rounding out part two of the book, Scott Masten of the University of Michigan examines the tradition of shared university governance by governing boards and tenured faculty. Rather than, say, a CEO making decisions for colleges, power is distributed among boards of trustees, presidents, and tenured faculty. The results are certainly inefficient decision-making and an appearance, at least, that nobody—or maybe the wrong somebody—is steering the ship. But, argues Masten, the arrangement may actually work well. At the very least, it was successful for a long time, vaulting America's higher education system to arguably the top place in the world, and changes should not be made in haste.

In the third and final section of the book, we present analyses laying out the need for robust competition in higher education, including for-profit options. This starts with a reprint of a 2014 Pope Center essay by the late Henry Manne, former dean of the George Mason University Law School, written not long before his death. In it Manne posits that all universities—not just those with investors and a certain tax status—are for-profit operations. Officially not-for-profit institutions do not distribute the revenue they get in excess of costs of production to shareholders, but the people in higher education are certainly rewarded with higher salaries, or lighter teaching loads, and all sorts of benefits that are, for all practical purposes, profits.

William Shughart of Utah State University and Jayme Lemke of the Mercatus Center next compare for-profit and community colleges, institutions that often compete for the same, often more marginal, students but could not be perceived as more different. For-profit schools are often seen as "agile predators," whereas community colleges seem like soft, gentle bunnies. Neither sector, however, seems to perform very well in completion rates, although proprietary schools are much more responsive to consumer demands. In the end, Shughart and Lemke argue that changing how we finance higher education is a much more important factor for improving outcomes than vilifying or elevating any particular sector.

Delving deeper into for-profit schooling, Michael DeBow, professor at Samford University's Cumberland Law School, chronicles the sudden explosion of for-profit institutions in the early 2000s and their only slightly less spectacular decline in recent years. He argues that a normative bias against profit—which drove heated rhetorical, political, and regulatory assaults against proprietary colleges by the Obama administration and like-minded people in states and Congress—explains the steep decline, while the profit motive that incentivizes schools to quickly and efficiently offer programs that are in workforce demand and to phase out those that are not explains the initial ascent. Far from being dangerous, such incentives are what are sorely lacking in higher education, and they must be allowed to function if postsecondary education is going to be quickly and inexpensively made available to broad swaths of people in a fast-evolving economy.

Finally, David Hyman, a doctor, lawyer, and Georgetown University law professor, examines a sector in which both nonprofit and for-profit entities have been able to compete on a relatively level playing field: health care. Hyman argues that the evidence shows no meaningful difference in care or outcomes between for-profit and nonprofit hospitals. Overall, he concludes that there is no compelling evidence to support deep, knee-jerk hostility to profit in education or health care and that a lot of evidence suggests that we should, in fact, embrace profit and free markets in both areas.

We hope that by the end of this book everything feels tied together in a nice bow. Or, at least, the nicest bow possible. Because if anything is clear, it is that the ivory tower is in a significant shambles, and making it neat and tidy is going to take a lot of change.

PART I:

Historical Perspectives on Competition and Government's Role in Higher Education

CHAPTER ONE

What Really Spurred the Morrill Act?

Jane Shaw Stroup

This chapter stems from a hypothesis proposed by the late Henry Manne that there must have been a thriving for-profit education system in the first half of the 19th century, one that has been largely ignored in recent years. In a paper in honor of the late law professor Larry Ribstein, Manne argued that the 1862 Morrill Act, which authorized the creation of land-grant universities to teach the "agricultural and mechanical arts," was stimulated by the success of these for-profit schools—but also crushed them.[1]

This essay explores the for-profit postsecondary industry in the 19th century and then discusses the public choice argument that Manne applied to the Morrill Act. It concludes that there was indeed a thriving for-profit education system in the early 19th century. However, the impetus for the Morrill Act may have come from the producers of failed and struggling not-for-profit schools rather than, as Manne postulates, from the consumers of for-profit schools.

Background

Although Manne's paper, "How the Structure of Universities Determined the Fate of American Legal Education," focused on legal education, it also discussed the history of proprietary or for-profit higher education in America before 1862. Such education is, as Manne points out, "a subject woefully neglected by historians of American higher education." (In a footnote, he remarked that "standard histories of American higher education are simply appalling in their ignorance of or intentional ignoring of this topic.")[2]

The United States experienced major economic growth in the first half of the 19th century. Where did the technical and management expertise behind this growth come from? In Manne's words, "Who educated all the engineers, architects, chemists, metallurgists, financiers, accountants, lawyers, and other specialists necessary to operate such a [complex industrial] system?"[3]

Manne postulated three "possible sources" of their education: immigration, apprenticeships, and foreign education of American students. Whereas apprenticeships are certainly private modes of education, they alone cannot account for all the education that took place within the United States during those years. Manne suggests that there must have been an additional private source within the United States: an active for-profit higher education system. That does seem to be the case—there were, certainly, many proprietary schools—but to learn more about that system, we must pull from many sources and fill in some gaps.

Law Schools

Although most lawyers of the 19th century learned their craft as apprentices, there were also for-profit law schools. According to Craig Evan Klafter, writing in the *American Journal of Legal History*, early–19th century proprietary law schools graduated a "disproportionate" number of individuals who went on to take leadership positions in the bar and in politics.[4] For example, in Connecticut, graduates of such law schools represented 10 percent of the state's lawyers from 1820 to 1830 but 70 percent of the state's congressional representatives from 1829 to 1839.[5] Such schools were frequently owned by state court judges who had free time but could not practice law without incurring a conflict of interest, and they were often equipped with excellent law libraries, says Klafter.

Thirteen such law schools were founded between 1784 and 1828. While the number of schools grew after that period, Klafter says, they lost their reputation for quality because of competition from university law schools.

Medical and Dental Schools

In his famous 1910 report for the Carnegie Foundation, Abraham Flexner reviewed the history of medical schools. He said that 26 medical schools had been founded between 1810 and 1840, 47 between 1840 and 1876, and even more in later years, although many were "short-lived." Flexner personally visited more than 150 medical schools for his report. Most of those schools were for profit, although a minority of them were nonprofit schools affiliated with universities. Flexner wrote of the former, "These enterprises—for the most part they can be called schools or institutions only by courtesy—were frequently set up regardless of opportunity or need."[6] Although the Flexner Report earned respect by identifying poor medical schools, it probably wound up reducing access to health care, particularly among low-income people, because as a result of its findings, many medical schools were shut down and regulations were passed that controlled the number of doctors for many decades.

Then, in 1926, in another study for the Carnegie Foundation (along the line of the Flexner report), William J. Gies reported that 13 schools of dentistry had been created between 1840, when the Baltimore College of Dentistry was founded, and 1868, when regulation of dental schools began. All were proprietary except for Harvard's. Gies claimed that the reasons there weren't more dental schools were that dentists preferred apprenticeships to academics and that physicians disdained dentists. He noted that a number of attempts by dentists to affiliate with medical schools were rejected, in his words, because of "[i]gnorance, intolerance, and professional vanity."[7]

Schools for the Practical Arts

But what about other schools that taught practical arts and scientific techniques at the high-school or college level? (The two levels were somewhat conflated during the period preceding the passage of the Morrill Act.)

A surprising amount is known about for-profit schools of the colonial period. In 1925, Robert Francis Seybolt wrote *The Evening School in Colonial America* for the University of Illinois. He examined newspapers and found that "evening schools" were widespread in the 18th century, as demonstrated by the many advertisements they placed in colonial newspapers and publications. For example, in the *American Weekly Mercury* in 1734, one Theophilus Grew offered to teach:

> Writing, Arithmetic in whole numbers and Fractions, Vulgar and Decimal, Merchants Accompts [sic], Algebra, Geometry, Surveying, Gauging, Trigonometry, Plane and Spherical, Navigation in all kinds of Sailing, Astronomy, and all other Parts of the Mathematics.[8]

In 1935, Vera M. Butler expanded the analysis of newspaper advertisements to the post-colonial period before 1850, primarily limiting her search to New England.[9] Most of the schools she wrote about taught an "English" curriculum (a more modern and freewheeling curriculum than the traditional "Latin" curriculum) and rarely focused on "industrial" or "practical" learning. One that did was the Fellenburg School in Windsor, Connecticut, which taught a broad range of courses, including bookkeeping, surveying, and navigation. In addition, its prospectus said as follows:

> A farm is attached to the institution; and the students will have under their daily observation, the various operations of farming; and those, who are expecting to engage in agricultural pursuits, will receive a course of Lectures, by which they will be made acquainted with the improvements which have been made, and are making, in the science and practice of Agriculture.[10]

Specialized Training

Let us return to Henry Manne's specific question about specialized training. Where, for example, did architects learn their craft? In a historical overview of the architectural profession in the United States, starting with the colonial period, Cecil D. Elliott outlines changes in the profession over time.[11] In doing so, he also indicates the sources of architects' education during the period before the Civil War.

The definition of "architect" at that time was not too precise. As Elliott says, "little effort has been made [in this book] to distinguish among architects, technicians, carpenters, builders, designers, or businessmen engaged in architecture." But he notes that the "customary" categories in colonial America were carpenters, master builders (also called housewrights), and "dilettante" or "gentleman" designers (such as Thomas Jefferson).

Some of these architects went through formal training, even before 1800. Writes Elliott, "Formal schools in architecture and the methods of drawing architecture were frequently announced to colonists by newspaper advertisements inviting laymen to attend classes conducted by a local craftsman or builder." And, he says, "ambitious carpenters" attended the schools.[12]

When the federal government sought designs for the Capitol and what would become the White House, 13 of those who submitted designs were carpenters or builders, says Elliott; another was a well-known housewright; 4 were "gentleman designers"; and 2 were immigrants who had actual architectural training, one in Ireland and one in France.

Elliott's overview confirms the varieties of education cited by Manne: apprenticeship, immigration, foreign training, and schools set up by local carpenters, builders, or architects.

Engineering Training

Let us look at another category of skilled technicians mentioned by Manne: engineers. It is often stated that traditional colleges such as Yale, Harvard, Rutgers, and Brown resisted adding practical education to their curricula, even on an elevated level such as engineering. A 1992 article about the history of engineering education by Terry S. Reynolds attempts to rebut that view and, in doing so, discusses the ways in which engineers (primarily civil engineers) were trained before the Civil War.[13]

Apprenticeship was the traditional mode of learning for engineers, but it "could not produce engineers in the quantity needed" for the vast transportation systems—roads, railroads, canals, and bridges—that the country built during that time, says Reynolds.[14] Thus, engineers of that era were taught in a number of ways, including (a) the military college (especially West Point, which was founded in 1802, although there were at least six others), (b) the independent technical college or polytechnic school (of which there were a half-dozen by the middle of the century, with Rensselaer Polytechnic the most famous), and (c) the focus of Reynolds' paper, 50 or so nonprofit colleges, where engineering programs were "grafted to the trunk of the traditional, classical college in a variety of ways."[15]

In many cases, engineering was taught as a "partial" or nondegree curriculum at traditional colleges (Princeton, for example, placed it outside the normal curriculum), and engineering degrees were not necessarily called engineering degrees. Nevertheless, it appears that engineering education was fairly widespread.

Reynolds estimates, however, that of the 50 engineering programs founded in the antebellum period, only about 30 were still functioning by the Civil War. The demise of so many engineering programs at traditional colleges suggests that the apprenticeship system was still strong. "Through most of the early and mid-nineteenth century," writes Reynolds, "employers remained skeptical of engineers trained in science and mathematics at colleges and preferred those who had acquired their training in the traditional on-the-job manner."[16]

Daniel H. Calhoun, author of a 1960 history of the American civil engineer, expands on just what that "on-the-job manner" was. Rather than becoming apprentices per se, in the early 19th century civil engineers in training could learn their trade by being part of major public works projects. "What developed in place of the professional preceptor's office [a form of apprenticeship] was the organized, hierarchical engineer corps, typically within a corporation or a state department of public works," Calhoun writes. He specifically cites the New York state canal system and Ohio public works but adds that "it was commonly expected that any large public works project would become a 'school' for engineers."[17]

Business and Commercial Schools

Manne was also interested in the education of "financiers" and "accountants," professions that fell within the purview of business or commercial colleges. The 1854 edition of the *Michigan Journal of Education* (its first volume) has a nonbylined article, "Commercial Colleges," that begins, "As we are often asked for information as to the organization and courses of study pursued in these institutions, a short article on the subject may not be uninteresting." The author then discusses Detroit Commercial College, "a type of the higher class of these schools" (one founded by his brother). Pupils studied at their own pace, usually taking 12 to 14 weeks to complete the course. The school was designed like a "counting room." There were no textbooks; the student started out with a "Day Book, in manuscript, containing the opening, current and closing entries of a simple business." The student worked through a series of these "Day Books" and then could specialize in areas such as "Commission Business, Retailing, Banking, and Steamboating."[18]

A year earlier, the *Weekly Standard* of Raleigh, North Carolina, had offered a quotation from Edwin T. Freedley's *A Practical Treaties* [sic] *on Business*, a popular guide to many aspects of business, including investing. Freedley wrote, "When the youth has finished his course of preparatory education at a school or private seminary . . . he should go into a counting-house, whatever may be his future ocupation [sic]. . . . It is there that he will learn order, method, obedience, and acquire a knowledge of life, and the business of life. It is there that he will learn the value of time, and the value of money—two very important things to know."[19]

A 1976 essay in the *American Vocational Journal* confirms that private business schools grew significantly after 1850. Such schools taught bookkeeping, arithmetic, and handwriting—followed by stenography in 1863 and, later, by typing.[20] They became a fixture of American higher education for many years. The U.S. Commissioner of Education's voluminous 1887 annual report listed 239 "colleges for business training" in operation in 1886. His list was based on self-reporting, however, so there may have been many more.

Academies

We know that there were private methods of teaching architects, engineers, accountants, and others in business. But there were other types of schools as well during the mid-19th century. One such type was the "academy." While the term today suggests a scholarly education, the academies of that era were mostly schools meant to prepare young people of the rural or small-town middle class (both men and women) for the growing number of "white-collar" jobs available. Bruce Leslie, writing in the *History of Education Quarterly*, calls them "the dominant institution of nineteenth-century higher schooling."[21]

Academies were quasi-private schools, often owned by individuals but sporadically supported by state or local taxes. They were so diverse in curriculum that it is not clear whether they should be viewed as secondary schools or colleges (some later became colleges and others high schools, but most disappeared). How much practical teaching they did is also difficult to determine. Many academies were ephemeral schools established to meet a short-term need, and thus they tended to be relatively informal.

Vera M. Butler, in her dissertation about early American education, remarked that "this [i.e., my] study of academies before 1850 must of necessity be, incomplete. No attempt was made to count cases. Some accounts seem to end in thin air." One reason for this "incompleteness" may have been offered by the editor of the *Springfield* [Massachusetts] *Republican*, who commented that "few parents are guided in the choice of a school by ads. Most schools suppose themselves known, so they only send in news of exhibitions." Butler noted, however, that large academies that advertised their programs did get attention from the press.[22]

Sources of the Morrill Act

If a strong private education sector existed before the passage of the Morrill Act in 1862, as shown by the evidence above, what role did this sector play in the proposal and enactment of the law?

Manne stated in his Ribstein paper that governments are "most likely to offer a service [typically, a subsidy] to the public when the private sector is already satisfying the real demand for that service."[23] He then proposed that the Morrill Act itself was a sign that the demand for higher education was being met. "It is highly unlikely that Morrill and the others pushing for land-grant schools were inventing a new product that consumers had not previously demonstrated their desire for."[24]

This idea differs from the usual view of the act. More typical is the stance of John Y. Simon, who wrote in "The Politics of the Morrill Act" that the law "emerged from an idealistic concern for the adaptation of existing resources to a changing society in a nation which generally believed that education policy was a public concern."[25]

Let us look at the debate and discussion that led to the passage of the act. Whereas a number of historians have reported on the congressional deliberations that led to the passage of the Morrill Act, the long and tortuous background of the law is contained in Alfred Charles True's exhaustive history of agricultural education, written for the Department of Agriculture and published in 1929.[26]

Agricultural education began in the early 19th century with the formation of agricultural societies in a number of states. These organizations, often chartered by state legislatures, promoted agriculture through the presentation of scientific papers, exhibits, libraries, prizes, and discussions. The societies were often formed by distinguished citizens who were also planters.

The Philadelphia Society for Promoting Agriculture, which sought "a greater increase of the products of land in the American states,"[27] grew out of the American Philosophical Society, the scientific society founded by Benjamin Franklin. The agricultural society's first president was a former mayor of Philadelphia; the next president had been a representative to the Continental Congress. George Washington, who was constantly experimenting with new tools and plant varieties on his Virginia estate, was an honorary member.

The state of Virginia had several agricultural societies in the early 19th century. Thomas Jefferson helped found the Albemarle Agricultural Society in 1817, and James Madison was its first president. True reports that the society "published many papers . . . conducted fairs and exhibitions with prizes for agricultural implements, livestock, and domestic manufactures, interested itself in the University of Virginia, and endeavored to obtain funds for a professorship in agriculture in that institution."[28] True describes similar societies in Massachusetts, South Carolina, Maine, New Jersey, New Hampshire, Connecticut, the District of Columbia, and New York.

Some of the societies, like Virginia's, attempted to expand formal education to include agriculture (in some cases at lower grade levels than college). Initially, however, their major focus was on creating state boards of agriculture. These boards brought the authority and funds of the state to the promotion of the science of farming. Members of the societies often served on the boards, and the boards sometimes supported the societies financially with legislated funds.

For example, True reports that in New York, the leadership of Governor DeWitt Clinton, who also headed the New York Society for the Promotion of Useful Arts, led to the creation of a state agricultural board. In 1819, the legislature appropriated $10,000 a year for two years for this board, which was to distribute it among the state's agricultural societies to pay for "premiums and reports."

Massachusetts illustrates the full panoply of support offered by legislatures to these societies. As early as 1819, the state's legislature was giving $200 a year to each agricultural society that raised at least $1,000 for itself, with additional funds provided in proportion to the amount the society raised, up to $3,000.[29] In 1837, the legislature appropriated $2,500 for an annual report on the condition of agriculture in the state and how it might be improved, although this appropriation was repealed in 1841. In 1845, the legislature mandated that to receive their state funding, the agricultural societies had to provide their full reports and publications to the secretary of state, who could then publish those "most worthy of public notice" in abstract form. In 1851 the legislature exempted the societies from taxation, and in 1852 "their funds invested in real estate were to be counted in determining their State allowance."[30]

During this period, True said, the Massachusetts board and societies continually pushed for funding to establish an agricultural college, as did those of other states. "Petitions were constantly coming to Congress for land grants for agricultural colleges in different States," wrote True.[31] Thus, an elite group of "planters" seems to have played the biggest role leading to consideration of a federal land-grant program.

Another force that contributed to the eventual shape and passage of the Morrill Act was the movement to create schools for the mechanical arts. Following a pattern set in England, the early republic saw the creation of mechanics' institutes, organizations founded by skilled workmen such as bricklayers and carpenters. These institutes sometimes provided education for their members. For example, the Ohio Mechanics' Institute, founded in Cincinnati in 1828, sponsored lectures and gave training; it eventually became a college and in 1969 was incorporated into the University of Cincinnati.[32] However, most of the mechanics' institutes were fraternal organizations, and education was not a prominent aspect of their activities. Even the Ohio Mechanics' Institute's education program experienced poor attendance over many years.

Proposals for mechanical arts to be taught in colleges, rather than at these institutes, appear to have come from other sources. Whereas established mechanics such as Harrison Howard, who was described in Joseph Kett's book about adult education as a "self-educated carriage maker living in Lockport, New York,"[33] did play a role in that effort, the biggest push seems to have come from select members of the professional class familiar with engineering or science.

Alden Partridge, a professor of mathematics and engineering at West Point who later worked as a surveyor, made one of the first attempts. Partridge had studied at Dartmouth, but, perhaps out of frustration with the school's narrow Latin curriculum, he transferred to West Point and graduated from that institution instead. He later founded the successful Norwich Military College, which became second only to West Point in producing leading civil engineers (and still exists as Norwich University). In 1841, Partridge boldly asked Congress to appropriate $40 million from the sale of public lands to create a system of education that would "supersede the present *anti republic* and *monastic* system."[34] Nothing came of his request, but as a friend of Justin S. Morrill, he probably had an influence on the Vermont congressman.

Jonathan Baldwin Turner, a professor at Illinois College in Jacksonville, also had a major influence on Morrill. In 1851, the state of Illinois had obtained both substantial funds from the sale of state lands and a federal land grant for education (such land grants were not unusual before the Morrill Act, but they were made only occasionally, state by state). Debate arose over how to use this money and land.

Some argued that the funds should be used to support existing colleges. But Turner, a Yale graduate, questioned, as did Partridge, the ability of existing colleges to add mechanical and practical arts to their arcane curriculum. He wanted a university that would serve "the industrial classes, including all cultivators of the soil, artists, mechanics, and merchants."[35]

Turner pointed out that the professional class had many opportunities for education but that the much larger "industrial" class had hardly any. Thus, he outlined a plan for a state-funded university that would include the following:

> Buildings of appropriate size and construction for all ordinary and special uses; a complete philosophical, chemical, anatomical, and industrial apparatus; a general cabinet, embracing everything that relates to, illustrates, or facilitates any one of the industrial arts; especially all sorts of animals, birds, reptiles, insects, trees, shrubs, and plants found in this State and adjacent States.

The institution should also include an experimental farm and gardens, and the teachers should be "men of the most eminent practical ability in their several departments." (Turner was not very specific about the exact subjects to be taught, however.)[36]

Turner did not succeed in obtaining state legislative funds for the university—a normal school won out. His project had to await the passage of the Morrill Act; under its terms, the University of Illinois at Urbana-Champaign opened its doors in 1868.

Before turning to Justin Morrill's bill, we must look at another effort to start an "industrial" college, one which was also supported by prominent people: the lengthy process that led to the formation (but never the operation) of the People's College in New York.[37]

The idea for that college arose at a meeting of an organization called the Mechanics Mutual Protection in 1843, of which Harrison Howard, mentioned earlier, was a leading member. The attendees at that meeting created another society, the Right Worthy Mechanics Grand Mutual Protection, whose purpose was "to raise the mechanics of America to their true position in society." The means to do this included "a more general diffusion of the principles and sciences governing mechanics and the arts, to elevate our brethren in their varied capacities and thereby give them the greatest proficiency in their several callings."

The goal, as described by Howard, was also to improve relationships between employers and labor, especially after the panic of 1837. (In his wording, there is a hint of an effort to forestall unionization and strikes.) The plan was "to establish one central or State college of practical science, wherein our youth, aspiring to efficiency and eminence in life as architects, engineers, or artisans of any sort, might receive a thorough physical and mental training, laboring a part of the day and thus paying at first a part and afterward for a whole of subsistence and teaching."[38]

The influential *New York Tribune* editor Horace Greeley got behind the project, as did New York's governor (in campaign speeches, at least). Enormous effort went into promoting the school and seeking "dollar subscriptions" to finance it. But construction of the college building began only because a benefactor, Charles Cook, donated some land and topped off the subscriptions to attain the $50,000 minimum needed to start the school. The difficulty of obtaining private funds led Greeley and others to seek state and federal funds. However, even after the Morrill Act became law, the People's College was unable to obtain land-grant funds, and thus it never opened its doors.

The Bill Becomes Law

Justin S. Morrill was an energetic congressman from Vermont who entered the House of Representatives in 1855 and stayed in Congress until 1898, serving for many years as a senator. In 1856, he offered a resolution that the House Committee on Agriculture should look into the possibility of a national college of agriculture, but nothing was done. The next year, he introduced a far more specific bill, one that without much change became the Morrill Act five years later. It authorized the national government to give to states federal lands that they could sell to raise funds in support of state colleges in the mechanical and agricultural arts.

Funds would be apportioned based on congressional representation, with each state receiving 20,000 acres (later changed to 30,000 acres) for each of the state's senators and representatives.

While Morrill later said that the idea came to him alone, scholars such as True, Simon, and others concluded that he was responding to—and perhaps incorporating—plans laid out by Alden Partridge and Jonathan Baldwin Turner and the examples of schools such as the People's College.

Opposition to Morrill's bill was twofold: first, that the U.S. Constitution did not authorize the national government to support institutions within states (a principle that had been violated already) and second, that through the sale of the granted land, western states would lose large amounts of their land to speculators. As historian Burt Powell wrote, "Senators Lane of Kansas and Wilkinson of Minnesota were especially strenuous in their opposition, maintaining that the location of large bodies of land in their states upon the scrip proposed, would be exceedingly detrimental to them."[39]

But Morrill was an effective politician, and he got his bill passed twice. The first time, President James Buchanan vetoed it on constitutional grounds. By the time Morrill tried again in 1861, the South had seceded (although it's not completely clear how much that mattered to the bill's passage), and the new president, Abraham Lincoln, was sympathetic to Morrill's cause. Although the final votes (32-7 in the Senate, 90-25 in the House) were imbalanced in favor of the law, John Simon says that some congressmen only approved the bill knowing it was likely to pass: "few wanted to cast a worthless vote that would be interpreted as a vote against education"—an indication that then, as today, education had a special stature in society.[40]

It is generally agreed, however, that the initial effect of the Morrill Act of 1862 was quite limited.[41] As late as 1883, E. E. White, president of Purdue University, wrote, "The contributions made to agricultural science have been small, and the promising work of agricultural experiment is still in its infancy, even in the institutions first organized, and in most of them it has not been seriously undertaken."[42] It was not until additional laws (the Hatch Act of 1887 and the Morrill

Act of 1890) provided the land-grant colleges with more funding that the colleges began to increase in number and significantly expand their programs.

What Can We Learn?

What does the history recounted in this paper tell us about why the Morrill Act was enacted? Let us return to Manne's paper. In a footnote, Manne points out that "the best indication that the voters want a given service is the success of private markets in offering these services, since that willingness of individuals to pay for this service is the best demonstration that they value it highly."[43] He also points out that there must be an additional positive-sounding "rationalization" to "provide a cover for the real transfer of wealth that the politicians are actually engaged in."[44] These statements reflect public choice analysis of the actions of politicians.

If that is the case, what transfer of wealth were the politicians who supported the Morrill Act engaged in?

Manne hypothesized that the politicians were responding to the consumers of agricultural and mechanical education and, through the Morrill Act, subsidizing their purchase of education. This may be true, but, and I believe that Manne would agree with this, the long history of agricultural and mechanical promotion before the act suggests that the political entrepreneurs who supported it were the affluent and well-educated members of agricultural societies and perhaps of mechanical societies as well. These were the people who had tried to start colleges in numerous states but had trouble obtaining funds to support them—and even had trouble finding students who wanted to attend their schools.

Whereas John Simon was probably wrong about the Morrill land-grant movement being "idealistic," he does recognize that the group of people who pushed for the colleges were an elite. He claims that working farmers (presumably a somewhat different group than the planters who founded agricultural societies) were not eager for the product the elites were offering. He wrote that "the juxtaposition of the two words, 'agriculture' and 'college' caused many amused chuckles." He even pointed out that one of the agricultural colleges was named Farmers' High School "to avoid the popular prejudice against the concept of college."[45]

From the start, the agricultural societies wanted to improve agriculture, including their own farms and those of their heirs, through education and experimentation. They did a lot to promote agriculture themselves: writing articles, giving lectures, creating experimental gardens, and sponsoring exhibits, fairs, and even schools for orphans. But they wanted more—yet their efforts at actually starting agricultural colleges were largely unsuccessful; their schools lacked both attendees and support from investors. In the case of the People's College, a benefactor had to step in with a gift for the school even to be formed.

Thus, the agricultural college seems to have been the goal of an elite group of "planters" and some well-placed "mechanics." The subsidies they sought and received from legislatures over the years helped them achieve their goal of improving cultivation, a goal that helped them as much as or more than it helped the run-of-the-mill farmer. But they did need a clear public purpose, and the idea of teaching the state's young people about agriculture and mechanics may well have been the "rationalization" that gave a public face to a private desire. Finally, some proponents of agricultural and mechanical schools, such as Alden Partridge, were resentful of the traditional, church-affiliated colleges and their "Latin" curriculum—a factor that undoubtedly contributed to congressional passage of the law. This resentment of elite schools was a recurring issue in an increasingly industrial 19th-century America, as there was a growing feeling that traditional schools were clinging to a curriculum that no longer served young men and women well.

Conclusion

There was clearly a vibrant for-profit education system in the United States in the first half of the 19th century. Such education took various forms, including apprenticeships, in-house education, proprietary schools, and academies. But the motive for government subsidies for public higher education (i.e., for the Morrill Act) appears to have come from the elite—not from the workers who benefited from the for-profit schools, but from the educated planters and mechanics who wanted to improve cultivation and industry, including their own.

Those planters and mechanics were willing to support agriculture with their own efforts, but they wanted more. And as the potential for contributions from scientific agriculture grew, they saw opportunities for a broad, government-supported education apparatus. The land-grant colleges supported by the Morrill Act were the result. However, in light of public choice theory, more analysis should be applied to this case. A detailed and realistic understanding of the political forces that led to public land-grant colleges is needed; further exploration of the role private schools played before those colleges were founded would help build that understanding.

CHAPTER TWO
The Morrill Land-Grant Act: Fact and Mythology
Richard K. Vedder

The Morrill Land-Grant Act of 1862 has taken on an importance of near mythical proportions among many scholars and higher education leaders. One study opined, "Land-grant institutions have helped transform the basic nature of American society."[1] Another proclaimed, "The Morrill Act of 1862 set the stage for the most distinctive and most successful example of public service by American universities."[2] Two points are argued by those scholars. First, higher education in America was nonexceptional, elitist, and somewhat inadequate until the Morrill Act unleashed a flurry of new colleges and universities. American preeminence in higher education arose out of the changes wrought by the 1862 legislation. Second, the emphasis on research and practical learning at the newly emerging universities led to large increases in productivity that set America on course to becoming the planet's preeminent economic power in the 20th century. As one prominent historian of American higher education put it, "The act immediately affected the expansion and structure of higher education and, eventually, the productivity of the American economy."[3]

This essay argues that those expansive claims for the Morrill Act are, minimally, greatly exaggerated. American higher education was growing rapidly before the Morrill Act, and a large portion of post–Morrill Act growth, including the evolution of the modern research university patterned on the German model, had nothing to do with that legislation. America's economic exceptionalism began well before the passage of the Morrill Act, and the United States had the largest output of goods and services of any Western country before any significant number of students had even graduated from the new land-grant universities and colleges.

More broadly, in this chapter I argue that America's exceptionalism—both educationally and economically—was secured long before large-scale, sustained federal intervention in higher education occurred following the passage of the Higher Education Act of 1965. Going even further, a decent case can be made that such large-scale government involvement, including that of state governments, essentially was unnecessary for both American higher education and the economy to prosper. The involvement may also have led to an overinvestment in education that is—potentially at least—a mild drag on contemporary American economic life. Finally, much of the enhanced government-induced spending provided extra benefits (such as economic rents) to key members of university communities, often at the expense of students and taxpayers.

The Morrill Act and Early American Public Higher Education

The Morrill Act of 1862 was a byproduct of the Civil War. Had the Civil War not occurred, there is some question whether this or similar legislation would have ever passed. The act, named after Justin Morrill, who was a Vermont congressman and later a senator, had the following as its purpose:

> Without excluding other scientific and classical studies and including military tactics, to teach such branches of learning as are related to agriculture and the mechanic arts, in such manner as the legislatures of the States may respectively prescribe, in order to promote the liberal and practical education of the industrial classes in the several pursuits and professions in life.[4]

The Morrill Act narrowly passed Congress in a period of intense legislative activity, including bills that were then—and, I think, appropriately now—considered far more monumental: the Homestead Act; the National Banking Act (creating the first federal regulatory body, the Comptroller of the Currency); the approval of a transcontinental railroad; the passage of the first federal income tax; and others. The Morrill Act had been proposed before the Civil War, and it even passed Congress in 1859, only to be successfully vetoed by President James Buchanan, who somewhat presciently argued that "It is extremely doubtful, to say the least, whether this bill would contribute to the advancement of agricultural and the mechanic arts."[5] He thought it improper for Congress to appropriate resources (land) to the states for institutions without federal oversight; he viewed education as a state, not federal, responsibility; and he questioned the constitutionality of the measure.

Congressional approval in 1859 was narrow: 105 to 100 in the House and 25 to 22 in the Senate, with southerners nearly unanimously opposing the measure.[6] Even in 1862, with most southerners absent because of the Civil War, the vote to even consider the Morrill bill in the Senate passed by a narrow 23 to 19, and much parliamentary maneuvering occurred before final passage and President Lincoln's signature.

The Morrill Act gave land to states agreeing to the act's provisions, in most states leading to one institution benefiting from the land grants. The grant amounted to 30,000 acres for each member of Congress. Land was cheap, and much of the good land was already claimed under other land grants, such as the Homestead Act and railway land-grant provisions. New York State cleverly used the law to obtain relatively valuable land out west (little public land was left in New York), and Cornell University became the only relatively large beneficiary under the law, ironically today an Ivy League university best known for its private, non–land-grant colleges. The value of all the land under the grants was less than $10 million, a figure less than 0.03 percent of one year's national output. In relation to the size of the economy, it would be the equivalent of Congress today making a one-time appropriation for education of $5 billion, hardly enough to be of transformative importance. No cash was provided to colleges annually until a second Morrill Act in 1890 made relatively modest provisions for it (although beginning in the 1880s, some funds went to agricultural experimental stations that often were associated with land-grant schools). Federal support for higher education under the Morrill Act was extremely meager, with no schools getting a dime of regular direct support in the first 25 years after the act's passage.

Morrill advanced a number of economic arguments in support of his bill. He said the United States must work "not to become a weak competitor in the most important field where we meet the world as rivals. It touches . . . our national honor . . . as well as our private pockets," and he went on to lament the "conspicuous lead" the Russians had taken in education.[7]

Growth in U.S. Higher Education before 1862

Conventional wisdom is that American higher education was confined to a relatively small number of private schools before the Morrill Act and that public higher education begins to flourish only after that legislation, which helped radically expand enrollments. In my judgment, that "wisdom" is wrong.[8]

To begin this discussion, let us take perhaps the most quintessential grouping of American public institutions, the Big Ten athletic conference, which is known for having several large and famous land-grant institutions. Of the 14 schools in the Big Ten, 10 of them (Indiana, Michigan State, Penn State, Northwestern, and Rutgers universities, and the universities of Iowa, Michigan, Maryland, Minnesota, and Wisconsin) were founded well before the Morrill Act was even passed. The four post-Morrill land-grant schools were Illinois, Nebraska, Ohio State, and Purdue universities. Indeed, even in the narrow area of promoting agricultural colleges—the dominant goal of promoters of the Morrill legislation—both Michigan and Pennsylvania had created their own schools, which later became land-grant institutions, in the 1850s.

Or let us take the top 25 national universities on the *US News & World Report* "Best Colleges" list for 2015 (actually 26 schools because of a tie at 25). A majority (15) of the schools were founded before the Morrill Act was passed. And most of the post–Morrill Act schools had no tie to the land-grant legislation, including prestigious schools such as Cal Tech, the University of Chicago, Johns Hopkins, Stanford, and Vanderbilt. Stretching things a bit (by counting two University of California schools, Berkeley and UCLA, as land-grant schools), only four land-grant schools are in the top 26 list, with—in addition to the California schools—the Massachusetts Institute of Technology and Cornell (ironically, both predominantly private schools). Among schools widely considered to be America's best, the Morrill Act's effect is very, very small.

Moreover, even if one confines the analysis to public institutions, at least 10 states had created them before the Civil War. In no way was the Morrill Act the key event in the emergence of public universities in America. The College of William and Mary was America's second university, and—decades before the Civil War—Virginia had also created Thomas Jefferson's dream, the University of Virginia. Before the Constitution was signed, the University of Georgia had been founded, and the University of North Carolina began in the year George Washington assumed the presidency. In the first decade of the 19th century, far more than 50 years before the Morrill Act, Ohio created not one but two public universities: Ohio University and Miami University. One of America's premier educational institutions, the University of Michigan, was founded in 1819, long before Michigan became a state, and it was operating out of Ann Arbor a full generation before Morrill successfully got his bill passed.

Most of the boom in higher education before the Civil War came from privately created schools, most with some religious affiliation. But by 1860 some 24 percent of the schools in the United States were public institutions, which Claudia Goldin and Lawrence Katz consider "remarkably high" in their book *The Race between Education and Technology*.[9] Looking at data from a *Higher Education Directory* from the early 1990s, they concluded that about 150 schools that persisted into the 1990s were founded in the last pre-Morrill decades of 1840 to 1860, compared with roughly 220 institutions in the first two post-Morrill decades, 1865 to 1885.[10]

Numbers were rising, as expected over time through the antebellum era with rapid population growth. In the last two pre-Morrill decades, about 6.45 institutions were created per 1 million population (using the mid-period, 1850, population to calculate), compared with only 4.88 per million in the 1865–1885 period. To say that the Morrill Act ushered in an era of extraordinary expansion of institutions of higher education, as some might, is highly misleading. Indeed, the data suggest that the creation of public institutions under the Morrill Act may have *crowded out* some private institutions that would have been formed, so the total "Morrill effect" on enrollments is zero or even negative. That conclusion is not novel: the late Henry Manne, in a prescient paper written more than four decades ago, concluded, "With the advent of the public university, a great deal of the support that formerly had gone for private universities disappeared."[11]

Aside from the so-called not-for-profit schools, rather robust proprietary (for-profit) education institutions provided vocational training in such subjects as law and medicine, which students attended following a primary education that provided basic numerical and written literacy. Following on Manne, a good case can be made that rent-seeking individuals used the political process to promote so-called public schools that, because of a murky definition of property rights, conferred the gains of university "ownership" on special-interest groups within the institutions. Public support in the form of land grants, appropriations, or private philanthropy made it more difficult for proprietary institutions to compete. But the new not-for-profit schools were captured by various interest groups within the institutions for their benefit, conferring economic rents on them. Early on, those interest groups primarily comprised university trustees; later, faculty and university administrators came to predominate. The crowding out associated with the Morrill Act may reflect an attempt to redistribute the gains from higher education expansion to politically well-connected parties.

It is important to realize also that the words "private" and "public" with respect to schools before, say, 1880 largely related to the composition of the governing board, not financial assistance. Before the Morrill Act, relatively few so-called public schools received regular state appropriations (some had received initial grants of cash or land), and, conversely, some so-called private schools, including Harvard University, had periodically received some public funds. But those funds were small and sporadic. Tuition levels were as high at so-called state universities as at private schools. Around 1840, for example, tuition at the University of Virginia ($75) was the same as at Harvard and more than at Princeton.[12]

Taken as a whole, then, American higher education was almost exclusively funded from private sources before the Civil War.[13] Because of philanthropy, much of it church supported and some endowment income, however, tuition fees were less than the cost of education, encouraging students to enroll in greater numbers than market forces alone would dictate. As the 19th century came to a close, state government support of higher education rose, setting the stage for widespread governmental involvement in the 20th century. Higher education in the 19th century, though, is primarily a tale of growing private initiative and enterprise.

Higher Education after the Morrill Act

Did the Morrill Act, providing federal assistance and encouraging state creation of public universities, lead to a surge in enrollment growth? As Figure 2.1 demonstrates, enrollment growth was actually higher in the

Figure 2.1

Higher Education Enrollment Growth, 1840–1860 vs. 1870–1890

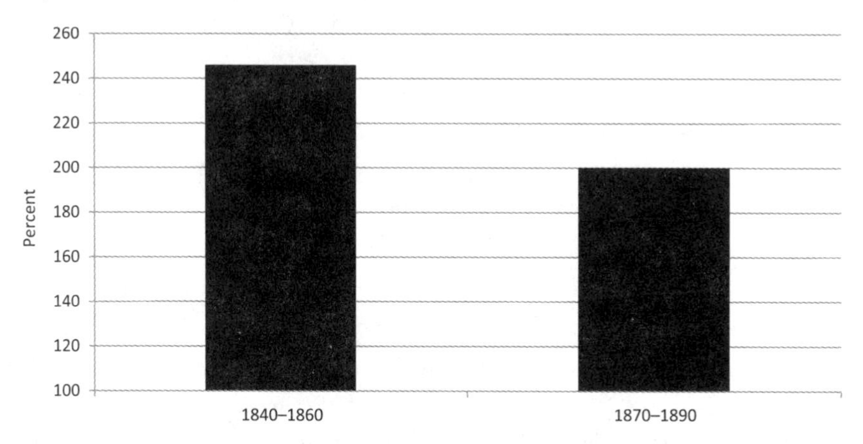

Sources: U.S. Bureau of the Census (USBOC), 1850 Census, Table CLIII; USBOC, 1870 Census, Table XII(a), https://www.census.gov/prod/www/decennial.html; U.S. Department of Education, National Center for Education Statistics, Table 301.20, *Digest of Education Statistics: 2015*, https://nces.ed.gov/programs/digest/d15/tables/dt15_301.20.asp?current=yes.

last two pre–Morrill Act decades than in the two decades after passage of the act (the 1860s was a transition decade, disrupted by the Civil War and the decade when land-grant institutions were beginning but had not graduated meaningful numbers).

Although it is true that enrollments more than doubled in the first full post-Morrill decade of the 1870s, the same is the case in the last full pre-Morrill decade of the 1850s. To be sure, some college enrollment was likely in preparatory departments where students were not truly receiving a "higher" education, and that problem may have declined somewhat over time, so the perceived *slowdown* in higher education enrollment growth after the Morrill Act may not have really happened. But it seems very unlikely that, in any meaningful sense, enrollment growth rose in the first generation or more after the Morrill Act.

Even if we expand our time horizon considerably and compare the 6.4 percent annual enrollment growth in the pre-Morrill period of 1840 to 1860 with the 4.8 percent growth in the 40 years from 1870 to 1910, the annual percentage of growth in enrollment is far higher in the period before the Morrill Act. The evidence supports Henry Manne's 1971 insight.[14] Moreover, although in the longer run the Morrill Act institutions grew relatively large, as late as 1940 a solid majority of students in four-year colleges and universities still attended private schools.[15]

Research and Innovation

Those arguing that the Morrill Act played a critical role in American economic and educational exceptionalism might dismiss the evidence of robust enrollment growth in the antebellum period with the observation that the pre–Civil War institutions were essentially colleges with no research function, and America's higher education primacy today revolves around research. The Morrill Act made promoting research a matter of national policy and led to the beginning of the modern research university.

Although the modern research university did evolve in the postbellum and post–Morrill Act period, the 1862 law had next to nothing to do with it. Indeed, just as the pre-Morrill enrollment growth was robust and involved little state or federal governmental involvement, the same is true of the evolution of the research university from 1870 to 1910. It is nearly universally agreed that the first great American university emphasizing graduate studies and research, which was built on the German model, was Johns Hopkins University, created in 1874. And what led to the creation of that institution? By far the largest gift in the history of higher education to that time: a $7 million bequest by Johns Hopkins, a major shareholder in the Baltimore and Ohio Railroad, to create a university.[16]

What was probably the leading research university at the end of the century? The University of Chicago, which was created by munificent gifts of well over $20 million by the world's richest man at the time, John D. Rockefeller. Rockefeller's gifts to Chicago far exceeded the amount of cash that *all* American land-grant universities received under the Morrill Act. Speaking about William Rainey Harper, the University of Chicago's first president, Roger Geiger asserts that he "created an institution that stood with Harvard and Columbia as the nation's finest research universities. Chicago, in fact, led in graduate studies."[17] None of the very "finest" universities that Geiger cites were land-grant schools or even other public schools.

It is true that by 1910 some of the land-grant schools were becoming respectable institutions. Yet they were distinct minorities among the greatest universities. In a precursor to modern college rankings, Edwin E. Slosson in 1910 authored a book on what he perceived to be America's 14 great universities.[18] Of the 14, 9 were private schools, and 1 of the 5 state universities, Michigan, was not a land-grant school and was founded decades before the Morrill Act.[19] Of the nine postbellum (and post-Morrill) universities, only five were land-grant schools, and one of them, Cornell, received a large part of its initial resources from a private donor, Ezra Cornell. Even today, it is a mixed private–public institution.

Looking nearly a half-century after passage of the Morrill Act, Slosson thought that about two-thirds of America's top universities had little or no association with that legislation. In 1924—some 62 years after the Morrill Act—an examination of faculty quality by Raymond M. Hughes of Miami University reiterated the primacy of the private non–land-grant universities.[20] Looking at 20 academic departments, Harvard was viewed in 13 cases as having the best or second-best faculty, Chicago had 12 firsts or seconds, and Columbia had 9. As Geiger notes, "What stands out is the dominance of Harvard, Chicago, and Columbia."[21]

Productivity Change, Innovation, and Economic Growth

But didn't America's emergence as a leading world economic power become obvious only in the very period in which the early land-grant universities were being formed? Although it is true that the world recognized the economic prowess of America more in the post-Morrill period, in reality the nation's march to become the world's leading economic power began long before the Morrill Act was passed. The great innovators, inventors, and entrepreneurial leaders of the nation in the post-Constitutional era up to World War I (1789–1914) mostly had no college education. The proportion of the growth in income attributable to technological progress or human capital formation was probably no greater—and, indeed, very likely even less—in the first few decades of the post-Morrill era when compared with the late pre-Morrill period. Government support for higher education played essentially no role in explaining economic growth during the period in which the United States emerged as a rapidly growing industrial nation. Yet by World War I, the United States led the world by any important economic indicator.

An oft-used taxonomy of economic change is that developed by Walt W. Rostow in *The Stages of Economic Growth*.[22] Rostow argued that each developed nation went through a critical stage, the takeoff, which lasted about 20 years, after which the conditions for sustained economic growth are secured. He claimed that the U.S. takeoff was from 1843 to 1860—before the Morrill Act. Although many have questioned the appropriateness of the "stages" approach to describe economic change, many American economic historians agree that growth accelerated after 1840, and some say even earlier, perhaps as early as 1820.[23] Incomes, output, and the standard of living clearly were rising robustly at least a generation before the passage of the Morrill Act. Those facts arguably suggest that much of the late 19th-century university expansion that occurred after the Morrill Act was more a consequence than a cause of American economic growth.

The leading global expert on national income accounting at the beginning of the 21st century was Angus Maddison. His estimate of the real average annual percentage growth of the gross domestic product (GDP) in the United States for the pre-Morrill period of 1840 to 1860 is an extraordinary 4.70 percent, compared with 3.98 percent in the first two post-Morrill decades of 1870 to 1890.[24] To be sure, population growth was larger in the earlier period, and most scholars consider per capita income growth a better measure of economic change and welfare. On that measure, the pre-Morrill growth of 1.59 percent a year still slightly exceeds the post-Morrill increase of 1.56 percent. To put it very conservatively, American economic growth did not accelerate in the first generation after passage of the Morrill Act. Of course, many factors determine economic growth, and the mere demonstration of a slight slowdown in growth rates in the post-Morrill era does not prove that the Morrill Act had no appreciable positive effect. The evidence, however, indicates that the extravagant claims that the legislation was vital to America's economic exceptionalism are likely not valid.

It is interesting to compare the United States with the world's previous leading industrial power, Great Britain, the nation that had the first industrial revolution in the late 18th and early 19th century. According to Maddison, in 1820 the GDP of the United Kingdom was almost three times that of the United States. Just 52 years later, in 1872, when very few people had graduated from a U.S. institution under the Morrill Act, the United States surpassed Great Britain to have the world's largest output.[25] Pre–Morrill Act growth led to the United States becoming the world's mightiest economic power. On a per capita basis, the Maddison data suggest that the United States passed Britain in 1903, when most leading American institutions of higher education were still private schools not affected by the Morrill Act.[26]

If the Morrill Act had positively affected economic growth, the effect should have shown up in what economists call "total factor productivity" growth—growth in output not explained by the mere accumulation of more land, labor, and capital resources. Total factor productivity growth would capture the gains arising from labor inputs becoming more educated and presumably more productive (possessing more human capital), as well as the gains arising from new inventions and innovations, which presumably were enhanced by having a more educated populace.

Drawing on the pioneering work of Robert Gallman, I once estimated the components of per capita growth in real net national product (an income construct highly correlated with the now more commonly used GDP measure).[27] I compared the period 1840 to 1880 (which was mostly pre-Morrill because there were almost no Morrill Act college graduates before the early 1870s) with the post-Morrill era of 1880 to 1920. If one looks at total output, net national product grew a good deal faster in the earlier period, and 0.86 percent of the 4.21 percent annual output growth was explained by total factor productivity, which was the component capturing human capital formation (more educated workers) and invention.

In the later period, total productivity growth explained 0.72 percent of a lower annual output growth, a somewhat *smaller* number. If one looks at the situation on a per capita basis and controls for the growth in population and associated growth in the labor force, roughly the same results occur, with total factor productivity growth explaining 59 percent of all growth in the earlier period, compared with 46 percent in the latter period. Those results make it difficult to think that the Morrill Act led to an upsurge in the growth effects of greater education or technology.

All of that evidence points to the same conclusion: there was no growth surge in the first several decades following passage of the Morrill Act. Moreover, the evidence suggests that the innovation and human capital enhancements that the Morrill Act supposedly brought certainly are not reflected in the aggregate statistics, which reinforces the conclusion that the legislation was of minor significance.

A closer review of the business history of the period supports that conclusion. The reality is that the overwhelming majority of the great inventors, innovators, and entrepreneurs—the economic movers and shakers during the period of America's rise to economic preeminence—mostly had little formal education. Looking at the period from the beginning of constitutional government to World War I (in other words,

1789 to 1914), I identified 30 important American inventors and entrepreneurs covering fields as diverse as fur trading, railroads, retail trade, and investment banking.[28] Of the 30, only 3 (10 percent) had graduated from college, and only 2 of them (Eli Whitney and Samuel F. B. Morse) had attended American schools; both went to Yale College (where they were also both members of Phi Beta Kappa). A third, J. P. Morgan, had received his degree from a German institution.

The vast majority of the other 27 entrepreneurs had not even made it to college, although a few had had noncollege experiences at academies or seminaries that, stretching things a bit, might be considered postsecondary but not precisely collegiate. It is fair to say that the bulk of the premier economic leaders of the United States in its formative period, both before and for the first two generations after the Morrill Act, were not college educated. Inventors of such important innovations as the telephone, the electric light bulb, and the airplane never saw a day of college.

The "Morrill-Inspired" Experience of Modern Times

If the Morrill Act did not in the first several decades after passage enhance human capital formation through greater enrollments, and if it did not promote economic growth, whom, then, did it benefit? Even more important, did later federal initiatives that built on the Morrill Act, especially the Higher Education Act of 1965, have similar results to the Morrill Act?

I will argue three issues. First, the vastly expanded governmental role in higher education that occurred in the 20th century (starting more than 80 years after the Morrill Act) has provided benefits to relatively small portions of the population. At first, benefits accrued to students collecting what Alfred Marshall and economists have since called "consumer surplus" but also to special-interest groups who are within the universities and who have captured many of the benefits of ownership (again, borrowing from Manne).[29] Indeed, those special-interest groups so exploit the federal government programs that arose from the Higher Education Act of 1965 that they essentially capture for themselves the consumer surplus that arises from such government spending and that was formerly captured by students. There has been an income distribution from the general taxpaying public and even from students to others associated with universities, including to faculty and alumni and—more recently and strongly—to nonacademic administrative staff members.

Second, I will argue that the vast government-supported expansion of higher education has not been associated with greater economic growth, again echoing the findings for the 19th century previously cited. Indeed, with growing governmental involvement, the political process has transferred resources from a relatively efficient private sector governed by competition and market discipline to an inefficient not-for-profit education sector that is largely insulated from the consequences of competition by government subsidies. Resources have flowed from a sector incentivized to be efficient to one incentivized to be inefficient.

Third, I will argue that because the magnitude of government resources used in American higher education has grown so large, diminishing returns to their use have set in, which leads to a whole variety of pathologies never intended. I will briefly discuss four examples: soaring tuition fees, an underemployment problem for graduates, a decline in academic quality, and a fall in the proportion of students from lower-income backgrounds.

The Growth of the Federal Presence in Higher Education

In its first half-century or so of existence, the Morrill Act had trivial effects on the magnitude of American higher education and the development of the research university. If one argues, however, that the Morrill Act inaugurated a precedent of a federal commitment to higher education, one can further argue that, with a lag of a century or more, its legacy today is profound. As was said about the Watergate investigations of the 1970s, "Follow the money." The three important pieces of legislation that enabled federal expansion of student support are the Serviceman's Readjustment Act of 1944 (the GI Bill); the National Defense Education Act of 1958; and, by far the most important, the Higher Education Act of 1965, which has been often amended—with expansions—since.

On the research side, legislation in the 1940s and early 1950s created several federal research agencies, such as the National Institutes of Health (with roots back to the 19th century but existing under that name since 1930 with large funding increases after World War II), the Atomic Energy Commission (1946 and now the U.S. Department of Energy), the National Science Foundation (1950), and the National Aeronautical and Space Administration (1958).

Federal spending on higher education grew steadily—but from an extremely small base—from 1940 or so to 1965 and very rapidly since. That spending has taken two forms: assistance provided to students and assistance provided to institutions. As Table 2.1 suggests, federal student aid in all forms (including tuition tax credits and work-study, as well as a variety of loan and grant programs) grew tenfold in inflation-adjusted terms in the 40 years from the 1970–71 academic year to the 2010–11 year, a compounded annual growth rate of 6.49 percent a year (it has declined some since). Second, direct support to universities has soared, even at so-called private universities. Indeed, in the 2011–12 academic year, private four-year universities received more than $26 billion in governmental support, almost all of it from the federal government, which constituted 21 percent of total revenue (excluding funding for auxiliary enterprises and hospitals). Tuition fees constituted

Table 2.1

Federal Student Financial Assistance Programs, in Constant 2014 Dollars, 1970–2014

Year	Total assistance (in millions of $)
1970–71	15,412
1980–81	33,373
1990–91	31,797
2000–01	68,655
2010–11	190,596
2014–15	161,314

Source: College Board, "Total Student Aid and Nonfederal Loans in 2017 Dollars (in millions). 2007-18," Trends in Higher Education: Trends in Student Aid, Table 1, https://trends.collegeboard.org/student-aid/figures-tables/total-aid#Total%20Student%20Aid.

49 percent of that revenue, and those fees were heavily financed from federal student financial aid, which was received by a large majority of students.

Thus so-called private schools received 70 percent of their revenue directly from the government or from individuals who received generous federal support to pay their tuition fees. Five universities (four of them private) each received more than $1 billion in federal revenue, almost all to support research.[30] Although the proportion of public support was even higher at state universities because of large state appropriations, the sharp delineation between "public" and "private" schools is more fiction than fact. Almost all schools are heavily dependent on governmental funding.[31]

With this explosion in federal expenditures on higher education in mind, observe in Figure 2.2 that spending per student (adjusted for inflation) more than tripled from the 1939–40 year, which marked the end of the Great Depression, to 2012–13, which was a time that enrollments were growing fourteenfold (from less than 1.5 million to almost 21 million). Total higher education spending was nearly 41 times as

Figure 2.2

Real Spending Per Student, U.S. Higher Education, 1939–2013

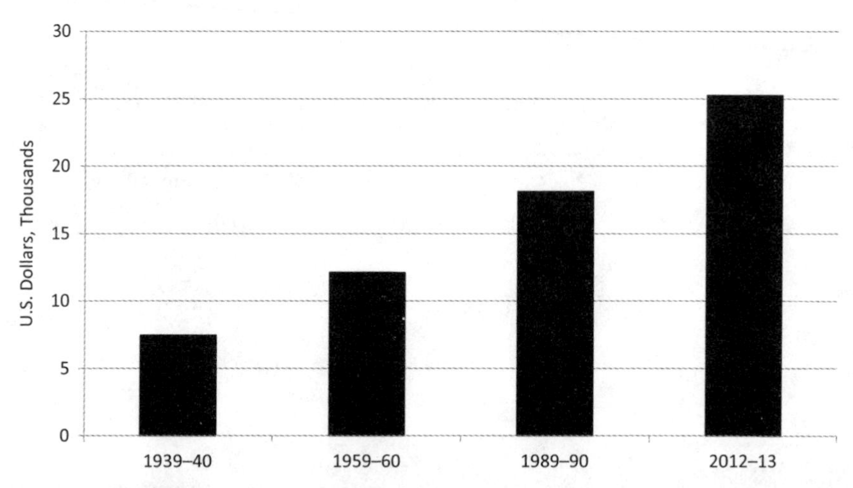

Sources: U.S. Department of Education, National Center for Education Statistics, *Digest of Education Statistics: 2015*, Tables 105.30 and 106.10, https://nces.ed.gov/pubsearch/pubsinfo.asp?pubid=2016014.

great—adjusting for inflation—in 2012–13 than in 1939–40.[32] The share of rising national output going for higher education roughly tripled.

Are students today receiving more or better instruction in smaller classes than they did in 1939–40? Possibly, although poor metrics make that conclusion hard to demonstrate. Some evidence, however—subsequently presented here—suggests that actual learning, broadly defined, is pretty meager and arguably declining in American universities. Even if the total university experience has gotten better for the typical student, have the incremental gains in the quality of the higher education experience justified a tripling in the price paid by students and the broader society?

The differential earnings between high school graduates and college graduates have grown, both in absolute and percentage terms, although the precise magnitude of the growth varies with which of many potential metrics are used in measurement. There are alternative definitions of the living unit used (individuals, households, or families); the work status of those examined (all persons, all workers, all full-time workers working year-round); and the measure of central tendency examined (mean or median)—not to mention gender (male or female).

That said, by most measures the work-related income differential between college degree holders and high school diploma holders in the 1970s was in the 40 to 70 percent range, whereas today it is in the 75 to 120 percent range; the differential has clearly grown. And that increase holds true for recent decades in particular. If one uses exactly comparable data and compares 1991 to 2015, the median income differential for all males grew from 67.4 to 92.8 percent; for females it grew from 79.7 to 118.4 percent.[33] To some, this is strong evidence that the Morrill Act–inspired expansion of higher education has been incredibly productive—indeed supportive of both income expansion and greater income mobility and equality—as a growing proportion of the population has degrees.

It is true that the composition of the labor force has changed and that an increasing proportion of jobs will use more cognitive skills rather than physical strength and endurance. That said, a significant part of the rising earnings differential associated with a college degree is almost certainly the result of public policy. In the early 1970s, the lament was that there was an oversupply of college graduates, as a distinguished Harvard labor economist argued in an oft-cited book.[34] The demand for college graduates was weak relative to supply.

A very strong case can be made that much of the rising high school–college earnings differential is not a consequence of a strong demand for highly skilled workers but more a consequence of a momentous public policy change occasioned by the U.S. Supreme Court's decision *Griggs v. Duke Power* (1971), one of the most important in the late 20th century.[35] Employers need to match job requirements to applicant qualifications, and doing so requires information about the potential productivity of those seeking employment. Before *Griggs*, an important tool that employers could use was testing: using one or more instruments to assess the potential worker's capabilities for a job. *Griggs* essentially outlawed much employee testing on the grounds that tests could have racially "disparate impact," which is in violation of Title VII of the Civil Rights Act of 1964. When in doubt, risk-averse employers eschewed the use of testing to avoid costly and distracting lawsuits. Later statutory enactments reinforced the reluctance to use testing.

In effect robbed of an important source of information, employers could still ask for employees' educational backgrounds, and a college diploma became a more important measure of potential employee competence. College completion always has been something of a screening or signaling device. Holders of college degrees typically are more literate, articulate, disciplined, and smarter that those with only high school diplomas, so they derive a wage premium for character traits that are at least partially independent of what they learned in college.[36] Employers increasingly relied on degrees as a means of certifying competence. As Bryan O'Keefe and I have explained elsewhere, that reliance increased the demand for college graduates and, after a lag of a few years, led to the beginning of a rise in the college–high school earnings differential.[37]

The secondary and tertiary effects of *Griggs* are hard to measure but are no doubt still material. By the 1980s, the now-rising college–high school income differential had become apparent, increasing the demand for higher education. As the financial return on investment in a college education grew, colleges could and did raise tuition fees aggressively to capture the excess investment return themselves. In technical terms, the demand for college rose relative to supply. The "nonprofit" nature of almost all of higher education at that time meant that, for many suppliers, few incentives existed to increase supply, an action that increases consumer choices and moderates tuition increases. Indeed, a sign of "success" in institutions of higher education is how many customers you turn away: Harvard has an admissions committee, but McDonald's does not—if you have $4 you can buy a Big Mac, but having $60,000 does not guarantee you admission to Harvard. In higher education, a low acceptance rate is a positive factor that *US News & World Report* uses in assessing institutional quality. But supply restriction also allows higher tuition fees. Higher education is one of the very few businesses in which firms actively try to turn away lots of customers.

Christopher Denhart, Joseph Hartge, and I have estimated that tuition fees in America, adjusted for inflation, typically rose around 1 percent a year in the period from about 1910 to 1978, but more like 3 percent a year since 1978.[38] It is not coincidental that 1978 marks about when the effect of *Griggs* was beginning to be felt, nor is it coincidental that 1978 is also about the time during which federal student financial assistance programs became huge—as Table 2.1 showed, those programs more than doubled in magnitude in the 1970s, even after adjusting for inflation.

A byproduct of both *Griggs* and the federal student financial assistance explosion was higher tuition fees, which meant more money for universities.[39] Other things equal, revenues rose relative to the cost of providing services, thereby offering a potential revenue surplus for schools, which in for-profit private enterprise equates with profits. How were the enhanced "quasi-profits" distributed?

Universities, which make their living by creating and disseminating information, are extremely reluctant to provide detailed information about how they operate. Nonetheless, a fair amount of evidence suggests that some of the incremental income that universities have received in recent years has been distributed to favored members of the university community in the form of economic rents—payments beyond those necessary to secure the provision of a service. Those favored employees are similar in many ways to stockholders in private corporations receiving dividends, implying, of course, that they have the equivalent of a de facto ownership interest in the universities. The payments can be the form of cash—higher salaries than necessary to secure employment—or in the form of amenities to make work more enjoyable, such as lower teaching loads for faculty members or having more subordinate employees to assist in meeting work obligations.

An exploration of the data reveals three things: (a) salaries of the most powerful and influential members of the university community—senior professors, top administrators, and so on—have risen more than the salaries of others, including the general population; (b) compensation has risen more in so-called private universities, where expanding federal financing has been particularly pronounced, and in four-year schools, where federal financing is far greater than in community colleges; and (c) professors have received economic rent in the form of lower teaching loads, whereas administrators have added to their bureaucracies with the passage of time. The general conclusion is that powerful persons within university communities have used their clout to capture disproportionate amounts of the vastly increased federal financial support.

Consider Figure 2.3. Nine-month salaries of full professors rose in inflation-adjusted terms in recent decades, whereas they fell for those

Figure 2.3

Change in Average Real Nine-Month Salaries, 1970–2014

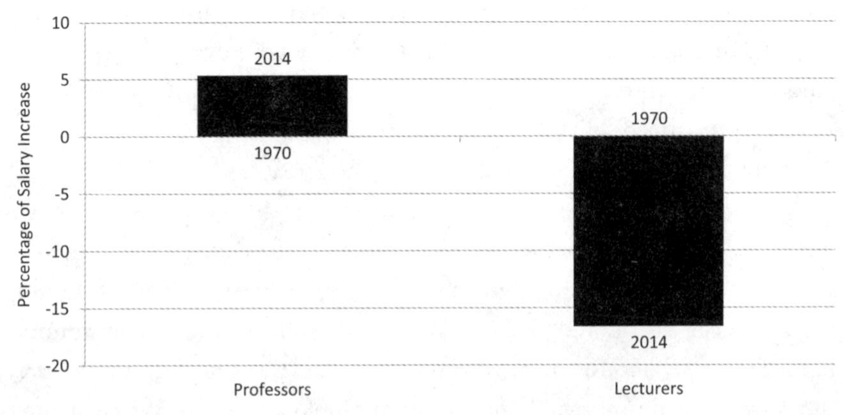

Source: U.S. Department of Education, National Center for Education Statistics, Table 316.10, *Digest of Education Statistics: 2015*, https://nces.ed.gov/programs/digest/d15/tables/dt15_316.10.asp?current=yes.

with the rank of lecturer. Full professors are generally tenured persons with some clout and an apparent quasi-ownership interest in the schools for which they work, whereas lecturers are nontenured, typically with little or no governance role, and are perceived as mere employees, not "stakeholders" (or stockholders in disguise). Those with political power within universities gained; those without that power lost.

Figure 2.3 significantly understates the increased compensation for professors for at least five reasons. First, the numbers exclude fringe benefits, which grew more than salary compensation over that period. Second, the data are for those on nine-month contracts. An increasing proportion of faculty members receive extra compensation in the summer months, very commonly for research but sometimes for teaching or administrative duties. Third, the consumer price index for all urban consumers used to adjust for inflation probably overstated inflation for at least part of the period examined. Fourth, the workload of professors eased over time, with faculty members teaching less, and thus professors have more time for discretionary research of their choosing. Fifth, almost certainly private nonuniversity income expanded through consulting, teaching for multiple universities (including in the expanding for-profit sector), and so on.

As previously indicated, the revolution in federal financing of higher education, for the most part felt indirectly through the effect on tuition fees, has turned so-called private schools into institutions that are at least partially dependent on the federal government for their funding. Figure 2.4 shows that this new largess, which was previously largely denied to private institutions, has now brought special prosperity to their faculties. The figure shows that real compensation for faculty members at four-year private institutions has risen far more than for their public university counterparts, because the federally financed tuition explosion has especially advantaged the private institutions. Meanwhile, teachers at two-year schools, which get little federal aid, have suffered.

The federal government's statisticians can tell you with pristine accuracy the number of female Hispanic professors of anthropology teaching in four-year private universities, but data are *not* systematically collected about faculty teaching loads. The evidence is clear, however,

Figure 2.4

Change in Inflation-Adjusted Faculty Nine-Month Pay, 1970–2014

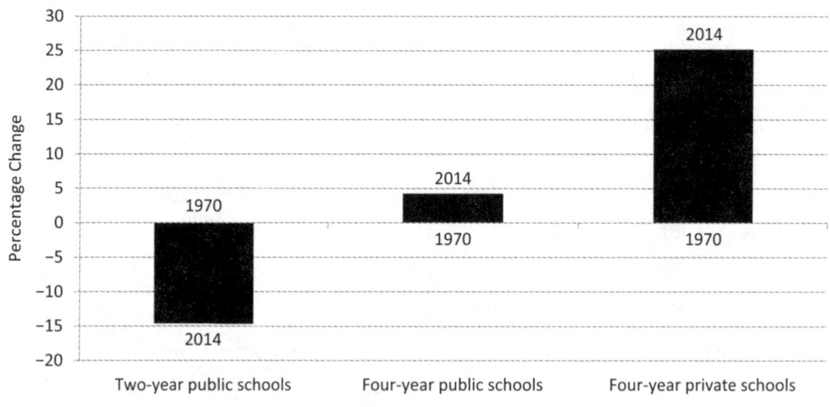

Source: U.S. Department of Education, National Center for Education Statistics, Table 316.10, *Digest of Education Statistics: 2015*, https://nces.ed.gov/programs/digest/d15/tables/dt15_316.10.asp?current=yes.

that teaching loads have fallen sharply over time; my guess is that the decline is somewhere between 25 and 50 percent since about 1960.[40] A survey of English departments, if one looks at undergraduate programs, found that in 1968 the typical teaching load was 12 hours a week; a 2013–14 Higher Education Research Institute Survey of more than 16,000 faculty suggests that the median teaching load today is about two courses, which usually means about six hours a week.[41] That survey, however, is of professors primarily teaching undergraduates; teaching loads at prominent research universities are even lower, with a one-course teaching load increasingly common.

It is interesting how the "Morrill Act–inspired" expansion of federal programs since 1970 has had almost the opposite of the effect intended by Justin Morrill. The people prospering the most are teaching in the elite private schools—not the "democratic" land-grant-style schools championed in the Morrill Act. The public schools serving the masses, in a relative sense at least, have suffered, and teaching faculties at two-year schools have probably had a modest decline in earnings, even adjusting for the data biases shown in Figures 2.3 and 2.4. The primacy of the so-called private schools over the public ones has accelerated in the modern era, has been aided and abetted by federal government subsidies (both direct and indirect), and has included favorable tax treatment for gifts and endowment investments.

But the faculty members, although generally faring reasonably well, are not the big winners in the dispersion of enhanced higher education monies. Indeed, their share of the pie has declined—and rather sharply. In the 1970s, "instruction" consumed about 40 percent of university budgets (and was mostly used to pay faculty), whereas in the modern era, it is about 30 percent.[42] There has been an explosion in the number of administrative staff members, and those new administrators have amassed power and increasingly high salaries.[43] This is particularly noticeable at the very top. The president of the University of Michigan, for example, in 1995–96 was paid less than $200,000 a year, whereas today's president makes well over double that amount, correcting for inflation, which implies inflation-adjusted increases of perhaps 5 percent a year over the past two decades.[44]

The new president of Texas A&M is receiving $1 million in base pay, an $800,000 "signing bonus," a $200,000 annual housing allowance, and other perks—about double the pay of his predecessor.[45] At the typical mid-quality state university at which I teach, the trustees contemplated allowing the president to move from a beautiful Victorian-era home in the middle of campus to a $1.2 million mini mansion miles from campus, presumably so he could avoid those annoying students. And, of course, this is nothing compared with the explosion in the salaries of college football coaches, which routinely reach into the millions of dollars annually at dozens of campuses around the country. Schools have spent massively on ever more elaborate football facilities to please the general public but especially the university, and this expense provides nonpecuniary income for them.

The tuition fee explosion, aided by the massive increase in federal student assistance programs, has financed an academic arms race that has provided a good deal of economic rent for many in the university community. But college graduates have incurred trillion-dollar debts, and a large number of them are forced to live with their parents after graduation to meet their debt obligations.

Universities and Economic Growth

The modern extollers of the Morrill Act speak of its ushering in an era of economic progress, which is simply not true on the basis of the national income accounting evidence for the 19th and early 20th century. But has the recent "Morrill-inspired" expansion of governmental support of higher education been accompanied by higher rates of economic growth? Do not universities have "positive externalities" or spillover effects that justify public subsidies, given the positive economic welfare effects on the population as a whole? The short answer to those questions is no.

As Table 2.2 indicates, the modern era of rising university attainment has been associated with a steady decline in the rate of economic growth. Whereas in the 1950s and 1960s GDP in the United States rose nearly 4.0 percent a year, which is almost reminiscent of late pre–Morrill Act America, in modern times 2.5 percent annual growth is more typical. Yet in those earlier years, well under 10 percent of adults had bachelor's degrees or higher, compared with an average of about 25 percent in the most recent period and nearly 33 percent today.

Of course, merely showing a negative association between rates of economic growth and rates of college attainment does not prove a causal relationship. Indeed, it is at least theoretically possible that if college attainment had not risen and that if our increased investments in higher

Table 2.2

U.S. Economic Growth and College Attainment, 1950–2014

Time period	Percentage annual GDP growth	Percentage over age 25 with college degree
1950–1970	3.93	7.7
1970–1990	3.25	16.2
1990–2014	2.47	26.7

Sources: U.S. Department of Commerce, U.S. Bureau of Economic Analysis, National Income and Product Accounts Tables, https://apps.bea.gov/iTable/iTable.cfm?reqid=19&step=2#reqid=19&step=2&isuri=1&1921=survey; U.S. Bureau of the Census, Table A-2, Educational Attainment Tables, https://www.census.gov/topics/education/educational-attainment/data/tables.html.

education had not taken place, the decline in the rate of economic growth would have been even greater. Obviously, lots of other factors explain economic growth, or the lack of it, including taxes, regulations, rate of immigration, proportion of the adult population working, dollar-yen-euro exchange rate, and many others.

Accordingly, a more sophisticated statistical analysis is needed, one using multivariate techniques that allow correction for noneducational determinants of economic growth. Data about legislative appropriations for higher education are available by state and can be related to the growth in real income per capita, thereby introducing a variety of other variables into the model to control for other factors. I have run hundreds of regressions looking at this relationship while using different variables, time periods, time lags, functional forms, and methodologies (e.g., time-series analysis, cross-sectional analysis, panel data), and they all fail to show a positive relationship between state spending on universities and economic growth. Indeed, often a statistically significant negative relationship is obtained: higher university spending is associated with lower economic growth.[46]

If college graduates are more productive than high school graduates, as indicated by the higher wages that the former can command, why, then, does spending more money on colleges not lead to higher rates of economic growth? There are a number of reasons, including that the correlation between higher education spending and the actual number of graduates is not very strong (perhaps further evidence that a good bit of incremental spending gets dissipated in economic rents). The major reason, however, relates to opportunity costs. Higher education appropriations are financed by taxation. Resources are taken from taxpayers, who mostly earn their living working and investing in the highly disciplined, competitive, market-driven environment of for-profit enterprise. In this sector, labor productivity historically rises 2 percent a year. Resources are redirected to the higher education sector, which is mostly not for profit, is highly subsidized, and has few incentives for efficiency. That sector shows actual *increases* over time in the amount of labor it takes to produce the ostensibly most critical output: educated students. Resources are redirected from efficient to inefficient modes of production.

Morrill-Inspired Legislation and the Law of Unintended Consequences[47]

The torrent of federal legislation that is related to higher education in the mid-20th century and is inspired in a sense by the precedent of the 1862 Morrill legislation has had profound and often relatively unintended effects on American higher education. The changes are so many and the effects so far-reaching that a complete accounting of them would be far beyond the confines of this essay, which focuses on the Morrill Act itself more than on the legislation later inspired by it. Accordingly, I will focus on only four major consequences of the extraordinary expansion of federal involvement in higher education over the past half-century. Most of these consequences were a direct effect of the massive federal programs for student financial assistance that mainly grew out of the Higher Education Act of 1965.

The Tuition Fee Explosion

Tuition fees have—for at least a century and probably much longer—risen faster than the overall rate of inflation. Writing coincidentally at about the time that federal expansion into higher education was beginning to grow exponentially, Princeton's William Baumol argued that higher education is a bit like theater: just as it takes as many actors to perform *King Lear* today as it did when it was written more than 400 years ago, so it takes as many professors today to teach a given number of students as in the past.[48] Wages have risen with productivity advances in the rest of the economy but not in the profession of teaching. Despite teachers' lagging productivity, if one is to make sure that professors are still attracted to the field, then their wages must rise with overall market conditions over time, thus tracking the overall productivity of the economy. That wage increase raises college costs. More recently, university presidents and others have argued that stagnating state appropriations are a major cost of rising tuition fees as well.

Yet Baumol's argument increasingly seems archaic because new technology allows professors to serve vastly more students and because the noninstructional share of college budgets has soared in recent years. The argument about state appropriations is of limited validity as well, because fees over time have also risen sharply at private schools that do not receive state appropriations.

Then–secretary of education William J. Bennett offered a third explanation for rising costs in a 1987 newspaper op-ed: colleges raise their fees because increasing federal student aid allows them to do so; that conclusion implies that the colleges, not the students, are the true primary beneficiaries of federal financial aid.[49] There are good reasons, which are based both on economic theory and on empirical evidence, to believe that Bennett is right.[50] Aside from the aforementioned study with Denhart and Hartge showing an uptick in tuition fees in the era of large federal student loans, new evidence from the Federal Reserve Bank of New York powerfully shows that increases in federal student financial aid are associated with tuition increases.[51] The "pass-through" effects of aid are estimated to be about 65 percent—a dollar more aid per student is associated with 65 cents more tuition. That analysis fits in with the story told previously: increased dollars flowing to colleges have allowed powerful interests to capture economic rents intended to help students.

The Underemployment of Recent College Graduates

A plethora of evidence shows that a large proportion of recent college graduates are "underemployed." They mostly have jobs, but ones that usually are held by those with less education (typically a high school diploma): baristas, clerks in big box retail discount stores, janitors, home health care aides, and others.[52] Whereas in 1970 there was only 1 college graduate to every 150 taxi drivers, now there are about 25. The new College Scorecard of the U.S. Department of Education reveals that at many schools, the average postgraduate earnings are no higher than those of high school graduates. Although slow employment growth following the 2008 financial crisis has aggravated underemployment, it is a long-term phenomenon; the way to largely eliminate it in the near future is difficult to see.

The vast federal assistance programs have increased the demand for education. Although supply has been relatively inelastic (see previous discussion), some providers have moved to expand capacity and accept more students. On balance, the federal aid programs have been successful in increasing enrollments—and the number of graduates—from what they would have been in the absence of such programs. That increase, in turn, has aggravated the underemployment problem. Employers, seeing the abundance of college graduates, often have raised the educational requirements for jobs such as bartender, for which no higher education experience was previously expected. Such requirements have given rise to credential inflation that is extremely costly and have probably aggravated unemployment among high school graduates.

The Decline in Academic Quality

Although good measures of the value added by college to a student's ability to function well in adult life are lacking, the evidence points to a likely qualitative decline in student learning and in the acquisition of critical thinking and reasoning skills. Tests of basic literacy given at both the national and international level show that American college graduates have relatively low rates of literacy, and those rates have been declining over time. To cite one factoid, between 1992 and 2003, the percentage of college graduates proficient in prose literacy declined from 40 to 31 percent.[53]

The path-breaking research of Richard Arum and Josipa Roksa shows that improvements in critical reasoning and writing skills during the college years typically are extremely modest.[54] Jackson Toby, in turn, has suggested that declining academic standards at the university level has led to falling standards at the secondary school level.[55] Moreover, whereas shortly before passage of the most important of the Morrill-inspired legislation (say, 1950 or 1960), students typically spent 40 hours weekly on academic pursuits, today they spend far less—less than 30 hours—but receive much higher grades because of grade inflation.[56]

In my judgment, the federal student financial aid programs have contributed to the qualitative decline in two ways. First, in contributing to higher enrollments, those programs have led to the admission to college of students who lack the cognitive skills and other attributes needed to master truly rigorous, difficult concepts that have historically been the hallmarks of higher education. That point has been made repeatedly and masterfully by Charles Murray.[57] One might reasonably assert that it takes persons with significantly above average cognitive skills (say, an IQ of 115, or about one standard deviation above the average) to master abstruse, abstract concepts that are the hallmark of at least part of traditional learning in universities.

By definition, in a society in which about 32 percent of the adult population has degrees, at least one-half of those graduates lack cognitive skills at that high level.[58] That lack has led to a "dumbing down" of the curriculum. Murray is echoing the sentiment of educators of an earlier era: Harvard's president James Bryant Conant, for example, opined even before World War II that "there are too many rather than too few students attending the universities of this country."[59] The equally prominent president of the University of Chicago, Robert Maynard Hutchins, after passage of the GI Bill in 1944, remarked even more caustically that American colleges would become "intellectual hobo jungles."[60]

Rent-seeking college administrators, not wanting to lose revenues and be accused of running failing institutions or denying access to disadvantaged members of society, have encouraged a loosening in academic standards to prevent rising dropout rates associated with a student body that is less capable. The most obvious manifestation of that is grade inflation, which has been continuous for more than half a century.

The second way in which the federal student financial aid programs have led to qualitative decline is that they do not reward academic success and high performance. Indeed, the opposite is true. Consider a marginal student, who has failed several classes but managed to stay in school—graduating, however, in six years. Consider also a superb student, who gets nearly all "A" grades, works hard, and graduates in only three years, perhaps aided by some credits earned from high school Advanced Placement courses. Suppose both receive Pell Grants. The mediocre student will receive probably about twice the federal aid that the good student will. Whereas traditionally scholarship monies were designed to prod students to be academically excellent, the federal programs work in the opposite direction.

The Declining Proportion of Low-Income College Graduates

The rationale behind the explosive expansion of federal student financial aid was that, in Morrill-like fashion, it would increase access to college by students of relatively modest means. It was to strengthen the attainment of the American Dream, thereby promoting income mobility by allowing poor students to use education as a tool for attaining income and even wealth. President Lyndon Johnson said in signing the Higher Education Act more than 50 years ago, "This act means the path of knowledge is open to all that have the determination to walk it."[61]

Fast forward 50 years to 2015. What happened to the proportion of college graduates from low-income families? *It had fallen* (see Figure 2.5). In 1970, about 12 percent of recent college graduates came from the bottom quartile of the income distribution; 45 years later, it was less than

Figure 2.5

Share of Recent Bachelor's Degrees Received, by Family Income Quartile, 1970–2010

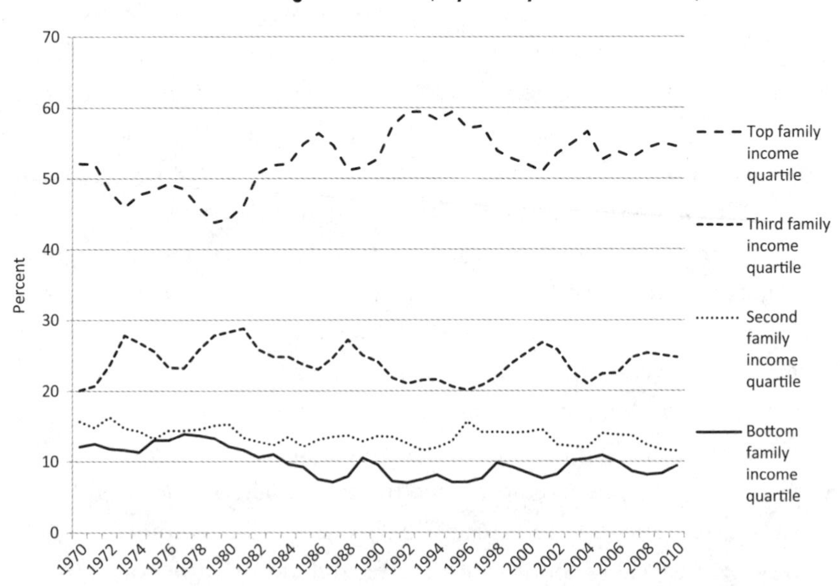

Source: Postsecondary Education Opportunity, "Bachelor's Degree Attainment by Age 24 by Family Income Quartiles, 1970 to 2010." http://pellinstitute.org/indicators/

Note: Definition of population of interest changes after 1986, from "Unmarried 18- to 24-year–olds" to "Dependent 18- to 24-year-old family members."

10 percent. Meanwhile, the proportion of graduates with above-average earnings actually grew.

These findings fit perfectly with Henry Manne's argument suggesting that the real winners of Morrill Act–inspired federal intrusions into higher education were not poor students but other groups. I think the federal financial aid programs pushed up tuition fees, scaring low-income students away from even applying, especially because the required Free Application for Federal Student Assistance form is byzantine in its length and complexity. Thus, the form deters some low-income students from filing for financial aid. Higher fees have provided income in both pecuniary and nonpecuniary form for academic *rentiers*, but they have hurt students, especially the ones that federal aid was most designed to help. There is some evidence that higher education has gone from lowering income inequality to raising it, as diminishing returns set in to its effectiveness.[62]

Conclusions

The Morrill Legacy—The Triumph of the Academic Beggars

Popular mythology has the Morrill Act and its legislative descendants such as the Higher Education Act of 1965 playing a transformative role, not only by elevating American universities to greatness but also by propelling the entire economy to unprecedented heights, thus serving in many ways as the fountain of American economic exceptionalism. I think that interpretation is fundamentally wrong.

In *The Wealth of Nations*, Adam Smith (1776) made the point that economies advance not from altruism but from greed and self-interest: "It is not from the benevolence of the butcher, the brewer, or the baker, that we expect our dinner, but from their regard to their own interest. . . . Nobody but a beggar chuses [*sic*] to depend chiefly upon the benevolence of his fellow-citizens."[63] Universities are beggars, depending heavily on the good-heartedness of others. Not content with magnificent gifts from private citizens, they have used the political process to propel their begging—and rent seeking—to a new level.

The Morrill Act can be viewed like a play having two acts. In Act One (1815–1914), higher education grew rapidly. But the growth was at least as great in a meaningful sense in the antebellum era before Justin Morrill successfully introduced his legislation. The one major difference in the post-Morrill era of 1862 to 1914 was the introduction of the concept of the research university, although that was not led by the land-grant colleges created under Morrill but by private entrepreneurs such as Johns Hopkins and John D. Rockefeller. Moreover, the evidence is clear that the United States' ascendency to economic superpower had nothing to do with the Morrill Act. Indeed, economic growth was higher in the pre-Morrill era than in the period following passage of the legislation.

Act Two involves the legislation of the modern era that was inspired by the precedent of the Morrill Act.[64] That era has seen unprecedented growth in the federal government's involvement in higher education. And what has it achieved? The era has been noteworthy for a slowdown in the rate of economic growth; within higher education, pathologies have included soaring tuition fees, growing underemployment of college graduates, declining academic quality, and even a relative decline in participation in higher education by low-income groups.

At the same time, powerful people within university communities behave as if they are stockholders of private corporations, and they have exercised some of their clout to capture, in some meaningful sense, partial ownership of allegedly nonprofit enterprises that, in fact, generate large financial surpluses each year. The "dividends" emanating from those surpluses have brought about troubles, including—but not limited to—powerful and increasingly affluent university bureaucracies, million-dollar university presidents with most of the accoutrements of corporate power, and faculty members whose contact with the classroom is in consistent decline. Rent seeking has gone amok.

Government support of colleges is usually justified on two grounds. First, there are positive externalities to universities; if the private sector were left to its own devices, too few higher education services would be provided. The 19th-century record with respect to the Morrill Act calls that issue into question, as does the economic growth–higher education empirical evidence. The 20th-century government involvement leading to vast numbers of underemployed graduates suggests that we may have actually *overinvested* in higher education.

The second big argument for public higher education is that it opens up access for lower-income Americans—it is a way of realizing the American Dream. Again, the evidence suggests otherwise. In their successful pursuit of economic rents manifested in legislation such as the Higher Education Act of 1965, academic leaders have in effect priced some poor persons out of the market for college.

In *Capitalism and Freedom*, classical liberal economist Milton Friedman argued against most government interventions, but he said that government spending on higher education was probably justified because of its positive externalities.[65] When I asked him more than 40 years later about that statement, he said, "I have not changed my view that higher education has some positive externality, but I have become much more aware that it also has negative externalities. I am much more dubious than I was when I wrote *Capitalism and Freedom* that there is any justification at all for government subsidy of higher education."[66] Reviewing the history of the Morrill Act and how it has morphed into the federal legislation of the past half-century suggests that Friedman's skepticism is justified.

CHAPTER THREE

Accreditation: Market Regulation or Government Regulation Revisited?

Joshua C. Hall

There is growing dissatisfaction with higher education in the United States. A recent national poll from the Robert Morris University Polling Institute found that less than 50 percent of parents gave institutions of higher education an overall "positive rating for demonstrating that they stay current with the demands of the job market and that they maintain relationships with employers."[1] To put this decline in perspective, the same poll found a steep decline in the perceived value of a bachelor's degree. Just a decade ago, 68 percent of parents placed a positive value on a bachelor's degree; today that number is less than 45 percent.

Criticism of higher education is, of course, not new. For proof one needs only to read old issues of the *Journal of Higher Education*. A particularly interesting example can be found in 1934, written by Stanford education professor Walter Crosby Eells. With the exception of a couple of introductory paragraphs and a conclusion, the entirety of the article consists of then-contemporary criticisms of the academy. The following charges leveled at the academy at that time sound similar to some of the arguments made today:

> They say that our universities are aimless institutions that have prostituted themselves to every public whim, serving as everything from a reformatory to an amusement park; they are only service stations for

> the general public; they are a bargain-counter system presided over by quacks; they are places where pebbles are polished and diamonds dimmed. The trustees according to the critics are men entirely unfitted for their tasks, ridiculously conservative and fearful, controlled body and soul by Wall Street. The presidents are liars and hypocrites, academic Machiavellis, who dull the intellectual life of the colleges, cow the faculty, and stultify the student body.[2]

Clearly, dissatisfaction with higher education is not new. It would be easy to look at the persistence of those criticisms, combined with the continued growth of the higher education sector, and believe that nothing needs to be done. In my opinion that would be wrong. Numerous pressures are facing U.S. higher education that, when combined with the rising visibility of the academy's critics, are going to lead to change. Those pressures include but are not limited to stagnating economic growth,[3] declining birth rates,[4] Medicaid and Medicare crowding out state support for higher education,[5] and the increased perception that for many, the costs of higher education exceed the benefits.[6]

A variety of reforms have been suggested. Although reform means different things to different people, most suggestions involve lowering costs, improving productivity, or doing things differently to achieve some broader social goal. For example, I edited a volume of essays devoted to the topic of reforming institutions internally.[7] Suggestions made in that volume primarily focused on ways that colleges and universities could save money in the area of operations,[8] athletics,[9] and management.[10] In addition, a couple of chapters highlighted two entrepreneurial efforts to lower costs and improve productivity, one at a for-profit university and another within an economics department at a major state university.[11] More recently, Richard Vedder listed 36 steps that could be taken to reform American higher education.[12] Other examples include proposals from Derek Bok, Richard DeMillo, Mitchell Stevens and Michael Kirst, and Robert Zemsky.[13]

A prominent reform that is often raised is changing accreditation, the voluntary self-regulation process for colleges and universities. Accreditation historically provided quality assurance and quality improvement for the consumer, but recently some have questioned its value. For example,

Vedder lists "Eliminate or reshape academic accreditation" as Step 17 of his 36 reform steps—in fact, he denotes it as a most important step. Vedder gives several reasons to eliminate or change accreditation, including (a) accreditation provides little useful information because both high- and low-quality schools receive the same accreditation; (b) accreditation is poor at measuring quality because it focuses on inputs, not outputs; (c) accreditation restricts entry into the higher education marketplace; and (d) accreditation is riddled with conflicts of interest.[14] Others calling for reform or elimination of the accreditation process include Leef and Burris,[15] the American Council of Trustees and Alumni,[16] Andrew Gillen et al.,[17] and Lindsey Burke and Stuart Butler.[18] Perhaps most important, accreditation was listed as having significant shortcomings in the report of the Spellings Commission for reforming higher education.[19]

There are four types of accreditation organizations in the United States: regional, national faith based, national career related, and programmatic accreditors.[20] Regional accreditors primarily accredit degree-granting two- and four-year institutions, such as Beloit College, Ohio State University, or West Virginia University. National faith-based accreditors focus on accrediting degree and nondegree-granting religious institutions, such as the Moody Bible Institute in Chicago. Career-related organizations accredit career-based, single-purpose institutions, such as West Virginia Junior College in Morgantown, West Virginia.[21] Programmatic accreditors focus on specific academic programs and schools, such as Association to Advance Collegiate Schools of Business (AACSB) International, which accredits degree programs in business administration and accounting.[22] Although all four types of accreditors are important, the discussion here primarily focuses on the regional accreditors because that is where the majority of students, activity, and criticism are centered.[23]

Initially, I was very skeptical of accreditation being a large problem. It seemed that many of the critics were engaged in some form of what Harold Demsetz termed the "nirvana" fallacy.[24] In its simplest form, the nirvana fallacy assumes that there exists some ideal compared to the current system. That assumption is problematic for at least three reasons. First, reforms often can make situations worse if reformers do not understand what drives the current system. Changing or eliminating an institution without some other institution in place to meet the outstanding need often will lead to a worse situation.[25] Second, the proposed solution might be worse because reformers fail to understand how the new system will change the incentives of those within it.[26] Third, the implemented solution might not be as efficient or effective as what had existed before.

I have argued that given the demand for quality regulation in higher education, economists' default should be that free individuals left to their own devices will produce institutions that meet their needs. As I stated in 2012, "The institutions that solve problems at the lowest cost cannot be known a priori; they must be discovered through trial and error and the marketplace's information revelation process."[27] The "right" level of regulation or assessment is not something that can be determined scientifically; instead it has to be discovered in the marketplace. What is the optimum minimum quality standard for a hotel that wants to call itself a Best Western? The answer, of course, depends on the benefits that member hotels receive from the Best Western assurance to consumers weighed against the costs of compliance with Best Western's voluntary standards.[28]

Although I stand by that general statement, with respect to higher education accreditation I have become convinced that calls for reform have merit. My thinking on that issue began to change while reading Daniel Bennett, who shows that higher education in the United States has never been laissez faire.[29] I began to see how the institution of accreditation, which solved a problem at one point in time, was now making things worse because of its interaction with the political system.[30] We are no longer in the world of the first or second best, as the federal government's involvement has severely distorted the information and incentives provided through the current "voluntary" system of regional accreditation.

This chapter is organized as follows: The second section discusses the history of accreditation in the United States up to World War II. I show that accreditation before the G.I. Bill was primarily self-regulation and that consumers buying education largely with their own money put pressure on schools to keep value high. The third section moves on to the post–World War II period, where I discuss how the G.I. Bill fundamentally changed the incentives of students, schools, accreditors, and the federal government in a way that has led to increasing costs and uncertain quality. I conclude that the G.I. Bill set in motion changes that have transformed accreditation from a voluntary process to an implicit form of government regulation that exacerbates the problems created by third-party payment in higher education. The fourth section concludes with some general thoughts and a possible proposal for reform.

Pre-G.I. Bill Higher Education Accreditation

Institutions of higher education predate the establishment of the United States as a nation. In 1745, there were only three colleges in North America: Harvard, William and Mary, and Yale.[31] As detailed by Bennett and Wilezol, nine colleges were established during the colonial period. Although they were primarily religious institutions, they were creatures of the state insofar as they required a charter from the colonial government or the Crown to begin operation. Those charters essentially granted colleges a monopoly over the awarding of degrees in each colony.[32] In that manner they acted like a very weak form of accreditation, especially given that the goal of most colonial colleges was to train ministers and other community leaders.[33] After all, the only college allowed to operate in a colony had to be of high quality.

Accreditation as we know it today only developed around 1900.[34] As the president of the Council for Higher Education Accreditation (CHEA), Judith Eaton, put it, "When accreditation was created 100 years ago, it sought, first and foremost, to serve higher education institutions and programs."[35] The issue at hand was really about signaling quality in a growing market that was highly decentralized. The number of students enrolled in institutions of higher education had doubled in just 20 years, and the number of institutions had increased by 166. In that expanding environment, old measures of assessing incoming students were becoming less accurate, more costly, or both.

The earliest forms of what we now know as accreditation arose from 1880 to 1900.[36] Four of our current regional accreditation associations had their start during that time, although the reason for their creation was not accreditation. Historically, schools had relied on direct knowledge of specific national preparatory schools or secondary schools in their limited geographic area. As secondary education began to grow, especially outside the northeast United States, the information problem of adequate preparation for college-level work became more acute. That was especially true for midwestern or southern students who wanted to go east for college, as there was great concern among college administrators in the East about the quality of preparation in midwestern and southern secondary schools. Schools tried to deal with those concerns in a variety of ways. In New England, many schools developed a common entrance exam. Other schools developed their own entrance exams and, for those students who did not make the cut, eventually developed their own preparatory schools to get students up to speed. That was especially common in areas with weak or nonexistent secondary schools.[37]

Eventually, colleges and universities in different regions realized that they had the same concerns and formed associations to deal with the issues they had in common.[38] Although the most pressing issue was determining what constituted an adequate education at the secondary level for admission to higher education, they eventually turned to accrediting themselves. It was a logical outgrowth of their certifying secondary schools, and it addressed the information problem arising from students crossing regional lines for colleges or universities. In 1905, for example, the North Central Association (NCA) created the first list of certified secondary schools in a region.[39] Those regional associations filled a very important quality assurance need at the time by providing some basis for college admissions officers to determine whether or not a student's secondary preparation had prepared them adequately for college.

It is important to remember that absent local knowledge or a letter of recommendation from someone who was well known to the college, the alternative was to create a written or oral entrance exam. The information was important not only to colleges and universities, it was important to students who wanted to make sure that they were studying the right material or at the right school to get into the higher education institution of their choice. Not only did students of that time not have the ability, given the technology of the day, to assess quality but that inability was significant given the geographical constraints that many students faced.

During the early part of the 20th century, more students were transferring between institutions both domestically and abroad. The regional associations began to certify colleges and universities as meeting minimum quality standards to be a member. For example, the NCA provided its first list of accredited schools in 1913 and the Southern Association of Colleges and Schools in 1919.[40] Those lists were designed with an eye toward distinguishing between preparatory schools, normal schools, secondary schools, and colleges and universities.[41] Consider the list of requirements the NCA said that a college must meet:

1. Follow respectable entrance requirements.
2. Offer courses selected from the classics.
3. Ensure a minimum of eight departments headed by full-time instructors, each possessing at least a master's degree.
4. Provide a good library.
5. Properly prepare students for post-graduate study.
6. Have a maximum class size of 30.
7. Have a productive endowment of at least 200,000 dollars.[42]

That was during a period when employers and other colleges and universities had real concerns about the quality of graduates of a number of schools.[43] For example, foreign institutions, with the University of Berlin leading the way in 1912, began to not recognize degrees from U.S. universities unless they were members of the Association of American Universities (AAU).[44] A special committee of the AAU was led by Charles Eliot, the president of Harvard, to evaluate whether the AAU should assess the quality of U.S. institutions beyond providing a list of its own members and criteria for membership. The report concluded the following:

> It is the duty of this Association either to standardize American Universities, and thus to justify the confidence which foreign governments repose in them, or to notify those governments that there are American Universities outside this Association whose work and standing are not inferior to universities now members of the Association.[45]

Ultimately, the AAU decided not to review colleges and universities. The U.S. Bureau of Education during the Taft administration briefly considered undertaking the task, but President William Taft put a stop to it in 1912 in response to public outcry over the idea of federal involvement in higher education.[46] The American Council of Education tried taking on the role of accreditor for a brief period, but they gave up being a national accreditor in 1935.[47] What remained at the end were the regional accrediting agencies. In spite of the fits and starts that accreditation undertook, before 1936 it was a voluntary system designed to provide information about quality to students, employers, and other colleges and universities.[48] Customers used the information provided by those accreditation agencies, and colleges and universities were willing to expend their own resources in the accreditation process.[49]

Very little evidence indicates that colleges and universities during that period used accreditation in an anti-competitive or rent-seeking manner. With the intent being to distinguish high-quality institutions from low-quality ones, the barriers to accreditation suggested by the early NCA criteria seemed appropriate to the period given the nature of higher education production. To the extent that colleges and universities were being anti-competitive or rent seeking during that period, it seemed mostly to occur through public institutions lobbying state legislatures for special favors. For example, in Ohio supporters of Ohio State University made numerous attempts to limit the operations of Ohio and Miami Universities.[50] This makes sense: most public support to higher education at that time was given to institutions, not to students.

Important to highlight is that after President Taft stopped the U.S. Bureau of Education from publishing an assessment of higher education institutions in 1912, there was very little government involvement in accreditation.[51] The lack of government involvement in education, especially with respect to regular financing of tuition (even at many state universities), meant that accountability was only to students, employers, and other higher educational institutions. The latter were voluntary membership organizations, which worked well because if the information they provided was inadequate or in error, they received feedback from other member institutions. Even if they wanted to use accreditation in an anti-competitive manner to limit entry into the higher education marketplace by raising everyone's costs, they did not have sufficient market power. Economic barriers to entry were low, and with little government funding, new entrants were not at a competitive disadvantage. As a result, new institutions, such as professional schools focused on business or law, flourished.[52]

The rise of new institutions not only shows how little market power accreditors had at the time but also how the higher education marketplace responded to a growing number of high school graduates eager to take advantage of the returns to additional education.[53] The high labor market returns to increased education, combined with relatively low tuition, led to growing enrollments during that period at both public and private institutions. Important to note, however, is that students and families were still paying tuition and room and board out of pocket during that period, as there were no Pell Grants, federally subsidized student loans, or federal G.I. Bill. As a result, families were very sensitive to differences in both price and quality.

According to Goldin and Katz, enrollment at public institutions of higher education grew relative to that of private institutions during that period because students responded to their lower tuition and room-and-board fees. Goldin and Katz also find that students were responsive to changes in public school tuition during that period, with lower public school tuition and room and board leading to higher enrollment. Direct state support to institutions of higher education therefore affected tuition and enrollment decisions but did not weaken consumer incentives to care about cost and quality.

In this marketplace in which students and families were largely paying out of pocket, the standards of accreditation agencies were sufficient to distinguish across types of institutions. Gillen and colleagues note that "those institutions that were accredited by reputable accreditors stood out as better than those that were not (or were accredited by a lesser accrediting body)."[54] Accreditors at the time were largely focused on distinguishing across different types of institutions based on easily observable standards such as faculty size, library volumes, and size of endowment. Although measures of "quantity" rather than "quality," those features of higher education institutions were enough to differentiate across institutional types for both consumers and member institutions. And because government support came in the form of direct support to institutions of higher education or land subsidies, accreditation did not serve any public accountability purpose.[55] Students were free to go to any type of institution they wished—accredited or unaccredited—and policymakers were free to directly monitor institutions that received public funding to ensure that public funds were being used in a manner consistent with their legislative purpose.

The period leading up to 1940 seemed to be a well-functioning higher education marketplace, with few reasons for citizens and policymakers to be concerned about cost or quality in general. Students and families paid for tuition and room and board out of their own funds and thus had strong incentives to ensure that college was worth what they were paying.[56] Federal and state support of higher education was typically for specific purposes, such as research or the promotion of agricultural and mechanical field of study.[57] In that environment, policymakers could easily monitor outcomes (whether the research was completed, how many graduates there were in mechanical fields) to hold institutions accountable for public funds. Finally, accrediting agencies competed with one another for reasonable ways of differentiating across institutions. According to the American Council of Trustees and Alumni, the competition among agencies kept the information component of accreditation high while not becoming overly burdensome because "the knowledge that institutions could drop accreditation kept associations from becoming dictatorial or attempting inappropriately to influence the content of education."[58] No single entity had enough influence to directly capture or impede market forces, and as a result the system largely worked well for all involved.[59] Things would change, however, following World War II.

The G.I. Bill and the Transformation of Accreditation

Like the enrollment boom of the late 19th century, the increase in higher education enrollments after World War II introduced new problems.

Institutions faced problems of where to put all the students and how to deal with the *in loco parentis* doctrine for older students who had been through war and were not willing to be subject to institutions' strictures.[60] The biggest change, however, was in the federal government's role in higher education. The original G.I. Bill and its reauthorization in 1952 introduced the federal government as a significant direct financier of higher education in the United States.[61] Julie Morgan notes that the "G.I. Bill introduced the concept of national, student-centered support for higher education."[62] Not only did it change the scope of federal government activity in higher education, it changed the scale, with more than 1 million students enrolled in higher education institutions on the G.I. Bill in 1946. According to John Bound and Sarah Turner, that was about 70 percent of male higher education enrollment in the postwar period.[63]

No longer was the government just directly funding institutions. Under the 1944 G.I. Bill, funds were paid directly to institutions based on the enrollment decisions of veterans. Students still had the freedom to attend the institution of higher education of their choice. For the veteran, however, the calculation had changed. Because tuition dollars no longer came out of his pocket, the question was no longer whether or not the degree was worth the cost. Veterans could take advantage of the higher education benefit of the G.I. Bill only if they enrolled in an institution of higher education, so the question was whether the degree was worth more than the cost of their time going to school. For veterans who were indifferent between going to college or entering the workforce, free tuition and room and board made going to college or university—any university—a no-brainer.

Not surprising, many veterans using the G.I. Bill were less concerned about the degree they were obtaining than were pre–World War II applicants who were paying the full tuition cost. Almost immediately widespread reports claimed that some veterans were going to "diploma mills," constituting a significant scandal. On the supply side, some for-profit institutions recognized that a number of veterans wanted to take advantage of the benefit but were less concerned about quality.[64] Under the original G.I. Bill, the only restriction on an institution's ability to receive federal aid was state authorization, which was a mere formality that did not involve issues of quality.[65] As a result, writes William Beaver, "Some schools existed to collect government funds and offered little actual education."[66] Those, and other abuses such as the overstating of costs, occurred with colleges and universities of all types that enrolled veterans under the G.I. Bill. For example, a General Accounting Office study at the time noted that 65 percent of colleges and universities employed questionable financial practices that led them to overcharge the federal government.[67]

The G.I. Bill and the influx of students who were not contemporaneously paying for the good they were consuming transformed the higher education marketplace. By and large, when consumers pay for a product out of their own pocket, they have an incentive to minimize expenditure given a certain level of quality or to look for the highest quality given a specific amount of expenditure. If they don't find a price–quality combination that they like, consumers can choose not to spend their hard-earned dollars on that good or service and instead spend it on other goods and services that provide them with more value. When consumers are not paying out of their own pocket or cannot use the resources on other goods and services, the incentive for cost containment and quality control are lessened.[68] Once such a higher percentage of college students were no longer paying the direct cost of education, consumer discipline could no longer be counted on to push schools toward cost minimization and quality.

In the wake of the diploma mill scandal and the subsequent General Accounting Office report, Congress took steps in 1952 to try to fix the accountability problem that they had created with the G.I. Bill. In passing the Veterans' Adjustment Act of 1952, which extended G.I. Bill–style higher education benefits to Korean War veterans, Congress required the Commissioner of Education to publish a list of nationally recognized accrediting agencies.[69] Only schools recognized by known accrediting agencies would be eligible to receive federal student aid.[70] Commissioner of Education Earl James McGrath listed the six accrediting agencies that then oversaw higher education accreditation in the United States, thereby imposing on private accrediting associations a new purpose: public accountability.[71] That new charge—a government-sponsored cartel with access to federal funding—substantially changed both accreditation and higher education.

Linking access to federal funds with regional accreditation fundamentally changed accreditation from a voluntary member organization that provided quality assurance to a government-sponsored cartel. As Gillen, Bennett, and Vedder note, "Some critics of accreditation have thus described the regional accreditation system as cartel-like, with each accreditor granted a regional monopoly with a guaranteed market for customers without having to provide much benefit."[72] Colleges and universities that wanted to enroll students using federal funds had to be accredited, which by itself was not problematic. The regional accreditation system established in 1952 by Commissioner McGrath, however, essentially ended competition among accreditors for members.[73] The lack of competition among accreditors meant that the standards of accreditors stopped responding to feedback from members and instead largely converged toward one another. That fundamentally changed accreditation in the United States from self-regulation similar to Underwriters Laboratory to an indirect form of government regulation.

Like the imposition of rent control in New York City after World War II, the implications of that change to the marketplace took some time to become apparent even though the underlying market institutions had been radically changed. The G.I. Bill and its subsequent incarnations, although large, were still fairly modest and temporary for many institutions. For smaller institutions it was still often not worth going through the costly accreditation process, thus accreditation was not absolutely necessary during the 1950s.[74] With passage of the Higher Education Act (HEA) of 1965, however, accreditation became a necessity for nearly all higher education institutions.[75] An important part of President Lyndon Johnson's "Great Society" programs, the HEA greatly expanded and made permanent a financial role for the federal government in higher education.[76] It was what Gillen and colleagues call a "massive and permanent expansion of federal funding," solidifying the federal government's involvement in higher education that began with the G.I. Bill.[77]

The pre–World War II system of higher education worked well for cost containment and quality control because no individual person or entity had too much power. Individual self-interest was harnessed by the competitive forces of entry and exit. Students and families chose institutions on the basis of a combination of academics and cost. They were paying with their own funds and so would evaluate their options against other potential uses. Accreditors wanted to differentiate among types of institutions to benefit their members. They were limited in what they could do for their members, however, by competition in accreditation and entry into the higher education marketplace. Accreditation was a form of quality assurance, but there was no way to turn that quality assurance into anti-competitive behavior or to act in a way contrary to member wishes because colleges and universities could always find another accreditor. The states and the federal government intervened in targeted ways that limited their influence, such as by urging the creation of universities, encouraging the study of agriculture or mining, or financing institutions directly. Despite distorting the market process, they did not impede the competitive forces that are crucial to cost containment and quality control.

The G.I. Bill fundamentally changed higher education in the United States by short-circuiting the low cost and decentralized accountability that comes with people spending their own money on goods and services that they value. The rise of diploma mills in the wake of the G.I. Bill is clear evidence that people never spend others' money as carefully as they do their own. Once the normal accountability system that exists in the marketplace was broken, the federal government "fixed" the problem by making the accreditors the gatekeepers to federal funding. Not only did this cartelize the regional accreditors, it effectively eliminated competition among accreditors. In addition, it meant that accreditors then had two bosses: their members and the federal government.

Understanding that accreditors have spent the period since 1965 torn between their two bosses helps explain two salient features of accreditation post-1965: (1) accreditors largely trying to continue the status quo and (2) the federal government increasingly ratcheting up its oversight of the accreditation process. First, accreditors have largely continued measuring quality by inputs.[78] Measuring quality by inputs such as physical infrastructure, size of the faculty, qualifications of faculty, degree program length, and so forth, clearly serves members by acting as a barrier to entry while not inquiring whether students are actually learning. The compliance costs to members are substantial, however, and certainly contribute to the rising cost of higher education.

Institutions are willing to put up with such high costs for several reasons. First, accreditation means access to federal funding, which is nearly essential to survive in today's highly subsidized higher education marketplace.[79] Second, many of those input-based measures, such as lower teaching loads, make the lives of faculty and staff at institutions much easier. Whereas normally, activities that raise costs to consumers without any concomitant value increase would be eroded by competition, requiring all higher education institutions to be accredited by roughly the same standards puts limits on institutional competition that would drive costs down. Similarly, new ideas and innovations in well-functioning markets tend to come from new entrants. The cost to new universities of obtaining accreditation, however, is substantial. One estimate put it at $10 million and 10 years of effort for a 50 percent chance of success.[80] Those costs thus act as a barrier to entry, especially against entrants with the potential to be extremely disruptive, such as low-cost and online entrants.[81]

A second salient feature of the post-1965 period has been increasing calls for greater accountability by the accrediting agencies, which has resulted in more federal oversight. Just as the post–World War II diploma mills led to the linking of accreditation and federal funding, as rising costs and quality concerns have become more prominent in higher education, the federal government has become increasingly involved in the "voluntary system of self-regulation." For example, in the early 1990s default rates on student loans were substantial, averaging about $3 billion a year.[82] Congress blamed accreditors, in part, for those losses, with the inspector general of the Department of Education testifying before the House Committee on Education and Labor that the accrediting agencies were not effectively accrediting schools and that that was partly responsible for the high default rates.[83]

The result was a significant number of changes to accreditation in the 1992 Reauthorization of the HEA. Judith Areen calls the 1992 HEA reauthorization a "serious federal challenge to private accreditation."[84] The legislation required each state to establish an entity that would review higher education institutions. In addition, it placed limits on distance learning, limited the percentage of an institution's budget that could come from federal funding, and gave accreditors learning assessment requirements.[85] Although state oversight was eventually unfunded and then eliminated, the federal government continues to push for increased assessment of student achievement in a variety of ways. For example, in 2006 the U.S. Department of Education proposed that accreditation agencies set and enforce minimum standards for student achievement.[86] That level of direct intervention was politically unpalatable, and Congress prohibited the U.S. Department of Education from directly regulating the manner in which accreditors assess student learning in the Higher Education Opportunity Act of 2008.[87]

It would be wrong to call this fighting back on federal oversight the preservation of self-regulation; clearly, the damage has been done. In 2009 longtime chancellor of Western Carolina University, John Bardo, wrote an essay about the "balance between federal and self-regulation" related to student learning and assessment. In that essay he spoke candidly about the balance that exists between the historical approach of peer review and the new one of government regulation:

> [B]ecause of the legal tie between federal financial aid and regional accreditation, it should be expected that the regional accrediting bodies will continue to be used by the federal government as a major instrument to effect change in colleges and universities. . . . And it should be expected that there will be pressure on these associations to incorporate increased institutional regulation. The long-term question, then, is to what extent regional accreditation will be based on federal regulation and to what extent it will reflect the professional opinions and stances of academic professionals.[88]

As Bardo points out, pressure from the federal government has already caused accrediting bodies to change their behavior. The Southern Association of Colleges and Schools, for example, broke with tradition and began a mandatory fifth-year interim report to address assessment concerns raised by the U.S. Department of Education. In the past, only colleges or universities that had failed to meet certain standards were required to undertake a fifth-year report. If there was any doubt whether the activities and decisionmaking of the regional accreditors occurred in the shadow of future federal government policy decisions, consider CHEA president Judith Eaton's recent essay at *Inside Higher Ed.* In the essay, which discusses the proposed Postsecondary Institutions Ratings System, Eaton says that "establishing the system may mean the end of more than 60 years of accreditation as a partner with government, the reliable authority on educational quality to which Congress and the Education Department have turned."[89] That certainly sounds as if the accreditors and the government are moving in tandem, unrelated to the fundamentals that first brought institutions together to set standards of quality.

Two issues are clear from the post-1965 period. First, in an era with significant third-party payment for higher education and no competition among accreditors, the information content of accreditation has little or no value in ensuring something beyond a very low level of quality. When Fuller Theological Seminary, the Laguna College of Art and Design, and Stanford University are all accredited by the same accreditor, how can accreditation have any information content regarding quality? Second, conflicts between the accrediting agencies and the federal government will continue to occur, as the accrediting agencies would like to continue with the status quo (input-based measures of quality and accreditation ensuring access to federal funds), and the federal government would like to keep program costs down and ensure that students are learning.

Concluding Thoughts

After a review of its history, higher education accreditation clearly seems more government regulation than self-regulation. Why is this important, and what does it mean for higher education reform? That is an important question to answer because many conservatives and libertarians are extremely hesitant to tinker with nongovernmental solutions to market failures that have survived the test of time.[90] If higher education accreditation is not market regulation and instead a type of government regulation, then concerns about changing the current system should be reduced. The question then becomes, which is the best way forward if the goal is to ensure that consumers get something of value? Pre–G.I. Bill, we knew that consumers valued the education they received because they paid for it. Is it at all possible to get back to that situation?

I suspect that the answer is no. The federal government seems to be here to stay as financier of higher education. Taking that as a binding constraint, what can be done? One possibility would be to cut the tie between the accreditation agencies and federal funding. After all, accreditation arose in an era in which very little information was publicly available about colleges and universities. Now there exists a plethora of information about colleges and universities from both government and nongovernment organizations, such as *U.S. News and World Report* and *Forbes*. Let a thousand flowers bloom for information providers. Accreditation agencies could still exist if they were to provide value to their member institutions, as do professional accreditors such as the Association to Advance Collegiate Schools of Business International. The value of accreditors would rise and fall with the value of the assurance they provide to consumers, as well as the other bundled goods they might provide to their members.

How should the federal government decide which institutions should be eligible for its funding? One possibility, suggested by Mary Watson, would be to entrust the job of quality assurance to the states.[91] The federal government could make state authorization to operate the prerequisite for receiving federal dollars. Such a system would have two important benefits. First, having 50 different state accrediting agencies would inject some much-needed competition into the accreditation process, especially with respect to new colleges and universities that might want to open. Second, such a system would align state- and federal-level political incentives.

Like the federal government, states care about keeping higher education costs low and quality high while ensuring access to higher education. States would thus have a strong incentive to discover the best way to minimize waste and ensure quality while also remaining politically accountable to voters.

This is but one possible reform to the current dysfunctional accreditation system, which has led to increased costs and reduced innovation. Although higher education accreditation once served the laudatory purpose of quality assurance, it has evolved into a cartel caught between entrenching the status quo and responding to calls for greater public accountability. Ultimately, the roots of our higher education accreditation problems are political in nature, and any reform must try to incorporate stronger feedback from voters who are fed up with waste and inefficiency in the system.

PART II:
The Current State of Higher Education in America

CHAPTER FOUR

Understanding the Runaway Tuition Phenomenon: A Soliloquy with Footnotes

Daniel D. Polsby

There is a mess in higher education. It is of relatively recent origin, it is extremely serious, and it could lead to industry-wide retrenchment and numerous failures of institutions of higher learning. It is not likely to get better by itself, the way to fix it is not obvious, and a growing number of respectable people are beginning to question whether it is worth fixing anyway. Actually, this is a fair appraisal for any of several messes in higher education; this paper is primarily concerned with only one of them: tuition. Going to college or graduate school has recently become much more expensive. As a result, young people have borrowed unprecedented amounts to pay for it. A reasonable fear is that because such big debt burdens are being assumed so early in life by so many members of the birth cohorts of the mid-1980s to mid-1990s, the risk-taking behavior of an entire generation—their inclination to engage in socially useful actions that entail risk—will shift in an undesirable direction.[1] Family formation and home ownership may be postponed. And there are increasing doubts, of a kind not much heard in the past, whether the product—a college, graduate school, or professional school education—is ultimately worth it.

During the 2016 presidential election we heard a good bit about higher education, and some of what was said will probably make its way into legislation. If the usual pattern holds, lawmakers will supply even more money to the system, and regulatory authorities will place various additional, onerous burdens on colleges and universities including, one supposes, price controls in one form or another. But what *is* the problem? Is it access—that is, are young people prepared and motivated but unable to afford college? My research suggests that access is a minor if not nonexistent problem at the moment, but that of course wouldn't stop politicians from spending lots of money on it if doing so would help them politically. Or is the problem that once students get to college, they are not being assigned the right readings and are not acquiring the right knowledge? I am pretty sure this second issue will always be worth at least some careful reflection because teaching and learning are activities we can always do better even if we are doing them very well already. But *are* we doing them well already? I doubt it, but less is known about this subject than one would wish to know before proposing comprehensive solutions. My aim is much more limited. I want to understand the implications of the ballooning debt load on young people, what is causing it to happen, and how it relates to tuitions, which have been exploding at more or less the same rate as student debt.

Wholly apart from the question of how loading young people with big debts is apt to affect the virtue of the state is the mundane matter of how we are going to finance higher education. Current financing arrangements are unstable and therefore unsatisfactory. A large fraction of college bills are paid with student debt. Both tuition and student debt have been increasing at a nearly exponential rate, which cannot be sustained. This matters because in the 20th century, higher education became, for all its foibles, one of America's greatest good works, creating and sustaining dozens of world-renowned research universities, many hundreds of excellent if less-famous schools, and a democratized undergraduate, graduate, and professional training regime allowing nearly anyone who can do the work to take the shot.

One often hears of a "bubble" in higher education,[2] for which we can thank Glenn Reynolds, who writes about it often and well.[3] It is a useful figure of speech for calling attention to the situation, maybe less so for getting people to care—or anyway, to care about the right things.[4] Hardly anyone expects formal higher education to disappear in a "pop" such as the South Sea Bubble or Bear Stearns. A lot of the industry's invested capital ought to be quite safe, and it will be if it is covering sound bets about what kinds of "educational experience" will continue to be valuable to people into the future.[5] But I think the whole subject will not be worth worrying about unless the broad general public—the taxpaying public—carries on believing that higher education is a source of substantial public good.

Management of public perception is a crucial if often unarticulated piece of the industry's business model. College and university budgets more or less assume that their market tuitions will cover only a portion of the cost of production of the education services that tuition is supposed to buy. That means that institutes of higher learning assume subsidies, from rich private donors or from the government. Do people in general still think that the spillovers of higher education have a positive rather than negative value? It is certainly what they used to think. In the mid 20th century, hardly anyone respectable in this country would have publicly doubted that the cultural, economic, social, and civic emanations from colleges and universities were *good* goods, if not national treasures; I doubt that is true anymore. Attitudes began to change noticeably around the Vietnam War, when colleges and universities became hubs of an angry counterculture. Some of those old estrangements seem to have never gone away, and some new ones may have accumulated since. People aren't favorably impressed when they see university presidents and other leaders quailing and stammering when presented with foolish demands to police people's speech on and off campus or to fine-tune institutional policy for exacting political correctness while making no real effort to denounce acts of vandalism, threats, "hate" hoaxes, and so on.[6] The "monoculture" of political sensibilities and commitments in many of the learned disciplines is not news, but it has been increasingly noticed—and it increasingly rankles.[7] No one seems to have much confidence that schools will be able to straighten things out for themselves, handicapped as most of them are with obsolete (or anyway, poorly functioning) structures of governance and institutional organization that blunt accountability for the effective use of resources and more or less guarantee a lack of mission focus. Bit by bit, old reservoirs of good will that higher education built up with the general public over decades and even centuries are drying up; one should expect skepticism about the claim that there is a crying need for more college than market tuition will pay for.

The sheer magnitude of the tuition problem is daunting. Student debt has grown very rapidly over the past 20 years, and it is now approaching 1.5 trillion dollars—a lowball number, actually, because it doesn't count intrafamilial transfers but only loans that are visible to the Federal Reserve. The best depiction I have seen is in Figure 4.1, which has been widely circulated on the Internet. The graphic originates with Mark Perry at the American Enterprise Institute. I will make reference hereafter to the ascent of the dotted line as I try to explain it to myself, if not the reader.

Figure 4.1

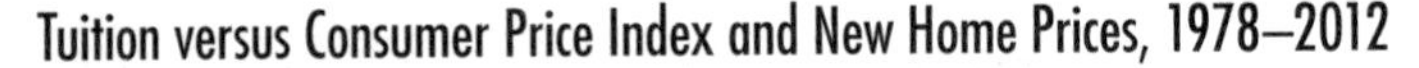
Tuition versus Consumer Price Index and New Home Prices, 1978–2012

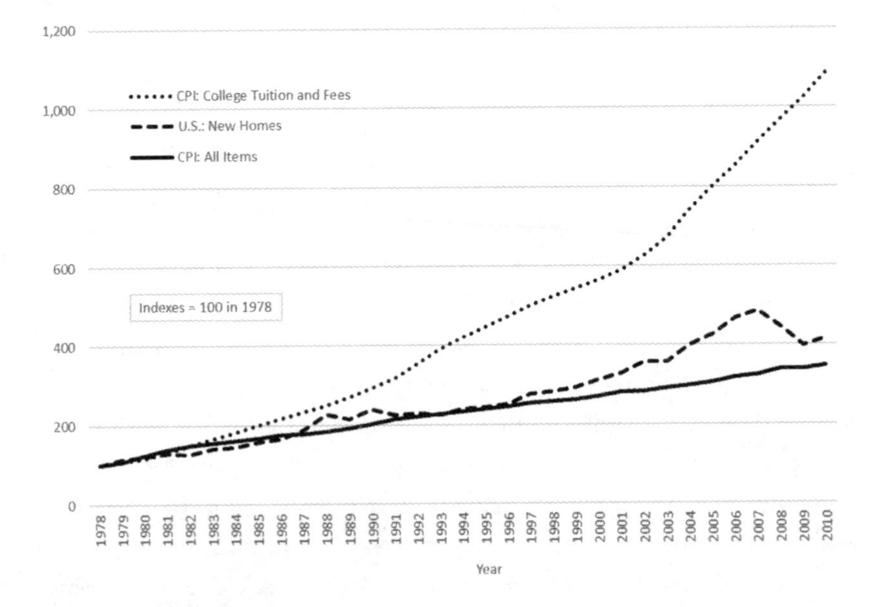

Note: CPI = Consumer Price Index.

Source: Mark J. Perry, "Higher Education Bubble: College Tuition Doubled Over the Last 10 Years vs. +52% for Medical Care," *Carpe Diem* (blog), July 26, 2011, http://mjperry.blogspot.com/2011/07/higher-education-bubble-college-tuition.html.

What could explain this picture? There's no shortage of theories, some of which I will mention. But I might as well say at the outset that all but one are incorrect: what explains the tuition picture is government subsidies; the other theories are mistaken, and I will do my best to exorcise them. The name usually attached to the correct theory is the Bennett Hypothesis, so-called because it was propounded by then–Secretary of Education William Bennett. Whether the Bennett Hypothesis is indeed correct has been a matter of controversy for at least 30 years, but the evidence for it at this point looks good enough to persuade an open-minded skeptic.

The other side of the argument is that, on the contrary, tuition goes up for reasons of its own, and the wherewithal to finance it has to go up too, unless higher education is to be the preserve of only the wealthiest families. No one has suggested that the supply of subsidized loans and the increase of tuition aren't related. Both have been increasing more or less simultaneously, which has made it difficult to say whether increasing tuitions are causing increasing loans or whether it's the other way around. Lucca, Nadauld, and Shen have a recent paper that persuasively sorts out what's causing what; together with other evidence (mentioned in the footnotes), there no longer seems to be much good reason to doubt that the Bennett Hypothesis is basically correct.[8]

Whether there are good reasons to doubt the hypothesis or not, doubted the Bennett Hypothesis will surely be, because if it is correct it raises by implication the question of whether the offending federal subsidies should continue. Federal loans involve annual outlays of hundreds of billions of dollars. Colleges and universities wind up with most of that money; that has to continue or many, if not most of them, would collapse. The money may not yet have been printed, but lots of it has been spent already, at least implicitly baked into budgets, which depend on enrollment assumptions, which depend on student loans. Enrollment assumptions roll out into staffing and facilities plans, which are hard and expensive to unwind.

One shouldn't say that government loans "contribute to" or are "a" cause of runaway tuitions but that they are *the* cause—the one and only thing that deserves to be blamed for the problem. Pretending complexity in the case of runaway tuitions is only misdirection. During many booming years of the 1980s and after, the business plans of many colleges and universities had been tacitly based on the indefinite persistence of fast growth in demand for higher education, something that schools could take advantage of in several ways, typically through higher enrollment, greater selectivity, or a mix of both. Fast growth through this period was not continuous and uninterrupted, but as a trend it was unmistakable, and it was one of the dominant facts of life through practically the entire careers of the now-receding generation of senior academic planners and administrators—up until 2008 or 2009, when the financial crisis hit. After the great wring-out of those years, constantly increasing enrollment while constantly increasing tuition was self-evidently no longer a tenable plan. But it wasn't obvious what, in concrete terms, Plan B was going to entail. In many ways this is still where we are.

As the country moved from financial crisis to recession and then a diffident recovery, nominal tuitions seldom receded and in many cases crept higher, which meant bigger bills for individuals in school (or their families) while labor markets were yielding stagnant returns to people lucky enough to have jobs. Congress responded, as it had done before, by facilitating more below-market credit to help students go to school. At the same time, schools responded—as they had done before—by raising tuitions to capture most of that new cash, leaving students no better off than they had been before.

Why is all this happening? And why is it coming to a head now? The first big indictment of the tuition problem was drafted by an anonymous headline writer at the *New York Times* in 1987: "Our Greedy Colleges." Tuitions going up? Blame greed.[9] William J. Bennett, the author of the article, wrote no such thing, but simply argued that government subsidies cause college tuitions to rise.

But the "greed" meme took hold and is still often heard. Yet greed has nothing to do with the abnormal spiking of tuition in comparison to most other prices, and that is not because colleges aren't greedy (of course they are) but that everybody is. Greed is a sort of universal constant than cannot possibly, in principle, explain change. If greed were all it took to generate phenomena like the dotted line in Figure 4.1, that line would depict the price of *everything*. Let us confidently put this idea aside.

Other possible candidates that might explain the dotted line fare no better than greed in the end. An interested and sympathetic friend of mine suggested that maybe there wasn't really a puzzle to be solved after all. Why shouldn't we expect to see tuition spiking, he asked, if there's continually increasing demand for the product? Isn't that just good old supply-and-demand in action? The main, visible products of higher education—bachelor's, master's, doctoral, and professional degrees—have become more and more valuable to their possessors in recent years because they help the degree holders to find and to keep jobs and to get paid more, which should, in turn, feed back into increasing demand still further. This is wrong, as will be explained presently.

University leaders want to tell a different story about the ascent of the dotted line in Figure 4.1. Public colleges and universities—two-thirds of the higher education market, as measured by enrollment—were always supposed to depend on state legislatures covering a major portion of their cost of operation. But for the past 20 or 30 years, state legislatures—almost all of them and to roughly the same extent—have been backing off those longstanding previous commitments to higher education. State subsidies that might at one time have covered two-thirds or more of schools' operating budgets have dwindled to covering one-third or less (at my school, for example, it's fallen to less than one-fourth). In most cases, those subsidies are the only large source of recurring revenue that a school would have apart from tuition. The unavoidable arithmetic of this situation is that as subsidy dollars diminish, tuition dollars must step up to take their place—hence the ascending dotted line. This account, too, is wrong.

Another much-trafficked explanation for soaring tuition—probably the most oft-repeated of the lot—is schools' poor management of their costs. This claim is that without the disciplining factors that hold for-profit businesses in check, colleges and universities spend—that is, waste—prodigious sums on gold plating and featherbedding. "Gold plating" means spending too much money on physical plant embellishments; "featherbedding" means spending too much money on nonessential personnel and consultants whose functions are extraneous to the actual education of students. Gold plating and featherbedding have to be paid for by someone, it is said, and so their costs are passed along to consumers. Wrong again.

None of those explanations works, at least not in any straightforward way. Soaring demand—there has been plenty of this over the past generation—certainly doesn't. To be sure, enrollments grew by more than two-thirds in the 30 years following 1980, while the population as a whole increased only about half as fast.[10] But just as basic microeconomic theory would predict, increasing demand called forth increasing supply. Over that same 30 years, the number of degree-granting institutions in the United States, including branch campuses, grew by 42 percent.[11] Many schools already in existence were in a position to add capacity if they didn't have excess capacity to begin with and therefore could (as many did) increase enrollments. More schools, more seats, plenty of supply, and plenty of room for more—there seem to be no reasons at all for generalized demand-driven price increases in higher education, and certainly no reason for anything like the dotted line.

"Appreciating value of the product" doesn't work either, although this is not because higher education hasn't become increasingly valuable in an economic sense. There can be little doubt that, at least if the metric is "degree earned," higher education is indeed valuable (and, depending on how and what one measures, having a degree might show up as increasingly valuable relative to not having one). Having a degree adds to lifetime earnings both through increased rate of compensation and workforce persistence, and does so in a more or less scalar fashion. Master's, doctoral, and professional degrees each confer an increment of benefit that seems, on average, to exceed their costs. But so what? The value of the product to the purchaser doesn't determine the price at which educational services can or should be sold.[12] Showing that the value of higher education has been increasing (as apparently has been the case through most of the past century or more) doesn't justify the inference that sellers would be in a position to grab that increment of value for themselves. All else being equal, the price of something that trades in a market, be its value great or small, should rise if it becomes relatively scarcer in relation to other things for sale in the market and fall if it becomes relatively more abundant. The *value* of the thing to its prospective buyer and its *price*—that is, how much the seller can get the buyer to pay for it—are two different things. The dotted line depicts a *price*. An explosive increase in the price of some commodity should lead us to suspect that some kind of scarcity-inducing kink has developed somewhere in the supply line. Yet instead of scarcity we find increasing abundance: more colleges, higher enrollments, plenty of competition, and plenty of room for all of these to increase—nothing, in other words, to explain the dotted line.

Academic leaders' favorite explanation—the continual erosion of state support for higher education over most of a generation—fares no better. This concern would be specific to state schools, but public higher education is by far the largest segment of the industry, so perhaps it is fair to see these schools' predicament as belonging in common to the sector itself. When state subsidies started tapering off in the late 1980s, tuitions escalated hand in hand. That increase was everywhere defended as unavoidable and inevitable—dollars that disappear from the "subsidy" column *must* be replaced with dollars from the "tuition" column, hence the increasing prices.

That bad explanation trades on an equivocation between two different senses of "must." That public subsidies have been shrinking in relation to schools' budgets is true, and that this shrinking blows up the long-subsisting business model is also true, but the next move is false. When one source of expected revenue goes down, it is *not* the case that another source "must" go up except in a trivial, bookkeeping sense (i.e., holding all else constant, books won't balance without the dollars required to balance them). But it is not actually necessary to hold all else constant; the *business* sense of "must"—the thing that matters—is what has to be explained. In the business sense it is false to say that diminished subsidies mean that tuition "must" go up. No one, other than regulated monopolies and governments, gets to jack up prices *ad libitum* like that. In a competitive environment, raising the price of a commodity above its market value shouldn't lead to a seller getting more money, it should lead to the seller getting *no* money because the customers will defect. That means that businesses whose income is diminishing, or whose costs are increasing, or whose expectations have been disappointed will have to deal with the resulting shortfalls from reserves, either of cash or credit. If that turns out to be impossible, too bad. Bankruptcies happen; not every story has a happy ending. The "dwindling subsidies" explanation, in other words, doesn't actually explain anything. Instead it raises a further mystery. Because if sellers find they are able to get more money by charging a higher price for their product, why would they have waited for a financial embarrassment before raising prices? Why wouldn't they have raised them as soon as they could? Cuts in revenue subsidies have nothing to do with a business's ability to raise prices. This whole line of argument just doesn't add up.

Finally we come to cost-related explanations for spiking tuitions. It's easy to see the attraction of this story. Not only is it intuitively grasped, it lends itself to amusing, sometimes lurid illustrations from real life. The basic idea is that colleges and universities must be especially bad at controlling costs for some reason, leading them to waste so much money that they have to charge ever-higher prices to make up for it. The antidote to this state of affairs, often mentioned as a corollary, is that to avoid charging ever-higher prices, colleges and universities have to get good at controlling costs, or at least get adequate at it. It is in this connection that one usually hears the bromide that an educational institution should be "run like a business."

The claim that poor control of costs leads to ever-escalating prices isn't plausible, but because nearly everybody believes it, I will pretend, *arguendo*, that there's something to it, although it trips over the logical disconnect mentioned in the preceding paragraphs. To generalize the point made there: higher costs don't automatically lead to higher prices. Products costing a lot to make won't fetch higher and higher prices just because they cost more and more to produce; conversely, products with low production costs won't necessarily be sold more cheaply. Cost and price are two different things.[13] Production costs are important only to whether one can sell a product at a profit, not to how much people can be induced to pay for it. If the costs of producing a product exceed the price at which it can be sold, then sellers simply have a loss on their hands; in normally functioning competitive markets, sellers *can't* pass the cost of production along to the customers by demanding a higher price.

For that reason, I think it is misguided *ever* to cite "cost" or "waste" as a reason for rising tuitions.

Yet I have persuaded very few people with that line of argument. Let us therefore consider some alleged cost items in more detail to judge whether their peculiarities might make them an exception to the generality just stated. One of these let me mention at the outset simply to be rid of it: phony nonsense classes, galling whenever one hears of it. Everyone has heard or read about colleges and universities offering academic credit for foolish courses. The caricature is that those are stupid classes on stupid subjects meant for stupid students (and guaranteed to make them stupider), taught by professors who are not necessarily stupid (but it helps).[14] There is no denying that courses like that do exist; I doubt, although, that they are very common. I don't recall having seen very many courses like that myself.[15] But for the sake of argument let us say that courses like that are common enough to worry about, and let us accept that they are wasteful more or less by definition because they are at cross-purposes with the stated and ostensible educational mission of the institution. Is there any possible way to connect all of those assumed facts back to the explosive growth of college tuitions? More likely, the exact opposite is the case. One would expect undemanding classes to be popular. Why wouldn't they be? My then-colleague David Haddock and I years ago described the incentives that should lead to students demanding fluff courses,[16] and it shouldn't be surprising if courses like that did turn out to be popular. Courses of that kind may be a pox on civilization, but if students like them they're probably making the institution money at the margin. That *could* connect back to tuition. Instructional programs that generate surpluses could subsidize other, possibly loss-making programs: popular fluff courses would not only fail to explain the dotted line, they would tend to push it downward rather than up.

Gold plating and featherbedding are the two main headings under which waste complaints seem to be organized; there may be others but I will limit myself to those two. Gold plating is the cheerfully tendentious name given to certain extravagances that colleges supposedly indulge in—building fancy gymnasiums, natatoriums, student centers, workout facilities, lavish dorms, amusement park–type rides, upscale dining facilities such as sushi bars and fusion cuisine bistros (and so on)—and what have any of those things to do with education?[17] If the answer is, little or nothing, then surely we could count *them* as waste, as deadweight contributors to cost, therefore a culpable part of whatever drives colleges' insatiable appetite for cash—so goes the argument.

Although exceptions may exist in the right tail of the opulence curve, over most of the range of experience those kinds of recriminations are way overdrawn. For one thing, students like that kind of stuff. At least until we get up toward that meretricious right tail—never have been there myself—students seem to be more than happy to pay for gyms and swimming pools and the rest. Over many years the student complaints I have heard on the subject (and it's one of the most persistent themes in our surveys) are almost always that we really don't have enough facilities like that and we really ought to have more. Furthermore, much gold plating, if we must call it that, should seem to everyone perfectly benign from the point of view of civilization—indeed, thinking specifically of gyms and swimming pools, downright constructive—*mens sana in corpore sano* and all that. Finally—being practical for just a moment—when it comes to recruiting an entering class, it is so very much easier to sell a 17-year-old kid on climbing walls and "lazy rivers" than on the lifelong value one acquires from enduring Professor Harshly's legendary interrogations on Dasein in *Being and Time*, even though we know that years from now that student will look back and appreciate the latter's greater ultimate value. There's a competitive market out there, after all. Vendors have to pay at least a little attention to what customers like, are happy to pay for, and complain about if they don't get. That's competition for you—red in tooth and claw.

Furthermore, if one comes across some instance of gold plating with an especially elevated aesthetic cringe quotient, the reason for it likely enough is that the donor whose gift made the thing possible would have it so. It's no skin off the school's nose to go along with these little sins against good taste and no dollars out of students' pockets. But in the end, a lot of what is called gold plating—and possibly most of it—will, if carefully considered, turn out to be fairly cheap. The cost difference isn't that great between building and maintaining a nice, inviting gym that is comparable to the better sort of private health club versus a hard-core, bare-bones facility that no one will like, few will use, and everyone will complain about. I grant that in this example, gold plating could have an effect on a school's operating budget (because, for illustration, the more people like and use a gym, the more people will have to be hired to staff it), but it's peanuts—nothing remotely adequate to explain the dotted line.[18]

Now let us consider "featherbedding," the hiring of excess staff, who often are paid excessively. Here we have a potentially more promising place to look for waste. Of course we can't really say whether an expenditure is superfluous until we first say what it is superfluous *to.* What are institutions of higher education supposed to do or be all about? That's too big an issue to get into here, so let's just assume this problem away and observe that *if* poor cost control is a big contributor to runaway tuitions, we can forget about gold plating. *Featherbedding* is where we need to look: payroll constitutes 60 to 70 percent of total outlays in higher education.[19] If we want to see money being wasted, that's where the money is.

And there are plenty of places to look. State and federal governments and regional and other accrediting agencies have forced copious additional administrative burdens on higher education in recent decades. Those bodies make laws and regulations, emit ukases, and occasionally send out "Dear Colleague" letters, all of which have to be dealt with by somebody. Compliance work often is specialized; staff must be hired to do it, professional staff at that—lawyers in many instances. Much—probably most—of that incremental regulation adds zero education value; the costs imposed, whatever they are, could thus be rightly denounced as pointless.[20] But compliance with pointless regulation is not pointless but a precondition to staying in business. And furthermore, no matter how pointless a regulation may be, schools will seldom criticize it. They wouldn't want to make a record of their skepticism about some new rule lest it be construed as antipathy toward its ostensibly important purpose when the next lawsuit is filed or the next regulatory intervention or investigation is begun. And even if a school did raise cain and a burden-lightening reform were actually adopted in response, free-riding competitors would benefit as well. Given all that, it's perfectly rational for colleges and universities to live by Rick Blaine's motto—"I stick my neck out for nobody."

Regulatory burden has priority over all education-related administrative outlays. In the case of large schools, regulatory compliance costs have been manageable, though far from trivial. How manageable they are at smaller schools unable to exploit scale economies isn't so clear—I expect that many or most of them experience compliance burdens as quite serious impingements on their mission. Yet this sort of hardship seems unlikely to have contributed much to the ascent of the dotted line. Employers all across the national economy have had to adapt to the same kinds of administrative law millstones—in some cases they must respond to the very same laws, in other cases, to industry-specific regulations, which could be practical counterparts to those in education. Extraneous regulatory burdens must surely hurt the resiliency and productivity of the national economy and the sector to which they apply, as well as hurt each firm's ability to capitalize on its peculiar strengths. But dotted-line phenomena—decades of uninterrupted price increases much greater than the consumer price index (CPI), for products that change, and have changed, rather little—do not typically result from regulatory burden.

But maybe there is something to be said about the growth of central administrative staff, apart from employees who look after government and accrediting agency compliance issues. We should also consider presidential and provostal helpers, many of whom will have been seconded from faculty appointments (and thus lost to the honest labor of instructional duties) or who will possess credentials and experience similar to faculty, and consultants of various kith and kindred. I actually looked at some of the experience that George Mason University has with staff proliferation, whose interesting but inconclusive results I report on presently.

Quite a lot of money is indeed spent on all this effort. And the nonmoney price tag can be costly, too—probably costlier.[21] Consultants are paid; people, often senior line personnel with high opportunity costs (in other words, actual jobs), then have to sit through the resulting presentations. Those presentations, in the best case, will merely be time wasters, and in the worst case they are initiatives in empty suits: innovative, sustainable, entrepreneurial, diverse, cutting edge, disruptive, and something or other to do with paradigms. As I later argue, the specific objects and projects that absorb whatever cash and time is devoted to them are the accidental rather than the essential properties of the exercise. The essence of the matter is that, to the extent resources are available—be they great or small—they will be effused on whatever enthusiasms are currently in hand (and fads are never in short supply in the education industry at any level). As academic administrators have relatively little to do with curriculum and research, those enthusiasms are most likely to be orthogonal, if related at all, to academic values.

As the plural of "anecdote" is "data," there are plenty of data about inept university administration and its make-work consequences.[22] And it is not difficult to find university administrators with a quite shallow comprehension of their business. That may be a partial explanation for why higher education is so vulnerable to fads: administrators who find themselves with a big, sprawling asset in their hands without a clue what they're supposed to do with it (other than "innovate!") need all the fads and other mental prostheses they can get. Here we are referring, however, to a phenomenon that isn't at all university specific. It is to be found in varying measure and proportion in almost any good-sized business organization in its maturity, especially those in which intangibles are a big component of the deliverables. Anyone who had been in the white collar labor force of a big, established company will have seen plenty of the same sorts of thing. Some big companies have been quite famous for it, actually, despite the fact that they're disciplined in a market in which the death penalty is a routine sanction.

Regulatory and compliance costs are endemic, and yet not all businesses ride on the dotted line. That is something only some of us get to do. Why? As I have shown, most of the usual suspects have alibis, and most of the rest look like small potatoes or are beside the point without any real bearing on the subject at hand. Federally subsidized student loans and nothing else are causing the ascent of the dotted line. That is where the education market differs from the widget market, and that must be the nub of the problem.

I came to this conclusion by quite a roundabout means, investigating the finances of my own university. At the outset it seemed to me that my university must surely be quite rich; I thought this because of the massive constant dollar increases in tuitions it had levied over many years, as well as its even more massive increases in enrollment. I discovered a number of possibly useful things about my university that I hadn't known before. It occurred to me rather late in the game that the answer to the mystery of the ascending dotted line was not going to be found in the university's public bookkeeping records but was hiding in plain sight.

In 2005 and 2006, not long after I became dean at my law school and well before the financial crisis, the situation with our own tuition began to bother me. Our law school was still cheap compared with the competition, but our tuition was going up fast, as were tuitions all over the university. At one of our annual university planning retreats, we were shown a five-year projection, with 10 percent across-the-board annual increases penciled in. (With slight modification, that plan was adopted.) Law school tuitions are multiples of the tuitions of most other university programs, so although several of the other deans felt concern about how this plan might affect their enrollments, especially in the out-years, I felt fear. At my university, deans are little more than spectators when it comes to setting tuition; along with its principal officers of administration, the governing board makes pricing decisions. I wasn't at the table when the cards were cut, nor were the other deans, but nothing was stopping me from remonstrating, so I started PowerPointing them—two can play at that game—about the risks that I foresaw and the advantages to be had from a less-aggressive pricing policy. I award myself partial credit because the risk I foresaw did indeed materialize, but not in the form I had imagined. I did not—and most other people did not—see the 2008 financial crisis coming, let alone what its consequences for my program were going to be.

My PowerPoint sufferers were not, most of them, stupid people; they knew that there were risks connected to an aggressive pricing policy. But sometimes brain knowledge doesn't get all the way to the viscera, where it might do some good. My story was that no one could be confident where the indifference point was between applicants enrolling and not enrolling at the university. We could be setting ourselves up for a fall by assuming that, as we approached the point at which the price was getting too high (whatever that point was), we would begin to see demand fall off little by little. My point was that we had no guarantees that we would be able to detect the softening of demand as it was happening, and therefore it was not clear that we would be able, when the market for legal (or other) studies turned sour, to keep matters in hand with rebates and few adjustments in our admissions work. Given the mighty annual chunks we were contemplating for increases, it seemed not all that improbable that tuitions might leapfrog the indifference point so that we could find demand for our product descending by a step function instead of a graceful curve. Worse, all at once a large fraction of prospective customers might just say "to hell with it." Such a thing would impose a painful "ignorance surtax" on the university revenues. Not only would we fail to capture the extra dollars associated with the increase in price, all the other dollars we were counting on customers bringing would walk out the door with them. A serious structural deficit could materialize quite suddenly. Alternatively, we could lower standards—painful to contemplate. That would degrade our almighty *U.S. News & World Report* rankings, the most important marketing tool in our toolbox. A more cautious tuition policy was therefore warranted. So I argued, but to little effect.[23]

I thought I might somehow improve my arguments if I had a better grasp of the history and development of George Mason, something that (perhaps surprisingly) I knew nothing about. I had to go through a lot of annual reports to figure out what the experience of the university had been with enrollments, tuition, and various kinds of trades-offs faced by previous generations of our academic administration. All I knew going in was that George Mason had opened its doors with a few hundred students in the early 1970s as a branch campus of the University of Virginia and that, by the first decade of the 21st century, it had upward of 30,000 students enrolled in many dozens of programs and disciplines, with a budget of about three-quarters of a billion dollars and big plans for further growth. I didn't know much else, nor was I required to.[24] But as runaway tuitions started to become a national story late in the first decade of the 21st century, I started hearing more and more increasingly anxious questions about tuition from alumni and members of the community—law students, too—especially around the time of year when tuition increases were announced. At about that same time the "wastrel" indictment started to be hung around the neck of the whole national higher education enterprise about our "edifice complex," as Ohio University economist Richard Vedder somewhere called it, and, as Johns Hopkins political scientist Benjamin Ginsberg later said, we were being laid siege to by "armies of functionaries—the vice presidents, associate vice presidents, assistant vice presidents, provosts, associate provosts, vice provosts, assistant provosts, deans, deanlets, deanlings, each commanding staffers and assistants."[25]

It was frustrating that smoking guns weren't in evidence—or much of anything else to help me understand what was going on or to further the argument that tuition policy ought to be more cautious. Then came the financial collapse of 2008, followed by the slow-motion collapse of law school enrollments, which affected nearly every law school in the country. By then, no one needed any PowerPointing from me on the perils of too-high tuitions. But the university's numbers, as far as I had progressed with them, had planted some seeds of skepticism in my mind about the usual explanations for soaring tuitions. I was beginning to think that the prodigies-of-waste stories that were so prominent at that time (as they still are) must have been missing a crucial point.

I managed, eventually, to assemble a run of 30 academic years of George Mason data (1979 to 2010), showing year-by-year changes in enrollment, tuition, "student revenue," numbers about various categories of employees—all sorts of things, actually—and on the first read through the data, we came up with an interesting and suggestive picture. George Mason's expenditures per full-time equivalent (FTE) student nearly doubled over those 30 years in constant dollars, going from $8,476 to $16,739.[26] Growth of enrollment was more rapid still—in fact it much more than tripled over those 30 years, from 7,654 to 24,900. Tuition more than *quadrupled:* $2,328 per head in 1979 and $9,667 by 2010.

Those numbers confirmed my conjecture that the university was not simply doing okay financially, it was actually raking money in. Even taking account of the ever-shrinking subsidy from the Virginia General Assembly, the numbers looked sweet. The state had cut our allowance as expressed in constant 2011 dollars from $6,000 per FTE student in

1979 to around $1,500 by 2011—painful even when stretched out over 30 years. Still, a budget calamity did not result.[27] After all, the student body (total FTEs) had tripled in size, and tuition revenue had quadrupled. Much more revenue was arriving than debouching. On paper it seemed there must have been plenty of cash around. But I never saw that treasure trove and never met anybody who had—or anyway, who would admit it. A mystery. *What are they doing with all that money?*

Where was it going? To all those famously overpaid and underworked professors (that would include me)?[28] Or maybe to Ben Ginsberg's multitudinous myriad minions and functionaries (me again: dean at the time)?

Thirty years of data were bound to reveal a swelling in the ranks of faculty if there was one. But the full-time instructional faculty—and the part-time faculty too—grew at practically the same rate as the student body: very slightly faster after 2005, but close to even. Of course one understands that there are other ways to extract rents than by doing less work. But there was no big increase of professors relative to the scale of the overall operation, nor was there some kind of compensation hypertrophy. According to my numbers, faculty compensation had increased quite slowly—a 25 percent real dollar increase in faculty compensation over 30 years.[29] Paychecks of our "classified" (i.e., clerical) staff grew faster than that, but there are not nearly enough of them to have driven the dotted line. It must be the administrators, then, by a process of elimination. Sometimes it seems that is what everybody thinks. Is what everybody thinks true?

It would take more preliminary work before one could answer that question. The category "administrators" is a catch-all. It has to be more clearly specified before one could know whether complaints like Ginsberg's would hold water. A lot of the people tracked by the George Mason human resources department as "administrators" plainly are not the sort of useless make-workers Ginsberg had in mind. National data have the same discrepancy. So far as the computer is concerned, an "administrator" (called "administrative faculty" in our local jargon) is any employee who has earned an advanced degree and has been hired for a noninstructional job that is in support of the teaching and research mission of the university.

The physicists who run the functional magnetic resonance imaging equipment would be an example; librarians—neither a small nor extraneous group—another. Leaders in admissions and placement offices are yet another—they are critical assets, hardly supernumeraries. The university has several billion dollars' worth of physical plant, requiring facilities managers, architects, and engineers to look after it. The scale of our operation (disbursing nearly a billion dollars per year in payroll and invoiced goods and services) demands professionally trained accountants and auditors. We also count institute directors and academic deans—what I used to be—as administrative faculty. None of the foregoing list of "administrative faculty" should strike a fair-minded person as excess baggage. But based on readily available public documents (once again, my exclusive source of George Mason information), we simply cannot say what proportion the superfluous administrators bear to the whole of the administrative faculty.[30]

We really ought to find out. Over 30 years, administrative faculty paychecks, on average, have been growing faster than those of the instructional faculty. Also, the number of administrators has been growing faster than the student body, the faculty, or the university overall. If the administrators-to-students ratio of 1979 had held until academic year 2010–2011, the university's administrative faculty would have comprised 200 FTE employees; instead, there were 450. That sounds like a significant difference, but what it may signify is impossible to say without more information. For all I know (in fact I suspect this), it might signify that the 1979 number was just untenably low to begin with—there's nothing special in the ratio as it stood in 1979; that's just the first year for which I could find data. If, for the sake of argument, we anoint the 1979 ratio as the correct proportion, it implies that—worst case—as of 2011 we had 250 FTE administrators who could be counted as superfluous. Average administrative faculty budget lines that year were about $90,000, including fringe, which works out to $22,500,000 of annual payroll devoted to hypothetical budget zombies—nonfunctional bodies that we have to pay for—which amounts to a tick less than $1,000 per FTE student per year.

If we assume the worst case,[31] it's nothing to sneeze at, but neither is it a fire bell in the night. It wouldn't begin to explain all the spending that must have been going on to leave us, if not broke, at least in perpetually straitened circumstances.[32]

Growth is the big thing that meets the eye about George Mason since 1972 or so. It's been one almighty construction project on three separate campuses for most of the years of its existence. By 2010–11 it had, to accommodate its more than 30,000 enrolled students and thousands of employees, to spend billions of dollars on classrooms, offices, labs, parking decks, library facilities—none of it "gold plated" by any reasonable definition, by the way. How many billion? At least two; I can't be sure about it. I wasn't able to assemble a comparable run of capital budget data, and some of what I found looks wrong. But I do have reliable numbers for the most recent period, 2002–2011, which show about a billion dollars (nominal, in this case) of capital outlays. I'm attributing the other guesstimated billion to pre-2002 construction.

Building construction money comes from a capital budget that is separate from the operating budget. Once a building is completed, though, those two budgets begin bumping into one another. Debt service, amortization, HVAC (heating, ventilation, and air conditioning), utilities, maintenance—all are charges against operating budget. They are competitors, in other words, with everything else that the operating budget has to pay for, including instructional services. The more building there is, the higher those physical plant charges are and (all else constant) the less money that is left over for everything else.

When buildings are planned and built at a fast-growing institution, they have to be built in contemplation of a future that is quite different from the present. University leaders expected George Mason to be quite big, with 50 or even 60 percent larger enrollments than currently. If buildings in such a campus are designed so as to line up with enrollment plans, new construction will be inherently biased toward what at first blush will look like overbuilding. When a building first opens, and for a certain number of years after, it is apt to seem that the university leaders built too much building for not enough program. That perception should change over time as the Big Plan comes to fruition. It may be perfectly sensible to proceed that way, much like buying children's clothing too big, to allow for growth. Buildings have a long—usually at least 50-year—service life. It would make little sense to have brought a classroom building online in 2010 scaled to that year's expected student census when average enrollments of the 50 following years are expected to be much higher. At some point in the future, equilibrium will be reached, in which current students are no longer being asked to pay for facilities that they will not use but that future students—if they indeed materialize—will.

There may have been—probably were—other esoteric expense items scattered around where I couldn't see them, but they didn't seem to be big enough to eat up all the extra cash or to drive big price increases. And so I began to think about other schools that, like my school, had been getting big fast and raising tuitions fast. Our price increases were always (so we were told) consistent with "the market." (That wasn't exactly true, as I found out—George Mason tuitions were growing a bit faster than others'—but it was approximately true.) That should mean that whatever dragon's-lair hoard of cash we had would be duplicated or nearly so at dozens of other schools.[33] The question therefore wasn't just where *our* money went—where did everybody else's money go? A plausible theory relies on cost disease, the phenomenon that keeps the wages of some workers, such as artists and professors, growing in step with the economy even though their own productivity may not have increased at all; in a cost disease scenario, rising productivity elsewhere means higher wages for those workers whose productivity does not and cannot rise. That may explain some of the increasing costs, but not nearly all.[34] Unable to find any smoking guns or salacious details, I was becoming discouraged until it occurred to me to wonder whether I was asking the right question. Might it be that putting "profligate expenditure" first in my explanation was getting the whole thing backward?

Of course it was. Gold plating, featherbedding, all the aimless intensity of consultants, all the cracked marketing plans and mission statements and strategic initiatives, the investments in unproven fads and fancies—all, to be sure, are found in constant conjunction with tuition increases. But they are not the cause of tuition spikes; *those are the effects.* Tuition causes revenue; revenue causes waste.

I wish I could claim credit for this great insight, but I can't. Almost as soon as this happy thought crossed my mind I realized that the principle, or conjecture, was actually put forward in a 1980 book, *The Costs of Higher Education,* by the late Howard R. Bowen.[35] He called it the "revenue theory of cost." It is one of the most famous things that has ever been written about financing higher education. The Bennett Hypothesis is simply a special case of the revenue theory of cost, what is sometimes called Bowen's Law. "The basic concept underlying the revenue theory of cost is that an institution's educational cost per student is determined by the revenue available for educational purposes."[36] The reason it happens is that in pursuit of "prestige, excellence, and influence," every institution will raise as much money as it can and spend approximately as much money as it raises, with no other real boundary.[37] Spend on *what*? On whatever the university's managers think, at the time, will produce the greatest effect on their institution's perceived "prestige, influence, and excellence."

Bowen, a prominent economics professor who became president of Grinnell College and later Iowa State University, could qualify as an expert witness on the question of what such institutions are trying to do. His canon of objectives squares with the altogether understandable, rational project of increasing the standing of an institution's entire community of constituents: boosting the economic value of the school's degree, thereby directly benefiting students; augmenting the psychic income, hence the total compensation of the faculty; and delivering a windfall to alumni as the economic and social value of their already-earned degrees are seen to have increased. Those are benefits that colleges should want, and if PEI (prestige, excellence, and influence) is the elixir, one should expect steady demand. But the trouble with trying to buy PEI on the open market is the demandingness of those attributes. Because they are positional goods, there can be no such thing as enough of them or even, in this context, a solid understanding of what "enough" could mean. One's competitors, who are locked on the same target because they have the same incentives, will ensure that the quest never ends.

A large part of the college cost problem does seem to be explicable with Bowen's Law; whether it's the whole story is less clear. If all we have on our hands is a public choice problem, there is an obvious solution—one that would have, I suspect, a large built-in political constituency.

The way to put a stop to the unproductive scrambling after status markers in higher education is simply to have government set up bigger and badder cartels for the industry. Of course, "cartel" is a naughty word; a suitable euphemism would have to be used for an organization whose function was—let us choose words carefully—not to restrict entry or limit production (which is what cartels do and which is bad) but to ensure minimum quality and protect easily misled consumers from fly-by-night operators. While we're at it we might have this organization take care that the prices being charged by the regulated constituents were fair, reasonable, uniform, scalar, just, and appropriate. Anyone can see that this does not amount to "fixing prices" (which is what cartels do, and which is bad) but is only a way to prevent races to the bottom, unlevel playing fields, and the abuse of consumers.

Even if we went down that road, however, I doubt it would solve the problem. Indeed, if it did anything of significance to solve the problem, it would be the first time a cartel had done such a thing. But there is something else about the demand for PEI that I suspect would survive all efforts to change the demand for it, even if dog-eat-dog competition were out of the picture altogether. PEI speaks to one of the most fundamental characteristics of the product. Higher education is a credence product, the kind of economic good that makes continuing demands on the confidence not only of people who are thinking about buying it or are in the process of buying it but also the people who have already bought it.

Credence products, so called, give their promisors (i.e., those who are selling the product) a distinctive set of communication challenges with respect to their customers and potential customers, their "promisees."[38] Promisors have to convey value and quality information that their promisees do not know but want to know—and may insist on knowing—before they buy the product. Those promisees aren't like gas station customers, who drive up knowing exactly what they want to buy, buy it, and then drive away happy with a full tank of gasoline.[39] Buying a tank of gas exemplifies the normal and simplest case of a contract for the sale of goods; buying and selling doesn't involve many—if any—uncertainties about either the price of or, more especially, the quality of the product; gasoline is gasoline (and for people who are particular about brand, Shell, Exxon, Mobil, etc., are what they are pretty much everywhere). Other species of transactions may be a little more complicated. Suppose a customer is in the market for a certain kind of product—shoes perhaps—for which value, attributes, and quality may vary considerably. Buying shoes is not like buying gasoline. Not all pairs of size 7 shoes are like other pairs of size 7 shoes; not even all pairs of size 7 Buster Brown brogues are the same one with another. Some size 7s fit properly, others do not. The customer has to try them on to be sure. There is thus a search cost attached to the transaction. Phillip Nelson called that sort of product a "search good," in which, more or less inspection and effort on the part of the buyer can resolve questions about attributes and value before the sales transaction occurs.[40]

A next level of communications difficulty for the vendor occurs with so-called experience goods, in which the buyer knows what is wanted but not whether the good or service being tendered for sale to satisfy that want actually fills the bill, and indeed, will not be able to tell for sure until actually consuming ("experiencing") the product. Wine is the example tendered by Dulleck and coauthors, and apparently by everyone else: how does one convey information to a customer about the experience of drinking a certain wine without allowing it actually to be drunk?

Credence products are a closely related but still more challenging sort of product, for which uncertainty about the value and quality of the product will persist even *after* consumption has occurred and the experience has been had. Many kinds of professional services are in this class. Consumers of credence products ("credence promisees") often have to take on faith that they have in fact received the performance they have paid for because even after all is said and done, they have no sure way of knowing. Information failure in contracting never gets more thoroughgoing than that, yet buying and selling can continue because the missing information is taken on faith.

Information failures, as a rule, militate against efficient levels of contracting occurring, and could, at a limit, prevent contracting from occurring at all. Efforts by credence industries to correct for that problem may be their greatest collective challenge. Higher education seems to be a compound, both an experience and a credence product in different respects. The inspection-proof uncertainty before contracting makes it an experience product. But uncertainty can persist after the contract is fully executed and years have passed. Promisees may still not know whether the thing that they paid for, the thing they thought they were buying, was the deliverable that was delivered. So in that sense it is a credence product as well.

The perplexity of the promisee must be the target of the promisor's efforts to cut uncertainties down to size. Promisors of experience products—movies, wine, and restaurant meals, for example—are, in effect, selling a pig in a poke. Their promisees will already know that they want a pig—but not necessarily whether they want *that* pig. When the experience of consumption is exactly what constitutes the subject matter of the contract, there is no getting around the need for the promisee to pay up front.[41] But promisors of experience products will want to make the poke less opaque if they can. They should seek to pump out as much information as possible to depict the attributes of the product that interest the promisee without actually supplying it. Hence there are movie trailers, and probably movie producers' well-known preference for brand name ("bankable") performers, often indulged at the cost of miscasting. Also hence the oenophile's fanciful vocabulary. In addition to teasers and insinuations, experience goods promisors are apt to depend on critics—disinterested arbiters whose expressed judgments can have an interpretable meaning to a prospective promisee. Restaurateurs address their version of the problem by offering freebies, as at the widely imitated Taste of Chicago festival, where cheap teaser portions of house specialties from many different restaurants are on offer.

Credence promisors that also have ex ante information problems to overcome will look and act like experience promisors before the contract is executed. Lawyers are an example—they are credence promisors who also have ex ante promisee uncertainties to deal with. Not many people wish to take time with a lawyer's YouTube highlights reel or would know how to evaluate it if they ever saw one. But opportunities to appear on bar association panels or programs on which potential clients could see them in action are highly prized. Such appearances provide potential clients at least some flavor of what an individual might be like as one's own lawyer.

Universities, like lawyers, have to deal with uncertainties both before and after a transaction, and they have been energetic at least with the "before" piece of the assignment. They hold many free events, including open houses for applicants, even for people only thinking about applying (sometimes parents are invited too); information sessions; mock lectures by star teachers; and special events for admitted students, not uncommonly stretching these things out for a whole weekend so that people can get a feel for the dorms and other facilities. Occasionally potential applicants will ask to sit in the back of a classroom and listen in to the real thing for a while. It's impossible, really, to convey much of what a years-long college experience will be like, of course, or how one school differs from another in the ways that most matter; but the effort is made, and it is likely better than nothing.

It is ex post that credence promisors have their peculiar information problem with their promisees. Experience promisees, once they have experienced the purchase, will know, for example, whether they liked the movie or the wine. But credence promisees, to the extent they are such, may never have their uncertainties fully resolved. Some of the best, worthiest law practice has to do with increasing the probability that a certain bad thing will not happen to the client. Good, careful planning and thinking through a legal strategy for a business can add untold value by avoiding trouble, but if trouble never comes, whether good lawyering was the reason may not be possible to determine. To the same point, excellent criminal defense work by lawyers is completely consistent with a client going to prison because without that good work, the outcome might have been even worse. But how can anyone know? You've got to trust me on that.

Over centuries the legal profession as a whole has evolved various means of substituting ethos for information; it has done so in recognition that the value of services rendered can be difficult for lay people to assess.[42] The profession strives to construct a public identity of lawyers and the legal system as the ligature that connects sacrosanct abstractions, such as justice and the rule of law, to concrete needs of clients in the everyday world. The objective is to solicit clients' visceral assent to the proposition that laying out large sums of money on unmeasurable performance was not a fool's errand. Preparing the ground for that faith to take root is the object of a very considerable investment by the bar. Lawyers entering the profession must swear an oath with legal consequences, in the presence of magistrates, generally in open court, and often with their families present. All their lives lawyers must observe an exacting published code of professional conduct that possesses the force of law and that applies to lawyers only. It is policed by an agency of the state's supreme court. Lawyers must subject their affairs to the scrutiny and jurisdiction of the state bar, with searching inquiries made about their behavior in the event of a complaint. Lawyers holding assets in trust for clients can expect to be severely sanctioned for commingling their own property with that of their client's, even when actual malversation is not remotely suspected. Most states require law licensees to potlatch a portion of their inventory annually for the benefit of generally recognized good works (service *pro bono publico*). Surrounding all and usually adhered to with ostentation are ladings of customs and rules of decorum and of etiquette that, although not written down, might as well be put upon tablets of stone. And the players at the profession's status pinnacle, the judges, alone among civilian officers of government conduct their public business not only in a uniform but in the uniform of a wizard.[43] Everything that magic can do, including a mighty vocabulary of crafty words and spells in ancient tongues, is enlisted to perform the sacral appointment of the profession. Other than elevating the status and the credibility of lawyers, what purpose could all that rigmarole be meant to serve? *Res ipsa loquitur.*

Colleges have many of the same needs and for the same reasons, growing out of the credence nature of their flagship product, "education." Everybody wants one. The president, one's parents—everyone—says you need to have one. You're supposed to go to college to get one. Off you go—money changes hands; a diploma eventually is awarded if all goes well; but the piece of paper aside, *what is it that you have, exactly, when you have an education*? It doesn't have mass or extension or a known address in the sensible world. You just gave somebody a couple hundred grand for it. So where is it? For the same dime, you could have had a McLaren. If you think about it for a minute, don't you feel like an idiot? No? Why not?

Education is a credence product of a very high order. Few credence promisors go to the lengths that lawyers do to protest their bona fides, but few are climbing a hill so steep: people find lawyers distasteful until they need one and discover that no adequate substitute exists. But educators come close to lawyers in their need to prove themselves. Unlike lawyers, they have not had a headwind to deal with and indeed have benefited from high general esteem, although that has surely been fraying in recent times. But they labor mightily all the same to preserve the credibility of their basic product. Ceremony plays a part. Academic pomp and circumstance may be in a bit of decline; professors in America don't conduct classes in robes, for example, as is the custom in some other countries. Most schools, though, still dignify convocations and graduations with ceremony and regalia, much of which alludes to the university's medieval origin. The ceremonies also show how the roots of these schools are profoundly intertwined with that foremost credence product, religion, more specifically the Christian religion, which since the time of St. Paul has been in all of its branches absorbed with the injunction that *faith* is required for members of the church.[44] The avidity for acquiring PEI is surely wrapped up in a felt need to—whatever else—keep one's credibility intact. When all other suppliers are likewise squabbling over PEI, one of the few things that all parties to these transactions, promisors and promisees alike, will usually agree on is that more resources need to be spent supplying adequate proofs. Subsidies for education therefore have been continuously politically popular—and continuously forthcoming.

Perhaps the credence hunger is therefore connected to the remarkable faddishness that seems to oppress the industry. One after another, a series of big themes is offered to recast and re-present the enterprise to the world (and to oneself), to become the paramount lens through which the whole thing should be viewed, understood, and interpreted.[45] Yet if so, why? Hypersensitivity to fads ought to be the incubus of those who are unsure of their standing with their constituency, who need to be seen as obsequious to its needs, with the big rewards going to whoever is quickest to respond. One thinks of the "fast fashion" apparel industry trying to keep up with the latest style demands of their unpredictable clientele, capitalizing on short supply chains to jump on this fad and then that fad, quickly getting stores stocked with whatever that is, and just as quickly moving on.[46] But the first institution of formal higher education I know of—something that was recognizably a university—was the Pandidakterion of Constantinople, founded in 425 CE. So far as appears, it had about the same mission that modern universities have (namely, facilitating the projects of the sovereign). Sixteen hundred years of practice speak to the robustness of the general plan. If any institution in the world can afford to be serene about its identity— what it is supposed to be doing, why, and even to a great extent, how—higher education should be it. But it is not. In its slavishness to ever-changing fashion, one senses in universities an inconsolable anxiety about eliciting faith that their product does indeed supply a privileged means to the useful, enriching end of connecting the past with the present and the future. For the moment, at least, the public seems to have internalized the idea that, dollar for dollar, education beats McLarens, but a dangerous current of skepticism is undeniably present and increasing. Skepticism is a potentially terminal sentiment to attach to a credence product. God forbid anyone gets the idea that the whole college thing is a scam. It seems reasonable to think, then, that the cost predicament Bowen identified is not an artifact of some kind of collective action problem buried in the structure of the higher education industry, nor is it simply an artifact of competition. It is rational for a university to fear that people might conclude that its basic product was adding little or no value to the world's stock of useful capital. Even for a monopolist, this would be a terrifying thought.

Concluding this soliloquy, I want to return to the relationship between subsidized student loan programs, enrollments, and the ascent of the dotted line. Washington public relations counselors love to say things such as "The first law of holes is, stop digging." But one cannot expect that precept to be followed where college enrollments are concerned, for reasons already explained. Still, let us suspend disbelief one last time and just imagine. Imagine there were no federal student loans—all the programs just disappeared overnight. How would that affect the demand for higher education? I have thin credentials as a seer, as I have studied the elasticity of demand for an educational product in relation to price only at my own law school. Yet here is my guess: applications to four-year schools would drop by 35 or 40 percent in the next admissions cycle, with overall enrollments eventually following. Colleges' income accounts would be hard hit nearly immediately. Subsidized loans for most student borrowers cover only a part of what they pay to schools. Every student in the margin between enrolling and not enrolling because of an available subsidized loan would (by assumption) not enroll if that loan facility disappeared, and out the door with them would go the part of the tuition that they were going to pay from personal savings, parental contribution, or whatever other source. The loss to the colleges, in other words, would far exceed the revenue from student loans that it could no longer capture; it would include *all* the revenue they would expect such students to bring. Only a handful of institutions, and very few of the public ones, could avoid something like bankruptcy within a year or two of such a sudden change—wild guess.

Reducing the loan program by half over 10 years would be survivable for many if not most institutions—another wild guess—but it would entail rescaling and redefining their missions. Colleges so affected would become less attractive compared with community colleges, to which they could expect to lose business. Under any scenario that contemplates significant reduction of federal student loans, haircuts[47] would be imposed on tens or hundreds of thousands of employees—large enough numbers that one could expect Congress to step up with a Distressed Professors Relief Act to transfer some of the losses to taxpayers.

Those large matters are smaller than the question of what happens, in any reduction scenario, to the margin-dwelling students, who now will have been priced out of the market (my guess, remember, is that there are 7 million or 8 million such people). Some of them would go to the community colleges and some others into the labor market—small numbers, I suspect, in both cases, especially the labor market, which is increasingly inhospitable to newcomers of any kind and especially brutal to college dropouts. We conceivably might have an ever-bigger population of young people with no real jobs, no educational opportunities they can pay for, no nothing—just unending video games and cable TV in mom's basement. They wouldn't have big student loan liabilities hanging over their heads, to be sure, but it would hardly matter because they would participate very little in the sociocultural economy at all unless public provision were made for them.

If that analysis has any relation to reality, only one way seems possible to stop the ascent of the dotted line, and that is to decouple federal subsidies to higher education from student loans. Congress could find another way to get money to this industry than through student loans. Doing that would displace pressure from the dotted line to something else. For example, think of straight subsidies. Colleges could get money from the U.S. Treasury if they ticked off some set of legislatively specified objectives (although one shudders to think what those would eventually become). Who would prefer to be in that world than one in which there were less central control but a rapidly ascending dotted line?

It is hard to avoid the conclusion that no matter how subsidies are delivered to higher education, they are going to have to shrink—whether quickly or slowly. Shortfalls in budgets that are associated with shrinking subsidies can be made up for in only a certain number of ways, most obviously, haircuts for faculty and staff (i.e., pay cuts) or outright layoffs, either of which would accelerate the already obvious trend toward substituting away from tenure line faculty and toward adjunct and other contract faculty, and relying much more on part-time staff work (and in many instances, less staff work). In such an austerity scenario, the research mission of universities, a big part of those institutions' contribution to public goods creation, would not necessarily have to be abandoned completely and all at once, nor probably would they be. By reinforcing recent trends, however, research activity would become ever more institutionally concentrated, at first in the top-quartile and then in the top-decile schools, and ever more dilute down the pecking order of this most exquisitely status-conscious industry. Almost all the rich schools are private ones—and one might notice in passing that they are the schools in which the political monoculture in the learned disciplines is most deeply entrenched, culturally influential, and remote from the current mainstream view of how the world actually works.

Industrywide retrenchment of this kind would reach private universities indirectly no matter how rich they were or became because as research effort dwindles in the industry as a whole, the job opportunities formerly open to the most talented graduate students would dwindle too. One should therefore expect that the demand for graduate education would diminish across the board. After all, second- and third-tier research universities have been one of the most important sources of employment for talented PhDs from the most highly ranked universities. As those kinds of jobs go away, so will the demand for the training it takes to get them. What research remained could be expected to shift toward being less dependent on graduate assistants; possibly a new profession, career research assistant, would be born.

It will be bad news if things develop that way. Graduate students—academics in their twenties whose attention is focused on a frontier of knowledge—often are the ones who come up with the best ideas, and if they don't think of those ideas themselves, they prod their mentors to do so. It is very much a numbers game as well: the more, the merrier, in general. Ideally, one would like to have a research infrastructure big enough to accommodate a substantial fraction of the people—small numbers, admittedly—able to excel at creative work. The price to be paid for withdrawing much public support from the most creative and energetic part of the academic enterprise is that the flow of new ideas will slow down. That is bad news for those of us who have been counting on their arrival. The saving grace is that one cannot experience, as such, a loss that is literally incalculable, because what might have been is a matter of idle speculation. If the idea of progress has merit, however, then loss there must assuredly be. On the other hand, if progress is *not* all it is cracked up to be (and one should concede that is possible), then retarding the pace of the growth of knowledge could be a gain—indeed, a benediction to all humanity. What if those crazy professors and their apprentices—the ones we have been subsidizing all these years—were, although they did not suspect it, about to invent a doomsday machine of some kind? Slowing things down would not seem to be such a bad move in such a case; exponents of the precautionary principle should actually prefer it. But it seems, at the end of the day, like a pretty un-American way to place a bet—which for me is reason enough to be against it.

CHAPTER FIVE

Academic Tenure and Governance

Roger E. Meiners

Academic tenure as we know it would not exist in a world of for-profit colleges. We do not observe voluntarily instituted near-life sinecures in any major for-profit institutions. The efficiency consequences of such an employment practice make it undesirable.

The common justification for tenure is well known: it permits faculty members to speak the truth (as they see it) without fear of retribution by intolerant administrators, board members, or legislators irritated with the statements of outspoken professors. It also protects faculty members from attacks by competing academic factions within and across disciplines at their own colleges. Changes in dominant ideologies within the academy can lead to witch hunts against unprotected faculty members. The risk of such retribution demands the presence of tenure for higher education to be capable of producing greater social benefits.

Those arguments are not without merit, yet we do not see tenure in other areas of productive activity in which professionals may also be involved in high-stakes arguments. Higher education is simply called "special," and tenure is justified because of the supposed unique status of college teachers. That self-anointed specialness is meaningless in economics. Higher education is likely less important than are food, housing, medical care, and security, yet it, and the people who operate within it, are declared unique. As the American Association of University

Professors (AAUP) has pronounced, "Institutions of higher education are conducted for the common good and not to further the interest of either the individual teacher or the institution as a whole."[1] Balderdash.

This chapter looks at tenure from an economic perspective; however, to understand the incentives created by tenure, it is helpful to consider its history and legal status. I argue that the original purpose of tenure was sensible, but it was perverted into the de facto life sinecures we now see. High-minded statements about universities' purity of purpose are little more than wishful thinking in a world of normal economic behavior by teachers employed by universities. After reviewing the legal status of tenure, I consider the economics of tenure; then I show that the way tenure operates is largely a symptom of the governance systems of non-profit and state universities.

A World without Tenure

Consider a thought experiment. What would happen if tenure were abolished? Setting aside legal issues, suppose the board of overseers at Harvard abolished tenure. What would happen? There would be shrieking about the impending demise of Western civilization, but would there be mass resignations by faculty members or an exodus by students? No. A few students may decamp for other Ivy League schools, but other students of comparable ability would fill their slots. Harvard faculty members—even if deadwood by Harvard standards—would still have employment alternatives elsewhere, so they would likely suffer little.[2] Parents, students, and donors have no reason to care about the issue except that some may see such changes as a good sign that weaker faculty members will be weeded out. Would prospective faculty members refuse to accept appointments at Harvard because of the no-tenure policy? Probably not enough to matter; there are always substitutes.[3]

Now change the thought experiment to the same thing happening at a slightly less-sainted university, George Mason University. There would be spleen-venting at AAUP and faculty senate meetings, but then life would return to normal.[4] In the event that some faculty members were dismissed, they would likely have inferior options compared with those of faculty members dismissed from Harvard, but the net effect would be small.[5] The university may be marginally more efficient because of the loss of deadwood and the scare thrown into other faculty members, but that possible effect is likely overblown, as will be discussed herein.

How tenure works in practice is a result of the structure of the state and nonprofit organizations. Without a change in governance structure, a change in tenure only would not likely make a significant difference in the efficiency of the organizations.

The Origins of Tenure

Tenure as we know it began to develop a century ago.[6] Before tenure was adopted, little evidence indicates that colleges casually dismissed faculty members. Most college charters noted that faculty members held their positions at the pleasure of the trustees. Faculty members generally were allowed to continue in office "during good behavior";[7] when dismissals occurred, those individuals had little chance for legal recourse. By 1820, Harvard was appointing professors with "indefinite" terms; other colleges followed suit. Faculty rankings evolved so that professors had incentives to work for advancement, but a faculty member who was not promoted was not prevented from remaining indefinitely at that college at the same rank.

Before formal tenure was adopted, most faculty appointments were technically year to year, but it was rare for a college not to reappoint all members. A survey of 22 major schools in 1910 found that only faculty members at the rank of instructor were appraised annually. Those of professorial rank were said to hold their positions with "presumptive permanence," although some schools did appraise assistant professors for multiyear renewals. As Charles Van Hise explained in 1910, "In all cases the meaning is the same, that the appointment is for life to the age of retirement, provided the appointee is efficient. . . . Appointments of professors and associate professors are practically permanent."[8] Another professor of the pretenure era noted, "In practically all of the larger institutions professors enjoy indefinite or permanent tenure upon the first appointment."[9]

Leading scholars formed the AAUP in 1915.[10] They suffered no employment threat from the lack of formal tenure; they lived under presumptive permanence, and, because of their prominence, they could easily find other positions. Nevertheless, the founders proposed that the AAUP undertake "the gradual formation of general principles respecting the tenure of the professorial office and the legitimate ground for the dismissal of professors."[11] A key part of the proposed process was the use of faculty committees to help review faculty appointments rather than leave decisions completely at the discretion of administrators.

The history of the early AAUP evinced a demand for standards that made tenure more difficult to achieve. The 1910 survey of leading universities showed that "governing bodies simply ratified the president's nominees for faculty positions."[12] Presidents could do what they wanted, which was usually to reappoint everyone. The initial AAUP standards for tenure and promotion moved away from presumptive permanence upon initial hire; they called for a 10-year tenure track. Assistant professors could be dismissed at any time during that period. Peers in a given field would actively participate in those decisions rather than administrators only. The following was written by the AAUP's Committee on Academic Freedom:

> If this profession should prove itself unwilling to purge its ranks of the incompetent and the unworthy, or to prevent the freedom which it claims in the name of science from being used as a shelter for inefficiency, for superficiality, or for uncritical and intemperate partisanship, it is certain that the task will be performed by others . . . who lack certain essential qualifications for performing it.[13]

Colleges gradually adopted the 10-year tenure track standard, but a report in 1924 found that still at some colleges, "after the first year's service a man is practically a fixture unless something very unforeseen happens."[14] Some schools that adopted tenure tracks made them only 2 or 3 years long, not 10. An unsurprising statement from the report claimed that reappointment of an annual contract for an assistant professor "especially if made more than once, carries with it a strong presumption of permanence."[15] A report in 1932 found "a presumption of permanency for assistant professors in 91 [of 283] of the institutions studied."[16]

Setting a higher bar to achieve tenure than administrators and trustees generally adopted would be consistent with the interests of established professors. One could argue that the established faculty members wanted to close the door behind them, but little financial benefit would result from that action. Given the prestige of the faculty members involved in the AAUP process in its early years, tenure seems to have been an effort to help ensure that administrators did not stick productive faculty members with colleagues the administration foolishly hired or failed to dismiss despite weak performance. Specialization exists in all occupations. Chemists are better able to discern a good chemist and economists are better able to discern a good economist than is the sociologist president of a university who controls all hiring.

For reasons not clear in the AAUP records,[17] the organization amended the recommended tenure track standard to 7 years, down from 10, in 1940; it is the standard most universities follow today.[18] Perhaps it was a compromise by advocates of the 10-year standard in an effort to get a stronger standard adopted by schools that still employed presumptive permanence or adopted very short tenure tracks. Given the economic conditions of the Great Depression, universities certainly did not have to lower their standards for tenure to attract faculty members.

Common Tenure Standards

The definition of tenure has not changed much over time. The most commonly adopted definition comes from the AAUP's 1940 statement: "After the expiration of a probationary period, teachers . . . should have permanent or continuous tenure, and their service should be terminated only for adequate cause, except in case of retirement for age, or under extraordinary circumstances because of financial exigencies."[19]

Most colleges subscribe to the AAUP statement. The AAUP does not recommend specific standards for granting tenure or for exactly how it can be revoked. A 1958 "Statement on Procedural Standards in Faculty Dismissal Proceedings" is still endorsed by the AAUP. It states that dismissal of tenured faculty members will be "rare" and likely "caused by individual human weakness," and it focuses on the kind of procedures (such as hearings and appeals) that most schools follow.[20]

Universities have formal standards for promotion and tenure and, increasingly, periodic post-tenure review.[21] Promotion to tenure usually is granted on the basis of research (scholarship), teaching, and—to a small extent—service.[22] Some schools include "collegiality" as a criterion, which vaguely means that the person is regarded as reasonably cooperative. At highly regarded universities, tenure is difficult to achieve, as the scholarship standards (and expectations of success at obtaining grant money in the sciences) are significant. The lesser the school, the lesser the scholarship requirement.[23] For most professors, the amount of time devoted to scholarship is, as measured by output, relatively low; therefore, they have plenty of time to devote to teaching.

How much does teaching matter? Most people would agree that candidates for promotion and tenure must be perceived as competent teachers. Administrators do not know much about the quality of teaching by faculty members, but they know a lot about complaints. A junior professor who causes problems for any reason is unlikely to be retained. Teaching evaluations provide feedback, but they are far from foolproof. Student rankings can be affected by grading standards, telling jokes in class, or other things not much related to instructional quality. Over time, tenured faculty members and administrators get a sense of whether someone is basically competent or not in the classroom and whether they should be supported for tenure—at least in that dimension.[24]

Legal Realities

Tenure, once granted, means a near-life sinecure; but legally, permanent tenure is not guaranteed. Nontenured faculty members (presuming away restrictions that may be caused by unionization) are usually retained at will, and their contracts can be not renewed without formalities. The U.S. Supreme Court noted, in the case of a nonrenewed tenure-track assistant professor, that there was no property interest protected by the Fourteenth Amendment that required a hearing; the university could simply not renew his contract.[25] As the court observed in a companion case, the claim to an entitlement of a faculty position must rest on more than a "subjective 'expectancy'"[26] of continued employment. As legal commentators have noted, however, tenured faculty members have the "right to procedural safeguards in case of termination."[27] The "heart of the tenure system is the requirement of specified cause for dismissal."[28]

At most colleges, private or public, procedural rights largely rest on contractual relationships between faculty members and colleges. Those relationships can be specific to an individual contract or, most commonly, by reference to the institution's tenure policy as published in a handbook—that is, colleges lay out the terms of tenure and specify procedural rules. If the procedural rules are competently drafted and, even more important, if they are followed properly within the university, schools routinely prevail in suits brought by those denied tenure initially or who have it revoked later.[29] An examination of recent cases does not reveal vindication of dismissed tenured faculty members, but that absence does not mean that such instances do not occur. When universities know that they are likely to lose, like most defendants they probably settle before trial, so the matters often are confidential.

Lowering the Boom on Inept Tenured Professors

As a result of complaints about the poor performance of some tenured professors, most states have instituted post-tenure review. Some colleagues assured me that, as professors in Texas, we are subject to barbarous treatment at the hands of a legislature dominated by troglodytes and by governors incapable of appreciating our enlightened scholarly efforts. Seemingly bolstering that claim, after offering rhetoric about professorial malfeasance, the legislature mandated post-tenure review to begin in 1998.[30] Texas law holds that all tenured professors are "subject to a comprehensive performance evaluation process conducted no more often than once every year, but no less often than once every six years."[31] At least in the University of Texas System the option is for the fewest reviews possible: once every 6 years. Texas law now states that tenure may be revoked, after proper due process, for "incompetency, neglect of duty, or other good cause."[32] "Incompetency" is not defined. "Neglect of duty" is "continuing or repeated substantial neglect of professional responsibilities."[33]

What has happened? The University of Texas System implemented a formal post-tenure review process. The Board of Regents details the procedure,[34] and each institution within the system has adopted a consistent procedure.[35] The system reported the results for the years 2009–2011;[36] in those 3 years, 995 tenured professors at nine universities were reviewed. More than 96 percent were performing satisfactorily. Less than another 2 percent were "marginal"—that rating is a warning to up performance or possibly face trouble later. A little more than 2 percent, 21 professors, were declared unsatisfactory in their performance.[37] I do not know if any of those persons were terminated as a result of that finding. My guess, based on some experience with the process, is that some faculty members have been "rehabilitated," whereas others were coaxed into retirement—perhaps encouraged by a bit of extra cash.

A declaration of unsatisfactory performance does not result in immediate dismissal. I have been told that the procedure is costly, especially to administrators. There may be a 2-year period of intensive review for the faculty member before the issue of dismissal may arise. Often, the issue is bad teaching, which may include a behavior that is easily remedied, such as showing up for class regularly. The professor is given a chance to improve, and he or she must be provided "coaching" about how to do so. If the professor contends that the claims are inaccurate, faculty members from other universities may be brought in to sit in on that professor's classes and take notes to help document the ability of the professor. The department chair must have frequent counseling sessions with the professor in question to review progress or the lack thereof. The administrative cost is high, so few administrators want to take that route—they bear a high burden.[38] Just letting it ride, or encouraging the person to retire by making his or her life a bit more miserable, is not uncommon.

In sum, dismissal of tenured faculty members is legally possible, but it involves a high cost to the employing institution. Administrators who take on such costly duties will not be showered with glory for improving their schools. Why are the procedures so detailed and costly? Procedure is necessary to demonstrate due consideration of the rights of the professor; however, the process goes beyond what would be required to demonstrate to a court that the review was adequate. The costliness of the process discourages its use.

Managers also dislike litigation. Extensive procedural protections for affected faculty members reduce the odds of loss in litigation *and* discourage the attempts of administrators to dismiss inept professors. I do not know how many cases have been settled out of court or how much money has been paid to get someone to resign, but I know that it happens regularly. In any event, the rate of dismissal of tenured professors is low.

As a side note, it is possible both to offer tenure and to design contracts that avoid a sinecure at a fixed salary. In Texas, where salaries are public, we find some professors being paid about $1 million a year, whereas most are paid less than $100,000 a year.[39] The highest-paid professors are those in medicine. They could earn significant salaries in private practice, so they must be bid away from that occupation. Professors in most disciplines do not have such attractive alternatives.

Medical schools have adapted. They must compete with private practice to attract faculty members, but those schools know that they cannot afford faculty members in life sinecures at very high salaries who become unproductive. Practices vary, but most medical faculty members have flexible contracts with relatively low base salaries. Professors who bring in big grant money commonly get paid a lot more and are released from other obligations to work on the research. Professors who bring in no grant money see their salaries go down, may be assigned to teach more, and may work more in the clinic run by the school, treating patients to help generate revenue to cover their salaries. Administrators bargain with professors about their workload and compensation.

Those bargains avoid some of the downside of tenure, with professors locked into a guaranteed salary for life. Nothing prevents other, nonmedical universities from being similarly creative in contracts with faculty members. If universities face greater budget problems, administrators might take a lesson from medical schools.

Economic Rationales for Tenure

Tenure does not exist as a near-lifetime sinecure because of the law. Armen Alchian explained many years ago that tenure works the way it does because of the nonprofit status of universities. This paper will return to his argument after considering rationales offered by other economists who have tried to devise arguments to assert that tenure is, at least in part, economically sensible for other reasons.[40]

One contention is that tenure exists because job performance is difficult to monitor.[41] Faculty jobs are highly specific, and the jobs require continual learning. Unlike in corporations, where workers may be shifted around, academics are stuck in particular disciplines (job rigidity) and are not mobile within the organization. Specializations are tied to academic fields, not to universities. As Michael McPherson and Gordon Winston have argued, senior administrators cannot effectively monitor the performance of faculty members in different fields, so having a "general attitude of autonomy and mutual respect which universities try to foster among faculty" members is efficient.[42] Renewable multiyear contracts are not desirable because evaluation of faculty members under such contracts "would prove very costly."[43]

Those claims are weak. It is true that professors have training in specific fields, and, say, economists cannot be shifted over to teach chemistry; but economists at corporations also cannot be shifted over to, say, product development. If the services of a corporate economist are no longer needed, that person is back in the economics job market. Why could the same not be true for economists who wish to consider themselves academic economists? Just because someone prefers to be in a particular job market, such as a university, does not mean that employers in that market must have an interest in them.

The claim that reviewing the performance of academic employees is too costly, so that granting tenure is economically sensible, is highly suspect. Monitoring performance can be difficult but need not necessarily be costly. How does Google measure performance? With lines of code written? No, a Google administrator makes a judgment call that someone is worth keeping on the payroll. The cost of making a determination of whether an academic term contract should be renewed—looking at teaching evaluations and counting the number of articles written—is unlikely to be greater than the cost imposed by a deadwood tenured lifer on the faculty.[44]

Another explanation for tenure is that academic departments are internal labor markets within universities. Employees—members of various departments—hold the knowledge of who is best to hire. As H. Lorne Carmichael suggests, without tenure, "incumbents would never be willing to hire people who might turn out to be better than themselves."[45] That would be especially true if budgets were tight, so faculty members knew that the few rewards available would go to smart, productive young professors. In a world of tight budgets, the "most brilliant of the young scholars would actually find their job prospects reduced."[46]

That line of reasoning is another "universities are special" argument. Apparently in no other area of economic endeavor are the incentives of employees so perverse that they want to hire weak colleagues so that the incumbents look good by comparison.[47] Where nonmarket constraints exist in labor markets, such as union work rules that protect established workers at the expense of younger workers, we do not see incompetent junior workers being hired.[48] The author's claim could be made about any organization that annually divides a limited pot of rewards among employees based on some measure of productivity, but the problem seems peculiar to universities because of their "special" nature. Employees in many organizations participate in the hiring process, yet the problem of incumbent employees desiring inept colleagues that causes a race to the bottom is not pervasive.[49]

Another argument, made by Richard McKenzie, is that tenure is economically sound because it is "a mutually beneficial trade between professors and their universities. However, we add that the tenure arrangement gives professors some (but not total) employment protection from the ebbs and flows—the ravages and vagaries—of institutional politics inside universities, while universities gain by paying lower wages."[50]

That argument is similar to the one made by supporters of various price controls, union work rules, and import controls. The claim is that markets will be disrupted and not work well if prices or supplies fluctuate. Market stabilization by price or quantity controls is needed or we will not have adequate mohair or milk supplies. Economists routinely scoff at such claims and have obliterated them in countless journal articles; those critics doubt that price stabilization or market shares must be guaranteed. The argument here, though, is that individual suppliers (professors) need protection against market fluctuations—that is, if a college has a department of basket weaving, and the demand for basket weavers evaporates so that few students sign up for basket-weaving classes, the professors nevertheless should be kept on the payroll for decades.[51]

No private-sector industry engages in voluntary labor transactions that provide life tenure.[52] When the dot-com boom hit in the 1990s, the demand for software writers went through the roof. Kids dropped out of college to take high-paying jobs. After the bubble burst, they were often scrounging for work or they were back in school. Should they have been given life tenure to protect them from market "ravages and vagaries"?

Another argument is that tenure has efficiency-enhancing roles. Professors make universities better by monitoring university administrators and trustees. Tenured professors, as compared with nontenured professors, are more likely to undertake "increased governance duties" because of reduced fear of reprisal.[53] The author of this argument, William O. Brown, also claims "tenure should be common in institutions that specialize in either teaching or research."[54]

The first claim, that tenure likely makes faculty members more willing to comment on the decisions of administrators, is true. The reason that such freedom may be useful is consistent with Alchian's argument, as discussed subsequently—nonprofit administrators need monitoring because private-sector financial metrics are lacking.

Contrary to the second claim, however, I am not aware of any for-profit research-intensive organization that provides tenure, and Brown does not mention one. Most for-profit organizations want employees to feel secure and not continually worry about being shown the door, but the expectation of a long career for productive employees is not the same as a near-life sinecure that requires minimal performance.

Another argument arises from concern about asymmetric information. Economists discovered a few decades ago that some people know more than other people in most transactions. Employees know more than employers about how much effort they provide at work. Sellers know more than buyers about the details of a product. Many devices are employed to deal with that discrepancy. Tenure is asserted to help solve the problem in academics of unequal information. After all, writes Aloysius Siow, "[S]pecialization exacerbates the informational asymmetries."[55] The problem of imperfect information leads to such things as the up-or-out rule in tenure; by fulfilling a tenure track, junior professors show senior faculty members if they are worth keeping. Most faculty members do not have much firm-specific knowledge—their intellectual capital easily transfers to another school. Tenure gives faculty members an incentive to stay at a school.

Siow asserts that up-or-out is used in some for-profit organizations—which is true, but it is not followed by tenure, so the analogy is poor. Before being tenured, junior professors are at-will employees who can be dismissed any year before the up-or-out decision. Most organizations are like that. In a for-profit firm, however, those promoted and declared to be a partner, director, or vice president can later be shown the door.[56] Even those senior managers have no near-guarantee that merely by appearing in the office and shuffling papers, they will be able to stay for life at a set salary, so comparisons with nonacademic institutions are not parallel. Furthermore, a lack of firm-specific knowledge is not uncommon. People in sales frequently switch employers, lawyers change law firms, mechanics move from one repair shop to another, doctors change hospitals or group practices, but people in those knowledge-based occupations are not given sinecures.[57]

Two other authors—João Ricardo Faria and Gonçalo Monterio—have argued that the tenure track is largely a training period in which "departments can use tenure rules and standards as an incentive system to make scholars develop work habits that ultimately lead to a successful and productive academic career."[58] If that were true, we would see it in other professions that have long learning curves, such as surgery, but we do not. We also do not observe that practice in for-profit settings, which makes the explanation suspect.

Other articles have also attempted to provide a formal economic justification for tenure, but the ones reviewed here are representative. Most proponents of tenure develop an argument couched in economic terminology for the proposition posited, but counter arguments are not difficult to offer, so the explanations are not convincing.

One argument seems stronger, and—unlike the papers reviewed—it has empirical evidence behind it. The argument is that tenure allows schools to save on labor cost, which McKenzie (it should be noted) also mentioned in his comment. If job security is strong, faculty members will accept lower salaries than if they must worry about continued employment.[59] For example, departments of economics where the odds of tenure are low, which includes most elite schools, tend to pay higher salaries to untenured assistant professors than do schools at which the odds of tenure are higher.[60] If a school does not value academic scholarship, operating costs can be reduced by offering easy tenure.[61]

Job tenure, as in length of service, is beneficial, but not in the academic sense of a near sinecure. A meta-analysis of 350 empirical studies, primarily of businesses, found that "longer tenured employees generally have greater in-role performance and citizenship performance."[62] Even accounting for age, however, longer tenure was related to more aggressive behavior and more absences not related to health. Although tenure was generally beneficial, the longer the tenure the weaker the benefits to the employer; when employees averaged more than 14.2 years' tenure, the benefits to job performance turned negative.[63] Nonacademic "tenure" and academic tenure are apples and oranges. Stable employment can be beneficial to an organization; being unable to remove indolent employees is not.

The proponents of various economic arguments for university tenure gloss over the consequences of a stagnant workforce.[64] Unless budgets rise continually, universities must make do with a faculty base that changes only when someone retires. That means that few new faculty members can be hired, and resources are not easily moved into new areas of interest. Dying European language departments with costly tenured professors continue in operation for decades. Schools find it difficult to shift resources to, say, Mandarin and Hindi, where there may be rising demand. Administrators cannot eliminate faculty members who, even if competent, are simply of little value.[65] Even if very few students wish to take Romanian or Hungarian, the university is stuck with tenured Romanian and Hungarian professors who contribute less value than if the resources could be moved to growing areas, such as Asian languages. That circumstance has nothing to do with protection for faculty members against attack for political reasons; it is an inefficient allocation of resources.

Universities, allegedly at the cutting edge of innovation, are not nimble institutions; they move like glaciers and become seemingly ever less responsive in a world in which change occurs ever more quickly. That quality is likely the highest cost imposed by tenure, but as discussed next, colleges are still unlikely to be nimble players in a fast-changing world even setting tenure aside.

Institutional Constraints Matter

Most economics articles regarding tenure do not focus on the implications that arise from the institutional structure of higher education. With the exception of a small number of proprietary schools,[66] colleges are state bureaus or nonprofit organizations. They are not subject to the normal discipline of market forces.

Armen Alchian explained in 1953 that tenure "springs from the special ownership arrangement and financial structure of our colleges . . . it arises from an absence of the ordinary kind of property rights that exist in profit-seeking businesses."[67] He noted that managers in nonprofit organizations can be more arbitrary in hiring and firing people because monitoring the performance of the nonprofit manager is very difficult.[68] Managers can shirk their duties or engage in nonproductive activities, and their monitors—board members—may have no clue. Employees seek protection from such managers through tenure.

Recall that a century ago, leading scholars, who had no reason to worry about job security or opportunities, promoted the creation of 10-year tenure tracks. Their concern was not job security but getting rid of presumptive permanence that resulted in their being stuck with less-able colleagues hired by administrators ignorant of the details of their field. That goal was likely quality enhancing. If tenure were abolished, something like presumptive permanence could take its place. At least the tenure process forces the issue of retention of junior faculty members. Those who think that college administrators would be tougher on indolent faculty members are likely off the mark; government employees rarely are subject to dismissal once they have completed a brief probationary period.[69]

Alchian predicted that tenure would dominate in nonprofit colleges but not in for-profit colleges. He also predicted that tenure would be stronger at schools that did not need to rely as much on current tuition dollars because of large endowments or state subsidies. That analysis was confirmed in an empirical study in a leading finance journal. The author found that tenure is rare at for-profits and is stronger at universities with larger state subsidies, and, among nonprofit schools, tenure is more common when the school has large endowments.[70] At schools where economic rents are greater, the faculty members have a better chance of capturing a portion of them in the form of job security, rather than administrators having full control of those rents. When faculty members are tenured, they are more likely to be openly critical of actions of administrators, which can serve as a check on administrators' actions. Because nonprofit schools do not distribute profits to shareholders, the rents can be captured by employees—administrators and faculty members. And there is no reason to think that administrators will do admirable things with surplus funds—they can devote it to their own salaries and perquisites.

Universities Are Not the Real World—As Everyone Knows

Proprietary firms have two key features, note Alchian and Harold Demsetz: "metering input productivity and metering rewards."[71] Those tasks are not simple, do not work perfectly, and are greatly affected by regulation.[72] The owners of capital want rewards for the risks they take, but they generally rely on administrators to run the organization and to manage workers. If the managers fail, they are dismissed. All inputs should earn their opportunity cost or they should not remain with the organization—that is, the revenue each input helps to generate should be greater than its cost, or the input is not economical.

The necessities of life—food, clothing, housing, and medical products—are provided primarily by for-profit firms in our society.[73] And no, colleges do not have a nonprofit structure because they produce public goods.[74] It is true that an educated populace is more productive than an uneducated populace and so provides social benefits, but given the returns of lifetime earnings from higher education, people have strong personal incentives to obtain a college degree. People invest in education for the benefits it provides them.

If subsidies to state colleges ended, for-profit colleges would likely expand, although provision by private nonprofit colleges may also expand as people look less to the state.[75] Metering input productivity—faculty cost and the services they provide—is not especially difficult. Faculty members teach and—if the employer cares about it—produce scholarship or some service. A major difficulty in education is measuring the value added of the education provided. Students move among majors based on perceptions of job opportunities, but they cannot discern the value added by a particular major or professor. The problem is compounded because most college curricula look quite similar.

Although proprietary colleges could do much of the job, they would have difficulty competing with state subsidies and schools with established reputations. Given that state and private nonprofit schools dominate and fight to retard encroachment by proprietary firms, current producers can be expected to continue to dominate. Next let us consider incentives within colleges that stem from their nonprofit status and domination by tenured faculty members.

Missing Property Rights

Not-for-profit organizations are missing governance mechanisms key to the efficient functioning of for-profit organizations. The lack of a profit motive, the lack of clearly identified residual claimant owners, and, therefore, the weak boards that oversee colleges are critical factors in how colleges operate. I will focus on public colleges because nonprofit colleges have some different features, but much of the analysis of public colleges also applies to nonprofit schools.

Colleges do not have clear owners; state governments establish colleges. State assets usually are entrusted to a board of trustees that has the authority to impose some changes, primarily affecting college leadership.[76] The boards are akin to corporate boards, but there are major differences:

- Colleges have no shareholders or legal residual claimants who have property rights in the organization.
- Shareholders do not elect the board.

- Board members have no direct financial stake in the institution.[77]
- Most boards of state universities are political appointees with limited terms; at private schools the boards often are self-sustaining, with the president playing a major role in determining who gets picked for the board.
- The lack of ownership and weak incentives of the board mean that the operators of the organization—faculty members and administrators—are more likely to capture rewards that might otherwise go to the equity owners of private firms.[78]

Consider two schools of higher education in Northern Virginia: the state institution George Mason University and the for-profit Strayer University. The nominal owners of George Mason, Virginia taxpayers, do not capture its benefits except, possibly, by sending their children there. Most nominal owners of George Mason have little reason to think much about it. George Mason faculty members and administrators think a lot about it, as is true in the labor-managed firm. Those employees have incentives to think of how to gain control of resources that benefit their well-being. At Strayer, the owners capture the benefits of success, and they suffer the consequences of bad decisions or market or regulatory vagaries.[79] They think hard about those matters.

Incentives of College Boards

If university boards are the legal equivalent of boards of a corporation, then they are the principals of the organization responsible for the execution of its mission. Corporate board members focus on the financials and on choosing and monitoring top managers.[80] Some have significant personal wealth tied up in the corporation; others are outsiders paid to bring expertise. It does not work with scientific precision, but firms are subject to the market for corporate control if poorly managed, so resources are allocated more efficiently over time.[81]

College boards generally look like corporate boards—a group of successful people. Most have little knowledge of the details of higher education, but that does not matter; many corporate board members have no specific knowledge about the products or services of company boards on which they sit. They are not there to discuss product details—the focus is on performance. Unfortunately, colleges lack many financial metrics available to firms.

College boards can look at factors such as the budget, changes in tuition, and success at fundraising. They can consider other measures, such as growth in enrollment or applications, changes in average SAT scores, graduation rates, *U.S. News & World Report* rankings, or whatever is thought useful. Regardless of how a college is run, however, there is no market for college control. There are no shares of stock as there are for private corporations where dissidents who believe they can do a better job acquire enough ownership to get control of the board and, thereby, of operational policy. Hence, what college board members *should* measure is unclear.[82] Who the board answers to—other than taxpayers very indirectly and the legislature or governor somewhat more directly—is also unclear. Students, alumni, faculty members, and others often assert that they are *stakeholders* in colleges, but they are not *shareholders*. They have interests in school assets and revenues but no ownership.

Being on a college board has prestige, but it is not the same as being on a corporate board. Even if board members devote a lot of time to absorbing information about a college, they have a hard time knowing whether it is performing as well as it should, given its revenue and its relative place in the academic world. Lacking the kind of bottom line that matters in the market, no metric dominates; what direction to take is a judgment call.

College board members are unlikely to know what the best strategy is—one cannot be all things to everyone—and every school is not going to rise in the rankings. Except in Lake Wobegon, half of all schools are below average—but average of what? Some low-ranked schools may provide greater value in knowledge gained by students than do most schools, but that value is unmeasured.[83] The metrics tend to be vague, and a college naturally gloms on to those that purport to indicate some measure of success. Regardless of how diligent board members and administrators are, they have a hard time knowing what "quality" performance is.

Board members also are often fed a diet of selective information by top administrators, who have strong incentives to manage information so as to minimize damage to their own positions. Where no bottom line exists other than a balanced budget, board members have a hard time knowing what information to demand beyond what they already receive.[84] Given that they have no concrete stake in the school, they also have limited incentive to seek out hard-to-get data.

Incentives of Administrators

Boards usually remove presidents not because of bad financial performance but because of some event that brought bad press to the school. Lawrence Summers was forced out as president of Harvard for saying something *seen* as politically incorrect by some members of the faculty, who played the matter up to the media. That was embarrassing, so he had to go. Few said that he did a poor job otherwise. Less discussed was the fact that some faculty members were unhappy about an expected realignment of resources at the school.[85] Presidents and other administrators learn to be trouble minimizers—offend no one, speak in platitudes, devote significant time to building coalitions, and go with the flow. Few faculty members may love an administrator, but if no one hates him or her, negative news is unlikely to appear about this or that group being up in arms about something, the merits of the matter notwithstanding.

The structure breeds cautious administrators. Had Summers spoken only in vague generalities, it would have been more difficult for disgruntled faculty members to find effective ways to oppose him. Most presidents previously served as provost, dean, department head, or other positions along the way. In most cases, the process for administrator searches is spearheaded by a faculty-dominated committee. The committee narrows down the list and gives it to the administrator or board, who makes the decision. A search firm often is used, but that fact matters little because the list of candidates looks much the same.

Even if a search committee is filled with academic stars, they all have vested interests. The engineering rep cares little about architecture, the architecture rep cares little about philosophy, and so on. The committee members are looking for danger signals, such as indications that a candidate would push a disproportionate share of resources to a particular department, such as engineering. Such fears generate opposition from non-engineering people, regardless of the quality of the candidate or how beneficial his or her hiring may be for the future of the institution. Compromise rules through the logrolling process.

Those most likely to make it through the screening process are consensus builders. They are not risk takers who may shut down a French department that has few students and move resources into environmental engineering, which looks to have better opportunities. Because most people who rise through academic administration have been through two or more such screenings and have track records in previous positions, a hatred for French—or any curriculum—will likely be exposed. The search process creates a bias toward cautious people who focus energies on matters that will not generate controversy. If an administrator makes enemies, including deadwood faculty members, the knives come out. Tales pass from one school to another about how a certain candidate is a madman.

Faculty members—and, likely, the college's board members—look for signs of positive accomplishments in previous postings, such as fundraising. Everyone loves more revenue. An administrator who leaves the faculty members to their own devices while she works to raise cash is likely to generate positive reports. If an administrator must deal with a problem, rather than simply settle the matter, the career-enhancing method is to appoint a committee to fiddle with it. The time costs may be high, responsibility defrayed, and higher opportunity costs incurred, but those costs rarely are calculated.

General Electric has a policy of dumping divisions that are not performing to expectations. Long famous for household appliances and a major player in financial markets, General Electric is getting out of those businesses because of better opportunities elsewhere. That rarely happens in universities.[86] For example, despite the crash in law school enrollment, few moves have been made to thin the number of competitors.[87] It is inconceivable that in a market subject to financial metrics, in which demand had fallen year after year, some competitors would not have thrown in the towel; but that rarely happens in universities.[88]

The net value of a third-rate law school in a state burdened with too many law schools is negative. But the president who takes the sensible step of closing it will be seen as a wild woman, willing to shut down any program and dump the faculty. She would unlikely be considered for employment elsewhere because cautious academics would worry that they could be next. Law today, French tomorrow, then—who knows?—even economics could be under assault! Better to stay with candidates who are not boat rockers and who promise to raise revenue to benefit all.

Many academic administrators are talented, but their incentives are to focus on areas such as fundraising and to avoid problems that could raise the ire of faculty members and thereby create bad career publicity. That tendency skews the set of job candidates available over time, abetted by cumbersome internal rules that make change costly. Administrators could adjust to other expectations, but who would create expectations to close marginal programs or to fire deadwood tenured faculty members? Proprietary firms adjust or go bankrupt; but, like Soviet steel mills, state schools bumble along, drawing resources from taxpayers and, increasingly, from students, who have no interest in needless programs or faculty members saved from extinction.[89]

The rules of tenure do not prohibit the dismissal of incompetent tenured professors, but it rarely happens because the administrative cost is high. Not only does the income of an administrator not rise because of dismissals, it may mean the end of other employment alternatives, as faculty-driven search committees are likely to weed out barbarians who fire faculty members, the merits of such matters aside.

Tenure Faces Hard Times

The defenders of tenure recognize the problems it creates, such as the protection of deadwood. The problems go beyond that but are just as likely to be insurmountable, given the current structure of higher education—that is, the abolition of tenure may matter less than detractors hope because of the nonprofit status of colleges.

The job security provided by tenure likely means lower average wages. Faculty members enjoy the security, and their employers enjoy the somewhat lower wage bill; however, the savings to employers are overstated. Universities are notorious for *salary inversion*: in fields in which demand for new, high-quality graduates is high, new assistant professors may be paid more than are older full professors, an indication that wages have adjusted somewhat to compensate for the security of tenure. But that does not mean that the older faculty members are a bargain. With strong job security, some faculty members will be less diligent, thereby providing less value for the employer. And despite the security, faculty members continue to lobby for wage increases, travel benefits, and reductions in workloads. That is what we expect of *homo economicus*.[90]

A few years ago an administrator for the University of Phoenix called me to see if I would teach a class in their Master of Business Administration program in Dallas. I asked what the pay would be. I was assured that, given my learnedness and experience, I would be at the top of their pay scale: $1,200 per course.[91] It was not a happy moment to learn a bit about my market value. That example is not indicative of what all pay would look like in the free-market alternative to the current system, but many well-educated people now are willing to teach courses for what existing professors see as low wages. Public and nonprofit colleges know that too, so only a minority of faculty members are now tenured, as lower-cost substitutes are employed.

When markets are constrained from free operation by various regulations, price controls, subsidies, and so forth, the winners under that structure will resist change, and the inefficiencies may persist for decades. American automakers and airlines and their union workers feasted well for decades until the forces of competition finally worked their way in. Consumers wanted better deals, workers were willing to work for less than union scale, and foreign competitors added to the pressure. Employers looked for lower-cost new workers. As long as the senior employees had been protected, they did not complain as much.

Similarly, the forces of change are at work in higher education. The number of tenured positions is declining. Schools adjust to changes in relative prices. From 1975 to 2011, although college enrollment at least doubled, the number of full-time tenured and tenure-track faculty members nationally grew by 23 percent. In contrast, full-time faculty members who are not on a tenure track (usually paid on a lower scale with higher teaching loads) grew by 259 percent; part-time faculty rose by 286 percent; graduate student employees rose by 123 percent; and full-time nonfaculty professionals increased by 369 percent.[92] Schools are saving resources by substituting away from tenured faculty members in favor of contract faculty members. The increase in the number of administrators likely reflects using less-costly nonacademics for administrative chores and the need to deal with burdens imposed on colleges by ever-growing and intertwined federal, state, and accrediting requirements.[93]

As the University of Phoenix knows, many people with graduate degrees are available to teach.[94] Colleges have less need to engage in costly tenure employment. Still, labor rigidities persist. Entire departments that could be abolished because of low demand remain for decades, as administrators wait for voluntary retirements. It is as if buggy-whip makers had to be kept on the payroll until their retirements despite the invention of the automobile.

State subsidies to colleges have been dropping. Schools make up the deficit by raising tuition rather than by cutting costs, as administrators try to save themselves from the wrath of the faculty members that would result from closing unneeded programs or raising teaching loads. But hanging on to the past is not a stable model if innovative competitors exist. Proprietary competitors such as Strayer University are more common now than they have been in decades past, but even more significant is the rise of online education as seen in Massive Open Online Courses (often just called MOOCs), charities such as Khan Academy, and organizations such as Coursera.

Faculty members often oppose recording their lectures, asserting that the university would just play it again and again and squeeze out the faculty. Those faculty members are kidding themselves; most of us are not that interesting. The online productions that are now available blow away a boring video of most of us lecturing. The problem for online higher education seems not to be in the production of alternative delivery methods—which is occurring—but in the existence of mechanisms or metrics to assure employers that the prospective employee with a diploma possesses a certain level of knowledge.

Increasingly, it will matter less and less if the knowledge possessed by a potential worker came from a traditional university or from free online courses.[95] If someone can write software, who cares where the knowledge came from? Universities still focus on traditional knowledge that increasingly is transferrable by alternative delivery methods. If employers signal that such knowledge—not a traditional diploma—is key and that the knowledge can be demonstrated, students will seek lower-cost alternatives via their laptops.

Final Thought on Tenure

Assume away state schools. In a world of private proprietary schools and nonprofit schools, we would likely still see tenure—not at proprietary schools; their markets are quite different from nonprofit schools. Proprietary schools focus on effective, no-frills delivery that appeals to a relatively distinct segment of the market. It is hard to imagine that they would become research institutions. Proprietary schools would be plentiful, but they would likely not be considered to have high academic prestige and would have little interest in faculty members who want compensation for publications.

Nonprofit colleges already dominate the rankings of comprehensive universities and undergraduate schools. They may not change greatly, but there would likely be more such schools in the absence of state-subsidized schools.[96] Harvard and other highly regarded schools are not going to throw out tenure; when someone becomes intolerable, they are encouraged with lump-sum payments to move on.

Harvard and other such major institutions are research and graduate-education driven; undergraduate teaching is a sideline. Numerically, most private schools focus on undergraduate education.[97] They see the value in the long-term retention of professors. Alumni like to see their old professors when they visit campus. Continuity seems important for fundraising and for assistance in recruiting new students. These schools seem to screen better for quality of instruction than does the average public school. Their professors know that they will devote a lot of time sitting in their offices talking to students, and those professors often are much more involved in campus activities than is the case with faculty members at generic state universities. Tenure gives private-teaching-school professors more incentive to invest in school activities (called "firm-specific capital" in economics) and to provide meaningful service to the school and its students, rather than to view themselves as independent research contractors who are always ready to move.

Regardless of how professors see themselves—special or not—they just have a job that must be done. Getting the incentives right is critical for increasing the value of higher education.

CHAPTER SIX

The Changing of the Guard: The Political Economy of Administrative Bloat in American Higher Education

Todd J. Zywicki and Christopher Koopman

Something has happened to the structure of higher education in America. Universities have increased spending, but very little of that has been related to classroom instruction; rather, it has been directed toward nonclassroom costs. As a result, academic bureaucracies have grown significantly, as universities focus on hiring employees to manage or administer people, programs, and regulations. Between 2001 and 2011, those sorts of hires increased 50 percent faster than the number of classroom instructors.[1] The trend toward growing academic bureaucracies has become ubiquitous in the landscape of American higher education.

With the increased growth of academic bureaucracies has come increased focus on the problems resulting from that growth. In his recent book *The Fall of the Faculty*,[2] Benjamin Ginsberg describes the problem as such:

> Every year, hosts of administrators and staffers are added to college and university payrolls, even as schools claim to be battling budget crises that are forcing them to reduce the size of their full-time faculties. As a result, universities are filled with armies of functionaries—the vice presidents, associate vice presidents, assistant vice presidents, provosts, associate provosts, vice provosts, assistant provosts, deans, deanlets, deanlings, each commanding staffers and assistants—who, more and

> more, direct the operations of every school. Backed by their administrative legions, university presidents and other senior administrators have been able, at most schools, to dispense with faculty involvement in campus management and, thereby to reduce the faculty's influence in university affairs.[3]

Ginsberg diagnosed it as "administrative blight."[4] Others, such as Greene, Kisida, and Mills, have termed the dramatic shift in spending "administrative bloat."[5] Regardless of what term is given, many have concluded that spending by American universities has been shifting away from faculty and classroom instruction and toward university administration.

Trends in employment of nonacademic personnel have received particular scrutiny as a result of the dramatic rise in university prices in recent years and the simultaneous increase in student indebtedness to pay for it. Despite that scrutiny, no one has yet provided an explanation for why expenditures and headcounts on nonacademic employees have risen so dramatically. Those trends are especially puzzling in light of the governance structure of the modern university, in which faculty seemingly play a decisive role, and the overall operation of the university is supervised by the board of trustees. Our goal in this chapter is to take a critical look at the rise of administrative bloat within the modern university in an attempt to answer the general question, "If the faculty is the effective owner of the university, why has the bureaucratic arm within the university grown while the academic arm has not grown in proportion?"

The explanation that we provide is that the role of the administration in the modern, nonprofit university is best understood as analogous to the nature of a bureaucracy in another famously nonprofit industry: the government. Unlike private business enterprises, in which allocation of employment and other resources is measured by reference to the value that they contribute to the company's bottom line, managers and directors of nonprofit entities have no inherent profit-and-loss device for measuring the contribution of staffing to the overall outcomes of the enterprise. That inability to measure results and monitor outputs effectively in a nonprofit organization gives an opportunity for academic administrators to pursue their self-interest at the expense of the enterprise, which they do by increasing the size of their discretionary budgets and staffing, much as government bureaucrats traditionally have been thought to do. Yet those developments present a puzzle, as the growth of the administration apparently has resulted in siphoning off of resources from the university's academic mission. We explore possible explanations for how this development has come about. In the remainder of the chapter we will attempt to ascertain the scale of those developments and to understand why they have occurred.

The first section of this chapter is a brief review of the history of university governance structures in the United States, from the founding of early religious-oriented and proprietary schools through the creation of faculty-dominated nonprofit and government-supported universities beginning in the late 19th century. That brief and familiar history sets the stage for a discussion in the next section of the dominant trends of the past several decades—the growth of university bureaucracies as an independent and coequal power source within the modern university. We review various studies that have been conducted to estimate the size of the growing administrative burden in modern universities.[6] Next we examine the various explanations that have been proffered to explain the tremendous growth in nonacademic employment and expenditures during that period. We suggest that the most persuasive explanation for the growth of administrative bloat has been the self-interested tendency of bureaucrats to consciously or unconsciously pursue an agenda to increase the range of their responsibilities and, hence, to increase the size of their office's budgets and staff. In that sense the objectives of education bureaucrats are best understood as being akin to the objectives of government bureaucrats, who have been modeled as having similar motivations. Like some academic analysis of government bureaucracy, our analysis here rests on the assumption that the relationship between academic administrators and other stakeholders in the university is characterized by agency costs, which permits those administrators to pursue their own interests at the expense of the overall enterprise. The final section turns to the particular question of why faculty, trustees, and others have permitted this growth of runaway bureaucracy to occur. We examine several possible explanations but do not—in this case—suggest that any one is most persuasive.

How Academic Bureaucrats Conquered the Modern University

In their earliest incarnations, American universities were structured according to two basic models: for-profit proprietary institutions that typically provided skills-based learning (such as professional schools in law, medicine, engineering, and the like) and religious-based schools that primarily existed to train future ministers in a particular faith or a missionary-type education function, such as evangelizing Native American populations.[7] In the for-profit model, the curriculum, course offerings, and fees were all established by an entrepreneur responding to market forces and the need to meet the demand of students for relevant, timely, and adequate training to pursue their chosen career. The curriculum and course of study of religious-oriented universities, by contrast, were established by a board of trustees, typically chosen by the sponsoring religious denomination or a self-perpetuating board with a similar orientation. In both cases, the objectives of the institution were clear, and that clarity also directed resource allocation. Those elements that did not conduce to higher profits in the first case or to the education of ministers and propagation of the faith in the latter were set aside as wasteful and unnecessary.

Beginning in the 19th century, those traditional models of university governance began to break down. First, the founding of government-sponsored land-grant colleges (such as through the Morrill Act) introduced a political element to university governance and organization—universities implicitly were required to serve political as well as educational ends. Second, private nonprofit colleges increasingly abandoned their religious orientation, retaining their traditional nonprofit status and governance structure but adopting a broad, vague mission of providing "education" through teaching students and performing research. As such, the curriculum of those schools began to take on a broader, less-focused structure, particularly with the inclusion of the natural sciences and social sciences in addition to the traditional focus on the classics and other humanities. Nonprofits implicitly and imperfectly accepted the mission of preprofessional education, taking over the role traditionally played by for-profit schools. Eventually, many traditional proprietary schools in law, medicine, engineering, and other fields of study were merged into nonprofit education institutions and came to take on the governance structure of those institutions.

What was the governance structure of those new nonprofit institutions? On paper they continued to bear a resemblance to the denominational universities out of which they had emerged, particularly the retention of a board of trustees that provided fundamental governance over the institution. As Henry Manne has noted, however, that continued control by the trustees over the university was nominal only.[8] In fact, the increased complexity of the university's structure and its lack of a clear mission created a power vacuum and a fundamental inability of the trustees to manage the organization. In fact, control had effectively shifted to the faculty, which now determined personnel decisions (hiring and tenure), curriculum, and, implicitly, the mission of the university. More important, the assumption of control by the faculty brought with it fundamental changes in university governance because the self-interest of individual faculty members was not necessarily aligned with the desires of other university stakeholders, such as students, parents, trustees, financial supporters, or political actors. Although a bit of an overstatement, it is somewhat accurate to state that the faculty essentially ran universities for their own personal benefit, adopting policies that benefited them, and which they rationalized as being good for the university as a whole. Faculty salaries and perquisites increased, teaching loads decreased, and faculty increasingly asserted control over many of the core functions of the university.

Recent years, however, have seen an unexpected development in university governance: the rapid growth of a huge administrative bureaucracy that seems to bear little relationship to the core educational mission of the university. Indeed, as is discussed herein, even as more and more resources have poured into universities from tuition dollars and public and private support, an increasing share of those dollars has been gobbled up by administrators and other university bureaucrats instead of supporting academic programs. Indeed, even as the army of bureaucrats has grown like kudzu over traditional ivy walls, full-time faculty are increasingly being displaced by adjunct professors and other part-time professors who are taking on a greater share of teaching responsibilities than they have in the past.

Even more striking, academic bureaucrats increasingly have assumed control over many areas traditionally thought to be part of the faculty's scope of control. For example, at most universities today the faculty has little or no input or control over student admissions, a task that has been completely delegated to bureaucratic specialists. Decisions with respect to hiring and promotion are increasingly hemmed by a raft of guidance and limits imposed by administrators, such as diversity mandates. Perhaps most astonishing, core policies regarding academic freedom for students and professors—such as the existence and terms of a university speech code—have increasingly been ceded to student life offices and other nonacademic university administrators.[9] Bureaucrats operating through institutional review boards can approve or reject research protocols on the basis of their subjective assessments of the ethics and merit of the projects, a decision often tainted with ideological bias and favoritism.[10] Administrators also have unilaterally imposed student and faculty disciplinary procedures for certain controversial topics, such as allegations of sexual assault, routinely overriding faculty objections. Thus, not only do university bureaucrats consume an increasing amount of university resources, they also have gathered an increasing amount of power and decisionmaking authority.

How Big Is the Problem?

As college costs have soared in recent years, analysts and the public have increasingly sought to understand the dynamics bringing those developments about. As a part of this growing focus, several studies and reports have been published that feature the spending trends in American universities. Those studies have had varying focuses and have set out to achieve different goals; however, they provide evidence of several distinct trends that are occurring in university spending. First, studies have found that the cost of attendance in higher education is rising. Some of the cost drivers are beyond the scope of this chapter, such as the exploding costs of buildings, including palatial student dorms, gourmet dining halls, and state-of-the-art student amenities, such as student centers, gyms, and even water parks. Second, a primary driver of higher spending is increased revenues, especially increases in federal student financial aid funding.[11] Although the underlying empirical importance of that factor also is beyond the scope of this essay, the surge of revenues into universities has loosened schools' budget constraints and enabled them to increase spending dramatically. Thus, increased revenues seem to be one catalyst for the growth of bureaucracy, as increased cash flow from student financial aid has swelled the coffers of universities. Third, and most significant, the data demonstrate that most of the increased personnel spending by universities has not been used to increase instructional employment and classroom instruction; instead, it has been focused primarily on administrative employment and expenditures. Essentially, the studies have found that increased revenues to American universities have not funded instructional functions but have been used to fund "administrative bloat."

Overall, those studies provide some insight into university spending trends over the past 20 years. The remainder of this section highlights findings in three distinct areas: (a) revenue, (b) spending, and (c) employment. Each of those areas is broken down, and the findings of the studies highlighted with regard to those subareas. This section also provides insights into those trends within both private and public universities.

Revenue

To understand "administrative bloat," it is important to understand from whence universities are receiving the revenue. Donna Desrochers and Jane Wellman, in their study *Trends in College Spending 1999–2009*, concluded that "shifts in revenue sources are significant to spending patterns because the source often dictates how the money can be spent."[12]

The study provided what Desrochers and Wellman found to be the major sources of revenue for universities: (a) net tuition revenue;[13] (b) state and local appropriations;[14] (c) private gifts, investment returns, and endowment income;[15] (d) state and local grants and contracts;[16] (e) federal appropriations, grants, and contracts; (f) auxiliary enterprises;[17] and (g) hospitals, independent operations, and other sources.[18]

Further, Roger L. Geiger and Donald E. Heller, in their study "Financial Trends in Higher Education: The United States,"[19] found that, from 1980 through 2009, unadjusted for inflation tuition had increased by 235 percent in public universities, 179 percent in private universities, and 150 percent in community colleges.[20] Those data are further confirmed by Jay P. Greene et al. in *Administrative Bloat at American Universities: The Real Reason for High Costs in Higher Education*.[21] Greene and his colleagues note that both tuition and government subsidies increased during the period 1993 through 2007. Further, from 2001 through 2011, although all institutions saw an average decline in state and local appropriations of approximately 25 percent, federal appropriations and federal, state, and local grants rose by 22 percent.[22] Net tuition during that period also rose across all institutions by an average of 31 percent. Notably, little evidence supports the hypothesis that rising tuition prices are materially related to the reduction in state funding.[23] Regardless, those tuition increases have not translated into increases in instructional employment and expenditures.[24]

As the cost of tuition has increased, the federal government has dramatically increased its student-directed financial aid programs through grants and loans. According to a study by economists at the New York Federal Reserve, however, approximately 65 percent of the increased funds provided to students through increased financial aid are captured by the universities in the form of higher tuition payments.[25] A separate study concluded that increased revenue was a larger contributor to increased tuition costs than were increases in the underlying cost of providing education.[26] That study also found that during the tighter budgetary conditions that followed in the wake of the financial crisis beginning in 2008, universities scaled back their hiring of nonacademic employees. Ironically, therefore, one reason why total costs paid by students and their families have risen so dramatically is that financial aid to students has risen substantially.

Finally, a long, relatively uninterrupted bull market has dramatically increased the value of universities' existing endowments. Because those endowments generate free cash flow without requiring university leaders to promise tangible results or other accountability, they provide a large amount of discretionary income to the university administration to direct as it sees fit. Roaring endowment returns—money that comes to the university without any additional implicit or explicit promise to any private or public supporter—might also be a contributor to the growth in administrative spending.

Spending

Looking at how that money was actually spent, Greene and colleagues, Geiger and Heller, and Desrochers and Wellman have all found that significant increases in spending have gone toward noninstructional expenditures. Desrochers and Wellman, looking at spending in 2009, noted the following:

> Total spending was boosted by spending on research . . . and auxiliary and other enterprises. Spending on research and its related administrative costs continued its steady increase at public institutions . . . but showed an uptick in private institutions after several years of fairly steady spending. Across all sectors, spending on auxiliaries, hospitals, and other independent operations grew faster than spending in most other areas in 2009, maintaining recent patterns across public institutions and in private research institutions.[27]

The study concludes that total spending grew faster than spending on "educational and related expenditures" alone.[28] It also finds that

> [t]he proportion of compensation spent on faculty has remained steady or decreased slightly over time. Looking only at full-time faculty, there has been little or no increase in the average salaries . . . at public institutions between 2002 and 2009; salaries at private institutions increased modestly. Full-time professors, however, only represent between 40 to 60 percent of faculty at four-year institutions.

> A growing reliance on part-time rather than full-time faculty has likely kept full-time faculty costs down and has also trimmed overall salary costs per employee in most sectors.[29]

Those findings are confirmed by Geiger and Heller. Looking at university expenditures as four areas of spending (instruction, student services, academic support, and institutional support), they found that from 1980 through 2009, instructional expenditures lagged the three other categories for both public and private universities.[30] Greene and colleagues also found that spending per student from 1993 through 2007 increased by 61.2 percent for administration whereas spending on instruction increased 39.3 percent.[31] More recently, between 2007 and 2011, expenditures on instruction increased by an average of 1 percent across all institutions, whereas all other expenditures increased by an average of 4.9 percent.[32]

Employment

Over the past two decades, universities have increased employment just as they have increased enrollment, tuition, and spending. Employment statistics, however, show that the increased employment—much like the increase in spending—is not directed at instruction but at administration and related services. Again, all three of the studies surveyed here produced findings that support this conclusion.

Greene and colleagues, who looked at employment trends at 198 leading universities from 1993 through 2007, found a 13.1 percent increase in university employees per 100 students.[33] For every 100 students in 1993, universities employed 31.4 employees (22.4 full-time and 9 part-time employees).[34] By 2007, however, that number had increased to 35.5 employees per 100 students (24.3 full time and 11.2 part time).[35] Greene and colleagues also found that the increases in employment were more telling when broken down by category:

> [U]niversities actually have more full-time employees devoted to administration than to instruction, research, and service combined. Even in 1993, these leading universities were flush with administrators, employing 6.8 full-time administrators for every 100 students

> compared with 6.0 full-time employees engaged in instruction, research, or service. By 2007, the preponderance of administrators relative to educators grew even larger at these leading universities, as there were 9.4 full-time administrators per 100 students compared with 7.0 full-time instructors, researchers, and service providers. In terms of growth, the number of full-time administrators per 100 students at America's leading universities increased by 39.3 percent between 1993 and 2007, while the number of employees engaged in teaching, research, or service only increased by 17.6 percent.[36]

In addition, Greene and colleagues explain that those numbers paint an even more drastic picture of administrative bloat when full-time administrators and full-time instructional staff are compared:

> In terms of growth, private universities increased their full-time staff involved in instruction, research, and service by almost the same rate as they increased administration, a 39.8 percent increase compared with a 40.1 percent increase.
>
> Leading public universities were also already administrative-heavy in 1993, but the rate of growth in administrative employment was even higher than the growth in educators, leaving these institutions even more administrator heavy in 2007. . . . Full-time employment in the instructional, research, and service category grew by 9.8 percent between 1993 and 2007, but the number of full-time administrators grew at nearly four times that rate—39.0 percent. It now takes 39.0 percent more full-time administrators to manage the same number of students than it did in 1993. Put another way, there are now fewer than 13 students for every full-time administrator at public institutions. Apparently, public universities are trying to keep up with private institutions in administrative bloat even if they cannot compete in the areas of teaching, research, and service.[37]

The authors concluded that discussion of employment with some statistics regarding part-time instructional employees, explaining that universities have increased the number of part-time employees. Between 1993 and 2007, part-time instructional employment increased by 82.7 percent in private universities and 31.5 percent in public universities.[38]

In addition, a recent study of employment trends in higher education found that between 2000 and 2012, professional positions (e.g., business analysts, human resources staff, admissions staff) grew twice as fast as executive and managerial positions at public, nonresearch institutions.[39] The authors also found that part-time faculty and graduate assistants accounted for at least half of the instructional staff in most higher education sectors and were providing additional capacity at larger, well-funded institutions while replacing new full-time positions at many others.[40] Between 2000 and 2012, four-year institutions averaged between 10 and 20 additional part-time instructors per 1,000 full-time equivalent (FTE) students. During that same period, public research institutions averaged no increase in full-time faculty and increased part-time faculty by an average of 12 positions per 1,000 FTE students. Public undergraduate schools averaged a decrease of 2 full-time positions and averaged an increase in part-time positions by 6 per 1,000 FTE students. Private undergraduate schools averaged a decrease of 1 full-time faculty position and averaged an increase of 10 part-time faculty positions per 1,000 FTE students. The largest gains in full-time faculty occurred at private research institutions, which averaged an increase of 16 positions between 2000 and 2012; however, those same institutions also averaged an increase of 21 part-time positions. Finally, by 2012, less than half of the full-time instructional staff at four-year institutions held tenure, which represents a 4 to 5 percent decline since 2000.[41]

Employment Trends in Public versus Private Universities

Spending and employment trends broken down by private versus public universities also provide some insights into the current growth in administrative bloat. Administrative costs have grown at a relatively rapid rate at both public and private institutions. The studies surveyed here, however, indicate that administrative bloat has grown differently at private versus public universities.

Greene and colleagues found that in 1993, private universities employed 11.3 full-time noninstructional employees and 8.2 full-time instructional employees for every 100 students.[42] By 2007, private universities were employing 15.8 noninstructional employees and 11.5 instructional employees for every 100 students.[43] In growth rate, the number of full-time instructional employees increased by 39.8 percent from 1993 to 2007, whereas the number of noninstructional employees increased by 40.1 percent.[44]

In contrast, public universities employed 5.7 full-time noninstructional employees and 5.4 full-time instructional employees for every 100 students. By 2007, public universities were employing 7.9 noninstructional employees and 6.0 instructional employees for every 100 students.[45] In growth rate, full-time instructional employment grew by 9.8 percent between 1993 and 2007; however, at 39.0 percent, the number of full-time noninstructional employees grew nearly four times as fast.[46]

In Search of an Explanation

The studies just cited show that over the past several decades, the amount of noninstructional employment and expenditures has risen drastically relative to instructional employment and expenditures. In addition, even as revenues have increased, spending related to full-time faculty has not increased as quickly as has spending related to administration, and those institutions were already administrative heavy before the current growth in administrative bloat. Further, the recent increase in part-time faculty members undermines the claim that the recent increase in employment in American universities is an attempt to increase the quality of education.[47]

What explains the dramatic growth in the size, expense, and pervasiveness of academic bureaucracy over the past two decades? There is no definitive answer to date, but several hypotheses present themselves, with varying degrees of persuasiveness. Those hypotheses can be divided into exogenous explanations (outside forces that have acted on universities and led them to increase the size of their academic bureaucracies) and endogenous explanations (internally generated forces that have prompted growth).

Although development in previous scholarship on this topic is limited, the literature that does exist provides several useful analytical perspectives. This section will highlight four different explanations from the literature.

A New Source for Administrative Spending?

The first explanation for the rise in administrative bloat is that administrators have access to funds that are unavailable to the faculty. Second, the sources of funding that universities have come to rely on, particularly funds from the federal government, have created increased reporting and regulatory compliance issues that have necessitated increased administrative growth.

The first of those two propositions, regarding funds unavailable to faculty, is the reason given by Greene and his colleagues in their study of administrative bloat.[48] They argue that the reason that universities have a growing administrative arm is because they can afford it.[49] Greene and his colleagues propose that the reason that university administrations are growing—and faculties are not—is because the administration holds ownership and control. The authors explain as follows:

> Growth in enrollments and higher rates of government subsidy have made universities flush with extra funds. Being nonprofits, they do not return excess profits to shareholders; instead, they return excess profits to their *de facto* shareholders, the administrators who manage the institutions. These administrators are paid dividends in the form of higher compensation and more fellow administrators who can reduce their own workload or expand their empires.[50]

In this telling, the administration has effectively come to supplant the faculty or trustees as the true owner of the modern university. Although there is some element of truth to this, few observers would be likely to agree that the administration is the effective owner of the university. Instead, it seems that a shared governance model has arisen between the faculty and administration. Notably, students do not seem to be a primary owner of the university but instead seem to be largely bystanders in the battle over university funding.

In addition to the sources of funds, the reporting and compliance requirements that come with certain funds may also account for the rise in administrative bloat. In particular, when an institution receives government funding, it rarely (if ever) receives those funds without some sort of restrictions or requirements. As universities receive more government funding, more administrators are needed to ensure proper reporting and compliance. Larry L. Leslie and Gary Rhoades explain that "[r]egulation and ever-expanding requests for information by state and institutional governing boards result in the addition of administrative staff and expenditures."[51] The authors put forward what they call the "administrative clone theory":

> Whenever legislation bearing on higher education was passed by the (federal) government, a new office was established in government to administer the law, and subsequently a "clone" of that office appeared on most major university campuses in America. Resource dependency theory would also point to organizations' increasing administrative expenditures to ensure compliance with state regulations and avoid economic penalties. At the same time, colleges and universities are increasing revenues from sources other than the state, which could have led many institutions to create still other structures complementary to external organizations other than the state.[52]

The authors continue by stating that, as universities continue to search out new, alternative revenue sources, resources will be diverted away from instruction and toward administrative costs, as new offices and administrative assignments are created to lead, encourage, manage, and support such revenue sources.[53]

Although they say nothing of the theory that administrations build to procure funds, Greene and his colleagues support Leslie and Rhoades' conclusion that federal subsidies necessitate administrative growth:

> The growth in government subsidy for higher education means that there is more government regulation and more government bureaucracy that universities must handle. Compliance with and management of government bureaucracy also contributes to administrative growth in universities because of the additional people it takes to navigate red tape.
>
> The increasing government role in universities also means that universities have to consider more political issues in their operations. To please political constituencies, universities need more diversity administrators, sustainability administrators, or anyone who might improve the prospects for subsidies from politicians.[54]

Although Greene and colleagues' study, as well as that of Leslie and Rhoades, concludes that federal subsidies are a cause of administrative bloat, the question remains, how much of the administrative growth in recent years is attributable to the compliance, reporting, and procurement costs of those federal funds.

Demand for Noneducational Services

In addition to the demands of government regulators, some argue that the demands of potential students also have increased administrative bloat. In the paper "College as Country Club: Do Colleges Cater to Students' Preferences for Consumption?" Jacob and his colleagues attempt to model the demand-side pressure that institutions face regarding consumption demands.[55] The authors find the following:

> [M]any students do appear to value college consumption amenities. More importantly, we find significant heterogeneity of preferences across students, with higher-achieving students having a greater willingness to pay for academic quality than their less academically oriented peers and wealthier students much more willing to pay for consumption amenities. . . .
>
> Preference heterogeneity has important implications for the postsecondary market since it results in different colleges facing very different resource allocation incentives depending on the characteristics of students on their enrollment margin. More selective schools have a much greater incentive to improve academic quality since this is the dimension most valued by their marginal students. Less selective (but expensive) schools, by comparison, have a greater incentive to focus on consumption amenities. The elasticities implied by our demand model can account for sixteen percent of the total variation in the ratio of amenity to instructional spending between colleges, and including them on top of key observable characteristics (sector, state, size, selectivity) increases the explained variation by twenty percent. [56]

Essentially, the authors argue, schools have an incentive to spend on the noninstructional aspects of the school. That incentive is especially strong given the finding that wealthier students are particularly interested in consumption amenities, as those students are more likely to pay full or near-full tuition rather than seek financial aid and thus represent a particularly valuable revenue stream. But that allocation of resources arises in response to student demand, both prospective and current. If prospective students value consumption amenities (such as palatial dormitories and hand-holding university bureaucracies) more than they value investments in educational quality, then universities would be expected to allocate resources accordingly, including a larger administrative staff to manage and provide those "consumption amenities." That, in the end, might account for an increase in the administrative growth that has taken place. The authors find that these incentives have driven universities to allocate resources differently:

> Colleges that face the highest demand elasticity for consumption amenities and the lowest elasticity for instructional spending . . . provide the highest level of spending on the latter, relative to the former. These schools spend nearly $0.90 on consumption amenities for every dollar spent on instruction. In contrast, colleges that face the greatest pressure to spend resources on instruction only spend $0.45 on consumption amenities for every dollar spent on instruction.[57]

The strong incentive that universities have to spend on "consumption amenities" in an attempt to attract students is increased because spending per student makes up 10 percent of the current *U.S. News & World Report* rankings for colleges and universities.[58] At the end of the day, when faculty compensation makes up 7 percent of the ranking, and spending on public service, academic support, student services, instruction, research, and institutional support are weighted more heavily, universities have a strong incentive to increase those expenditures that have the potential to attract more students and increase a university's coveted ranking.

In the end, student demand for consumption amenities might explain some of the growth in administrative expenses for a variety of student services. Moreover, it certainly explains the growth in spending on amenities such as gourmet food and the construction of new luxurious dormitories, recreation centers, and athletic facilities. It seems unlikely, however, that much of the growth of administrative spending can be explained by a demand by students and wealthy families for the particular services that those employees provide.

Nonprofit Bureaucrats as Government Bureaucrats

The preceding two explanations are exogenous—they explain the growth of academic bureaucracy in reference to external factors. If that is the case, however, then the growth of academic bureaucracies should cause little dissatisfaction; they are simply responding to outside forces that presumably provide value-increasing resources to the institution. Yet the growth in administrative overhead has been widely criticized, which indicates substantial agreement that the growth in administrative cost is problematic and does not increase value to the university. That circumstance suggests that the growth in university bureaucracy is not being driven in response to outside pressures but instead by endogenous forces.

One of the authors of this chapter has argued elsewhere that the behavior of bureaucrats within a nonprofit organization can be accurately analogized to that of government bureaucrats and in distinction to employees in a for-profit firm.[59] This similarity seems apt in that unlike for-profit firms, both government and nonprofit institutions lack clear profit and loss signals by which to determine the marginal return to the organization from investments in personnel and other activities of the organization. Zywicki, for example, discusses the growing power of university institutional review boards (IRBs), which are established purportedly to articulate and implement standards for ethical research protocols. Over time, however, the power of IRBs has grown, as has the number of employees that they oversee and the salaries of IRB administrators. Yet little evidence indicates that those increased expenditures and power have increased either the efficacy or efficiency of their operations.

Economist William Niskanen argued that government bureaucrats are motivated by a desire to increase their power and the discretionary budgets of their agencies.[60] Doing so, Niskanen asserted, will also redound to the personal benefit of the bureaucrats by enabling them to gain promotion, salary increases, prestige, and potentially higher outside earnings if bureaucrats choose to go through the revolving door to the private sector. Zywicki notes that many of those features are present for academic bureaucrats operating in a nonprofit setting because they likewise possess incentives to build larger staffs and claim a wider range of authority for themselves.

That model of endogenous bureaucratic expansion seems to be consistent with much of the observed behavior and growth in university bureaucracy. Martin and Hill conclude that growth in employment and noneducation spending in universities is driven predominantly by the university's growth in resources available to it. In other words, when revenues increase (such as by increased endowment returns or increased federal support) the university responds by increasing its expenditures on noneducation employees and services. By contrast, when colleges faced tighter resource constraints following the 2008 financial crisis, administrative spending slowed or even declined among higher education institutions as a percentage of university expenditures.[61] That suggests that increased spending on administration may be explained by administrators seeking to promote their own interests, and they are constrained only by the funds available to them.

Agency Costs and Bureaucratic Growth

Growth in university bureaucracy being driven by the self-interest and opportunism of the bureaucrats presents a puzzle, because those expenses divert scarce resources from educational ends to employees who add little value to the university enterprise. As already noted, even as expenditures on administration have risen dramatically, expenditures on faculty have remained flat over time, and full-time tenure-track faculty members increasingly have become a shrinking share of the university faculty, as they are being replaced by lower-paid adjunct and other temporary professors.

That development raises the question of why those supposedly in charge of the university—either the board of trustees or, more realistically, the faculty—are content to allow such a situation to develop and persist. After all, the services provided by the university president and other administrative employees are not the primary function of the university; they exist to support the academic functions of the institution. Why then does that situation persist?

Faculty and Academic Bureaucracies

One possible explanation for faculty acquiescence in a growing administrative bureaucracy is that those developments occur with the express or implicit blessings of the faculty, as faculty members have outsourced many of their traditional duties, such as student advising, to academic administrators. Ortmann and Squire, for example, model the modern university as a series of principal–agent relationships that involve the trustees, administrators, and professors.[62] The authors then demonstrate how "academic ratchet and administrative lattice" (i.e., administrative bloat) are predictable results given each group's particular goals.

Ortmann and Squire argue that both faculty and administrators have incentives to allow administrative bloat to occur.[63] Prototypical professors, according to the authors, have three related objectives: job security, freedom to spend their time on activities they prefer, and maximization of professional reputation and income.[64] Prototypical administrators seek to keep their job, build their reputation, and free their own time for outside income opportunities.[65] Further, administrators share the goals common to all managers, such as desire for status and power manifested in a large office and support staff.[66]

Given professors' goals of maximizing professional reputation, income, and freedom to spend time on preferred activities, professors have an incentive to delegate to administrative staff certain roles that were traditionally performed by faculty members. Given administrators' goals of freeing time for outside income opportunities and building power through a growing support staff, administrators have an incentive to delegate roles to a growing support staff. Ortmann and Squire characterize the situation as follows:

> Here, we see how the academic ratchet drives the administrative lattice and serves the interests of both Professor and Administrator. The ratchet allows the Professor to devote his time to activities that are more rewarding financially and professionally; in its wake it creates a series of neglected duties that the Administrator can use to justify the administrative lattice.[67]

In this model, the growth of the administrative bureaucracy occurs with the implicit approval of the faculty. A couple of assumptions presented by Ortmann and Squire might still explain the trend toward administrative bloat, regardless of the principal–agent relationship between faculties and administrations. First, faculty members ultimately work to maximize professional reputation, income, and freedom to spend their time on activities they prefer. Second, administrators work to build power through a growing support staff (as suggested by Zywicki as well).[68] If those two assumptions are true, then it may not matter how the principal–agent relationship between faculty and administration is defined; in either case, both the administration and the faculty are prone to allowing overdelegation to administrative staff members, which drives administrative bloat. The hypothesis that administrative growth has occurred with the implicit blessing of the faculty, however, seems inconsistent with the general hostility that faculty members generally express about those trends (exemplified by Ginsberg's views, previously described).

Monitoring Costs

An alternative explanation suggests that the growth in administrative bloat in modern universities has *not* occurred with the implicit or explicit consent of the faculty but against the faculty's wishes. Nevertheless, despite the preferences of the faculty as a whole, individual faculty members face severe collective action and free-riding problems if they monitor administrators effectively. Monitoring administrative bloat can be a tedious, time-consuming, and frustrating experience for faculty members. Moreover, although those firm-specific investments benefit the university, they do not increase the professor's market value in comparison to time spent on research and similar activities because they do not raise the professor's professional profile. For increasing one's salary, prestige, and other similar goals, overseeing the university's administration comes with a high opportunity cost of time and distraction from activities such as research.

Against those high individual costs, each faculty member gains very little personal benefit from time spent on the thankless tasks of monitoring the university's budget and reducing wasteful staffing by university bureaucrats—tasks that benefit the entire university community, not the vigilant professor. Moreover, although most senior faculty in the modern university have tenure and cannot be dismissed for standing up to the college president and senior administration, the senior administration still retains the ability to make a faculty member's life miserable with onerous and unpleasant teaching assignments, time-consuming service obligations, and denial of raises and sabbaticals. Administrators hold many possible threats over uncooperative faculty members, and faculty members are well aware of that. As a result, from the perspective of each faculty member, the personal costs of monitoring activity outweigh the personal benefits. That suggests that rational faculty members will be unwilling to invest in monitoring activity and will seek to free-ride on the efforts of other faculty members, leading to a general underproduction of monitoring activity.

From that perspective it is easy to see why individual faculty members are not interested in incurring the costs associated with continued monitoring of the administration, which thereby allows the current administrative bloat to continue.

Reforming Administrative Bloat?

Given that analysis, what is to be done about administrative bloat in America's universities? As noted, some of the growth in bureaucracy is a reflection of ever-greater entanglement between higher education and the regulatory state. As governments at all levels have imposed heavier and heavier administrative burdens on universities, a small army of university administrators has arisen to meet those challenges. Some growth in administration also reflects a response to growing demand by students and parents for various amenities, such as counseling services and the like, that universities have increasingly come to provide.

Yet those trends probably do not explain all of the growth of administrative bureaucracy. As noted, for example, in the financial crisis and its aftermath, beginning in 2008, many universities did tighten their belts with respect to administrative employment, slowing or even reversing their growth in bureaucratic employment. That suggests that at least some of the growth in administration is a response to opportunity—roaring endowments and rising tuition rates have brought in fabulous amounts of money that have enabled university bureaucracies to grow rapidly. To some extent, then, university bureaucracies have grown of their own motivational force, either through the implicit blessing of the faculty or through an internal expansion process.

Clearly, the recent growth in administrative expenditures and personnel cannot go on forever. The growing cost of college is increasingly unsustainable, and the rapid growth of nonacademic units of the college budget is increasingly difficult to justify. Conversely, understanding the underlying causes of the growth in administrative bureaucracy also presents challenges for reform.

Indeed, the growth in academic bureaucracy in recent years may have actually been an unintended consequence of an earlier generation of reform efforts, namely the efforts by university trustees and administrators to tame the seemingly overwhelming power of the faculty in university governance.[69] An earlier generation of reformers, perhaps best exemplified by William F. Buckley in his famous book *God and Man at Yale*,[70] railed against the undue control of faculties over university governance. Buckley suggested that one remedy for the problems caused by faculty control of the university was greater influence by the board of trustees and, in particular, that the trustees should run universities more like a business and the board should comprise successful business executives who would insist on accountability and tight governance.

Yet, as with any complex organization, it is difficult for the board to run the enterprise directly, especially a charitable enterprise such as a university. As such, the trustees generally began to delegate their authority to a newly empowered university president, who was implicitly given the powers of a chief executive officer (CEO) and the board's deference thereto. In theory, the new CEO-style university president would be expected to bring accountability, cost control, and mission focus to the university, with the support of the board.

In practice, this charge to run the university has encountered a fundamental problem—the university is *not* a for-profit business but is a nonprofit enterprise. As such, the university lacks the profit-and-loss feedback signals that guide management conduct in a for-profit business setting. Instead, as suggested by Zywicki, modeling the behavior of university bureaucrats like government bureaucrats, who are in another nonprofit setting, is seemingly more accurate. In that model, the university president would not be expected to align expenditures according to rigorous marginal costs and marginal returns but instead would engage in empire-building enterprises that increase the influence and range of control of the university administrators. Rather than provoking conflict with faculty members by challenging them to improve academic quality and reduce costs, university presidents would leave the faculty largely undisturbed and build a parallel structure of academic bureaucracy. Because neither the university president nor members of the board are the residual claimants of increases in productivity or cost reductions, one would expect that university presidents would have little incentive to provide such outcomes and even less reason for board members to insist on them. Instead, as the head of a nonprofit organization, a university president would be expected to try to increase the share of university revenue that flows to the administration and to minimize conflict over those resources. Unlike a CEO in a for-profit firm, the task of a CEO in a large nonprofit university seems to be more political than economic. That fundamental difference in the institutional structure between for-profit and nonprofit enterprises seems to have been overlooked by earlier champions of the CEO model of university presidents, who instead of taming the problems associated with faculty governance have simply exacerbated them by erecting an administrative apparatus next to it.

That historical experience also provides a cautionary tale for an alternative proposed by Benjamin Ginsberg, which is to reinstate the traditional supremacy of the faculty in the university governance scheme.[71] But just because administrative control of the university has turned out to be inefficient does not imply that faculty control of the university is more desirable. After all, faculty members also lack well-aligned incentives to manage the university efficiently. Indeed, the effort to reform university governance to empower administrators and counterbalance the undue influence of faculty members was a response to real problems caused by the self-interested and subpar character of faculty governance. That the proposed solution (increasing the power of administrators) failed to address the problem should not be read to imply that the problem itself was not real.

Henry Manne suggested an alternative approach to university governance reform—a return to for-profit university ownership and governance systems. The presence of a residual claimant with incentives to maximize productivity and reduce costs for customers is the most effective means for aligning university decisionmaking and resource allocation with the demand of student-customers. Not surprising, for-profit colleges generally are recognized as being more nimble and responsive to changes in market demand for students and employers. Manne argues that equity holders motivated by profit will be focused on maximum efficiencies. In such a governance system, runaway growth in administration is unlikely because it reduces the bottom-line profit. To be sure, one difficulty with realigning colleges along a for-profit axis is the reality that with federal funding and student financial aid so pervasive in higher education, the incentives for cost reduction and productivity increases is not as clear as in other industries. Still, adoption of a for-profit ownership and governance model could better align the incentives of owners, managers, and students in a way that the current structure does not. Whereas the current nonprofit structure rewards price increases, eschews cost savings, and encourages internal empire building, a for-profit ownership and governance structure would tend to push in the direction of a more streamlined administrative structure. Absent the introduction of a profit measurement for universities, however, reform of university administrative bloat may remain elusive.

Conclusion

In this chapter we have sought to answer the question, "If the faculty is the effective owner of the university, then why has the bureaucratic arm within the university grown while the academic arm has not grown in proportion?" One contributing factor seems to be that the increasing subsidies that the modern university is receiving have provided a new source for administrative spending that is otherwise unavailable to the faculty. The sources of that funding, particularly the federal government, have created increased reporting and regulatory compliance costs that have necessitated administrative bloat. Another contributing factor may be the increased demand that universities face to provide students with noninstructional services, which have also necessitated increased administration, although that, too, seems to be a small contributor to the problem.

Of particular concern and importance seems to be the relationship between the faculty and administration that has, in many ways, created a permissive culture in which administrative bloat has been allowed to thrive. Namely, faculty members are either unwilling or unable to take on the growing administrative bureaucracies. As noted previously, that is likely the result of the benefits that have come from overdelegation—and the costs that would be incurred by individual faculty members if they were to attempt to increase their monitoring of those bureaucracies.

Understanding the causes of administrative bloat is a necessary first step toward its reform. Zywicki noted the following:

> Just as efforts to "reinvent government" have done little actually to reduce the cost of governmental bureaucracy or increase its effectiveness, repeated studies and complaints about the inefficiencies of [university] bureaucracies standing alone will do little to reform the system. It is necessary to start with an accurate model of how the current situation came to be before we can come up with a plan for how to improve the situation.[72]

Much in the same way, simply pointing out the problem of administrative bloat is an ineffective means to finding solutions to the problem. An accurate model is necessary to understand the causes of the problems facing modern universities. We hope that this chapter is a step toward creating such a model.

CHAPTER SEVEN

The Senseless Monstrosity in Our Path: Academic Bargains and the Rise of the American University

Scott E. Masten

> *[N]obody has any business to destroy a social institution until he has really seen it as an historical institution. If he knows how it arose, and what purposes it was supposed to serve, he may really be able to say that they were bad purposes, that they have since become bad purposes, or that they are purposes which are no longer served. But if he simply stares at the thing as a senseless monstrosity that has somehow sprung up in his path, it is he and not the traditionalist who is suffering from an illusion.*
>
> —*G. K. Chesterton,* The Thing

Anyone with even passing familiarity with the governance of American universities is aware of its failings and sometimes absurdities. (For anyone else, casual browsing of the *Chronicle of Higher Education, Inside Higher Education,* or other higher education coverage on pretty much any given day should provide an adequate primer.) Critics across the board disparage the existing system of shared governance in which boards, administrators, and faculty participate in institutional decisions, as a primary obstacle to solving—if not the ultimate cause of—the many problems confronting higher education: "Almost every contemporary issue facing higher education . . . is impeded and frustrated by a hundred-year-old system of governance practices that desperately needs modification."[1] American colleges and universities are hobbled by "an outmoded and dysfunctional set of organizational structures, processes, and policies . . . [in which] everyone claims a veto but no one takes responsibility for results."[2] Democratic decision processes in academia result in "a web of inefficiency" that "undermines the very well-being of the nation's colleges and universities."[3] The system of shared governance has become, "in effect, governance by multiple veto by campus groups with vested interests[;] it can stymie necessary reforms."[4]

A consequence of the diffusion of authority in universities is that everyone disclaims control. Trustees, who possess ultimate legal authority, deny exercising it "in any meaningful sense," contending that the "real power in any university . . . is the faculty."[5] Professors, in turn, complain that—notwithstanding formal structures affording faculty nominal authority in certain areas—faculty possess little power in practice, the true locus of control residing with administrators who simply ignore faculty advice with which they disagree.[6] For their part, university presidents profess an absence of latitude to make decisions in a system of "powerful governing boards at the top, a culture of faculty governance at the bottom, and between them a relatively weak central administration."[7] With no one in charge, it is little wonder that the public displays "widespread skepticism about how universities and colleges are run."[8]

And yet, somehow, despite all of these faults, American universities managed to dominate higher education for much of the 20th century. In the words of one admirer, "the American higher education system has become the worldwide 'gold standard' for higher education, respected for its leadership in research and scholarship and for providing access to large numbers of students."[9] Apparently, the governance defects of U.S. colleges and universities—as bad as they are—did not prevent American higher education from outperforming educational systems elsewhere.

It is possible, of course, that with better governance the achievements of American higher education would have been greater still. The extent to which universities have been held back by bad governance, however, leaves the question of how we ended up with our current system and why it has persisted: If superior arrangements exist, why were they not adopted? With more than 3,000 four-year, degree-granting institutions, the U.S. higher education industry is, by any conventional measure, highly competitive. In any other industry with so much competition, we would expect an enterprise that discovered and adopted a better way to manage its resources to outbid its less efficient rivals for customers and employees. Why not in higher education?

To be sure, longevity is not proof of superiority. Conceivably, malign motives, deficient incentives, or even chance events could have set universities on a path from which it has been difficult to deviate. Or perhaps today's governance arrangements were appropriate to the circumstances when they were adopted but have since become obsolete. But before declaring longstanding practices mistaken or outmoded, we ought to be reasonably confident that those arrangements have not served some valuable, possibly undiscerned, purpose that justifies their continuation. To do that requires that we understand why the system arose, how it evolved, and why it has endured.

The Emergence and Diffusion of Shared Governance in the United States

Criticism of the role of faculty in academic governance has a long and illustrious history. Adam Smith famously assailed faculty control of universities in *The Wealth of Nations* (1776), observing that, when professors control the institutions of which they are members, "they are likely to make a common cause, to be all very indulgent to one another, and every man to consent that his neighbor may neglect his duty, provided he himself is allowed to neglect his own."[10] The situation at Oxford was so bad, according to Smith, that "the greater part of the public professors have, for these many years, given up altogether even the pretence of teaching."[11] A couple of centuries later, Thomas Sowell, echoing Smith, identified faculty governance (combined with tenure) as "[a]mong the leading liabilities of American colleges and universities," opining that "it is the wholly unaccountable nature of faculty self-governance which makes it so dangerous."[12]

Although critics often treat governance arrangements in modern American universities as ancient, static, and universal, none of these is the case. Unlike Smith's Oxford, early American colleges did not have a tradition of faculty control. The typical institution of higher learning in the United States before 1865 was a small denominational college headed by a cleryman.[13] Authority, both formal and effective, resided in the president and outside governing boards composed mainly of clergy.[14] Colleges of this era mostly offered a standard classical curriculum that emphasized ancient languages, philosophy, rhetoric, and theology, supplemented eventually with studies in the natural sciences, English, and agricultural and mechanical arts.[15] There was little specialization; a professor was expected to be a "jack-of-all-disciplines."[16]

The distinctive organization features that we associate with the modern American university—large administrative bureaucracies, departmentalization, and faculty governance—began to take shape only toward the end of the 19th century. Of these features, faculty participation in university decisions was the last to emerge. As late as 1874, there was, in the view of one prominent Harvard scholar, "no university in the United States the intellectual interests of which [were] managed by professors, but always by a corporation outside."[17] Histories of American universities in the late 19th and early 20th centuries are remarkable more for their accounts of autocratic presidents than for faculty inroads into governance.[18] Even with the establishment of academic departments—"a logical outgrowth of size and specialization and of the pressing necessity to delegate and decentralize if major administrators were not to find themselves overwhelmed"[19]—the locus of power merely shifted from presidents to department chairs: "The turn of the century was a time of conspicuous departmental dictatorships" as control over appointments and promotions allowed department chairmen to demand personal loyalty and to inhibit rival viewpoints from being expressed in classrooms.[20]

Eventually, faculty at some institutions began to acquire a formal role in university decisions, as trustees delegated powers and responsibilities through bylaws and organizational constitutions. By 1890, faculty senates had been established at Cornell, Michigan, Illinois, Wisconsin, and other Midwestern institutions.[21] For the most part, however, those developments afforded professors little real authority. In Laurence Veysey's assessment, "Except for producing some unwieldy academic 'senates' and for encouraging somewhat greater departmental autonomy in the area of appointments, [the movement for more faculty control at the turn of the century] bore little substantial fruit."[22] At other institutions, such as Johns Hopkins and the University of Chicago, professors managed to acquire de facto control over matters of education and research.[23] But such gains were also subject to reversal. On becoming president of Columbia University in 1902, Nicholas Murray Butler substantially weakened the system of faculty self-governance that had developed during the 1890s.[24] Early faculty participation at Berkeley was similarly curtailed under the autocratic administration of Benjamin Ide Wheeler (1899-1919).[25] Almost everywhere, presidents remained the dominant force. "Whatever faculty voices may have been raised to the contrary, university government by the twentieth century centered upon the office of the president."[26] As American higher education entered the new century, "even the most fundamental of faculty prerogatives—strong influence over, if not outright control of, decisions concerning faculty appointments and tenure—was very much in a 'state of play.'"[27]

A series of surveys conducted over the course of the 20th century indicate that, although faculty roles in university decisions increased, such gains were gradual and selective. A 1911 poll of science professors at top universities revealed overwhelming support for "a change in administrative methods in the direction of limiting the powers of the president and executive officers" through more democratic participation by faculty.[28] A 1925 survey of local chapters of the American Association of University Professors (AAUP), however, found "formal involvement" in "the selection of members of the teaching staff" in fewer than one-fourth (38 of 167) of responding institutions and no clear faculty role in hiring decisions at more than two-thirds (114).[29] A subsequent survey suggested only modest change by 1940: Although a plurality (47 percent) of 217 responding AAUP chapters reported a trend toward more faculty governance at their own institutions, "the typical American college or university still . . . provided for faculty consultation on appointments, promotions, dismissals, and budgets only through department heads or chairs," who were, in turn, appointed by deans or presidents without formal faculty consultation at four of five institutions.[30]

Faculty authority expanded in the period after World War II as "faculty were sometimes able to negotiate gains in shared governance with presidents and boards," but, as earlier, that authority "remained highly uneven across the institutional landscape."[31] The extent and unevenness of faculty roles across institutions and decision areas were captured in a 1970 AAUP survey that asked representatives of colleges and universities to "specify the level of faculty participation" in each of 31 decision areas in terms of the following categories:[32]

> *Administrator Determination*: decisions or actions over which administrators have unilateral authority
>
> *Faculty Determination*: decisions or actions over which "the faculty of an academic unit or its duly authorized representatives have final legislative or operational authority with respect to policy or action"
>
> *Joint Action*: decisions or actions that require "formal agreement by both the faculty and other components of the institution" and are subject to "veto by any component"

Figure 7.1 summarizes the distribution of authority among these categories across decision areas at the 826 institutions that responded, representing about one-half of the roughly 1,650 four-year, degree-granting institutions in the United States at the time.[33] The bars in the figure indicate, for each decision type, the percentage of institutions governed by faculty determination (dark bars) or joint action (light bars).[34] Immediately apparent is the large variation in authority across decision areas. Whereas faculty at a majority of institutions were likely to exercise some level of authority over instructional and curricular matters and some internal organization issues (decision areas 1–11), faculty authority over compensation, budgets, or the appointment of presidents or deans was rare (areas 24–31). Moreover, where it existed, faculty authority was most often shared with administrators (*Joint Action,* represented by the light bars). The only decision for which faculty at a majority of institutions enjoyed exclusive authority (*Faculty Determination*) was academic performance of students (area 1)—essentially, grading. For every other decision category, administrators at most institutions possessed at least veto power but frequently

Figure 7.1
Faculty Authority by Decision Area, 1970

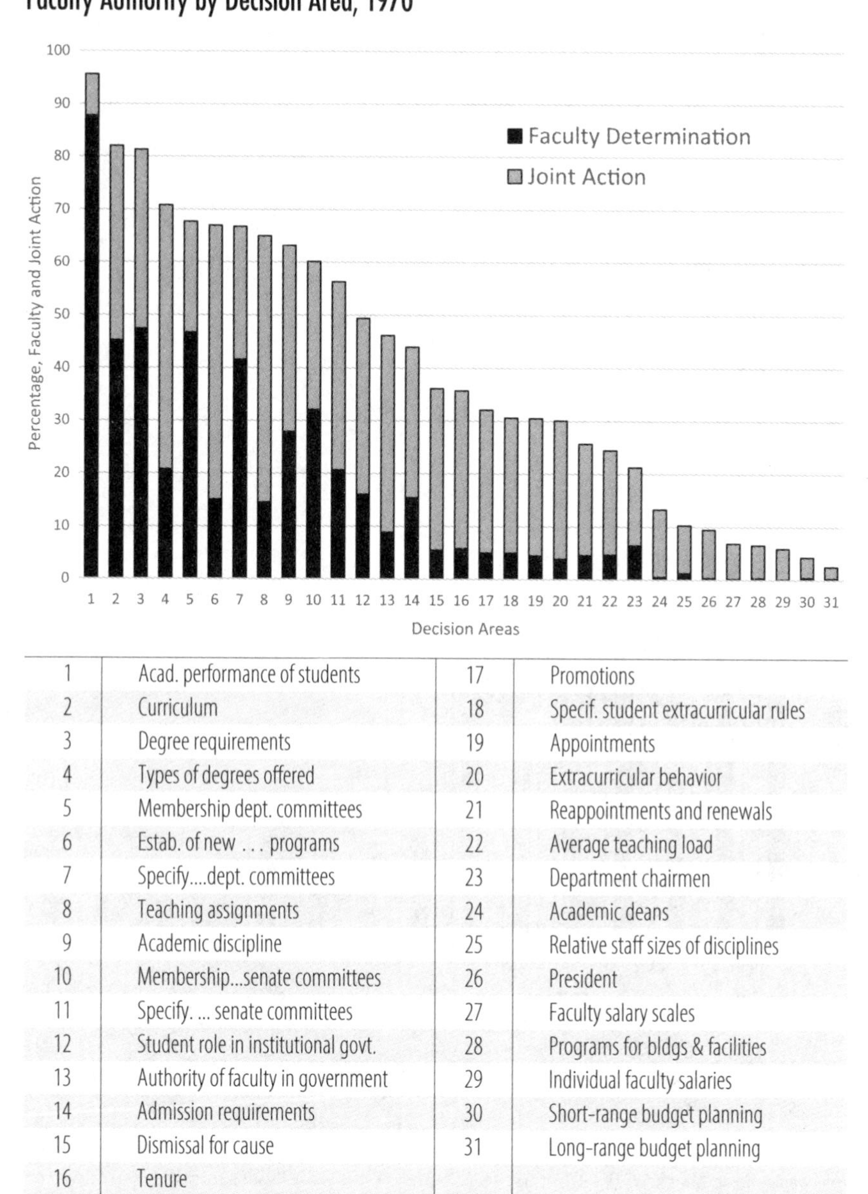

1	Acad. performance of students	17	Promotions
2	Curriculum	18	Specif. student extracurricular rules
3	Degree requirements	19	Appointments
4	Types of degrees offered	20	Extracurricular behavior
5	Membership dept. committees	21	Reappointments and renewals
6	Estab. of new . . . programs	22	Average teaching load
7	Specify....dept. committees	23	Department chairmen
8	Teaching assignments	24	Academic deans
9	Academic discipline	25	Relative staff sizes of disciplines
10	Membership...senate committees	26	President
11	Specify. ... senate committees	27	Faculty salary scales
12	Student role in institutional govt.	28	Programs for bldgs & facilities
13	Authority of faculty in government	29	Individual faculty salaries
14	Admission requirements	30	Short-range budget planning
15	Dismissal for cause	31	Long-range budget planning
16	Tenure		

Sources: American Association of University Professors, "Report of the Survey Subcommittee T," *AAUP Bulletin* 57, no. 1 (March 1971): 68-124; Scott E. Masten, "Authority and Commitment: Why Universities, Like Legislatures, Are Not Organized As Firms," *Journal of Economics and Management Strategy* 15 (2006): 649–84.

complete authority; *Administrator Determination* was the predominant governance mode for 20 of the 31 decision categories (decision areas 12–31). Even for hiring, promotion, and tenure decisions (areas 15–17, 19, and 21)—"the most fundamental of faculty prerogatives," according to Bowen and Tobin—faculty exercised effective authority at only about one-third or fewer colleges and universities in 1970, three-quarters of a century after the outlines of the modern American university first appeared.

By the end of the 20th century, that picture had changed significantly. Figure 7.2 presents a side-by-side comparison of the allocation of faculty

Figure 7.2

Faculty Authority by Decision Area, 1970 and 2001

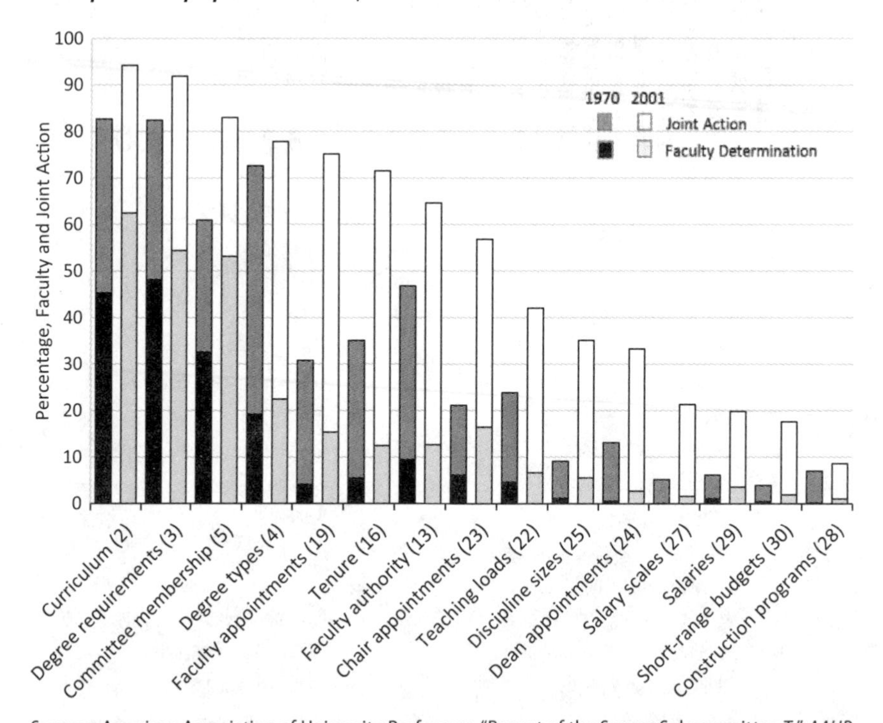

Sources: American Association of University Professors, "Report of the Survey Subcommittee T," *AAUP Bulletin* 57, no. 1 (March 1971): 68-124; Gabriel E. Kaplan, "Preliminary Results from the 2001 Survey on Higher Education Governance," American Association of University Professors, 2002; Scott E. Masten, "The Enterprise as Community: Firms, Towns, and Universities," in *Handbook of Economic Organization: Integrating Economic and Organization Theory,* ed. Anna Grandori (Cheltenham: Edward Elgar Publishing, 2013), pp. 105–6.

Note: Numbers in parentheses refer to the decision area numbers in Figure 7.1.

authority in 1970 and 2001 for the 15 decision areas covered in a follow-on survey.[35] As seen in the figure, faculty gained authority across the board over the 30-year interval between the surveys, with the largest increases occurring in the areas of faculty appointments (decision area 19), tenure (area 16), and department chair appointments (area 23). Administrator determination, which had been the prevalent governance mode for 11 of those 15 decision categories in 1970, dominated only 7 categories in 2001, with faculty at a majority of institutions having obtained control or veto authority over decisions that determined the authority of faculty in governance at the institution level (area 13), in addition to hiring, tenure, and chair appointments. The gains in faculty authority notwithstanding, substantial variation in governance remained both across decision areas and, for decision categories in the middle range of Figure 7.2, among institutions. Notably, faculty at more than one-fourth of responding colleges and universities had no authority over the fundamental areas of faculty appointments or tenure as American higher education entered the 21st century.

In sum, early American colleges and universities, unlike some European institutions, did not have a tradition of faculty governance. When faculty in the United States did begin to gain decision authority, they did so only gradually and selectively. Although formal structures of faculty governance have now existed at some universities for a century, the extent and scope of faculty authority has varied both among institutions and over time. And although the trend throughout the 20th century was toward more participation, faculty authority—with a few exceptions, such as over curricular matters—is rarely exclusive: Most decisions over which faculty have formal authority require mutual agreement with administrators.

Staring at the Senseless Monstrosity

Critics mostly let the defects of modern university governance speak for themselves without displaying much interest in how such a purportedly inefficient system arose and persisted. When the origins of shared governance are considered, detractors tend to blame a combination of rent seeking, market power, and, occasionally, chance or idiosyncratic events. In Henry Manne's account, for instance, faculty came to control universities by default, the result of "an accident of history that caused our higher educational industry to be not-for-profit or government-owned in its structure."[36] In such organizations, Manne claimed, control tends to be "somewhat arbitrary or political in nature," going "to whatever group just happens to be best positioned to capture the benefits, regardless of whether they are the best qualified or the most efficient ones or the most deserving ones. In this case, where there was really no one else contending for quasi-ownership of physical assets, the faculties were almost guaranteed to emerge in charge of the institution. No one else really wanted it."[37] Happenstance is similarly implicated in historical accounts that portray faculty demands for greater control at particular institutions as a backlash against especially autocratic presidents or other "local conditions."[38]

As with the prevalence of nonprofits in higher education, faculty governance has been too pervasive and durable to be explained by chance events and path dependence alone.[39] Among more systematic explanations proffered by critics, growing faculty market power has been a favored culprit. Noting the correlation between growth in demand for professors and "the timing of grants of authority to faculty," Bowen and Tobin, for example, argue that "the strong expansion in demand for professors in the late 1890s and early 1900s . . . had a pronounced impact on their role in governance—and especially . . . their role in the faculty appointment/advancement process."[40] The accelerating demand for professors after World War II similarly produced "gains in income, power, and prestige"[41] and "increased leverage,"[42] which enabled faculty "to negotiate gains in shared governance with presidents and boards."[43]

Faculty governance and the demand for faculty definitely rose together over time. The number of instructional staff (regular faculty, junior faculty, and research assistants) grew tenfold—from roughly 60,000 to more than 650,000—between 1921 and 1973, a period during which the U.S. population approximately doubled (from 106 million to 203 million between 1920 and 1970).[44] Higher demand for professors implies higher rents accruing to faculty (assuming less than perfectly elastic supply). It does not by itself, however, explain why faculty would have chosen to take those rents in the form of greater authority or more security rather than in higher compensation, even if increased demand somehow conferred monopoly power on tens of thousands of professors. More broadly, insinuations that faculty governance and tenure were manifestations of monopoly power on either side of the academic marketplace are hard to reconcile with the competitive nature of the industry. The number of postsecondary institutions grew rapidly in the decades following the Civil War through the end of the century, rising from 563 in 1870 to 977 in 1900 and 1,041 in 1920, with continued increases thereafter.[45] Table 7.1 shows the number of four-year, degree-granting institutions at the end of each decade from 1919–1920 through 2009–2010, plus the most recent figure for 2014–2015. Higher education in the United States consisted of large numbers of institutions at any point in time, but—of arguably more importance—the market experienced significant entry over time: The

Table 7.1

Number of Four-Year Postsecondary Institutions, 1919–2015

Year	Public	Private	Total
1919–20			989
1929–30			1,132
1939–40			1,252
1949–50	344	983	1,327
1959–60	367	1,055	1,422
1969–70	426	1,213	1,639
1979–80	549	1,408	1,957
1989–90	595	1,532	2,127
1999–00	614	1,749	2,363
2009–10	672	2,102	2,774
2014–15	701	2,310	3,011
Change 1949–2015	357	1,327	1,684

Sources: Thomas D. Snyder, *120 Years of American Education: A Statistical Portrait*, [Washington: U.S. Dept. of Education, 1993], Table 26; and Thomas D. Snyder, Cristobal de Brey, and Sally A. Dillow, *Digest of Education Statistics 2015* [NCES 2016-014], [Washington: U.S. Department of Education, 2016], Table 315.10.

Note: Data for years before 1974–75 include main campuses only. Data for later years include both main and branch campuses. Inclusion of branch campuses increased the number of public institutions by 85 and private institutions by 9 in 1979–80.

number of institutions has roughly doubled every 60 years and has more than tripled since 1920.

Beyond the sheer number of competitors and entrants, higher education histories describe the industry's dynamism during its formative years. By all accounts, higher education in the late 19th and early 20th centuries was characterized by high degrees of institutional autonomy, experimentation, and competition.[46] Following the 1819 Dartmouth College case, which, among other things, constrained state authority over private institutions, private colleges faced few constraints on their operations or organization. With an "almost total lack of federal involvement . . . colleges and universities—and their donors—were spared government intrusion and allowed to innovate."[47] The result was an industry characterized by "fluidity, uncertainty, and diversity," as institutions experimented with organizational and governance arrangements.[48] Successful experiments persisted and were copied: "Again and again the first widespread occurrence of a particular academic practice may be traced to those years, usually after preliminary pioneering by one of two institutions during the seventies or eighties."[49] Arrangements that proved unworkable, on the other hand, were abandoned. In 1919, Berkeley's Board of Regents created "a Council of Deans to exercise presidential responsibilities," an experiment that "proved to be a disaster" and lasted only a year.[50] More durable was the California Institute of Technology's (Caltech's) creation in the 1920s of an executive council, comprising four trustees and four faculty members, "to exercise the authority normally assigned to a college president."[51] Although Caltech as an institution experienced considerable success during that period, its novel governance had few imitators and was replaced with more conventional governance arrangements in 1946.[52] Eventually, the basic structure and organizational features of the American university emerged through a process of experimentation in a "competitive market for money, students, faculty, and prestige" as "truly deviant ideas on academic structure were all but impossible to reconcile with success."[53]

Even if survival in the face of competition supports a presumption of efficiency, it leaves unanswered the question of why faculty governance came to dominate other possible arrangements. The most conspicuous development coincident with the rise of faculty authority was the introduction and diffusion of research as a function of universities. Scholarship emerged fairly abruptly in the United States:

> [I]n the 1870's research played no important role in American higher education. . . . Around 1880 a definite change occurred. . . . Ten years later research had become one of the dominant concerns of higher education. . . . As far as official demands upon faculty were concerned, by 1910 research had almost fully gained the position of dominance which it was to keep thereafter.[54]

The growth in research over the educational landscape is reflected in the number of institutions granting doctorates and in the number of doctorates granted. The first true American research university, Johns Hopkins, opened in 1876. By 1900, more than 14 U.S. institutions were granting PhDs.[55] Between 1920 and 1971, the number of institutions awarding doctorates grew from fewer than 50, roughly 5 percent of all four-year institutions, to 260, about 15 percent.[56] American universities were granting doctorates at the rate of about 40 per year in the late 1870s, a figure that rose to about 300 annually by 1900; 1,200 by 1925; 33,000 by the mid-1970s; and 55,000 in 2015.[57] Roughly 3,600 PhDs were granted in the first decade of the 20th century, more than 400,000 in the last.[58]

Expectations of scholarship, initially concentrated in research universities, eventually extended to faculty in many liberal arts colleges as well: "The ethos of research . . . spread throughout the tertiary educational system, and even institutions where teachers ha[d] historically done little or no research now encourage their faculty members to undertake research. . . . In the late 1960s, only a minority of those working in American four-year higher educational colleges tended to publish regularly; today over sixty per cent do."[59] Coincident with this growing emphasis on research, faculty participation in the decisions of liberal arts colleges increased significantly.[60]

Although the emergence and diffusion of faculty governance broadly parallels the introduction and spread of research in higher education, the causal connection between scholarship and faculty authority is less obvious than is their temporal correlation. The higher education literature posits two main avenues through which research may have affected governance. The first associates the rise of faculty governance with changes in faculty self-perceptions that accompanied the professionalization of academic careers as scholarship gained prominence.[61] As their stature increased, the argument goes, professors came to view themselves as more akin to doctors and lawyers—deserving of comparable autonomy and respect—and to regard treatment as mere employees as inconsistent with their newfound professional status as experts.[62]

Research, as has been widely noted, also severely diminished the ability of nonspecialists to evaluate faculty performance and expanded the range of university activities. Trustees found "less and less of an opportunity for usefulness in a machine so elaborate that any incursion into it, by those unfamiliar, may do infinite harm."[63] With growth in the size and complexity of institutions, boards increasingly delegated policymaking and managerial decisions to presidents,[64] who, in turn, found it necessary "at least to consult with departmental faculty who had the relevant expertise in order to make an informed evaluation of the credentials of individuals being considered for appointment or promotion."[65] Greater specialization eventually left "university-wide administrators, and at times deans as well, unable to do more than respond to initiative on matters of personnel, facilities, teaching, curriculum, and research."[66] In the absence of anyone else competent to evaluate their activities, "[p]rofessors, as the authorities for their respective specializations, assumed more and more control over academic affairs."[67] In this view, faculty gained authority not because "no one else really wanted it" but because no one else really was capable of exercising it.

Although plausibly contributing factors, neither faculty self-perceptions nor expertise offers a fully satisfactory explanation for the form, appearance, and spread of governance arrangements observed in U.S. higher education. Arguments made on the basis of tastes are difficult to refute, of course. Nevertheless, historical accounts provide little support for the claim that faculty governance resulted from heightened professional self-regard or preferences for control over time. Then, as today, most faculty regarded engagement in the affairs of governance as a burden: "At the large universities, faculty meetings were often tedious and relatively inconsequential affairs; the fastidious professors either attended them for amusement or else avoided them whenever possible."[68] Even if changing status altered attitudes, an absolute preference for autonomy or control does not automatically translate into authority when other objectives and costs are taken into account: "Desires for security, status, and income sometimes found further expression in a more sweeping demand for power," but of these, achieving power was "the least realistic."[69]

The proposition that changes in control were related to changes in relative competence finds some support in the observed distribution of authority across decision areas in Figures 7.1 and 7.2: Faculty generally possess greater authority over areas in which they possess the most expertise, such as curriculum design, and less over issues about which they are likely to be less well-informed—budgeting and construction programs, for example. Strictly speaking, however, the ability to make effective decisions in the presence of dispersed information and expertise implies only a need to communicate or consult with knowledgeable parties and does not necessarily require the delegation of authority over those decisions. As noted previously, the earliest response to scholarly specialization was the decentralization of decision authority, first, from boards to presidents and, later, from presidents and deans to autocratic department chairs rather than to faculty. In modern universities, administrators continue to draw on the specialized knowledge and judgment of faculty on many decisions through consultation while retaining full authority over those decisions.[70] Finally, although the distribution of authority among decision areas is broadly consistent with differential expertise, the relatively late diffusion of faculty authority over hiring and promotion decisions and the still scant authoritative participation of faculty in salary determinations are hard—without additional considerations—to reconcile with the need to rely on faculty expertise.

Academic Bargains and University Governance

The establishment of research as a central function of universities very likely was a major factor in the evolution of academic governance—but not directly or primarily for reasons of faculty status or expertise. Rather, the production of scholarship changed academic employment relationships in ways that made academic bargains more difficult to secure.

Specifically, research increased the cost of institution-specific activities, reduced faculty mobility, and, by increasing faculty heterogeneity, impeded collective responses to administrator opportunism.

Before the introduction of research (and, to a large extent, for adjunct and other temporary faculty today), the relationship between a college and a professor did not differ fundamentally from employment relationships in other settings. Professors received compensation for their services on an at-will or short-term contract basis. If a professor became dissatisfied with his compensation or work conditions—or the college, with his services—the relatively standard curriculum of early colleges facilitated the substitution of alternative trading partners. In such settings, mobility and reputation served to discipline the academic labor market in the conventional way.

With the emergence of research as a major academic activity, what were previously relatively discrete, simultaneous exchanges acquired a temporal dimension. Because academic reputations depend on a scholar's cumulative contributions, interruptions in research production acquired the potential to reduce an individual's professional standing and market value throughout his career, particularly if delays or disruptions resulted in a loss of priority for a discovery or contribution.[71] Research thus raised the opportunity cost of time spent on teaching and in service to an institution. More important, the long-term consequences of current research effort introduce a sequential component to academic bargains that increases the risk of opportunism. As long as administrators value faculty time spent on institutional activities more than the cost to professors of forgone research, a bargain in which administrators compensate faculty for research sacrifices—with promises of higher salaries, promotions, future appointments of desired colleagues, or anything else that faculty value—will leave both better off. Discrepancies between the timing of actions and the accrual of benefits expose such bargains to the risk of reneging, however: the possibility that the dean (or the next dean) may fail to honor his or her end of the bargain will (or should) make a professor hesitant to serve on committees, schmooze with alumni, or pursue research favored by the institution or its patrons (e.g., by redirecting research toward practical rather than basic research or away from controversial topics), lest he or she find his or her academic credentials and market opportunities diminished relative to those who spurn such requests. (Future dean: "I don't know or care what deals you may have struck with my predecessor; what matters to me is your record, and what I see is less than expected for someone at your career stage.") By the same token, administrators will be wary of fully compensating faculty up front for the expected value of research sacrifices (even if doing so did not run afoul of the nondistribution constraint) for fear that faculty, having received the benefit, will provide less than consummate effort.

Contracting—a common response to holdup and reneging problems in commercial bargains—offers little recourse in academic transactions. Although some dimensions of academic employment, such as current salary and teaching loads, are contractible, the complexity and subtlety of academic responsibilities and the need to adapt to changing circumstances make conventional contractual solutions to reneging on academic bargains ineffective.[72] As a result, academic bargains must be largely self-enforcing. Unfortunately, not only does research exacerbate the hazards of one of the parties reneging on the academic bargain, it also weakens the supports for such bargains. First, by reducing faculty mobility, research diminishes the credibility of termination as a response to administrator opportunism. Although research itself typically is not institution specific, greater specialization—by reducing the likelihood of finding suitable positions at institutions of comparable status and resources within increasingly narrow fields and subfields—tends to complicate the academic matching problem. Second, because the sanctions that an individual faculty member can bring to bear on opportunistic administrators (or colleagues) are few and small, effective deterrence often will require collective actions—faculty revolts, protests, and the like. The private costs of participation in such actions, however, are potentially large, especially in light of an administrator's (or majority faction's) ability to target rewards and retaliation selectively. In general, the prospect of overcoming the individual incentive to free ride will be greater to the extent that members of the "community" agree on what constitutes acceptable behavior and can identify and communicate violations and settle on appropriate responses thereto. By increasing the heterogeneity of faculty interests and beliefs, research reduces the ability of faculty to assess the outcomes of substantive bargains between administrators and faculty (and among faculty) and thereby makes the coordination necessary for credible collective "self-enforcement" of academic transactions harder to achieve.[73]

Faculty governance can be seen in this context as serving a role analogous to democratic institutions in securing political bargains. In the political domain, constitutionally prescribed democratic decision rules enhance confidence in governmental policies by (a) broadening the interests of the government[74] and (b) providing a relatively verifiable criterion—namely, that proposals receive the consent of designated individuals or groups—by which to evaluate the legitimacy of decisions.[75] In general, the more parties with veto power, the greater the stability of bargains. In institutions that vest authority exclusively in administrators, a discrete change in policy or practice (such as a change in program emphasis or in the relative weights assigned teaching and research in tenure decisions) requires only a change in the priorities or identity of a single individual. Effecting the same policy change under rules that require the concurrence of a specified majority of enfranchised faculty, by contrast, would necessitate a shift in the overall distribution of faculty preferences or identities sufficient to make the new policy the preferred course of the decisive voter (or voters). By giving those who would be adversely affected by a proposal the potential to block its passage, faculty governance increases confidence in the continuity of existing policies and, thereby, the willingness of faculty to conform their behavior to standards and policies peculiar to a given institution. By the same token, requiring the assent of both faculty and administrators affords administrators (and the interests they represent) protection against faculty overreaching and, to the extent that it further contributes to the stability of academic policies, stands to help preserve minority interests within the faculty as well.[76]

The cost of adding veto points—in both academia and politics—is the increased difficulty of effecting adaptations, thereby, increasing the likelihood that opportunities for efficient adjustments will be blocked. Criticisms of university governance, not surprisingly, echo those of its political counterparts, particularly of divided democracy: policy incoherence; lack of accountability; capture by special, entrenched, or ideological interests; and an inherent propensity to preserve the status quo to the extent of fostering gridlock. The question in universities—as in polities—is whether the gains in securing the respective bargains outweigh the drawbacks of democratic governance.

The available evidence generally supports the proposition that university governance reflects and has been responsive to these tradeoffs. The emergence and subsequent spread of shared decision authority closely followed the introduction and diffusion of research. Among the institutions covered by the 1970 AAUP survey, faculty authority—and especially joint administrator–faculty determination—was more prevalent in large, heterogeneous research institutions than in liberal arts colleges and specialized institutions.[77] Those differences decreased significantly by 2001, however, at the same time that research expectations at liberal arts colleges increased.[78]

Conclusion

Adam Smith was, as previously noted, no fan of faculty governance. But as low as his opinion of faculty control of universities was, Smith regarded administration by an authority outside the faculty as worse:

> An extraneous jurisdiction [by someone outside the faculty] is liable to be exercised both ignorantly and capriciously. In its nature it is arbitrary and discretionary, and the persons who exercise it, neither attending upon the lectures of the teacher themselves, nor perhaps understanding the sciences which it is his business to teach, are seldom capable of exercising it with judgment. From the insolence of office too they are frequently indifferent how they exercise it, and are very apt to censure or deprive him of his office wantonly, and without any just cause. . . . It is by powerful protection only that he can effectually guard himself against the bad usage to which he is at all times exposed; and this protection he is most likely to gain, not by ability or diligence in his profession, but by obsequiousness to the will of his superiors, and by being ready, at all times, to sacrifice to that will the rights, the interest, and the honour of the body corporate of which he is a member.[79]

The inducement under autocratic governance to engage in what we would today call rent seeking or influence activities transformed professors in French universities, by Smith's account, into "the meanest and most contemptible persons in society."[80] Smith's solution was to subject professors to competitive market discipline by tying their compensation to fees paid directly by students. Their livelihoods dependent on "the affection, gratitude, and favourable report of those who attended upon [their] instructions," professors would thereby be induced to discharge their duties faithfully and diligently.[81]

Student sovereignty over the supply of education was hardly original to Smith. The first medieval universities of Europe were, in fact, organized much as Smith proposed: teachers at the universities at Bologna and Salerno during the 12th century were hired, paid, and even fined for poor performance directly by student guilds.[82] Yet despite the prominence of the so-called "Italian model" of education during the Middle Ages, student-run universities were ultimately displaced everywhere by alternative governance arrangements. Smith's market solution failed the market test of survival.[83]

By this standard, the American model of university governance would have to be deemed a success. Its many problems and deficiencies notwithstanding, the U.S. system of shared governance has survived in the face of substantial competition. The reasons for that success, I believe, derive from its role in sustaining academic bargains. More broadly, an appreciation of the functions of faculty governance in a modern research university requires an understanding of its relation to tenure and academic freedom. As Smith observed, uninformed decisions are necessarily arbitrary and capricious, inviting sycophancy and rent seeking. Giving authority to those with the relevant expertise increases the prospect that decisions will be made on the basis of academic rather than political, personal, or other nonacademic considerations. But decision authority cannot be meaningfully exercised if troublesome or uncooperative participants in the decision process can be easily replaced; voting authority without tenure would be of little value. The complementarity between faculty governance, tenure, and academic freedom is an important reason why faculty governance and tenure rights are granted conjointly and why comparable decision rights typically are not granted to non–tenure track faculty or to students, staff, alumni, donors, or other groups who also have interests in the operations of universities.

Criticisms of the system of shared governance that has long characterized American higher education continue. The *Chronicle of Higher Education* listed "widespread attacks on shared governance" as one of its 10 "key shifts in higher education" in its 2016 *Trends Report*, noting that "[t]he traditional model of shared governance is eroding as more governing boards make unilateral changes that ignore faculty opinion."[84] That university governance is rife with inefficiencies is indisputable. And it may well be that the nature and severity of the problems facing colleges and universities today have made once salutary organizational arrangements obsolete or have exacerbated the system's inherent defects to the point that the need for wholescale reorganization is now acute. Also possible, however, is that the commitment afforded by shared governance will be crucial to securing the academic bargain needed to elicit from faculty the effort and cooperation required to respond to that new educational environment.

PART III:

Competition in Higher Education

CHAPTER EIGHT

All Education Is For-Profit Education[1]

Henry G. Manne

We are all familiar with famous huge errors in economics, such as those of Karl Marx, errors that ultimately create vast human suffering.

But there are countless small errors that no one pays much attention to when they are published. They pass unnoticed, often gaining acceptance by default, until a large policy issue emerges that can use that idea to bolster its argument.

Just such a scenario was much in evidence a few weeks ago with the release of Robert Shireman's paper "Perils in the Provision of Trust Goods" by the Center for American Progress.[2]

Shireman was previously an official in the Obama Department of Education and has been a front man in the Obama administration's campaign against for-profit higher education. In his paper, he argues that nonprofit schools are more likely to treat their students fairly than are profit-seeking schools.

He draws heavily on a 1980 *Yale Law Journal* paper, "The Role of Nonprofit Enterprise," by the distinguished lawyer and economist Henry Hansmann of the Yale Law School.[3] In his paper, Hansmann introduced the concept of the "non-distribution constraint" as a principal reason why the not-for-profit organizational form is generally selected for the provision of certain goods, like education, rather than for-profit companies.

Hansmann's main argument is that charitably inclined folks are willing to entrust money to nonprofits because nonprofits must follow the "non-distribution constraint," which forbids personal benefits beyond some "reasonable" remuneration for the managers, including, in the case of schools, boards of trustees and administrators. This analysis applies even more strongly to government-owned institutions.

The non-distribution constraint, Hansmann argues, gives nonprofit managers better motivation to spend the organization's funds on its stated mission rather than on personal benefits. In contrast, the argument goes, for-profit enterprises motivate managers to maximize profits (all going to the owners) and disregard other interests, like those of the students in colleges.

This analysis is wrong in two fundamental ways.

First of all, it cannot be demonstrated empirically that for-profit educational enterprises perform worse on various measures than nonprofits. Efforts to show this disparity suffer from all manner of statistical errors, such as directly comparing the test results and loan-repayment rates of nonprofit schools, where higher ranked and wealthier students enroll, to those of for-profits, which mostly cater to weaker and poorer students.

More significantly, however, the argument is wrong because it totally overlooks the pressures for efficiency and responsiveness to consumer demand that exist in any competitive industry. And proprietary firms inevitably dominate competitive industries, while competitive forces will, for reasons to be shown below, always be weak in an industry dominated by not-for-profit firms.

The weakest part of Hansmann's theory, much exaggerated by Shireman, is that the baleful quest for profits is absent in the nonprofit sector. This is a hallowed and egregious myth. Human nature does not change with the legal structure of the employing organization. Managers of nonprofit organizations are no less interested in maximizing personal utility than are managers of for-profit firms. But the form of these gains will differ in the two kinds of organizations.

Can anyone believe that light teaching loads, generous research leaves, tenure, high salaries, political correctness, and so on represent something other than "profits" to faculties? Calling it an expense rather than a distribution of profits does not change the underlying reality; it merely tricks the uninformed.

Tenured faculties (and to a growing extent bureaucratic administrators) have long been the "owners" of our universities and, as such, have long participated in the real profits, the non-distribution constraint notwithstanding.

If an enterprise, whether for profit or nonprofit, survives over a period of time, it must be that it is covering all its costs. And since most schools survive for long periods, we also know that they cannot all be at the margin of survival, where one dollar less of revenue would spell bankruptcy. They must be realizing revenues (whether from taxes, tuition, or gifts) well in excess of their real costs.

Now the important thing to realize here is the connection between survival and what for lack of a better word we will call "profit." If there is none of this excess of revenues over costs—profit—the enterprise does not survive. So Shireman can shriek all he wants about the malignant influence of profits, but for the point he is trying to make, there is no such thing as a nonprofit organization.

What there is, of course, is a well-designed system of obfuscating the distribution of these profits.

Given that tenured professors have long enjoyed the protection of a cartel, it is impossible that they are not realizing supra-competitive returns. But a big difference between them and the shareholders of a corporation is that they usually cannot realize this above-market return in the form of greater take-home cash payments—the "non-distribution constraint" at work.

Rather, their benefits are hidden in various in-kind payments, like light teaching loads, short office hours, luxurious faculty clubs, generous research leaves, tenure, and myriad other academic delights, all of which pass university accounting muster as "costs" of education. But the underlying reality of the matter refutes both Hansmann's and Shireman's notion that the nonprofit schools are different from the for-profit schools mainly because of the absence of "profits" in the former.

But there is a significant difference in these two forms of organization that neither Hansmann nor Shireman acknowledges. That is the absence of transferable property rights in the assets and stream of income of the nonprofit organizations. (Note the emphasis here is on the non-transferability of property rights, not their absence, since, as we have already seen, faculties and administrators do indeed possess certain constrained "property rights" in the institution.)

Unlike the shareholder who can transfer a claim on corporate profits by selling shares, professors and administrators do not have that power.

It is the transferability of property rights, not the access to profits, that explains much of the greater concern for efficiency and responsiveness to consumers in the for-profit sector.

Therefore, if faculties or administrators are to enjoy any of the benefits that come from their protected positions (i.e., protected from competition), they must do it while they are alive and on the job. That is, they are not allowed to take this profit home with them or leave it to their heirs.

To take advantage of their position as owners, they must take these funds in the form of something that looks like an academic expense. This explains most of the differences in behavior of participants in for-profit and nonprofit higher education and a lot about why higher education has become so expensive and its quality often so low.

It is a far more robust theory than that advanced by Hansmann, and it reflects a reality light years away from Shireman's dream world of altruistic academics.

CHAPTER NINE

Assessing For-Profit Colleges

Jayme S. Lemke and William F. Shughart II

The higher education sector in the United States has experienced rapid growth over the past 50 years. That expansion has been both in scale—more people are pursuing postsecondary education than ever before—and scope—colleges are taking on more ancillary functions not related directly to their teaching, research, and public-service missions. In addition to education and credentialing, many colleges and universities provide housing, food, counseling services, athletic training, entertainment, and extensive social programming. Further, easy access to federally subsidized loans and grants means that the willingness of consumers to pay has not hit the ceiling it would have hit in the absence of those subsidies. The combination of rising demand, expansion in the scope of activities provided by institutions of higher learning, and little to no discipline from the demand side of the market has led to significant increases in the price tags of U.S. colleges and universities. Tuition cost inflation exceeds the rise in consumer prices overall as well as the Consumer Price Index's health care cost component.[1]

It should come as no surprise that an expanding customer base and dramatic increases in the prices those customers face have attracted new entrants to the higher education industry. The contemporary for-profit college can be understood as one such competitor. Students who find unappealing either the products or the prices of traditional educational institutions may instead elect to enroll in schools that are less expensive, more targeted to their education goals (e.g., two-year colleges and technical-training programs), or both. Indeed, for-profit colleges now account for at least 10 percent of all students in postsecondary schools. DeVry University alone enrolled more than 60,000 students at more than 75 campuses nationwide in 2014.[2]

Despite obvious demand, the discount-market position of many for-profit institutions of higher education has generated a great deal of criticism. Although no formal prohibitions have been imposed on for-profit colleges that attempt to provide high-cost, high-quality education experiences, the significant tax advantages enjoyed by private and public nonprofit colleges make that particular market one into which competitors find it difficult to enter. As such, for-profit colleges primarily have become lower-cost providers and, hence, frequently offer postsecondary education experiences of lesser quality. They are not the Neiman Marcuses and Saks Fifth Avenues of the education market; they are the Walmarts and Dollar Trees. The starting point of most of those critiques is to observe that trustees who manage nonprofit institutions have students' best interests as their primary objective, but individuals who manage for-profit institutions primarily seek to maximize profits.[3] The implication is that when the financial bottom line and the quality of the education experience conflict, the nonprofit college will prioritize education and the for-profit institution will prioritize its bottom line, thereby minimizing cost and maximizing revenue at students' expense.

Yet cost minimization is different from cost avoidance. It is not in a for-profit college's interest to zero out all spending allocated to educating its students because at the end of the day, the college must satisfy its customers to continue doing business. To the extent that remaining profitable requires providing the expected educational or credentialing benefits—or both—that students want, for-profit colleges are motivated, at least in the long run, to provide educational value that exceeds students' out-of-pocket expense. The question, then, becomes whether a nonprofit or a for-profit postsecondary education system is more likely to generate the desired combination of quality and price.

The answer to that question ultimately can be known only by observing consumer behavior. Which type of institution do students find most worthwhile to continue to attend? Evidence salient to that simple market test of success or failure is difficult to interpret in this context because of the extent to which the market for higher education is distorted by subsidies to both colleges and students. Because most students pay far less than the full price tag for their education, they are provided no guarantee that the value generated by the education experience exceeds its cost. So how can those with an interest in education policy understand the value and efficacy of the for-profit college system compared with the currently available nonprofit alternatives?

In this chapter, we attempt to answer that question.[4] First, we describe the current for-profit college system. Second, we summarize the evidence available on the performance of for-profit, postsecondary education institutions. Third, we compare the performance of for-profit colleges with the performance of their closest analogs in the public sector: community colleges. Fourth, we discuss the related question of whether more stringent regulation of for-profit colleges is likely to produce the results desired by advocates of higher-education reform. The conclusion considers a potential path forward for understanding the debate about the role of for-profit colleges in fulfilling the stated policy goal of enabling young people to obtain education and training beyond the high-school level that prepares them adequately for success in an increasingly competitive global economy.

The For-Profit Education Sector

The term "for-profit college" covers a wide range of education opportunities and types of education institutions. Traditionally, the main purpose of the for-profit college degree or certificate program was to provide vocational training and other education experiences that take two years or less to complete. The credential conferred at the end of the completed program usually was a certificate rather than a recognized college degree. After the passage of 2005's Deficit Reduction Act, another major player entered the for-profit college scene: institutions with massive enrollments that offer students instruction primarily or exclusively online. Before the passage of that 2005 federal law, postsecondary schools were required to offer "no more than half their courses online and have no more than half their students enrolled in distance-learning courses."[5] The 2005 law contributed to the viability of a mass-market, low-cost postsecondary education sector in which many for-profit colleges now specialize.

The governance structures of the for-profit sector also differ. Some for-profit colleges are publicly traded companies, whereas others are privately owned.[6] Many major players in the market are of the first type, including the former Corinthian Colleges and Adtalem Global Education (formerly DeVry Education Group). Apollo Education Group; Laureate Education, Inc.; and Full Sail University—the for-profit institution Mitt Romney was criticized for praising without disclosing the university's contributions to his 2012 presidential campaign[7]—are all privately held, for-profit institutions.

Despite differences in ownership arrangements, the programs offered by nonprofit and for-profit institutions are similar in many respects. Many for-profit colleges now grant two-year associate's and four-year bachelor's degrees. Some for-profit colleges even offer master's or doctoral programs. About 70 percent of for-profit college revenue comes from Title IV federal aid programs, which means that for-profits and nonprofits alike are part of the same regulatory structure and funding system.[8] Moreover, public and private nonprofit colleges and universities increasingly are attempting to compete in the "nontraditional" spaces of online education, distance learning, and evening programs for working adults.

Controlling access to Title IV funds is the primary way the U.S. Department of Education (ED) regulates colleges and universities. To receive the funds that ED disburses to institutions of higher education every year through programs designed to defray student tuition costs, colleges and universities must follow ED guidelines that are designed to ensure proper stewardship of those funds. Much of that authority originates in the G.I. Bill of 1952 and the Higher Education Act of 1965, both of which expanded the scope of federal higher education funding significantly.[9]

One of the guidelines established by ED is that the college or university must be accredited by an ED-approved accreditation agency.[10] That requirement ostensibly avoids direct federal regulation by allowing multiple accreditation agencies to function simultaneously. However, because the accreditation agency itself must be approved, the potential remains for ED to regulate indirectly the particulars of a given school's operating structure and practices by approving only those accreditation agencies that monitor and enforce compliance with particular kinds of policies. That requirement effectively subsidizes accreditation agencies by increasing a school's gains from accreditation. Establishing accreditation agencies as the de jure gatekeepers to Title IV funds gives those agencies a powerful carrot that they can dangle before administrators to compel cooperation with their recommendations about how an institution of higher education should be run. State governments serve a similar role by granting the college or university legal permission to exist.

In addition to those general standards, for-profit colleges must comply with other regulatory rules. For-profit colleges have a unique status with respect to such regulatory structure because ED considers them to be institutions of higher education for some purposes but not for others.[11] Their status as "proprietary" institutions of higher education means that revenue from federal aid programs (excluding veterans' benefits) can account for, at most, 90 percent of the total costs, and the institutions must function for at least two years before becoming eligible to receive any Title IV funds (known as the 90/10 rule).[12] The burden of the gainful employment rule, designed to ensure that students are enrolling in education programs that will help them advance their career prospects, will also fall disproportionately on for-profit schools, although there is some uncertainty about whether ED will decide to enforce that rule under the Trump administration.[13] This topic will be discussed in greater detail in a later section.

Performance of For-Profit Institutions

For-profit institutions awarded 18.1 percent of all degrees and certificates earned in the 2011–2012 academic year.[14] That percentage is all the more remarkable given that during 2011, only 9.3 percent of postsecondary students were enrolled in for-profit institutions.[15] Ten years earlier, in 2001, only 3.3 percent of postsecondary students were enrolled in for-profit institutions.[16] Although both for-profit and nonprofit private institutions are eclipsed in size by public colleges and universities, Figure 9.1 shows that for-profit institutions have been gaining market share for nearly 20 years.

The growing prevalence of for-profit colleges has attracted attention and criticism. Particularly given the extent to which attendance at for-profit colleges is subsidized through federal loan programs, the Health, Education, Labor and Pensions (HELP) Committee of the United States Senate has taken on the "duty to ensure that for-profit schools spend these Federal dollars efficiently and effectively."[17] On March 1, 2015, ED released a list of postsecondary institutions that would be subject to stricter monitoring subsequently because of concerns about their financial integrity. Of 556 institutions that made the list, 329—nearly 60 percent—were for-profit colleges.[18]

Figure 9.1

Percentage Enrollment by Type of Degree-Granting Institution

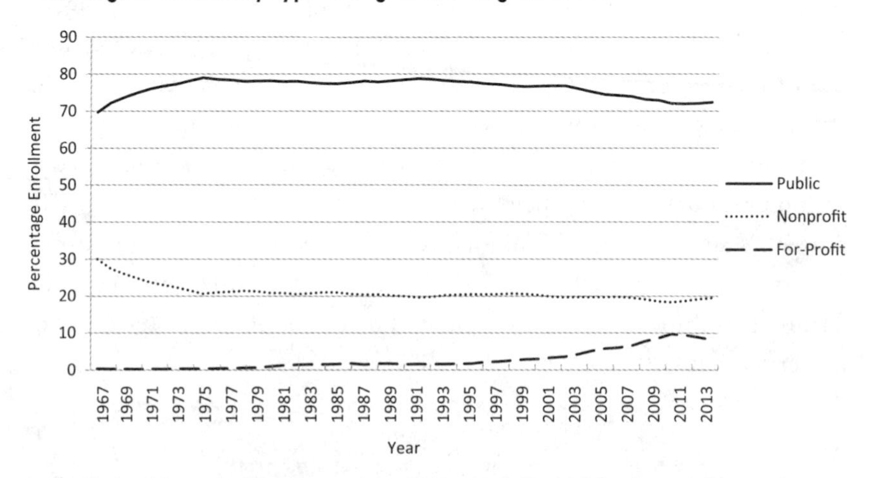

Source: National Center for Education Statistics, "Table 303.10: Total Fall Enrollment in Degree-Granting Postsecondary Institutions, by Attendance Status, Sex of Student, and Control of Institution: Selected Years, 1947 through 2024," *Digest of Education Statistics*, March 2015, https://nces.ed.gov/programs/digest/d14/tables/dt14_303.10.asp.

One criticism frequently leveled against for-profit schools is that they spend too much on marketing and recruiting relative to spending on education and that those expenditures often are being used in ways that are misleading or even predatory. For example, the Government Accountability Office testified in front of the HELP Committee that an undercover operation revealed aggressive, deceptive, and occasionally deceitful tactics employed by for-profit colleges to boost enrollment. Of the 15 for-profit colleges investigated, 4 encouraged prospective students to report inaccurate information on their Free Application for Federal Student Aid form, and all the colleges investigated "made some type of deceptive or otherwise questionable statement."[19] The fear that students are being exploited contributed to the HELP Committee's concerns about for-profit institutions increasing the amounts they were spending on marketing and recruiting relative to education.[20]

The proportion of postsecondary educational resources allocated to instruction is shrinking at all types of degree-granting institutions.[21] As the fraction of higher education budgets spent on administration is rising, the share of budgets going to instruction and physical plant maintenance is falling. However, instructional spending is a poor measure of how much knowledge actually is being imparted. Innovative instruction methods could allow students to learn more at a lower cost per professor, or adjunct faculty—who may be in their positions because of personal choices to focus on teaching rather than research—may (or could) be better classroom teachers and mentors of college students than are tenured research professors. For-profit colleges employ adjunct and other non-tenure-track faculty almost exclusively.[22] Tenured and tenure-track faculty members tend to be expensive. An effective way to hold down the education costs borne by students may be to replace tenure lines with so-called clinical instructors, who in many cases do not hold a terminal degree (usually a PhD); are hired only to teach assigned classes, with no research or service obligations; and agree to employment contracts with specified terms, usually of one academic year.

Another criticism of the for-profit system is that students at for-profit colleges often seem to get lower returns to education spending than do students at other colleges. Students who attend for-profit colleges are significantly more likely to borrow money than are students who attend other types of institutions: a total of 88 percent of for-profit college students borrow, relative to 41 percent of students at public, four-year institutions and 54 percent at private, nonprofit, four-year institutions.[23] Levels of student indebtedness are higher at for-profit colleges than at public, not-for-profit institutions but lower than the levels of debt accumulated by students at private nonprofits. The median for-profit college student enrolling in 2004 borrowed $13,961 within six years of enrollment. The median private, nonprofit college student borrowed more ($16,606), and the median public, nonprofit college student borrowed significantly less (only $6,000), largely because of the lower cost of tuition at directly subsidized public institutions.[24]

Furthermore, loans taken to attend for-profit schools go into default more frequently. Among students who attended schools offering a bachelor's degree or higher, approximately 18 percent of for-profit college attendees defaulted on a loan within three years compared with a 6 to 7 percent default rate at public and nonprofit private colleges.[25] Students at for-profit colleges also are less likely to graduate from four-year programs.[26] The primary difficulty with those stylized facts is a failure to compare like data. Lower four-year-program graduation rates and higher default rates are reasonable to expect among for-profit college attendees if the current focus of for-profit colleges is on the marginal student who would not otherwise be accepted by—or be able to attend—a college at all and who may not even be interested in a traditional, four-year education.[27] Further, there may be significant variation depending on the type of degree program. To truly understand whether for-profit colleges are offering an inferior product, for-profit students must be compared with public and nonprofit students with equivalent backgrounds and academic aptitudes who are matriculating in programs designed to develop the same skill set.

One reason the outcomes of today's for-profit college students are difficult to compare with the outcomes experienced by students at other institutions is that those student populations are so different from each other. Students at for-profit colleges are more likely to be age 25 or older and more likely to be supporting themselves financially, both characteristics that are used to identify populations that are at risk of not completing degree programs. For-profit students tend to be less wealthy. The family income of the median for-profit college student is only 60 percent of the family income of the median public-school student and less than half the family income of the median private-school student. For-profit students also are more likely to be drawn from minority populations.[28] In 2011, the University of Phoenix awarded more bachelor's degrees to black students than any other institution.[29] Comparative demographics are presented in Table 9.1.

Other characteristics associated with low completion rates also are overrepresented within for-profit institutions. For-profit college students are more likely to attend school part time, work full-time jobs while enrolled, have dependents other than a spouse, be single parents, or not hold a traditional high school diploma.[30] A study of career colleges in Texas found not only that a greater percentage of students at for-profit colleges were of lower income, more racially and ethnically diverse, older, and more likely to be supporting themselves but also were more likely to have a high school grade point average of 2.5 or

Table 9.1

Demographics of Student Populations, by Type of Institution

Student characteristics	For profit	Public nonprofit	Private nonprofit
Age 25 or older	56%	35%	38%
Financially independent	76%	50%	39%
African American	26%	13%	12%
Hispanic	19%	13%	11%
White, non-Hispanic	50%	66%	70%
Median family income	$24,300	$40,400	$49,200
Parents with associate's degree or higher	37%	52%	61%

Source: Government Accountability Office, "Proprietary Schools: Stronger Department of Education Oversight Needed to Help Ensure Only Eligible Students Receive Federal Student Aid," Report GAO-09-600 to the Chairman, Subcommittee on Higher Education, Lifelong Learning and Competitiveness, Committee on Education and Labor, U.S. House of Representatives, 2009.

below and to come from families in which neither parent had earned a bachelor's degree.[31] Single mothers who pursue higher education are more likely to choose to enroll in for-profit colleges than in any other type of institution.[32]

Education policy expert Watson Scott Swail analyzed the prevalence of risk factors associated with exiting an education program early.[33] Students in four-year programs at for-profit colleges are 5.8 times more likely to have three or more risk factors associated with dropping out before completing a degree than are students in four-year programs at private, nonprofit schools and are also 8.7 times more likely to have three or more risk factors than are students in four-year programs at public schools. That effect exists on a smaller scale for two-year programs and may not exist at all for programs that require less than two years to complete. In the latter programs, the percentages of students who have three or more risk factors associated with exiting before completion is 56 percent at for-profit schools, 44 percent at nonprofit private schools, and 70 percent at public schools.[34]

Those are some of the reasons underlying differences in outcomes at different kinds of institutions. Unfortunately, most studies that have been done do very little to attempt to control for particular student characteristics when evaluating student performance, largely because such particulars are extraordinarily difficult to come by. The situation at for-profit colleges looks significantly less bleak in studies that do include some kind of control. Among institutions in which at least 60 percent of the student population is low income, as measured by eligibility for need-based Pell grants, for-profit colleges actually have higher graduation rates (55 percent) than do private, nonprofit schools (39 percent) and public schools (31 percent).[35] Furthermore, when the comparison is limited to the two-year programs that are the focus of most for-profit institutions, for-profit colleges significantly outperform community colleges in graduation rates. Sixty-three percent of for-profit college students enrolled in a two-year program graduate within three years, as compared with the 20 percent graduation rate at community colleges.[36] That evidence suggests that attempts to place limits on for-profit schools in the name of protecting students from exploitation may disproportionately affect low-income students and other underserved populations, thereby harming the very populations that advocates of reform purport to help.

Comparing Apples to Apples: For-Profit and Community Colleges

Based on whom for-profit colleges are educating and what kinds of programs are being offered to those students, the most comparable public option is the community or junior college. Like for-profit colleges, community college enrollees are more likely to be nontraditional students with characteristics that put them at risk for not fulfilling their education goals. Relative to traditional, four-year college students, community college students are more likely to have delayed higher education, be supporting themselves, and come from lower-income families with parents who—at the most—completed high school.[37] Community college students also are more likely to be enrolled in programs lasting two years or less or to be enrolled with the intention of taking only partial coursework or transferring to another institution.

Overall, the profile of for-profit college students is significantly more like the profile of the community college student than the student at a traditional, four-year college, whether public or private. The relevant alternative for most for-profit college students is not attending a traditional institution of higher learning. Rather, those students, if they were not attending for-profit institutions, would be most likely to attend a community college or to not pursue postsecondary education at all. So, what are the primary differences between for-profit and community colleges, and why do some students choose the for-profit sector in the first place? The literature that addresses this question, much of which employs the case study method, suggests four key differences between the for-profit and the community college experiences: (a) accessibility, (b) program structure, (c) quality of product, and (d) sticker price.

One of the most significant differences between for-profit and community colleges is that, perhaps counterintuitively, for-profit education programs are significantly more accessible to most students. Community colleges have strict enrollment caps, which mean that students who do not apply for admission early enough simply are denied access. A study that compared a campus of an unnamed for-profit college chain with three community colleges serving the same geographic area found that the community colleges had lower acceptance rates, despite the for-profit technical college having stricter admission requirements in basic arithmetic and language skills.[38] The limited capacity of community colleges—which is an inherent feature of their artificially low prices and the fact that expansion is possible only by undergoing an extensive bureaucratic process that is likely to require action by the state legislature—may explain why for-profit colleges have seen such significant growth relative to community colleges.[39]

A focus group of for-profit college students identified lack of access as a major reason that students chose not to attend community colleges, despite their significantly lower tuition rates. In the words of one for-profit college student, "I wish I had done it [referring to community college] first but *I could not afford to*" [emphasis added].[40] In other words, the opportunity cost of delaying education in the hope of getting a spot in a community college program was costlier to that student than the higher price tag. Many other focus group participants also reported frustration with waitlists, lack of information, and even trouble reaching anybody when they attempted to explore the possibility of community college.[41] Here is what another for-profit college student had to say:

> [Getting into community college] is one of the most difficult things in the world! . . . First getting through to them [by telephone] is hard. Then they put you on a wait list just to possibly get into the school. There are prerequisites too I think. I thought to myself, do I really have time for this? There are schools that will let me in right away, like the one I am at now. Getting into a community college, it is just way too many barriers for no reason. I just want to learn.[42]

The difficulty of even getting a spot in a community college is particularly worrisome given the socioeconomic status of these students. If their access to for-profit colleges is limited and they cannot get into a community college, education opportunities for already disadvantaged groups—such as racial minorities, single parents, and those living in poverty—will be reduced even further.

Program structure also is revealed as a significant determinant of the for-profit versus community college choice. For-profit institutions that depend on continually providing a valuable product to ensure their survival may be more likely to experiment with curriculum structures and pedagogical techniques that may be more effective for the nontraditional student. For example, one analysis of higher education in Texas conducted case studies of four types of for-profit institutions to understand the recent high graduation rates from the state's for-profit institutions.[43] The case studies found that those institutions used a cohort-based model in which small numbers of students are admitted together and proceed through the same sequence of classes on the same course schedule. Classes often are clustered at the same time each day—8 a.m. until 1 p.m., for example—to enable students to maintain a regular extracurricular work schedule, and programs start on a rolling basis. That means that students who make the decision in March to pursue additional education do not have to wait until September to begin—they can often start taking classes the next week or month. Such a flexible, compact structure may explain why students at for-profit institutions are more likely to enroll as full-time students, mitigating one of the risk factors associated with dropping out.[44]

In addition to offering condensed, continual programming, for-profit colleges often have highly standardized curricula that make it easier for nontraditional students to find a combination of campuses and classes that align with their work and child-care schedules.[45] Evidence also suggests that for-profit colleges may be more sensitive to the fact that their students do not have much time to deal with the bureaucratic aspects of higher education. At least one comparative study found that administrative services such as admissions, registration, and financial aid were more centrally located and more easily accessible than at community colleges in the same area.[46] Other studies have found that students who choose for-profit colleges value such convenience because they often are putting schooling on top of their family and work responsibilities.[47] In contrast, at community colleges, one counselor is often assigned to 1,000 students, many of whom will not get the chance to speak to the counselor before or during the first four weeks of their program.[48] That observation is consistent with the fact that students report greater difficulty even getting basic information from community colleges.[49]

A significant related characteristic is that although tuition often is higher at for-profit colleges, the targeted nature of many for-profit programs means that the same goal can be achieved more quickly. For example, in a comparison of vocational nursing programs, Iloh and Tierney found that although the for-profit program cost $34,000 (compared with $5,000 at the community college), the for-profit program took only 13 months to complete, whereas completing the community college program required two years.[50] The income foregone during that extra year of schooling—not to mention potential delays in starting dates because of more rigid structures and the potential of being waitlisted by the community college's admissions office—is a significant burden that could make the for-profit school's higher tuition charge more acceptable to some students. As one for-profit student described it, "With this degree I get benefits much quicker and without distractions."[51] That is one reason students choose for-profit schools over community colleges.[52]

The third factor that determines college choice is the nature of the education experience provided. Education is not a homogenous product; it comes in myriad forms. For example, students may choose for-profit over community colleges because they prefer the fact that education offerings at for-profit colleges are more hands on and skills based—or at least they are perceived to be—and more likely to be taught by practitioners rather than academicians.[53] By contrast, many community colleges at least purport to emphasize a type of education that is broader and more focused on the inherent value of education than on particular skill sets. In the words of one community college administrator, "[Our college] is more suited to allow students to participate in the exploration process of education rather than getting locked into a program before they have a chance to really know what they want. [Our college] provides students with options, not simply a job."[54] We offer no opinion as to which of the two education approaches is better; that choice, after all, is up to individual students. However, given the significant differences that can exist across education programs, if even some students are more likely to succeed in the types of programs offered by for-profit colleges, eliminating those programs has the potential for significant downside risk. Can there be a compelling argument in favor of limiting variety in pedagogical aims and approaches?

Entwined with questions of quality are questions of adaptability to the needs and wants of student populations. For-profit colleges may find adapting to the changing needs of their students easier thanks to their greater distance from state education bureaucracies. One study found that although the curriculum at a for-profit technical college was determined centrally, curriculum changes still could be adopted more rapidly than at community colleges, which often require a multistage approval process extending all the way to the state's department of higher education.[55] The same study observed that although requirements for teaching at community colleges and for-profit colleges are similar, for-profit colleges are able to hire and fire teachers much more quickly than are community colleges, which often follow the same shared faculty governance model as their four-year counterparts.[56] That greater flexibility is another reason to expect more experimentation and more rapid adjustment to the type of education that proves most effective for current and future groups of students.

The fourth and final distinction that emerges regularly between for-profit and community colleges is that tuition charges at for-profit colleges often are significantly higher for otherwise equivalent programs—although perhaps only nominally so, given the above description of programmatic differences—than at community colleges. Students who do opt to attend community college often emphasize the lower price tag as the primary driver behind their decision.[57] That suggests, at the very least, that people face a range of tradeoffs when choosing to pursue higher education. Some students might value the low sticker prices of community colleges, whereas others may value the convenience and completion speed of for-profit colleges.[58] That, again, suggests that preserving a range of options will be beneficial rather than attempting to shift the full for-profit student population into community colleges.

A final question worth addressing in this comparison is whether it is demonstrably true that for-profit colleges are less ethical and more likely to be predatory in their pursuit of students.[59] Fortunately, Iloh and

Tierney supplement the literature on this issue with a "mystery shopper" study that compares five for-profit and five community colleges from the same city.[60] What the authors found was that it took multiple attempts to reach representatives at the community colleges, none of whom asked about who was calling, and four of five responded to questions by referring the caller to the school's website. Only one representative stayed on the phone even long enough to hear the prospective student's questions about graduates' job placement rates. The for-profit colleges were significantly more responsive, with a single representative answering all the caller's questions. Four of five for-profit representatives answered on the first ring, and three of five representatives asked more questions of the prospective student than she asked of them. For-profit college representatives did not answer questions about job placement with specific data; however, those data were not made available by the community colleges either.[61] That evidence suggests that individuals concerned about people enrolling in education programs with insufficient information may be wise to direct their concern toward community colleges rather than for-profit colleges.

The bottom line is that it is far from obvious that the admissions officers of for-profit colleges have a stronger incentive to "take advantage" of potential students than do the admissions officers of community colleges. Community colleges, in fact, may seek to "increase enrollments by accepting students who have little chance of success, since FTE [full-time equivalent] enrollments generate tuition, state, and sometimes local revenue."[62] That effect may be exacerbated by state funding of community colleges, which makes it easier for them to survive irrespective of the reputations of their courses and graduates.

Regulation in the For-Profit Market

A related question of importance is what effect regulation of the for-profit sector has had, or will have, on the sector's positive aspects, such as its flexibility and responsiveness to student demands. The previous section leads to the conclusion that many students prefer the for-profit option, but there may still be room for improvement. If improvements could be brought about by regulation, further public controls on for-profit colleges might be desirable. However, the history of regulation in that sector suggests that further regulatory efforts are likely to do more harm than good.

The primary way for-profit colleges interact with the regulatory apparatus is through federally subsidized student loan and grant programs. Many for-profit colleges are Title IV–eligible, meaning that they meet the requirements established by ED regarding where students spend the grant and loan monies they are awarded. An eligible institution may receive up to 90 percent of its income from Title IV programs, and many for-profit colleges take advantage of that opportunity.[63] In 2010, for-profit colleges received 79.21 percent of their revenue from various Title IV programs—a figure that does not include any benefits provided by the Department of Defense or the Department of Veterans Affairs.[64] Pell grants in particular often wind up in the coffers of for-profit colleges. The fraction of Pell grants going to for-profit colleges increased from 13 percent in 1999 to 25 percent in 2009 despite the fact that only 10 percent of students are enrolled in programs at for-profit institutions.[65]

Another source of government funding that often subsidizes for-profit college enrollments is veterans' benefits. A study of the 20 major for-profit colleges that provided data to the Senate's HELP Committee (30 were contacted) found that they received 683 percent more funding from the Department of Veterans Affairs and the Department of Defense in 2010 than they had in 2006.[66] That dramatic increase is explained in part by the expansion of veterans' benefits authorized by the amended post-9/11 Veterans Educational Assistance Act, which was first implemented in 2009.[67] Those funds do not count toward 90/10 rule compliance, which mandates a 90 percent revenue ceiling that a college or university is permitted to reach with its Title IV programs.[68] As such, the law opens a loophole for colleges and universities, allowing them to receive up to 100 percent of their revenue from various federal sources.

Evidence is mounting that the widespread taxpayer-financed subsidization of higher education through student aid and loan programs is driving up the cost of postsecondary education. In other words, colleges and universities are raising tuition to capture state and federal funds intended to defray students' costs. To the extent that it is true, federal higher education spending makes college more expensive rather than more affordable.[69] One study designed to test the hypothesis of whether postsecondary schools are capturing federal education funds compares tuition charged by Title IV–eligible for-profit institutions to tuition charged for similar programs at Title IV–*ineligible* for-profit institutions. The authors estimated that Title IV–eligible institutions charge students an estimated 78 percent more than do similar institutions that do not receive Title IV funds.[70] That finding suggests not only that those federal programs enable colleges and universities to increase tuition beyond what an unsubsidized market would support, thereby making college less affordable, but that the size of that effect is potentially quite large. Not enough Title IV–ineligible nonprofit institutions exist to conduct a study that looks specifically at nonprofit colleges and universities. However, a number of studies of nonprofit education institutions find significant tuition increases in response to changes in federal grant programs or increases in student loan caps, which suggests that the finding is generalizable.[71]

A major regulation that newly affects for-profit colleges is the so-called gainful employment rule. The original Higher Education Act of 1965 defined a proprietary—or, for-profit—institution of higher education as one that "provides an eligible program of training to prepare students for gainful employment in a recognized occupation."[72] However, the requirement that an institution's graduates be employed gainfully never was meaningfully enforced. In an effort to ensure that Title IV funds going to for-profit colleges are not spent in pursuit of unproductive degrees, ED announced the gainful employment rule in June 2011.[73] ED took several years to come to agreement over the specifics of the regulation, but an announcement eventually was made that for-profit institutions of higher education would be required to demonstrate their compliance as of July 1, 2015. An institution would get a "pass" if its graduates have annual loan payments that are less than 8 percent of their total earnings or 20 percent of discretionary earnings.

It would be in the "zone," as ED describes this category, if its graduates have annual loan payments between 8 percent and 12 percent of total earnings, or between 20 percent and 30 percent of discretionary earnings. And it would fail to meet the gainful employment standard if its graduates have annual loan payments exceeding 12 percent of total earnings or 30 percent of discretionary earnings. An institution would become ineligible for Title IV funds once it fails in any two out of three years or if it remains in the zone for four consecutive years.[74] When the gainful employment rule was initially announced, ED anticipated that 193 of the 3,695 programs falling under the purview of the new rule would be declared ineligible for Title IV funding moving forward.[75] Under the rule's 2015 formulation, ED estimates that "about 1,400 programs serving 840,000 students—of whom 99 percent are at for-profit institutions—would not pass the accountability standards."[76]

Although it is not yet clear whether the Trump administration will follow through on enforcing the rule, its treatment under the Obama administration highlights an inconsistency between the rhetoric surrounding education and actual education policy.[77] President Barack Obama argued that community college tuition should be fully subsidized because "[w]e can't afford to let striving Americans be priced out of the education they need to get ahead."[78] Senator Bernie Sanders of Vermont has proposed that all four-year colleges be tuition free so as not to bar admission to those who cannot afford the charges, and former secretary of state Hillary Clinton announced on the campaign trail for the Democratic Party's 2016 presidential nomination that she wanted to spend $350 billion over the next 10 years to ensure that no student leaves a public institution of higher learning burdened by loan debt.[79] If the goals of Title IV and other possible new federal programs are to make it easier for marginal students to pursue education opportunities, then pulling loan and grant money from only those programs that are disproportionately likely to serve marginal (and often marginalized) students is counterproductive. In addition, when the quantity of available, career-focused education programs is restricted, the predictable response of those institutions that remain in business—which then will have more students competing to get through their doors—will be to raise tuition even higher. Instead of more education at a lower cost, we would get less education at a higher cost.

For-profit colleges also are subject to regulatory oversight designed to establish and maintain quality standards. In the early 1990s, the Senate Permanent Subcommittee on Investigations found that state governments and accreditation agencies had failed to adequately oversee quality and maintain standards.[80] The result was that during the reauthorization of the Higher Education Act of 1992, the regulatory oversight authority of ED, state governments, and accreditation agencies was expanded.[81] That policy change was consistent with the idea that bureaucrats who specialize in regulation—such as those at ED—tend to find regulatory solutions to problems rather than to cede power voluntarily.[82] Mark L. Pelesh, writing during the time he was serving as executive vice president for legislative and regulatory affairs at Corinthian Colleges, Inc., pointed out the following:

> With the [Higher Education Act] student aid programs representing almost one-quarter of annual postsecondary revenues (not to mention additional substantial funding coming from public research grants and state appropriations to public institutions) it would be unrealistic to expect that government would, or could ever, choose to deregulate and allow competition among institutions . . . in fact, *none of the participants in the regulatory system would seriously consider arguing for such an approach* [emphasis added].[83]

One possible reason why an industry would vigorously oppose its own deregulation is that it has engaged in regulatory capture. For-profit colleges are a small, well-defined group of firms that stand to gain extraordinary benefits from regulation—exactly the type of industry that would be expected to be successful at capturing regulators.[84] The theory of regulatory capture can be interpreted in two general ways: (a) the broad interpretation that refers to any special interest that succeeds in influencing regulators or (b) the narrow interpretation that refers to a regulated monopoly that winds up influencing the individuals who were supposed to constrain it.[85] Both definitions seem to apply to today's system of higher education regulation.

Because of the contradictory interests existing within the higher education industry, the outcome of rent seeking has at various times helped or hurt the for-profit firms and, as a corollary, their competitors. The obvious boon was the initial 2005 rule change that permitted institutions to offer more than 50 percent of their classes online and still be eligible for receipt of Title IV funds.[86] As discussed in the section on the effect of regulation, for-profit institutions have been disproportionately successful in capturing those rents. On the other hand, regulation also has offered ways for the public and nonprofit higher education systems to insulate themselves from competition from the for-profit sector. Nonprofit institutions lobbied in favor of the 90/10 rule to place some limit on for-profits' receipt of federal funds, and they lobbied against a prospective amendment to the Higher Education Act that would have prevented public and private nonprofit institutions from refusing to consider transfer credits from for-profit colleges.[87]

Lobbying groups that represent various contingents in the nonprofit education industry also provided support for the initial gainful employment rule, which places additional regulatory burdens on the shorter, career-focused programs in which for-profit schools often specialize.[88] The interest that a public or nonprofit competitor would have in shutting down for-profit programs that offer courses similar to their own is obvious—the public or nonprofit schools get more students and, potentially, can even begin to charge more per student. More recently, however, those same lobbies have opposed the final version of the gainful employment rule. Twenty-seven major education lobbies—with the notable exception of the Association of Private Sector Colleges and Universities—lobbied against the regulation on the following grounds:

> In recent years the sheer volume, ineffectiveness, and cost of the regulations and related actions promulgated or proposed by the Department of Education have far exceeded what might reasonably be required for these purposes. While we share many of the Department's stated goals, and have made repeated efforts to inform and improve their regulatory approaches, the agency has been unable or unwilling to address our concerns. . . . We are alarmed that the two pending administrative actions under consideration by the Department—the college ratings

> system and a federalized teacher preparation program accountability system—will be similarly burdensome with no public benefit.[89]

In other words, those lobbyists' concern has nothing to do with harm to either the providers or the consumers of for-profit education. Rather, the lobby is taking action that is explicitly intended to forestall the adoption of additional regulation inimical to its own interests. So again, the higher education industry marshals political influence to shape the way in which it is overseen.

Conclusion

The modern higher education system is subsidized heavily and subject to regulatory oversight in ways that drive up the cost of tuition, benefiting colleges and universities of all types at the expense of students and taxpayers.[90] Introducing competition into higher education often is suggested as a means of disciplining the providers of higher education and making it more difficult for them to get away with capturing federal subsidies designed to reduce rather than increase students' costs. The profit motive is not inconsistent with the goals of higher education. Rather, a more competitive postsecondary education system, in which educators could profit by providing high-quality education, would create incentives highly compatible with the aims of the supporters of publicly financed education subsidies.[91]

However, for-profit education as it exists today does not much resemble a competitive market, and the profit motive as it currently operates encourages investment in rent seeking rather than investment in education. The extent to which the industry is subsidized by Title IV and other federal and state funding programs instead keeps for-profit providers more beholden to legislators and regulators than to students. Rather than being an alternative to the publicly funded higher education system influenced by special interest groups, for-profit colleges are deeply entangled within that system. Moreover, for-profit colleges are often at risk because of their status as the weakest sheep in the higher education herd. Consequently, regulatory capture within the higher education industry often targets the for-profit industry for the sake of securing more monopoly rents for the traditional public and private nonprofit institutions of higher learning. Rent seeking diverts federal subsidies from less wealthy and talented students to more wealthy and talented students, potentially reducing education options for the traditionally underserved populations that are the bread and butter of the for-profit higher education industry. The likely consequence of the nature of industries captured by the regulatory state is that future attempts to rectify current problems will result in even more regulation.

The untested assumption behind many federal subsidies for higher education is that education develops important skills that make both the student and society better off. In addition to the costs of rising tuition and the inevitable rent seeking for shares of ever-growing federal largesse, however, the drive to make postsecondary education opportunities accessible to progressively larger numbers of students has degraded the market value of the traditional four-year baccalaureate degree. That decline in market value is in part because opening wide the doors to public institutions of higher learning means that colleges are now offering programs of study that lack the obvious traditional benefits of either a broad liberal arts education or training in a specific skill or trade. As a result, the payoff from four years of college turns out to be much less than many students expect. As of 2015, the wage premium for college graduates seemed to have stopped rising, and 9 percent of college graduates under age 25 were unemployed.[92] In the words of Wharton management professor Peter Capelli, "Looking at the actual return on the costs of attending college, careful analyses suggest that the payoff from many college programs—as much as one in four—is actually negative. Incredibly, the schools seem to add nothing to the market value of the students."[93]

Given the failures of heavily subsidized public, nonprofit institutions of higher learning, one should not be surprised that for-profit colleges have begun competing successfully for students who seek alternatives to the traditional model of postsecondary education—alternatives that (for a price) offer more tightly focused and convenient programs aimed primarily at preparing students for higher-paying jobs, especially students from less well-off households and those who have fewer and less-respectable academic credentials. Nor should it be surprising that some of those institutions prey on their customers or that the traditional higher education sector wants to protect its rents against the inroads made by for-profit rivals. Ultimately, to introduce competition over cost and quality into the higher education sector requires more student choice and a transition to a system in which the true costs of college are borne by those who are in a position to be able to evaluate whether the purchase is worthwhile—the students and their parents, not the regulators.

CHAPTER TEN

Public Policy and the Future of For-Profit Higher Education

Michael E. DeBow

The Obama administration conducted a legal and regulatory crusade against for-profit colleges and universities. Investigations were launched, large fines assessed, and lawsuits filed (and some settled) alleging, among other issues, predatory lending, deceptive advertising, and securities laws violations. Bankruptcies and reorganizations followed. In what could be a coup de grace, in late 2016 the U.S. Department of Education withdrew its recognition of the accrediting agency responsible for most for-profit colleges,[1] a decision that went under review in federal district court in Washington and was remanded back to ED.[2]

At the same time the Obama administration was turning up the heat on for-profit colleges, it was pushing a dramatic expansion of public community colleges. In a January 2015 speech, President Obama announced "America's College Promise," "an ambitious new plan to bring down the cost of community college tuition in America. . . . I want to make it free."[3] The state of Tennessee adopted a "community college for all" program in 2014.[4] By August 2017, similar programs had been adopted by several other states and the city of San Francisco.[5] In April 2017, New York State upped the ante with its Excelsior Scholarship, which conferred free tuition at four-year as well as two-year public colleges on students from families with annual earnings of $125,000 or less,[6] at a projected annual cost of $163 million.[7] Numerous other states are considering that route to expand the percentage of high school graduates who go on to postsecondary education.[8] Obviously, the push for "free college" also poses a significant threat to the continued existence of for-profit colleges.

All of this raises the question: Should the for-profit college have any role in American higher education? In this chapter, I attempt to clarify the debate by considering both the costs and the benefits of for-profit colleges. My conclusion is that if ever-higher enrollment in higher education remains one of the goals of American public policy, then federal and state government officials would be unwise to seek to eradicate the for-profit sector of the higher education industry.[9]

The discussion that follows is quite timely. A new presidential administration offers the opportunity for a new relationship between the federal government and for-profit colleges, as shown by the Department of Education's June 2017 announcement that it will reconsider two of the most significant regulations aimed at the for-profit sector—the "gainful employment" rule and the "defense to repayment" rule.[10] It is at least possible that the federal government may adopt a regulatory posture toward for-profit firms in higher education that will not deprive students—and taxpayers—of the benefits of that organizational form.

For-Profit Higher Education: A Brief History

The origin of the for-profit sector as we know it was the 1968 congressional reauthorization of the Higher Education Act of 1965 (HEA),[11] which made funds from the College Work-Study Program and the National Defense Student Loan Program available to students at for-profit schools for the first time.[12] The HEA reauthorization of 1972 made even more government student financial aid funds available to for-profits.[13] The HEA provides that "[p]roprietary institution[s] of higher education" (that is, for-profit schools) and "[p]ostsecondary vocational institution[s]" are only eligible for Title IV funding if they "prepare students for gainful employment in a recognized occupation."[14] (Substantial additional federal funding comes through programs providing educational benefits to military veterans and active service personnel.[15]) Since the 1998 reauthorization, the HEA has prohibited for-profit colleges from receiving more than 90 percent of their revenue from Title IV funds—the so-called 90/10 rule.[16] Clearly, the availability of federal student financial aid fueled the rapid expansion of the for-profit sector, which enjoyed enrollment growth at an annualized rate of 11 percent from 1976 to 2008.[17]

With the advantage of hindsight, one can see that 2010 stands out as the peak year for for-profit colleges. In the fall semester they accounted for 2,022,785 students, or 9.6 percent of total postsecondary enrollment.[18] The largest for-profit, the University of Phoenix, taught 470,800 students in the third quarter of 2010 and took in net revenue of $4.5 billion that year.[19]

The adversarial posture eventually adopted by the U.S. government and numerous state attorneys general toward for-profits generated significant negative publicity for those institutions, which must have contributed to the decline of the for-profit sector since 2010. In 2015, enrollment in for-profits had fallen to 1,345,795 students—or 6.7 percent of total postsecondary enrollment.[20] Continuation of that trend into 2016 was indicated by data from the University of Phoenix, where enrollment fell from 206,900 students in the third quarter of 2015 to 155,600 students in the third quarter of 2016, and net revenue declined from $2.15 billion in fiscal year 2015 to $1.63 billion in fiscal year 2016.[21]

Those enrollment and financial setbacks resulted in a significant restructuring of the for-profit sector. Apollo Group, the parent company of the University of Phoenix, was purchased by a group of investors in a going-private transaction in February 2016.[22] Two of the largest for-profits declared bankruptcy after federal lawsuits were filed against them—Corinthian Colleges in May 2015[23] and ITT Educational Services in September 2016.[24] Most recently, for-profit Education Management Corporation agreed to be acquired by the nonprofit Dream Center Foundation in March 2017,[25] and for-profit Kaplan University was purchased by nonprofit Purdue University in April 2017.[26] Myriad federal and state investigations remain ongoing.[27] At this point the future of the for-profit form of organization in higher education is in serious doubt.

The Case against For-Profit Higher Education: Federal Financial Aid

Critics argue that for-profit colleges abused the federal student financial aid system and fraudulently marketed their degree programs. Three quotations from 2015 convey the gist of that critique. Sen. Elizabeth Warren (D-MA) charged that for-profits often "leave students with huge bills for useless degrees."[28] U.S. Secretary of Education Arne Duncan attacked for-profit colleges that "take advantage of students and leave taxpayers with the bill," and bring "the ethics of payday lending into higher education."[29] Nine state attorneys general condemned "certain large, predatory for-profit schools" because they "seem to exist largely to capture federal loan dollars and aggressively market their programs to veterans and low-income Americans."[30]

Consider first the argument that for-profits have gamed the federal financial aid system. More than 90 percent of the for-profits' revenue stream comes from the federal government and that is a higher percentage than that received by any other sector of the higher education industry. (Since 2010, all Title IV loans have been made directly by the U.S. Department of Education rather than through banks and other private lenders, a policy change that resulted in the government borrowing more than $1 trillion to fund student loans during the past eight years.[31]) During the 2009–10 academic year, federal student loans and grants flowing to for-profit institutions constituted more than 20 percent of the total aid extended under Title IV,[32] although enrollment in for-profits constituted only about 10 percent of the whole.[33] Critics have cited that statistic many times.

In addition to the for-profits taking more than a proportional share of federal student aid, critics point to the higher student loan default rate among their graduates. Recent data are shown in Table 10.1, with the category "Public" including both two-year and four-year institutions.

A question arises: Should we be surprised that the for-profit default rate is higher than that for nonprofits? If the students who attend for-profit colleges tend to have poorer educational backgrounds and face greater personal challenges than students who attend nonprofit colleges, then

Table 10.1

Three-Year Cohort Default Rates, by Sector

Fiscal year in which borrowers entered repayment	Type of institution from which borrowers graduated	Default rate (%)
2013	Private nonprofit	7
	Public	11.3
	For-profit	15
2012	Private nonprofit	6.8
	Public	11.7
	For-profit	15.8
2011	Private nonprofit	7.2
	Public	12.9
	For-profit	19.1

Source: "Official Cohort Default Rates for Schools," U.S. Department of Education, September 28, 2016, https://www2.ed.gov/offices/OSFAP/defaultmanagement/cdr.html and https://www2.ed.gov/offices/OSFAP/defaultmanagement/schooltyperates.pdf.

perhaps they face greater obstacles to financial success upon graduation and thus a greater risk of default on their loans. In that case, estimating what the for-profit default rate "should be" as compared with, say, graduates of public colleges and universities is a difficult proposition. That point, however, did not restrain critics of the for-profit sector from searching for regulatory solutions to the perceived problem.

In that vein, congressional Democrats introduced legislation to tighten the "90/10 Rule" by including veterans and military benefits in the amount capped, but those bills failed.[34] Those legislators also encouraged the Department of Education to take steps to include veterans and military financial aid, but ultimately that failed as well.

Nevertheless, the department has formidable powers with respect to financial aid issues, including the authority to set standards by which it can withhold Title IV funds from underperforming colleges and universities. Its primary sanction is framed by loan default rates.

Any institution of higher education loses its eligibility for federal student aid if its graduates' default rate on their federal loans—measured by the three-year cohort default rate—exceeds 25 percent for three consecutive years or is 40 percent or more in any one year.[35]

Recall also that the HEA makes Title IV funds available to "proprietary institution[s] of higher education" and "postsecondary vocational institution[s]" only if they "prepare students for gainful employment in a recognized occupation." In 2009 the department began work on a definition of "gainful employment" to be applied to for-profit and vocational institutions. The gainful employment rule (or GE rule) was plagued with bureaucratic delays and was successfully challenged in court by the for-profits' principal trade association,[36] which delayed its effective date until July 1, 2015.[37] A fact sheet released by the department on the effective date explains the rule and its intended effects:

> Under the new regulations, a program would be considered to lead to gainful employment if the estimated annual loan payment of a typical graduate does not exceed 20 percent of his or her discretionary income—what is left after basic necessities like food and housing have been paid for—or 8 percent of his or her total earnings. Programs that exceed these levels would be at risk of losing their ability to participate in taxpayer-funded federal student aid programs. Today, gainful employment programs will start to be held accountable to these outcomes, and the worst performing programs will lose eligibility for federal Title IV student aid if they do not improve. In addition, failing programs that may present a risk to students if they lose eligibility will have to start notifying students.
>
> *Based on available data, the Department estimates that about 1,400 programs serving 840,000 students—of whom 99 percent are at for-profit institutions—would not pass the accountability standards.* All programs will have the opportunity to make immediate changes that could help them avoid sanctions, but if programs do not make these changes, they will ultimately become ineligible for federal student aid—which often makes up nearly 90 percent of the revenue at for-profit institutions.[38] [emphasis added]

Although the GE rule became effective in 2015, questions of implementation remained to be worked out. The process was not completed before the end of the Obama administration, and President Donald

Trump's secretary of education, Betsy DeVos, expressed reservations about the GE rule. The upshot was the announcement in June 2017 that the department would begin a "negotiated rulemaking" process to rewrite the GE rule, followed by an extension of time for covered schools to come into compliance with the GE rule (as it currently exists) from July 1, 2017, to July 1, 2018.[39] Stated an article in the *Chronicle of Higher Education*, "The department said it anticipated that a committee would begin negotiations to rework the gainful-employment rule in November or December of this year, meaning a revised rule could not take effect until July 2019."[40]

The Case against For-Profit Higher Education: Dodgy Marketing

Critics roundly denounce the marketing efforts of for-profits, casting them as misleading and fraudulent. The earliest instance of an agency of the federal government bringing suit on a consumer-protection theory occurred in 2011, when the U.S. Department of Justice joined a False Claims Act case against nonprofit Education Management Corporation (EDMC).[41] The suit was originally filed in 2007 by former EDMC employees, who alleged that the company had falsely certified its compliance with a federal statute that prohibits a college from paying incentive-based compensation to its admissions recruiters. According to the U.S. attorney involved, the suit sought recovery of "a portion of the $11 billion in federal student aid which EDMC allegedly obtained through false statements."[42] EDMC settled the case in November 2015 for $95.5 million and simultaneously agreed to a conduct-oriented settlement with 39 state attorneys general.[43] In March 2017 EDMC announced it would cease to be a for-profit firm once its purchase by the Dream Center Foundation closed in the summer of 2017.[44]

In the latter days of the Obama administration, three more major federal lawsuits were filed against for-profit colleges on consumer-protection grounds. The Consumer Financial Protection Bureau (CFPB) filed two suits in 2014: one against ITT Educational Services in February and the other against Corinthian Colleges in September (ITT was also sued by the Securities Exchange Commission in May 2015[45]). Under pressure from those and other suits and investigations, both ITT and Corinthian[46] filed for bankruptcy protection, as noted earlier. In January 2016 the Federal Trade Commission sued DeVry University.[47] DeVry settled the matter for $100 million in December 2016[48] and is still in operation.

The saga of Corinthian Colleges Inc. provides a good case study. This section goes into the federal government's actions against the company in some detail so that the reader may decide whether Corinthian deserved the corporate equivalent of the death penalty.

In 2014, Corinthian was the fourth-largest firm in the for-profit sector, with approximately 70,000 students enrolled at its Everest College, WyoTech, Heald College, and other campuses. In January of that year, the Department of Education asked Corinthian to supply additional information concerning the job placement rates of its campuses during the 2010–2013 period, pursuant to the reporting requirements of 34 C.F.R. § 668.41. Corinthian responded but did not assuage the department's concerns. In June 2014 the department placed Corinthian on "an increased level of financial oversight after the company failed to address concerns about its practices, including falsifying job placement data used in marketing claims to prospective students and allegations of altered grades and attendance."[49]

In the face of the strong position taken by the department, Corinthian agreed to a settlement in July, committing to liquidate itself by "sell[ing] or clos[ing] its campuses across the country in the next six months."[50] The single largest sale—more than half of Corinthian's campuses—was to Educational Credit Management Corporation.

As Corinthian was in the process of selling all of its assets, on September 16, 2014, the CFPB sued the company in the U.S. District Court for the Northern District of Illinois.[51] The complaint contained five counts—two under the Consumer Financial Protection Act and three under the Fair Debt Collection Practices Act.

Many for-profit colleges make loans to their students to comply with the 90/10 rule. In doing so they become "covered persons" under the Consumer Financial Protection Act, which makes it unlawful for a covered person "to engage in any unfair, deceptive, or abusive act or practice."[52] An odd detail is that the act defines "unfair" and "abusive" but not "deceptive." An act or practice is unfair if "(A) the act or practice causes or is likely to cause substantial injury to consumers which is not reasonably avoidable by consumers; and (B) such substantial injury is not outweighed by countervailing benefits to consumers or competition."[53] Responding to the absence of a statutory definition of "deceptive," the CFPB has explained that it will act according to a three-part test: "For an act or practice to be deceptive, it must mislead or be likely to mislead the consumer, it must be material, and the consumer's interpretation of the act or practice must be reasonable."[54]

One count of the CFPB's complaint against Corinthian accused it of "deceptive" acts or practices; the other, "unfair" acts or practices. The CFPB press release at the time of the filing described its case against Corinthian as follows:

- "Corinthian inflated the job placement rates at its schools. Based on its investigation, the CFPB alleges that this included creating fictitious employers and reporting students as being placed at those fake employers."
- "Corinthian counted a 'career' as a job that merely lasted one day, with the promise of a second day."
- Corinthian schools secretly "inflated advertised job placement rates by paying employers to hire graduates on a temporary basis."
- Corinthian "promised students extensive and lasting career services that were not delivered. Students often had trouble contacting anyone in the career services office or getting any meaningful support. The limited career services included distributing generally available job postings from websites like Craigslist."
- "Corinthian sold its students predatory loans that typically had substantially higher interest rates than federal loans. In July 2011, the Genesis loan interest rate was about 15 percent, with an origination fee of 6 percent. Meanwhile, the interest rate for federal student loans during that time was about 3 percent to 7 percent, with low or no origination fees."
- "Corinthian expected that most of its students would ultimately default on their Genesis loans. In fact, more than 60 percent of Corinthian school students defaulted on their loans within

> 3 years. The Everest, Heald, and WyoTech schools did not tell students about these high default rates."[55]

Notice that the first four bullet points cover the same subject—the firm's placement record, then under investigation by the Department of Education. The only difference is that the CFPB's condemnation extends beyond Heald to other Corinthian colleges. The only entirely new allegations involve Corinthian's allegedly predatory lending. Thus a large portion of the CFPB's case duplicated the Department of Education's investigation and possible lawsuit.

The complaint asked for eight forms of relief: (a) permanent injunction against future violations; (b) a declaration "that Corinthian engaged in deceptive conduct that induced its students to take out private student loans"; (c) payment of restitution and damages to an unspecified group of "consumers harmed by their unlawful conduct;" (d) disgorgement; (e) rescission of all private loans made by Corinthian after July 21, 2011; (f) civil money penalties; (g) plaintiff's costs; and (h) "such other and additional relief as the Court may determine to be just and proper."

Seven months later, on April 14, 2015, the Department of Education fined Corinthian $29.6 million for the "misrepresentation of job placement rates" by officials of one of Corinthian's operations, Heald College.[56] The department arrived at that amount by looking at a total of 947 claimed placement reporting violations over a three- to four-year period, 2010–2014. The department found three major faults with Corinthian/Heald's performance, according to the notice of intent to fine Corinthian.

First, the department found that Heald's "placement rate disclosures omitted essential and material information concerning the methodology Heald used to calculate the rates." The department noted six specific shortcomings:

- Heald "failed to disclose in its 2013/2014 web-based disclosures that its placement rates excluded students it classified as having deferred employment."
- Heald "falsely represented in its 2013/2014 web-based disclosures that its placement rates were supported by attestations."

- Heald "failed in all of its placement rate disclosures to identify with specificity the cohort whose results were being reported."
- Heald "failed in all of its placement disclosures to state that it counted as placed graduates whose employment began prior to graduation, and in some cases even prior to the graduate's attendance at Heald."
- Heald "paid temporary agencies to hire its graduates to work at unsustainable temporary jobs at its own campuses and counted these graduates as placed."
- Heald "counted placements that were clearly out of the student's field as in-field placements in its placement statistics."

Unfortunately, the department does not provide much data to help assess the frequency or the materiality of those shortcomings. One exception is the observation that in the reported placement data for 2012 graduates, "over one-third (33.8%) of the graduates reported to have been 'placed in the field' started their jobs prior to January 1, 2012, and over one-quarter (25.5%) started their jobs prior to January 1, 2011." More systemwide information like that would be helpful in gauging the strength of the department's case; instead, the illustrations tend toward the anecdotal. Thus, the "temporary jobs" point is supported by reference to a single program at a single campus in a single year.[57]

Second, the department determined that Heald's Stockton, California, campus misrepresented the placement rate of its medical assisting program to its accrediting agency. The agency's minimum placement rate for accreditation was 60 percent. Heald Stockton reported a 78.27 percent placement rate; the department recalculation found that the actual placement rate was only 32.7 percent.

Third, the backup documentation used by Corinthian and Heald to support claimed placement rates often was flawed and incomplete, "missing key fields" such as the level of a student's program of study, and containing "numerous duplicates."[58] The department readjusted the placement rates downward to reflect only valid backup documentation and provided the readjusted rates in a chart that compared 23 reported rates with the corresponding adjusted rates.

The maximum fine the department could assess for violations that occurred before October 2, 2012, was $27,500 per violation. For violations after that date, the maximum became $35,000 per violation. The department treated every individual program report as a separate violation and imposed the maximum fine on all of them. Thus, $35,000 on each of 483 violations plus $27,500 on each of 464 violations produced a total fine of $29,665,000. The department concluded that Heald's "substantial misrepresentations" constituted "a blatant disregard for the [relevant] statutes and regulations." The department explained its choice of the maximum possible fine by stating that "the violations involved in this case are severe, and the potential harm to the government and to students is also severe."

After the fine was announced, Secretary of Education Arne Duncan released a statement that said, in part, "This should be a wake-up call for consumers across the country about the abuses that can exist within the for-profit college sector. We will continue to hold the career-college industry accountable and demand reform for the good of students and taxpayers."[59]

On April 27, 2015, the company ceased virtually all operations, affecting approximately 16,000 students who were enrolled at its 28 remaining campuses.[60] Corinthian's CEO blamed "the current regulatory environment" for not "allow[ing] us to complete a transaction with several interested parties that would have allowed for a seamless transition for our students."[61]

On May 4, 2015, Corinthian filed for chapter 11 bankruptcy protection, listing assets of less than $20 million against debts of $143 million.[62] Responding to news of Corinthian's bankruptcy, Undersecretary of Education Ted Mitchell issued a statement that began, "Students seeking better life options *should be assured that their investments will pay off* in increased knowledge, skills, and opportunity" [emphasis added].[63] Sen. Richard Durbin (D-IL) said that the company was "the canary in the coal mine for the for-profit college industry."[64] In the same vein, Duncan predicted that Corinthian "will not be the last domino to fall" and that "[t]his is our first major action on this but obviously it won't be the last."[65] As it turned out, Durbin and Duncan were right.

It apparently remains an open question whether the Department of Education realized how fragile Corinthian was. Mark Schneider of the group College Measures and Jorge Klor de Alva from the Nexus Research and Policy Center found the following:

> Among the more disturbing reports around the Department of Education's approach to Corinthian are the conflicting accounts of what officials knew regarding Corinthian's finances when they froze federal funds to the school. The Department claims it was unaware that its actions would have the effect of shutting down the school, while other reports make clear officials within the Department were fully aware of the shaky nature of Corinthian's finances. So either the Department inadvertently displaced 70,000 students without a plan for how to handle them, or it took actions knowing full well that a system incapable of absorbing these students would be their only recourse.[66]

After Corinthian filed for bankruptcy, the Department of Education decided to forgive the loans of all Corinthian students of record as of June 20, 2014. By one estimate, that included 15,000 students who owed $200 million in government student loans.[67] In addition, the department forgave loans to former students of Heald College, some 40,000 borrowers with about $544 million in federal loans.[68] The department also entertained petitions from students of other Corinthian colleges who applied for loan forgiveness "if they believ[ed] they were defrauded by their college under state law."[69] Those students' pleas for debt relief were heard by a "special master." As of October 2016 the department had "granted more than 15,000 claims for forgiveness—which, taken together, amount to more than $247 million in relief." It had received 7,815 "closed school claims" for loan forgiveness from more than 15,000 former Corinthian students "representing an estimated $247 million in loans."[70] Perhaps inevitably, there was criticism of the department's debt forgiveness as insufficiently generous.[71] By mid-January 2017, the department "had approved more than 28,000 applications for relief from former [Corinthian] students . . . amounting to more than $558 million in relief."[72] One estimate put the likely eventual cost to taxpayers at $3.5 billion.[73]

Assuming the veracity of Corinthian's bankruptcy filing, the Department of Education's fine amounted to about 150 percent of its assets. Government officials should take the Corinthian story as a cautionary tale: any plan to fund student loan forgiveness or other relief with the proceeds of fines and settlement extracted from for-profit colleges is likely to meet with only very limited success.

Should taxpayers applaud these federal prosecutions as tough-minded policing of the public treasury? It is certainly possible to look at the Corinthian Colleges story and conclude that the company was a bad actor. Even so, the question remains of the appropriate remedy, and in answering that question the rhetoric of prosecution is not very helpful. Prosecutors want to make a defendant's actions sound as contemptible as possible. Listening to the rhetoric used by some enforcement officials about for-profit college defendants, a casual observer might conclude that all students of a particular defendant were misled by it and subsequently harmed. To take just one example, consider again the CFPB's prayer for a declaratory judgment that "Corinthian engaged in deceptive conduct that induced its students to take out private student loans." One reading of that statement is that all Corinthian students were misled and acted on the basis of the misrepresentation. Student ignorance of the placement reports and other possible student reactions to them, for example, are completely ignored. It does not get any more sweeping than this: all the defendant's students were victimized, and the government must vindicate their injury.

To take another example: recall that much of the CFPB's case against Corinthian focused on its misrepresentation of job placement rates. CFPB alleged that at one Corinthian location in Georgia, its employees' misrepresentations "increas[ed] placement rates by as much as 37% per program on reports that Corinthian gave to accreditors in 2009 and 2010." Similarly, a Florida campus allegedly inflated its campuswide placement rate by 6.6 percent in a report to its accreditor. The reader might wonder how many of the Georgia locations had discrepancies that were less than 37 percent and also how important a 6.6 percent discrepancy might be to potential students. Such questions may weigh on investigators, but prosecutors are not prone to doubt. The bad guy had been identified and must be punished.

In October 2016 the Department of Education adopted a new set of "borrower defense rules" that had been slated to go into effect on July 1, 2017, and that was applicable to all educational institutions receiving Title IV funds.[74] The department's summary of the lengthy rule asserted that "the regulations replace a complicated, uneven, and burdensome standard for assessing claims that is based on the application of various State laws with a new Federal standard that will make relief available when there is:

- A breach of contractual promises between a school and its students;
- State or Federal court judgments against a school related to the loan or the educational services for which the loan was made; or
- A substantial misrepresentation by the school about the nature of the educational program, the nature of financial charges, or the employability of graduates."[75]

The new rules were criticized as confusing and burdensome by some nonprofit as well as for-profit colleges. In June 2017 the department announced it would delay the effective date of the borrower defense rules by one year and begin a "negotiated rulemaking" process to rewrite the rules.[76] Nineteen state attorneys general have sued to block the department's reconsideration of the rules.[77]

The Case in Favor of For-Profit Higher Education

In view of the criticism of for-profits, some may be surprised that the performance of for-profit colleges has significant positive aspects. Of course, if the power of the profit motive is kept in mind, the positive side of for-profit colleges should not come as a surprise. Instead, the private sector's superiority over the public sector in terms of efficiency[78]—surely one of the clearest lessons of the 20th century—gives for-profit colleges quite a head start in justifying their existence.

For-profits' efficiency-generating attributes were noted in an article titled "For-Profit Colleges Change Higher Education's Landscape," which appeared in the *Chronicle of Higher Education* in February 2010.[79] As its subtitle suggests, "nimble companies gain a fast-growing share of enrollments." The article showed for-profits as responsive to the needs of their target market—particularly adults working full-time jobs—and consciously innovative as to online teaching, staffing, and other operational details. Criticism of for-profits was mentioned, but it was not emphasized.

Another 2010 study, published by the Center for College Affordability and Productivity, expanded upon the operational strengths of for-profit colleges compared with traditional campuses:

- "They generally do not have fixed costs in a tenured faculty" and so can add or subtract teachers faster than can traditional campuses.
- "[T]hey do not follow the shared governance model common in most of higher education" and thus make decisions more quickly and without encountering opposition from entrenched interests on campus.[80]

A 2012 article by three Harvard economists published in the prestigious *Journal of Economic Perspectives* was similarly positive on balance. The authors—David Deming, Claudia Goldin, and Lawrence Katz—reported that "the vast majority of students from for-profits express satisfaction with their course of study and programs" and "for many, the for-profits have been a success."[81] Deming and his colleagues also praised the sector's "Responsiveness to Markets" in a section that deserves to be quoted at length:

> For-profits cater to the expanding market of nontraditional students, develop curriculum and teaching practices to be able to provide identical programs at multiple locations and at convenient times, and offer highly-structured programs to make timely completion feasible. For-profits are attuned to the marketplace and are quick to open new schools, hire new faculty, and add programs in growing fields and localities. . . . For-profits are less encumbered than public and non-profit schools by physical plant, alumni, and tenured faculty.[82]

The authors highlighted for-profits' provision of new, high-demand programs in health care occupations.[83]

Another area in which for-profits proved quite innovative is the marketing of their programs, identifying likely "customers" and tailoring sales efforts effectively to attract their patronage. For-profits engage in much more extensive marketing efforts than do traditional nonprofit colleges, and that kind of outreach is expensive. For example, in fiscal 2009, the University of Phoenix's parent corporation "spent nearly 33% of its total budget on selling and promotional activities."[84]

The for-profits' high levels of spending on advertising and marketing have many critics, who see it as mostly misleading and manipulative. For example, Sen. Sherrod Brown (D-OH) alleged that in 2009 the for-profit sector "spent 23% of their budgets" in that way, compared with only "one-half of one percent" of the budget of traditional colleges. In response, Brown introduced a bill to prohibit the use of funds received through federal student aid programs "for advertising, marketing, and recruitment."[85] One might think that the enormous difficulties in the rollout of the Affordable Care Act would make politicians somewhat careful in criticizing others' efforts to inform target audiences of the availability of a government entitlement program. However, the for-profits' critics are not so deterred.

At any rate, there is no denying that the for-profits' marketing efforts were quite effective—for a time. One particular achievement of the for-profits is that they reach people who most likely would not have enrolled in a postsecondary institution at all had they not enrolled at a for-profit. As a result, the students attracted by the for-profits' marketing efforts differ significantly from the student bodies of both public and private nonprofit colleges and universities. In a 2015 letter to the under secretary of education, the primary trade group for the for-profit sector (American Private Sector Colleges and Universities, or APSCU) described those differences as follows:[86]

Higher percentage of minority students: 52 percent vs. Public 42 percent, Private nonprofit 35 percent

Higher percentage 25 years or older: 63 percent vs. Public 37 percent, Private nonprofit 26 percent

Higher percentage employed full-time: 35 percent vs. Public 26 percent, Private nonprofit 17 percent

Higher percentage studying online: 46 percent vs. Public 8 percent, Private nonprofit 10 percent

In other words, for-profits enroll a higher percentage of "nontraditional" students than do other kinds of institutions, including community colleges. Deming and his colleagues compared students in for-profit institutions in 2003–04 with community college students and found that "for-profit students are disproportionately single parents, have much lower family incomes, and are almost twice as likely to have a General Equivalency Degree (GED)."[87]

The bottom line is that the for-profits succeeded in attracting and educating the very students whom politicians and others say they wish to encourage to attend college in greater numbers. Moreover, it seems that the for-profits were able to do that at a lower cost than were more traditional, nonprofit colleges, for two reasons. First, for-profits do not receive direct legislative appropriations, as public nonprofits do. Also, for-profits pay taxes, whereas nonprofits do not. A recent study of public expenditures on higher education in California, New York, Ohio, and Texas during the academic years 2007–08 through 2011–12 attempted to quantify those differences.[88] The authors, Jorge Klor de Alva and Mark Schneider, concluded that for-profits saved taxpayers in those states a total of $8.4 billion if one assumes that all the for-profits' students would have otherwise enrolled in public, taxpayer-subsidized, two- or four-year colleges.[89] The authors expanded their analysis to include the entire country:

> According to federal data, on average, over the last five years, there were approximately 2.9 million full-time equivalent students enrolled in four-year [for-profit] colleges in the United States. If these students were in public four-year colleges, the nation would have had to find nearly $19 billion in state subsidies. Additionally, around 1.7 million full-time equivalent students were enrolled in [for-profit] two-year institutions. If they were enrolled in community colleges, taxpayers would have been on the hook for an additional $9 billion—a total of $28 billion in additional state and local appropriations.[90]

It thus seems that large savings could be realized by taxpayers if a larger proportion of students attended for-profit colleges. That option has received almost no attention to date, for reasons that will be discussed.

For-Profit Colleges and Community Colleges Compared

President Obama proposed a huge expansion of the federal government's role in postsecondary education, specifically with respect to the first two years of undergraduate (or technical) education. He announced "America's College Promise" in a January 2015 speech[91] and later described community college as a "ticket to the middle class."[92]

Certainly the prospect of zero tuition would be a happy one for students. Conversely, if for-profit colleges disappear from the lower-division (freshman and sophomore) segment of the market, it would have a negative effect on students, albeit one that is difficult to quantify. We have already noted that for-profits emphasized such student-friendly features as flexible scheduling and online instruction, as well as more career-focused curricular offerings. If community colleges do not face the competitive spur of the for-profits, it is reasonable to predict that this part of the market would display less innovation in the future. How that compares with the redistributive aspect of America's College Promise, from the student's point of view, is very difficult to say.

From the taxpayer's point of view, the most important question is which model is more economically efficient. Although taxpayers would presumably enjoy more positive externalities from better-run purveyors of higher education, their primary interest would seem to be in minimizing the cost of sending all high school seniors on to college.

Tuition-free community college would greatly reduce the problem of student loan defaults by greatly reducing the amount of student borrowing. That is, a large fraction of the loans now granted would, in effect, be replaced by larger federal appropriations to public colleges, *none* of which would—of course—ever be repaid by students. The cost to taxpayers of America's College Promise was estimated at $60 billion over its first 10 years.[93] At first glance that does not seem an improvement over the status quo so far as the taxpayer is concerned, to put it mildly.

Worth noting is that students at for-profits and community colleges have similar loan default rates, with the rate for community college students being higher than that for for-profit students during the most recent three years for which data are available (see Table 10.2).

Table 10.2

Three-Year Cohort Default Rates, Community Colleges and For-Profit Schools

Fiscal year in which borrowers entered repayment	Type of institution from which borrowers graduated	Default rate (%)
2013	Community colleges	18.5
	For-profit	15
2012	Community colleges	19.1
	For-profit	15.8
2011	Community colleges	20.6
	For-profit	19.1

Source: "Official Cohort Default Rates for Schools," U.S. Department of Education, September 28, 2016, https://www2.ed.gov/offices/OSFAP/defaultmanagement/cdr.html and https://www2.ed.gov/offices/OSFAP/defaultmanagement/schooltyperates.pdf.

Although a much smaller fraction of community college students borrow as compared with students at for-profits, the similar default rates may nonetheless tell us something about the postgraduation financial difficulties faced by nontraditional students, broadly defined.

Comparison of the financial performance of for-profits and community colleges should also take into account the fact that community colleges receive substantial subsidies from taxpayers in the form of state appropriations, whereas for-profits do not. At one time APSCU estimated that each community college graduate cost taxpayers more than $32,000 via government subsidies.[94] Furthermore, for-profits pay taxes—about $1.7 billion in 2010, according to APSCU—whereas public and private nonprofit colleges do not. Taking into account state appropriations and for-profits' tax payments, for-profits clearly educate their students at a lower cost to taxpayers than community college do. That leads to the conclusion that, instead of greatly expanding the community college sector, contracting out the entire community college mission (at a minimum) to for-profit firms would be more economical.

Yet another strong reason for taxpayers to favor a continued role for for-profits is that in the past those institutions, as noted previously, proved more flexible and innovative than traditional campuses.

Because the owners of for-profit institutions can claim the additional profits generated by future innovations, they have more of an incentive to come up with future innovations than do their nonprofit competitors. The Obama administration claimed, as part of its pitch for America's College Promise, that it wanted to "promot[e] innovation and competition to bring down costs and improve college quality."[95] Taxpayers would certainly benefit from lower costs and improved quality; however, those benefits are much less likely to be realized if for-profit colleges are completely displaced by tuition-free community colleges.

Why the Fear and Loathing of For-Profit Colleges?

It does not seem to trouble most opponents of for-profit colleges that their criticisms can also be lodged, to one degree or another, against nonprofit colleges. Disappointing education outcomes, excessive debt and defaults, limited career prospects, sharp marketing practices, and the like are not exactly unknown in the nonprofit sector. See the following, for example:

- The most talked-about book about higher education in the past decade made a strong empirical case that almost half of American undergraduates experience "no statistically significant gains in critical thinking, complex reasoning, and writing skills" as a result of attending nonprofit private or public universities.[96]
- The marketing strategies pursued by nonprofit campuses have their own severe critics.[97]
- Colleges and universities seem to react to increases in federal student aid funding systematically by raising their tuition charges.[98] Obviously, public and nonprofit private schools also are keenly interested in "captur[ing] federal loan dollars," to borrow the characterization of for-profits made by the state attorneys general quoted earlier.
- Stories abound of career disappointment among graduates of even very prestigious private colleges. Statistics compiled on the Department of Education's newly released "College Scorecard"

provide college-specific placement data, such as the following from a story in the *New York Times*:

> At Bennington College in Vermont, over 48 percent of former students were earning less than $25,000 per year. A quarter were earning less than $10,600 per year. At Bard College in Annandale-on-Hudson, the median annual earnings were only $35,700. Results at the University of New Mexico were almost exactly the same.[99]

- Plenty of degree programs at nonprofit colleges produce more graduates than there are jobs to go around. To take just one example from graduate education, the Modern Language Association estimates that English departments across the country graduate 1,000 new PhDs each year to compete for only 600 available positions.[100]
- In 2013, *Forbes* magazine removed four nonprofits that deliberately misreported admissions data from its college rankings issue for two years: Claremont McKenna, Emory, Bucknell, and Iona.[101] Quite a few nonprofit law schools (including highly ranked ones) have played fast and loose with their reporting of admissions and job placement statistics.[102]
- Poorly performing four-year colleges can be identified through a *Wall Street Journal* database, "How Accredited Colleges Stack Up," that pulls together graduation and loan default rates at 1,513 colleges, both for-profit and nonprofit.[103] As of June 2015 the seven worst-performing schools for three-year default rates were private nonprofits, the eighth worst was a public school, the University of Arkansas–Pine Bluff. The first for-profit on the list, Salem International University, checked in at number 18 from the bottom, with a default rate of 27.6 percent. The University of Phoenix was 80th on the list, with a 19 percent default rate. The bottom 5 percent of the list contained 82 colleges: 38 private, 29 public, and 15 for-profit. Clearly, performance problems similar to the problems in the for-profit sector also exist in the public and private nonprofit sectors.

In light of the preceding data, a belief in the added trustworthiness of entities with nonprofit status seems ill founded. Why, then, did the Obama administration insist on treating for-profits as fundamentally different from—and much more in need of policing than—public and private nonprofit colleges?

One possibility is that it is a simple case of pork-barrel politics. Traditional, nonprofit higher education is a solid Democratic constituency, whose faculty and administrators overwhelmingly supported the Obama campaigns in 2008 and 2012.[104] If the Obama administration managed to shrink the for-profit sector through litigation and regulation and expand the community college realm through America's College Promise, traditional campuses would see a significant increase in public funding and enrollment—specifically, the kinds of students who would have attended for-profits in past years.

That the administration sought to confer those benefits on one of its key constituencies is certainly plausible, but that explanation runs into the possibility that the for-profit sector may be a (primarily) Democratic constituency as well. (One fact to consider: Bill Clinton received $16.5 million from for-profit Laureate International Universities to serve as its "honorary chancellor" from 2010 to 2013.[105]) Without more evidence on the political activities of the for-profit sector, the rent-conferring explanation of the Obama administration's adamant opposition to for-profits remains incomplete.

Another political angle is presented by the various plans to make college tuition-free. Obviously, the recipients of such a new entitlement would likely view it favorably—and with it the politicians responsible for its adoption. Certainly all students would prefer to not pay any tuition compared with having to take out and repay a student loan to attend college. Finally, the financing of the entitlement out of tax revenues would be consistent with the widespread enthusiasm for income redistribution though government spending.

Another ideological explanation might be that critics of for-profits view free enterprise generally with skepticism and so believe that for-profit colleges are intrinsically inferior to nonprofits. Robert Shireman, who was deputy undersecretary of education from 2009 to 2010, has offered one justification for that mindset in a 2014 essay, "Perils in the Provision of Trust Goods: Consumer Protection and the Public Interest in Higher Education."[106] Shireman based his argument in large part on the work of Henry Hansmann, a professor at the Yale Law School known for his analysis of nonprofit enterprises.[107] Hansmann's basic idea is that the legal requirement that nonprofit managers limit their personal remuneration and other benefits drawn from the enterprise—what he called the "nondistribution constraint"—ensures that nonprofits will behave in a more other-regarding fashion than do for-profit enterprises (whose managers may claim a larger share of profits for themselves). That differential is particularly important in the provision of "trust goods"—goods for which consumers are not likely to be well informed. For Shireman, this is the implication:

> Investor pressure to reduce costs and to grow an enterprise is constructive when the product or outcome is well defined. However, when the product is intangible—such as with higher education—those same pressures can destroy consumer value without the consumer even being aware. Nonprofit status addresses this problem by eliminating owners and investors from the equation, leaving the institution's management answerable to a board that uses criteria other than personal financial benefit to set organizational priorities.[108]

A very serious flaw in Shireman's analysis is that he discounts the importance of innovation in higher education and, by extension, the superior performance of for-profit colleges in generating new degree programs, scheduling formats, online components, and so forth. In fact, Shireman seems to view much, if not all, of the for-profits' innovative contributions as a negative:

> Will these "efficiencies" actually be achieved without hurting quality, or will they rob students of intellectual interactions in ways that are real but extremely difficulty [*sic*] to monitor or measure? There is no way for us to know because higher education is a trust good. We have no choice but to trust what the CEO tells us about the quality of the product.[109]

In such a hapless world, perhaps we would have no choice but to ask government to take over the production of trust goods. In the real world, we would have seen less innovation in a higher education industry without firms driven by the profit motive. Moreover, we will see less innovation in the future if for-profit firms are ruled out of the marketplace for higher education.

Another serious problem with Shireman's analysis was set forth by Henry Manne in a June 2014 essay—and reprinted in chapter 8 of this book—"All Education Is For-Profit Education."[110] Manne focused on the importance of nonpecuniary benefits to administrators and employees in nonprofit organizations. He asked, with respect to (nominally) nonprofit colleges, "Can anyone believe that light teaching loads, generous research leaves, tenure, high salaries, political correctness and so on represent something other than 'profits' to faculties?"

Administration and faculty on nonprofit campuses are maximizing something in their daily work; it's just not narrowly defined accounting profit. The costs of the search for nonpecuniary benefits in nonprofit institutions can be quite large. A 2011 study by the Center for College Affordability and Productivity looked at faculty teaching loads at the University of Texas at Austin. The study concluded that tuition there "could be cut by as much as half simply by asking the 80% of faculty with the lowest teaching loads to teach about half as much as the 20% of faculty with the highest loads."[111]

The power of the drive to seize nonpecuniary benefits in the nonprofit realm is succinctly captured in "Bowen's Law," formulated by three-time college president Howard R. Bowen in 1980: "[C]olleges raise all the money they can, and spend all the money they can raise."[112] The nonprofit side of the higher education industry is dominated by that mindset, thus taxpayers need every spur to cost containment and efficiency that the profit motive can provide.

Conclusion

The extension of federal student aid to more and more students necessarily involves the recruitment of students with objectively weaker academic backgrounds into the college ranks, and the outcomes for those new recruits are likely to be less impressive than are the outcomes for objectively stronger students. Thus it should be no surprise that relatively weaker students attend for-profits, community colleges, and lower-ranked four-year schools and then default on their student loans at higher rates than do academically stronger students who attend higher-ranked nonprofit colleges.

The Obama administration's plans for America's College Promise, as well as state-level free college programs, are understandable as a matter of redistributive politics, but they do not change the basic problem with attempting to send everyone to college. If making a federal loan to a student attending a for-profit college is fiscally imprudent, then it is also fiscally imprudent to give that same student a grant to attend a community college. There is no reason to expect something magical will happen because the student is attending a nonprofit rather than a for-profit institution. Undersecretary Mitchell's wish, noted earlier, that all students "should be assured that their investments" in higher education "will pay off" is simply unattainable.[113] A college degree has never been a guarantee that one's investment in it "will pay off in increased knowledge, skills, and opportunity," and that fact becomes ever more certain as more and more people are enticed into the college experience by federal financial aid. Certainly no such guarantee can be granted by the simple expedient of converting individually owed loans to taxpayer-provided grants.

To the extent that the country wishes to pursue the idea that everyone should go to college, the survival of the for-profit model holds out the prospect of a more customer-oriented business model, as well as more innovation. Unfortunately, the demonization of the for-profit organizational form for colleges may have reached a point of no return, at least as far as many politicians are concerned. Taxpayers should hope that the Trump administration's "reset" of the regulatory framework governing for-profit colleges gives due regard to the strengths that organizational form offers.

CHAPTER ELEVEN

Nonprofit and For-Profit Enterprise in Health Care: Birds of a Feather?

David A. Hyman

> We presume none sins, unless he stands to profit by it.
> —Talmud, 200 C.E.[1]

> The very word, 'profit,' is a signal that denies the trust relationship.
> —Kenneth J. Arrow, 1963[2]

In competitive markets, there are strong incentives to choose the optimal organizational form. But in educational markets, we observe the durable presence of both nonprofit and for-profit firms, along with government/public schools. To be sure, the distribution and market share of these three organizational forms varies by sector within the overall educational market. The nonprofit form dominates elite higher education and divides the market for near-elite and non-elite higher education with government/public schools. The for-profit form dominates tutoring, vocational and online education, and programs for nontraditional students. Government/public schools dominate K-12 education, although the nonprofit form is a significant niche player, particularly in some parts of the country.

In education, the for-profit form has become a lightning rod for controversy, with allegations of fraud, waste, abuse, and almost every other sin under the sun.[3] The U.S. Department of Education is forgiving the federal loans of students who attended Corinthian Colleges. It has also rolled out regulations conditioning access to federally subsidized student loans on the satisfaction of a "gainful employment" requirement—but that requirement essentially applies only to for-profit schools.

What do we actually know about the effect of organizational form on performance? In this chapter, I suggest that we can learn something about these matters by examining the role of nonprofits and for-profits in health care. In the United States, health care accounts for $3.2 trillion in spending per year, or roughly 17.5 percent of the gross domestic product. That spending pays for every conceivable type of product and service delivered by physicians, hospitals, nursing homes, nurses, respiratory therapists, physical therapists, home health care aides, pharmacists, managed care organizations (MCOs) and health maintenance organizations (HMOs), and so on. It also pays for products such as drugs, medical devices, and imaging equipment. Payments for those services and products are handled by health insurers, pharmacy benefit managers, behavioral health care management companies, and the like.

What organizational form do these providers employ to deliver these services? And what difference, if any, does the choice of organizational form make? These issues have proven to be hardy perennials. Over the past few decades, controversies have arisen over:

- Whether for-profit MCOs and HMOs should be allowed to participate in Medicare or allowed to exist at all;
- Whether for-profit hospitals and insurers have higher administrative overhead;
- Whether for-profit hospitals and nursing homes deliver lower quality care;
- Whether for-profit hospitals and nursing homes exploit workers, patients, and taxpayers;
- Whether nonprofit hospitals and insurers should be permitted to convert to for-profit entities, and the impact of conversion on their behavior;

- Whether nonprofit hospitals and insurers deserve a tax exemption;
- The role and virtues (or lack thereof) of for-profit enterprise in health care delivery.

Unsurprisingly, these disputes have given rise to both litigation and legislation, accompanied by a veritable tidal wave of heated talking points and advocacy briefs. Editorials have appeared in the most prestigious medical journals, and bioethicists have opined on the subject. Conferences have been held, and books have been published. The consensus view of most of those that have opined on the subject is quite simple: "nonprofit good, for-profit bad."

As it happens, there is a significant amount of empirical scholarship evaluating the real-world behavior of nonprofit and for-profit firms in the health care space. In this chapter I briefly explore that literature. It begins by outlining the distribution of organizational forms across the health care sector. Next, I document the existence of large subsidies and preferences for the nonprofit form in U.S. health care law and policy. Following that, I review the empirical literature on organizational form and performance, and then points out an unusual asymmetry in the way in which blame is allocated when things go wrong and one of these organizational forms is involved.

Organizational Form and Health Care

As noted above, health care and education are the two sectors of the economy in which we find a substantial number of nonprofit and for-profit entities. But in health care, unlike education, we observe the simultaneous and longstanding presence of the nonprofit and for-profit forms *within the same market segment*. More specifically, we observe a substantial number of nonprofit and for-profit hospitals, nonprofit and for-profit nursing homes, nonprofit and for-profit insurers, and nonprofit and for-profit MCOs and HMOs.

Depending on provider type, the market share of each organizational form varies significantly. The nonprofit form has long dominated the hospital sector. According to the most recent figures, nonprofits account for roughly 58 percent of community hospitals, and for-profit firms and government each account for roughly 21 percent of community hospitals.[4] For-profit hospitals tend to be smaller, so they account for a smaller share of beds than do nonprofit hospitals. There are also a variety of hybrid arrangements—with for-profit management companies running nonprofit and government hospitals—and outright conversions, which have gone in every possible direction.

The nursing home sector has long been dominated by for-profit firms. Before the mid-1970s, health insurers were primarily nonprofit, but there is now a robust for-profit presence, including entities that have always been for-profit (e.g., Cigna and Aetna), and those that converted from nonprofit status (e.g., Anthem). Finally, physicians have long practiced independently as for-profit entities, but an increasing number are now employees of hospitals (which, as noted above, tend to be nonprofit) or of group practices or HMOs (which may but need not be organized as nonprofits).

These patterns are longstanding. In a 2006 article, I observed that "roughly 70 percent of nursing homes, health maintenance organizations (HMOs), and dialysis centers; 50 percent of home health agencies and psychiatric hospitals; 25 percent of substance abuse centers and hospice programs; and 16 percent of hospitals are organized and operated on a for-profit basis."[5]

Geographic factors must also be taken into account. For-profit hospitals are much more prevalent in the South and the West than in the Northeast. Nonprofit HMOs and MCOs are more common in California and the Pacific Northwest than in most of the rest of the country. Within individual states, form also seems to affect the choice of locations—and therefore the competitive environment in which these institutions operate.

Finally, there is variation within entity status. Academic medical centers are almost all structured as nonprofit firms. But unlike other nonprofit hospitals, they tend to be located exclusively in large urban areas and are likely to be larger, have residency and fellowship training programs, and see a disadvantaged population. All these factors will affect the payer mix, profitability, and quality and type of care compared with other nonprofit community hospitals. Similarly, among for-profit hospitals, there are significant differences between physician-owned single-specialty (such as orthopedic and cardiac) hospitals and for-profit general community hospitals that are owned by large corporate chains. Such variation means that a comparison of all nonprofit hospitals with all for-profit hospitals will miss or obscure important variation within each category.

Preferences for the Nonprofit Form in Health Care

There are a series of longstanding preferences for the nonprofit form in health care, typically justified by the assumption that "nonprofits are particularly trustworthy, such as more likely to act in the interest of their patients or other beneficiaries, less likely to interfere in the medical judgments of physicians, and less likely to behave competitively in markets than comparable for-profits."[6]

What form do these preferences take? The most obvious, of course, is tax exemption. A nonprofit hospital may qualify for an exemption from federal, state, and local taxes, while an otherwise similar for-profit hospital will not. Although federal tax exemption has garnered most of the attention, for most hospitals the largest benefit is the exemption from local property taxes. One recent paper set the combined value of federal, state, and local tax exemptions at $24.6 billion.[7]

To qualify for this favorable treatment, nonprofit hospitals must be organized and operated to promote a charitable purpose. Importantly, "charitable" is not the same thing as "charity." In 1956, the IRS required nonprofit hospitals to be "operated to the extent of [their] financial ability for those not able to pay for the services rendered."[8] In 1969, the IRS eliminated this explicit requirement to provide charity care, and instead identified the "promotion of health," which benefits the general community, as the standard for whether a hospital could qualify for tax exemption.[9] In practice, the "community benefit" standard turned out to be almost entirely toothless, but more recent developments indicate that the federal government is becoming more serious about extracting more charity care for the tax exemption.

The campaign to encourage nonprofits to provide more charity care has involved two distinct strategies: public reporting and specific performance requirements. Public reporting is accomplished through a new form (Schedule H) that hospitals must file as part of their federal information return. The Patient Protection and Affordable Care Act (PPACA) also imposed specific performance requirements on nonprofit hospitals, including establishing financial assistance and emergency medical care policies; limiting charges to patients eligible for assistance under those policies; making reasonable efforts to identify eligible patients before engaging in extraordinary collection actions against them; and conducting community health needs assessments and adopting implementation strategies to meet those needs.[10]

At the state level, a significant number of states now require hospitals to document their provision of charity care and other community benefits. And when the local taxing authority is dissatisfied with the performance of a hospital, they can seek to revoke that hospital's exemption. Over the past decades, there have been bitter disputes over the propriety of granting exemptions to hospitals in Illinois, New Hampshire, Ohio, Pennsylvania, Tennessee, Utah, and Vermont. In Illinois, the law now requires hospitals to provide uncompensated care equal to or in excess of their estimated property tax liability. To defuse these controversies, some hospitals have made payments in lieu of taxes.[11]

What about tax exemption for health insurers and HMOs? Prior to 1986, nonprofit health insurers were exempt from federal income tax. Since then, Internal Revenue Code section 501(m) provides that nonprofit insurers that provide "commercial-type" insurance as a substantial part of their activities are not exempt from federal income tax. However, nonprofit insurers may still secure some preferential tax treatment as long as they meet certain requirements, such as maintaining high risk and small group plans.

HMOs are a special case. Many are organized so that they do not provide commercial-type insurance, thereby evading the strictures imposed by section 501(m). However, this does not mean that nonprofit HMOs automatically qualify for tax exemption; they must still satisfy the other requirements in section 501(c). After some initial successes, HMOs have had difficulty in obtaining a tax exemption, because they typically only provide services to their members and not to the general public.

In health care, there are also several less significant preferences for the nonprofit form, including an exemption from the prohibition on the corporate practice of medicine, and, at one time, preferences under antitrust merger analysis and protection from tort law (through charitable immunity). There are also a few instances in which nonprofits are subject to greater scrutiny, such as transactions with insiders and control transactions.[12]

Why does any of this matter? First, if you subsidize something, you will predictably get more of it. The prevalence/dominance of the non-profit form in the health care marketplace is likely to be at least in part a function of these subsidies, rather than the merits of the nonprofit form as such. More concretely, the nonprofit form may dominate the hospital industry because of the sizeable tax subsidy provided to nonprofits, and not any inherent efficiencies associated with that business form. Second, to the extent we observe performance differences between nonprofit and for-profit hospitals, some or all of that outcome may be attributable to the nonprofits' attempts to satisfy the requirements of tax exemption rather than to the nonprofit form as such. It is important to keep both of these points in mind as we evaluate the empirical evidence on the impact of organizational form on behavior.

What Difference Does Organizational Form Actually Make?

There is an extensive literature on the performance differences (and non-differences) between nonprofit and for-profit entities in health care. Most of the literature has focused on hospitals, but there are also studies of other entities, including insurers, nursing homes, dialysis centers, and hospice providers. There are two excellent recent reviews of the literature and two recent studies analyzing why the results are so varied and variable.[13]

The basic flavor of the literature is usefully captured by a paragraph from each of these pieces. I have sought to use the authors' own abstract or summary, but in one instance (Horwitz) I identified a paragraph from the chapter that provided the necessary summary. To simplify matters,

I present the abstracts and summaries in chronological order. First, in 2000, Sloan concluded his chapter in the *Handbook of Health Economics* as follows:

> Overall, the evidence suggests that for-profit and private not-for-profit hospitals are far more alike than different. If private not-for-profit hospitals are to distinguish themselves in terms of some nonpecuniary objective, they will have to define specifically what that focus is. In an environment of increased competition, to finance this objective, they will have to secure sources of funding other than patient dollars. On the other hand, given the transformation of health care in the United States toward price and quality competition that has occurred during the 1980s and 1990s, one might have anticipated much more relative growth of the for-profit sector than has actually occurred. Thus the evidence also calls into question the "knee-jerk" reaction that for-profit automatically means great efficiency.
>
> One of the questions we posed at the outset was whether or not other ownership forms than the for-profit form are more efficient ones for the hospital sector. The answer depends on much more than technical efficiency and allocative efficiency in choice or inputs. Viewed in such narrow terms, the for-profit form performs about as well as private not-for-profits. The answer also depends on whether or not hospitals with particular ownership forms produce the socially optimal combination of outputs. On this score, my review also suggests not much difference and, if anything, under competition, differences may be expected to narrow. Private not-for-profit hospitals will have less latitude than previously to produce outputs they deem to be socially worthy.[14]

Next, in 2007, Shen and her colleagues provided the following abstract of their study:

> This study applies meta-analytic methods to conduct a quantitative review of the empirical literature on hospital ownership since 1990. We examine four financial outcomes across 40 studies: cost, revenue, profit margin, and efficiency. We find that variation in the magnitudes of ownership effects can be explained by a study's research focus and methodology. Studies using empirical methods that control for few confounding factors tend to find larger differences between for-profit

and not-for-profit hospitals than studies that control for a wider range of confounding factors. Functional form and sample size also matter. Failure to apply log transformation to highly skewed expenditure data yields misleadingly large estimated differences between for-profits and not-for-profits. Studies with fewer than 200 observations also produce larger point estimates and wide confidence intervals.[15]

Then, in 2008, Eggleston and her colleagues summarized their own study:

> This systematic review examines what factors explain the diversity of findings regarding hospital ownership and quality. We identified 31 observational studies written in English since 1990 that used multivariate analysis to examine quality of care at nonfederal general acute, short-stay US hospitals. We find that pooled estimates of ownership effects are sensitive to the subset of studies included and the extent of overlap among hospitals analyzed in the underlying studies. Ownership does appear to be systematically related to differences in quality among hospitals in several contexts. Whether studies find for-profit and government-controlled hospitals to have higher mortality rates or rates of adverse events than their nonprofit counterparts depends on data sources, time period, and region covered. Policymakers should be aware of the underlying reasons for conflicting evidence in this literature, and the strengths and weaknesses of meta-analytic synthesis. The "true" effect of ownership appears to depend on institutional context, including differences across regions, markets, and over time.[16]

Finally, in 2015, in the Oxford Handbook of U.S. Health Law, Horwitz noted the following:

> In terms of quality of care, the research is mixed although several articles demonstrate that nonprofits differ . . . [from] for-profits, with the former often providing higher quality services, depending on the types of services studied and the data source. Research on the financial behavior of nonprofit health providers, such as the exercise of market power, pricing behavior, or hospital costs, has often shown few differences in such behavior. Although most recently, researchers have found that in response to financial shocks nonprofit hospitals that

> enjoy market power raise prices (indicating that they had not been profit maximizing previously) and other nonprofits reduced unprofitable service provision (indicating that they had been cross-subsidizing previously). In addition, for-profit hospitals are more likely than nonprofits to "upcode," billing for more profitable diagnoses for patients when doing so results in a higher reimbursement. They are also more likely to locate where there is relatively low demand for free and subsidized health care.[17]

To summarize the summaries, although one can find differences between the performance of for-profit and nonprofit entities, the evidence is mixed, and the distribution of nonprofit and for-profit performance significantly overlaps. Plus, many of the observed differences are not particularly robust to alternative specifications, indicating that the diversity of findings has a lot to do with the data sources, covariates, time period, region, and analytical choices made by individual researchers.

With that warning firmly in mind, I will briefly sketch out some of the findings of past research, broken into four discrete areas.

Uncompensated and Charity Care

There has been a veritable cottage industry of studies of the financial performance of nonprofit and for-profit hospitals, with many focusing on the amount of uncompensated care (that is, charity care and bad debt) provided. In general, these studies have found relatively modest overall differences, with outliers at both the top and bottom of the distribution. Some for-profit hospitals provide almost no uncompensated care, and some nonprofit hospitals provide a huge amount. More important, the overall distributions show significant degrees of overlap.

A 2006 report by the Congressional Budget Office (CBO) provides a representative example.[18] The CBO analyzed the provision of uncompensated care and concluded that "although nonprofit hospitals, on average, have slightly higher uncompensated-care shares than for-profits (by 0.5 percentage points), the distributions of uncompensated-care shares among those two types of hospitals overlap to a large extent." The cover of the report bears a striking histogram, which is reproduced as Figure 11.1.

Figure 11.1

Histogram of Uncompensated Care Provision by Firm Status, December 2006

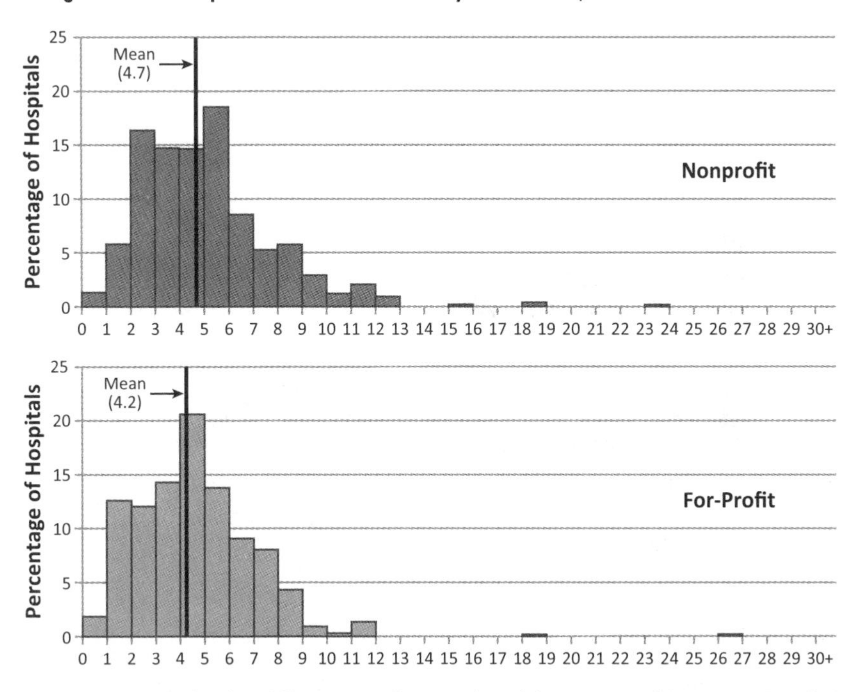

Source: Congressional Budget Office, "Nonprofit Hospitals and the Provision of Community Benefits," Pub. no. 2707, Washington, December 2006.

More recently, a study published in *Health Affairs* examined the same issue, using California data from 2011–2013.[19] The authors found that nonprofit and for-profit hospitals delivered equivalent amounts of uncompensated care (4.4 percent of total operating expenses). They also found and highlighted in the title of their article that nonprofits delivered more charity care (i.e., care for which payment was never expected) than did for-profits (1.9 percent versus 1.4 percent of total operating expenses). But even in that study, the distributions overlapped substantially—as Figure 11.2 makes clear.

And, when the authors looked at uncompensated care, they found that "spending was not related to not-for-profit status."[20] Thus, entity status matters in the delivery of uncompensated/charity care, but it matters much less than is commonly believed.

Figure 11.2

Charity Care at Nonprofit and For-Profit California Hospitals

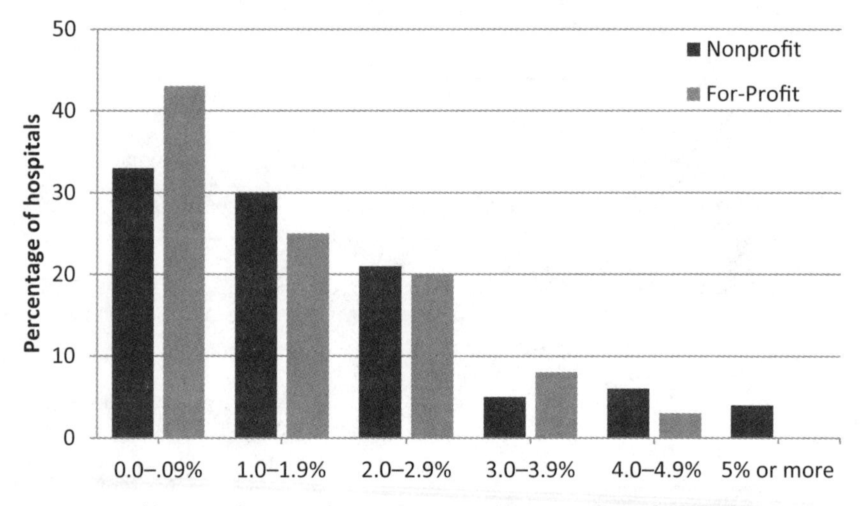

Source: Erica Valdovinos, Sidney Le, and Renee Y. Hsia, "In California, Not-for-Profit Hospitals Spent More Operating Expenses on Charity Care than For-Profit Hospitals Spent," *Health Affairs* 34 (2015): 1299.

Billing and Collection Practices

Policymakers have long been concerned about the impact of large medical bills on low-income and working-class Americans. For-profit hospitals have come in for their share of criticism on the subject; a recent study found that 49 of the 50 U.S. hospitals with the highest charge-to-cost ratios were for-profit firms.[21]

But nonprofit firms have also run into difficulty in this area. During the early 2000s, there was a huge outcry over nonprofit hospitals overcharging uninsured patients and using aggressive collection practices to secure payment. Hundreds of class-action lawsuits were filed in federal and state courts.[22] Some of these cases were settled, but most went nowhere, although the litigation helped trigger legislative action in several states and probably helped contribute to the inclusion of the performance requirements in the Patient Protection and Affordable Care Act noted previously.

More generally, this controversy and the associated publicity hurt the reputation of nonprofit hospitals. When Yale–New Haven Hospital was sued by a Yale Law School clinic for its billing and collection practices, the *Wall Street Journal* gave the story front-page coverage.[23] In 2004, the *New York Times Magazine* published a lengthy article about nonprofits garnishing the wages of grieving widows and having people arrested for nonpayment of their hospital bills.[24] More recently, in 2014, National Public Radio aired a segment on "When Nonprofit Hospitals Sue Their Poorest Patients."[25]

This controversy may not have entirely eliminated the presumption that nonprofits are inherently virtuous, but it certainly raised questions about their real-world behavior. When the pages of the *New York Times* note the "transformation of the nonprofit hospital from savior to scourge," there has been a seismic shift in the framing of the dispute over entity status in health care.[26]

Conversion Effects

Few issues have attracted more overheated rhetoric than the conversion of nonprofit hospitals to for-profit status. As I noted in an article that is now almost 19 years old, "horror stories about hospitals which were acquired by or fell under the sway of the evil for-profit empire are exceedingly popular. It is easy to get the sense that nonprofit hospitals throughout the nation are under siege, and for-profit hospitals are the barbarians at (and in many instances inside) the gates."[27] Commentators warned "of the 'dissolving' of the nonprofit sector, a 'Pac-Man like assault on community owned hospitals,' and the 'largest redeployment of charitable assets in the Anglo-American world since Henry VIII closed the monasteries.'"[28] Postconversion, allegations of misconduct and of dramatic cuts in the provision of uncompensated care are easy to come by.

What do we actually know about the impact of conversions on hospital behavior? There are multiple studies of this issue by different groups of authors. One team did two studies of conversions – first in California, and then in California, Florida, and Texas.[29] They found no statistically significant evidence of differences in uncompensated care, prices, or the provision of unprofitable services, such as trauma care, burn care, and substance abuse treatment. At some individual hospitals, there were significant changes, even though the overall effect for the entire sample was indistinguishable from zero. Needleman and his colleagues analyzed nonprofit hospital conversions in Florida.[30] They found that hospitals that converted delivered relatively low amounts of uncompensated care, both pre- and postconversion. Thorpe and his colleagues studied a larger group of conversions and found evidence of a moderate decline in uncompensated care post-conversion.[31] Other studies have found similarly mixed and modest to moderate overall effects.

That said, there are three important reasons to be cautious about generalizing from a comparison of pre- and postconversion behavior. First, nonprofit hospitals that convert are likely an unrepresentative sample of nonprofit hospitals as a group, and their postconversion behavior may also not be representative of for-profit hospitals. Second, some of these hospitals obtained approval to convert only by making certain (usually time-limited) commitments about their postconversion conduct. The behavior of hospitals that are subject to explicit postconversion commitments does not provide much insight into the behavior of hospitals that are not subject to such commitments.

Finally, and most important, there must be clarity about the relevant baseline. For-profit hospitals satisfy their community obligation by paying taxes, and they are under no obligation to provide uncompensated care. Even if it could be convincingly shown that postconversion, all hospitals provided much less uncompensated care, that finding does not provide a valid basis for condemnation. It is nonprofit hospitals (not for-profit hospitals) that must justify their subsidies by providing uncompensated care and other community benefits. Stated differently, for-profit hospitals may choose to provide uncompensated care, but they are certainly not under any obligation to do so.

Spillover Effects

A modest literature addresses the dynamics when nonprofit and for-profit providers are competing in the same geographic market. Horwitz and Nichols show that when nonprofits are located in a market with more for-profits, the nonprofits behave more like for-profits.[32] More specifically, they focus on more profitable services and more quickly change their mix of services in response to financial incentives. Earlier research similarly suggested that local market conditions are an important factor in the behavior of nonprofit firms, and more competitive markets tend to squeeze out the behavior that is attributed to nonprofit status in less competitive markets.[33] Thus it is an oversimplification to view nonprofit status as a clear predictor of firm behavior.

Attribution Bias

Over the past few decades, there have been multiple scandals involving for-profit entities operating in the health care and educational spaces. When these scandals break, there is usually strident criticism of the evils of the for-profit form, and the incentives that result from that choice of entity status, accompanied by proposals to simply ban the use of the for-profit form in the relevant space. Failing that, there is likely to be substantially increased oversight (which creates jobs for lawyers and compliance officers), fines, and a non-zero likelihood of criminal prosecution against either the for-profit entity or its top officers. The criminal charges will typically be settled with a deferred prosecution agreement, triggering criticism by left-wing populist scolds that no one has been sent to prison. In the pharmaceutical sector, some companies have reportedly dealt with the residual risk by designating a "vice president for going to jail."[34]

However, there have also been multiple scandals involving nonprofit entities operating in the health care and educational space.[35] When these scandals break, no one proposes banning the use of the nonprofit form. Instead, there is usually strident criticism of the character of the individuals involved, the institutional culture, or prevailing local norms, accompanied by proposals for a modest increase in monitoring and exhortations for the nonprofit entity to do better. Someone may lose their job, but criminal charges are almost never in the offing.

When the scandal involves a governmental entity, no one will be fired, although if the scandal is extraordinarily salient, someone at the top may be forced to resign. For example, after multiple scandals hit the

Department of Veterans Affairs, Eric Shinseki was forced to resign as secretary in 2014. Similarly, the Acting Commissioner of the IRS resigned in 2013 in response to the disclosure that the IRS had targeted conservative groups for additional scrutiny during the run-up to the 2012 election. Although his replacement requested the resignation of the IRS director of tax-exempt organizations who had overseen the process, she refused and was placed on administrative leave, retiring six months later with a full pension. As of this writing, no one has been fired at the Environmental Protection Agency for the spill of more than 1 million gallons of polluted water at the Gold King Mine in Colorado. Similarly, criminal charges are a nonstarter unless the responsible person can be shown to have cheated on his or her expense report or misused classified data.

Ironically, in many parts of the government, the bigger the screw-up, the less likely there will be punitive consequences. As Lieutenant Colonel Paul Yingling noted in a scathing article, "As matters stand now, a private who loses a rifle suffers far greater consequences than a general who loses a war."[36]

Finally, it is worth noting that when the scandal involves a governmental entity, the typical "solution" is to throw more money at the responsible entity. That hardly seems like a solution designed to create optimal incentives.

We should not be surprised that scandals occur, regardless of the choice of entity form; to believe otherwise is to indulge in the nirvana fallacy. But, the asymmetry in public reaction to such scandals demonstrates the existence of an extraordinarily high degree of attribution bias.[37] It is implausible on its face that entity status explains any and all bad behavior on the for-profit side and none of the bad behavior on the nonprofit and government side. If the quotes that lead this chapter are any indication, that attribution bias is longstanding. Regardless of its longevity, it is still bias—overt, explicit, and unjustified.

Summary and Conclusions

In health care, debates over the virtues and deficiencies of for-profits and nonprofits are policy perennials. There is no shortage of articles and books on the subject.[38] Unfortunately, "the debate about for-profit health care is fueled as much by values as by evidence."[39]

Empirical research indicates a sizeable overlap in performance by nonprofit and for-profit entities. Neither side has a lock on either virtue or vice, and evidence shows that more competitive markets result in behavioral convergence, regardless of entity status. Considerable heat has been brought to bear on this subject, but the light cast by empirical research indicates more provable similarities than differences in the real-world performance of nonprofits and for-profits.

There are four final issues to address. First, the existence of sizeable federal, state, and local preferences for nonprofit hospitals complicates matters. Until recently, those subsidies were tied to entity status, not performance. In effect, this meant that a hospital may receive a subsidy by adopting a prohibition on inurement, even if its behavior was otherwise indistinguishable from a for-profit entity.[40] A tailored strategy would be more sensible, such as tying the amount of the subsidy to the satisfaction of specific quantifiable and objective measures of performance, irrespective of whether that work was done by a for-profit or a nonprofit firm.

Second, for all the controversy over for-profit hospital conversions, it is important to note that similar heated disputes have erupted when nonprofit Catholic hospital systems have acquired or proposed to acquire nonreligious nonprofit and public hospitals. Those disputes involved the issue of whether the now religiously affiliated nonprofit hospital would continue to provide abortion services (or referrals for the same) and emergency contraception. The existence of these disputes shows once again that it is an oversimplification to treat nonprofits as a homogeneous category.

Third, the prohibition on inurement is at best a slight speed bump in the path of rewarding insiders, if one is so inclined. Incumbents may face some limitations in taking out the profits in the form of cold, hard cash, but there is no shortage of other creative means for doing so, in the form of various types of in-kind compensation, including plush working conditions, lobbies clad in marble and walnut, and the like.[41]

Finally, a personal note. Over the past two decades, I have taught at five law schools—two were nonprofit entities (Georgetown and George Washington), and three were government schools (Illinois, Texas, and Maryland). Across these five institutions, I have known many hard-working law professors who were devoted to their students, although many more were devoted primarily to their research. A distressingly large number treated the position as the best part-time job imaginable, and there was no shortage of partisan hackery.

These individual idiosyncrasies aside, the common element at all five institutions was that the terms and conditions of employment were systematically rigged to favor the interests of the incumbent faculty against all comers. There is no guarantee that the introduction of the for-profit form will disrupt this cozy cartel. But nothing else that we have tried has been up to the task. Perhaps it is time to put aside the visceral hostility to the use of the for-profit form in education and health care and try something different. Otherwise, social policy with regard to entity status in these large and dysfunctional sectors of the economy will continue to bear an uncomfortable similarity to *Animal Farm*: "four legs good, two legs bad."[42]

NOTES

Introduction

1. College Board, "Trends in College Pricing: 2017," Figure 4B, https://trends.collegeboard.org/college-pricing/figures-tables/published-tuition-and-fees-relative-1986-87-sector.

2. Farran Powell, "10 Most, Least Expensive Colleges," *U.S. News & World Report*, September 13, 2016, https://www.usnews.com/education/best-colleges/the-short-list-college/articles/2016-09-13/10-most-least-expensive-private-colleges.

3. Doug Shapiro et al., "Completing College: A National View of Student Attainment Rates—Fall 2010 Cohort (Signature Report 12)," National Student Clearinghouse Research Center, Herndon, VA, November 2016, Figure 5, p. 16, https://nscresearchcenter.org/signaturereport12/.

4. National Center for Education Statistics, *Digest of Education Statistics: 2016*, Table 331.95, https://nces.ed.gov/programs/digest/d16/tables/dt16_331.95.asp?current=yes.

5. Josh Mitchell, "More Than 40% of Student Borrowers Aren't Making Payments," *Wall Street Journal*, April 7, 2016, https://www.wsj.com/articles/more-than-40-of-student-borrowers-arent-making-payments-1459971348.

6. Mark Kutner et al., "Literacy in Everyday Life: Results from the 2003 National Assessment of Adult Literacy," National Center for Education Statistics, April 2007, https://nces.ed.gov/pubsearch/pubsinfo.asp?pubid=2007480.

7. National Center for Education Statistics, PIAAC Results Portal, accessed May 7, 2018, https://nces.ed.gov/surveys/piaac/results/makeselections.aspx.

8. Richard Arum and Josipa Roksa, *Academically Adrift: Limited Learning on College Campuses* (Chicago: University of Chicago Press, 2011), p. 3.

9. National Center for Education Statistics, *Digest of Education Statistics: 2017*, Table 502.30, https://nces.ed.gov/programs/digest/d17/tables/dt17_502.30.asp

10. Pew Research Center, "Is College Worth It?" May 15, 2011, http://www.pewresearch.org/wp-content/uploads/sites/3/2011/05/higher-ed-report.pdf.

11. Public Agenda, "Americans Are Losing Confidence in the Necessity of a College Education for Success in the Workforce," in *Public Opinion on Higher Education*, September 12, 2016, https://www.publicagenda.org/pages/public-opinion-higher-education-2016#finding1.

12. Scott Jaschik, "Pressure on the Provosts," *Inside Higher Ed*, January 23, 2014, https://www.insidehighered.com/news/survey/pressure-provosts-2014-survey-chief-academic-officers; Preety Sidhu and Valerie J. Calderon, "Many Business Leaders Doubt U.S. Colleges Prepare Students," Gallup, February 26, 2014, https://news.gallup.com/poll/167630/business-leaders-doubt-colleges-prepare-students.aspx.

13. Sandy Baum, "Myth: College Is Unaffordable for All but the Rich," *The Presidency*, Spring 2012, http://www.acenet.edu/the-presidency/columns-and-features/Pages/Myth-College-Is-Unaffordable-for-All-but-the-Rich.aspx.

14. Terry W. Hartle, "Statement of Terry W. Hartle, senior vice president, American Council on Education, before the Committee on Ways and Means Subcommittee on Oversight of the U.S. House of Representatives on the Rising Costs of Higher Education and Tax Policy," October 7, 2015, https://www.acenet.edu/news-room/Documents/Testimony-Hartle-Ways-Means-Oversight-Subcommittee.pdf.

15. Jason Delisle, "The Disinvestment Hypothesis: Don't Blame State Budget Cuts for Rising Tuition at Public Universities," Evidence Speaks series, Brookings Institution, June 17, 2017, https://www.brookings.edu/research/the-disinvestment-hypothesis-dont-blame-state-budget-cuts-for-rising-tuition-at-public-universities/; Neal McCluskey, "Not Just Treading Water: In Higher Education, Tuition Often Does More than Replace Lost Appropriations," Cato Policy Analysis No. 810, February 15, 2017; Preston Cooper, *Pennies on the Dollar: The Surprisingly Weak Relationship between State Subsidies and College Tuition*, American Enterprise Institute, June 7, 2017.

16. College Board, Trends in College Pricing, Table 2, "Average Tuition and Fees and Room and Board (Enrollment-Weighted) in Current Dollars and in 2018 Dollars, 1971–72 to 2018–19," https://trends.collegeboard.org/college-pricing/figures-tables/tuition-fees-room-and-board-over-time.

17. Robert B. Archibald and David H. Feldman, *Why Does College Cost So Much?* (New York: Oxford University Press, 2011), p. 84.

18. National Center for Education Statistics, *Digest of Education Statistics: 2016*, Table 303.10, https://nces.ed.gov/programs/digest/d16/tables/dt16_303.10.asp?current=yes.

19. Shapiro et al., "Completing College: A National View of Student Attainment Rates—Fall 2010 Cohort," Figure S-4, p. 58.

20. U.S. Department of Education, "Comparison of FY 2016 Official National Cohort Default Rates to Prior Two Official Cohort Default Rates," August 5, 2017.

21. Neal McCluskey, "For-Profits Have the Toughest Challenge," SeeThru-Edu, August 6, 2015, https://seethruedu.com/for-profits-have-the-toughest-challenge/.

22. Shapiro et al., "Completing College." Although eight-year completion rates for four-year for-profit schools are slightly lower than for two-year public schools, eight-year completion rates for two-year for-profits are much higher.

Chapter 1

1. Henry G. Manne, "How the Structure of Universities Determined the Fate of American Legal Education—A Tribute to Larry Ribstein," *International Review of Law and Economics* 38, Supplement (2014): 107–16. Manne also contended that the Morrill Act led universities to continue a form of governance, the trust, that was not well-suited to practical education. "The land-grant schools were highly vocational in their mission, but they retained the governing structure of their private not-for-profit predecessors, a structure consistent with the fact that no one in charge really wanted consumer sovereignty or a competitive market for students" (p. 107).

2. Manne, "How the Structure of Universities Determined the Fate of American Legal Education," p. 110n18.

3. Manne, "How the Structure of Universities Determined the Fate of American Legal Education," p. 110.

4. Craig Evan Klafter, "The Influence of Vocational Law Schools on the Origins of American Legal Thought, 1779–1829," *The American Journal of Legal History* 37 (1993): 307–31.

5. Klafter, "The Influence of Vocational Law Schools," p. 331.

6. Abraham Flexner, *Medical Education in the United States and Canada* (New York: Carnegie Foundation for the Advancement of Teaching, 1910), p. 6.

7. William J. Gies, *Dental Education in the United States and Canada* (New York: Carnegie Foundation for the Advancement of Teaching, 1926); quotation on p. 39, statistics on p. 42.

8. Robert Francis Seybolt, *The Evening School in Colonial America* (Urbana: University of Illinois, 1925), p. 26.

9. Vera M. Butler, *Education as Revealed by New England Newspapers Prior to 1850,* ed. Lawrence Cremin (New York: Arno Press and the *New York Times,* 1969 [1935]), pp. 199–200.

10. Butler, *Education as Revealed by New England Newspapers*, p. 197.

11. Cecil D. Elliott, *The American Architect from the Colonial Era to the Present* (Jefferson, NC: McFarland & Company, 2003).

12. Elliott, *The American Architect*, p. 14.

13. Terry S. Reynolds, "The Education of Engineers in America before the Morrill Act of 1862," *History of Education Quarterly* 32 (1992): 459–82.

14. Reynolds, "The Education of Engineers in America," p. 460.

15. Reynolds, "The Education of Engineers in America," p. 462.

16. Reynolds, "The Education of Engineers in America," p. 481.

17. Daniel H. Calhoun, *The American Civil Engineer: Origins and Conflict* (Cambridge, MA: MIT Press, 1960), p. 48.

18. "Commercial Colleges," *Michigan Journal of Education and Teachers' Magazine* 1 (1854): pp. 353–54.

19. "How to Educate a Man of Business," *Freeley's Treaties* [sic] *on Business,* published in the *Weekly Standard* (Raleigh, NC), August 17, 1853, p. 2.

20. Melvin L. Barlow, "200 Years of Vocational Education, 1776–1976: Independent Action: 1826–1876." *American Vocational Education* 51, no. 5 (May 1976): 35.

21. Bruce Leslie, "Where Have All the Academies Gone?" *History of Education Quarterly* 41 (2001): 263.

22. Butler, *Education as Revealed by New England Newspapers*, p. 199.

23. Manne, "How the Structure of Universities Determined the Fate of American Legal Education," p. 111.

24. Manne, "How the Structure of Universities Determined the Fate of American Legal Education," p. 111.

25. John Y. Simon, "The Politics of the Morrill Act," *Agricultural History* 37 (1963): 103.

26. Alfred Charles True, "A History of Agricultural Education in the United States, 1785–1925," U.S. Department of Agriculture Miscellaneous Publication No. 36 (Washington: Government Printing Office, 1929).

27. From the minutes of the society, quoted in True, "A History of Agricultural Education," p. 7.

28. True, "A History of Agricultural Education," p. 15.

29. I interpret this to mean that a society that raised $2,000 would receive $400 in total and that one that raised $3,000 would receive $600.

30. True, "A History of Agricultural Education," p. 26. If I interpret this correctly, societies could use their investment in real estate as matching funds.

31. True, "A History of Agricultural Education," p. 99.

32. See "Ohio Mechanics Institute," Ohio History Central, at http://www.ohiohistorycentral.org/w/Ohio_Mechanics_Institute?rec=782. Another thread in the development of mechanical arts colleges was the manual training

movement, but this movement was primarily a "health" effort to make sure that students, whatever their status, experienced the healthy effects of manual labor.

33. Joseph Kett, *The Pursuit of Knowledge under Difficulties: From Self-Improvement to Adult Education in America, 1750 to 1990* (Stanford, CA: Stanford University Press, 1994), p. 132.

34. True, "A History of Agricultural Education," p. 83, quoting Partridge's "memorial" read in the House of Representatives on Jan. 21, 1841. This statement was an allusion to the narrow educational objectives of most denominational colleges.

35. Quoted in True, "A History of Agricultural Education," p. 85.

36. Quoted in True, "A History of Agricultural Education," p. 86.

37. The discussion is based on True, "A History of Agricultural Education," pp. 53–56. Howard's quotations come from his papers collected in the Cornell University Library and cited by True.

38. Quoted in True, "A History of Agricultural Education," p. 54.

39. Burt Eardley Powell, *The Movement for Industrial Education and the Establishment of the University 1840–1870* (Urbana: University of Illinois, 1918), p. 124.

40. Simon, "The Politics of the Morrill Act," p. 106.

41. See Richard Vedder's chapter in this volume, "The Morrill Land-Grant Act: Fact and Mythology."

42. Quoted in True, "A History of Agricultural Education," p. 202.

43. Manne, "How the Structure of Universities Determined the Fate of American Legal Education," p. 111n27.

44. This idea has been developed and popularized by Bruce Yandle as the "bootleggers and Baptists" coalition.

45. Simon, "The Politics of the Morrill Act," p. 103.

Chapter 2

1. Frank Newman, Lara Couturier, and Jamie Scurry, *The Future of Higher Education: Rhetoric, Reality, and the Risks of the Market* (San Francisco: Jossey-Bass, 2004), p. 187.

2. Frank H. T. Rhodes, *The Creation of the Future* (Ithaca, NY: Cornell University Press, 2001), p. 195.

3. Roger L. Geiger, *The History of American Higher Education: Learning and Culture from the Founding to World War II* (Princeton, NJ: Princeton University Press, 2015), p. 281.

4. An Act donating Public Lands to the several States and Territories which may provide Colleges for the Benefit of Agriculture and the Mechanic Arts, 7 U.S.C. §301 (passed 1862).

5. Benjamin Perley Poore, *Veto Messages of the Presidents of the United States with the Action of Congress Thereon* (Washington: Government Printing Office, 1886), p. 262.

6. This exposition draws heavily on John Y. Simon, "The Politics of the Morrill Act," *Agricultural History* 37, 2 (April 1963): 103–11.

7. John H. Florer, "Major Issues in the Congressional Debate of the Morrill Act of 1862," *History of Education Quarterly* 8, 4 (Winter 1968), 474.

8. A former colleague has written an excellent account of early higher education relevant to this discussion. See Daniel L. Bennett, "Myth Busting: The Laissez Faire Origins of American Higher Education," *The Independent Review* 18 (Spring 2014): 503–26.

9. Claudia Goldin and Lawrence F. Katz, *The Race between Education and Technology* (Cambridge, MA: Harvard University Press, 2008), p. 255.

10. Goldin and Katz, *The Race between Education and Technology,* p. 257. The numbers reported here are author calculations from a graph and could be slightly in error.

11. Henry G. Manne, "The Political Economy of Modern Universities," in *Education in a Free Society,* edited by Anne Husted Burleigh, (Indianapolis, IN: Liberty Fund, 1973), p. 111.

12. Geiger, *The History of American Higher Education,* p. 167.

13. See Geiger, *The History of American Higher Education,* chapters 1 through 6, for more detail.

14. Manne originally gave his paper at a Liberty Fund conference from March 28 to 31, 1971. Publication came two years later. At the time of his death in early 2015, Manne was writing a book with Todd Zywicki and had prepared a paper for another Liberty Fund conference, purportedly a sequel to the 1971 paper and with themes that are in this paper, including the Morrill Act. At this writing, I have not read the second paper.

15. Geiger, *The History of American Higher Education,* p. 516.

16. See Hugh Hawkins, *Pioneer: A History of the Johns Hopkins University, 1874–1889* (Ithaca, NY: Cornell University Press, 1960) for a full account of the development of that institution.

17. Geiger, *The History of American Higher Education,* p. 348.

18. Edwin E. Slosson, *Great American Universities* (New York: Macmillan, 1910).

19. The other state universities were those of California, Illinois, Minnesota, and Wisconsin.

20. Raymond M. Hughes, *A Study of the Graduate Schools of America* (Oxford, OH: Miami University, 1925).

21. Geiger, *The History of American Higher Education,* p. 495.

22. Walt W. Rostow, *The Stages of Economic Growth: A Non-Communist Manifesto* (Cambridge, UK: Cambridge University Press, 1960).

23. Three particularly influential pioneering volumes making this point were as follows: William N. Parker, ed., *Trends in the American Economy in the Nineteenth Century,* vol 24 of *Studies in Income and Wealth* (Princeton, NJ: Princeton University Press for the National Bureau of Economic Research, 1960); Dorothy S. Brady, ed., *Output, Employment, and Productivity in the United States after 1800,* vol. 30 of *Studies in Income and Wealth* (New York: Columbia University Press for the National Bureau of Economic Research, 1966); and Lance E. Davis, Richard A. Easterlin, and William N. Parker, eds., *American Economic Growth: An Economist's History* (New York: Harper and Row, 1972). In each of these volumes, Robert Gallman had particularly interesting essays.

24. Angus Maddison, *The World Economy: Historical Statistics* (Paris: Organization for Economic Co-Operation and Development, 2003) and my calculations. Although I think the 20-year perspective is appropriate, a comparison using a 40-year period, which compares 1820–1860 to 1870–1910, shows higher growth in the earlier period (4.37 percent a year) than in the post-Morrill era of 1870 to 1910 (3.93 percent).

25. Maddison, *The World Economy,* pp. 47, 49, and 84.

26. Maddison, *The World Economy,* pp. 61 and 88.

27. Richard K. Vedder, *The American Economy in Historical Perspective* (Belmont, CA: Wadsworth, 1976), pp. 98–102. The calculations were based on the work of Robert Gallman. See his "The Pace and Pattern of American Economic Growth," in Davis et al., eds., *American Economic Growth: An Economist's History of the United States* (New York: Harper and Row, 1972).

28. The entrepreneurs and inventors included are Philip Armour, John Jacob Astor, Alexander Graham Bell, Andrew Carnegie, John Deere, Thomas Edison, Marshall Field, Henry Ford, Charles Goodyear, Jay Gould, Edward H. Harriman, George Hartford, James J. Hill, Cyrus McCormick, J. P. Morgan, Samuel F. B. Morse, Ransom Olds, John D. Rockefeller, Richard W. Sears, Issac Singer, Leland Stanford, Gustavus Swift, Lewis Tappan, Cornelius Vanderbilt, John Wanamaker, George Westinghouse, Eli Whitney, Frank D. Woolworth, Orville Wright, and Wilbur Wright.

29. See Alfred Marshall, *Principles of Economics*, 8th ed. (London: Macmillan, 1920) for the original exposition of the now widely used concept of consumer surplus.

30. The four private universities are California Institute of Technology, University of Chicago, Johns Hopkins University, and Massachusetts Institute of Technology.

31. A few schools completely eschew governmental assistance. Hillsdale College, for example, does not even participate in the federal government's Integrated Post-Secondary Education Data System.

32. U.S. Department of Education, National Center for Educational Statistics, *Digest of Education Statistics: 2015*, Table 106.10, https://nces.ed.gov/programs/digest/d15/tables/dt15_106.10.asp?current=yes.

33. U.S. Census Bureau data, https://www.census.gov/data/tables/time-series/demo/income-poverty/historical-income-people.html.

34. Richard B. Freeman, *The Overeducated American* (New York: Academic Press, 1976).

35. Griggs v. Duke Power, 401 U.S. 424 (1971).

36. Several economists, ironically writing at about the time of the 1971 Griggs v. Duke Power Supreme Court decision, developed the theory of labor market signaling. Michael Spence won the Nobel Prize for his work; see his "Job Market Signaling," *The Quarterly Journal of Economics* 87, 3 (August 1973): 355–74.

37. Bryan O'Keefe and Richard Vedder, *Griggs v. Duke Power: Implications for College Credentialing* (Raleigh, NC: John William Pope Center for Higher Education Policy, 2008).

38. See Richard Vedder, Christopher Denhart, and Joseph Hartge, *Dollars, Cents, and Nonsense: The Harmful Effects of Student Financial Aid* (Washington: Center for College Affordability and Productivity, June 2014).

39. A byproduct of the massive increase in federal student assistance was a decrease in the growth of state government appropriations, as state politicians thought that student financial needs could be met by the federal government. A consequence of that has been that so-called private institutional budgets have increased faster than that of state universities, thus widening the perceived gap in quality between private and public schools. Federal student aid provided a revenue bonanza to schools generally but to private institutions especially.

40. Fairly typically, I think, the teaching load at Ohio University in economics was 12 hours a week around 1955, 9 hours a week when I began teaching in 1965, and 6 hours a week today.

41. Higher Education Research Institute (HERI), *The Undergraduate Teaching Faculty: The 2013–2014 HERI Faculty Survey* (Los Angeles: HERI, UCLA, 2014), p. 27, https://heri.ucla.edu/monographs/HERI-FAC2014-monograph.pdf.

42. For a fuller discussion of this topic with some evidence, see Richard K. Vedder, *Going Broke by Degree: Why College Costs Too Much* (Washington: AEI Press, 2004), chapter 3.

43. The standard treatment here is Benjamin Ginsburg, *The Fall of the Faculty: The Rise of the All-Administrative University and Why It Matters* (Oxford, UK: Oxford University Press, 2011).

44. I am indebted to James Duderstadt (the University of Michigan president in 1995) for information about the 1995 salary.

45. Joel Connelly, "Ex-UW President Young Will Make More Than $1 Million at Texas A & M," March 10, 2015, http://blog.seattlepi.com/seattlepolitics/2015/03/10/uws-young-going-for-the-gold-lots-of-it-at-texas-a-m/.

46. See Vedder, *Going Broke by Degree*, pp. 128–38, or his "Private vs. Social Returns to Higher Education: Some New Cross-Sectional Evidence," *Journal of Labor Research* 25, 4 (Fall 2004): 677–86.

47. This section draws heavily on Vedder, Denhart, and Hartge, *Dollars, Cents, and Nonsense*, pp. 15–25.

48. William Baumol and William Bowen, *Performing Arts: The Economic Dilemma* (New York: Twentieth Century Fund, 1966) is where the argument was first presented. A modern-day account written very much in the Baumol-Bowen tradition is Robert B. Archibald and David H. Feldman, *Why Does College Cost So Much?* (Oxford, UK: Oxford University Press, 2011).

49. William J. Bennett, "Our Greedy Colleges," *New York Times*, February 18, 1987. Bennett's views have not fundamentally changed. See his book with David Wilezol, *Is College Worth It?* (Nashville, TN: Thomas Nelson, 2013).

50. A good study is Andrew Gillen, *Introducing Bennett Hypothesis 2.0* (Washington: Center for College Affordability and Productivity, 2012), https://files.eric.ed.gov/fulltext/ED536151.pdf.

51. David O. Lucca, Taylor Nadauld, and Karen Shen, "Credit Supply and the Rise in College Tuition: Evidence from the Expansion in Student Aid Programs," New York: Federal Reserve Bank of New York, Staff Report no.733, July 2015. For more specific data on tuition inflation, see Richard Vedder, "If in Doubt, Blame Ronald Reagan," *Forbes*, September 3, 2014, http://www.forbes.com/sites/ccap/2014/09/03/if-in-doubt-blame-ronald-reagan/.

52. A few examples can be found in Richard Vedder, Christopher Denhart, and Jonathan Robe, *Why Are Recent Graduates Underemployed?* (Washington: Center for College Affordability and Productivity, 2013); Jason R. Abel, Richard Deitz, and Yaquin Su, "Are Recent College Graduates Finding Good Jobs?," *Current Issues in Economics and Finance* 20, 1 (2014), https://www.newyorkfed.org/research/current_issues/ci20-1.html; and Jordan Weissman, "53% of Recent College Graduates Are Jobless or Underemployed—How?" *The Atlantic*, April 23, 2012, http://www.theatlantic.com/business/archive/2012/04/53-of-recent-college-graduates-are-jobless-or-underemployed-how/256237.

53. See U.S. Department of Education, *A Test of Leadership: Charting the Future of Higher Education* (Washington: 2006), p. 14. Organisation for Economic Co-Operation and Development data of international adult literacy more recently show poor performance by college-educated Americans. See http://www.oecd.org/site/piaac/publicdataandanalysis.htm.

54. Richard Arum and Josipa Roksa, *Academically Adrift: Limited Learning on College Campuses* (Chicago: University of Chicago Press: U.S. Department of Education, 2011). Also interesting is the sequel volume, *Aspiring Adults Adrift: Tentative Transitions of College Graduates* (Chicago: University of Chicago Press, 2014).

55. Jackson Toby, *The Lowering of Higher Education in America: Why Financial Aid Should Be Based on Student Performance* (Santa Barbara, CA: Praeger, 2010).

56. Several studies of students' time use show roughly similar results. See Arum and Roksa, *Academically Adrift*, pp. 96–104, for a good discussion. On grade inflation over time, see Richard K. Vedder, *Thirty-Six Steps: The Path to Reforming American Education* (Washington: Center for College Affordability and Productivity, 2014), pp. 36–37. For a more lengthy critique of the practice, see Valen E. Johnson, *Grade Inflation: A Crisis in College Education* (New York: Springer-Verlag, 2003).

57. See Richard Herrnstein and Charles Murray, *The Bell Curve: Intelligence and Class Structure in American Life* (New York: Free Press, 1994), or Murray's *Real Education* (New York: Crown Forum, 2008).

58. IQ tests have a mean of 100 and a standard deviation of about 16, implying that only 16–17 percent of the population have IQs higher than 115, which is about one-half the proportion of college graduates in the general population.

59. James B. Conant, "The Future of Our Higher Education," *Harper's*, May 1938, p. 563.

60. Robert Maynard Hutchins, "The Threat to American Education," *Collier's*, December 30, 1944, p. 21.

61. Lyndon B. Johnson, "Remarks at Southwest Texas State College upon Signing the Higher Education Act of 1965," November 8, 1965, in Gerhard Peters and John T. Woolley, eds., *The American Presidency Project*, http://www.presidency.ucsb.edu/ws/?pid=27356.

62. This point is discussed extensively in Daniel L. Bennett and Richard K. Vedder, "Public Policy, Higher Education, and Income Inequality in the U.S.: Have We Reached Diminishing Returns?" *Social Philosophy & Policy* 31, no. 2 (2015): 252–80, http://papers.ssrn.com/sol3/papers.cfm?abstract_id=2451152.

63. Adam Smith, *An Inquiry in the Nature and Causes of the Wealth of Nations* (Indianapolis, IN: Liberty Classics, 1981, the Glasgow Edition originally published in 1976 by the Oxford University Press; first published 1776), pp. 26–27.

64. Even here, we may be giving too much credit to the Morrill Act because land grants for universities preceded that legislation. Indeed, the Northwest Ordinance of 1787, before the nation's birth under the Constitution, proclaimed that "religion, morality and knowledge being necessary to good government and the happiness of mankind, schools and the means of education shall forever be encouraged." https://www.ourdocuments.gov/doc.php?flash=false&doc=8.

65. Milton Friedman, *Capitalism and Freedom* (Chicago: University of Chicago Press, 1962).

66. Milton Friedman, in email to the author, September 12, 2003.

Chapter 3

1. Jaqueline Thomsen, "Poor Grades from the Public," *Inside Higher Ed*, June 9, 2015, https://www.insidehighered.com/news/2015/06/09/national-poll-finds-overall-dissatisfaction-college-selection-process-while-parents.

2. Walter C. Eells, "Criticisms of Higher Education," *Journal of Higher Education* 5 (1934): 187.

3. Tyler Cowen, *The Great Stagnation: How America Ate All the Low-Hanging Fruit of Modern History, Got Sick, and Will (Eventually) Feel Better* (New York: Dutton, 2011).

4. Douglas Belkin, "U.S. Private Colleges Face Enrollment Decline," *Wall Street Journal*, November 11, 2013.

5. Jennifer A. Delaney and William R. Doyle, "State Spending on Higher Education: Testing the Balance Wheel over Time," *Journal of Education Finance*, 36 (2011): 343–68; Thomas J. Kane et al., "Higher Education Appropriations and Public Universities: The Role of Medicaid and the Business Cycle," *Brookings-Wharton Papers on Urban Affairs* (Washington: Brookings Institution Press, 2005), pp. 99–146.

6. Richard K. Vedder, *Going Broke by Degree: Why College Costs Too Much* (Washington: AEI Press, 2004); William J. Bennett and David Wilezol, *Is College Worth It?* (New York: Thomas Nelson, 2013).

7. Joshua C. Hall, ed., *Doing More with Less: Making Colleges Work Better* (New York: Springer, 2010).

8. Carrie B. Kerekes, "Privatize It: Outsourcing and Privatization in Higher Education," in *Doing More with Less: Making Colleges Work Better,* ed. Joshua C. Hall (New York: Springer, 2010).

9. William Shughart II, "Cost Inflation in Intercollegiate Athletics: And Some Modest Proposals for Controlling It," in *Doing More with Less: Making Colleges Work Better,* ed. Joshua C. Hall (New York: Springer, 2010).

10. Matthew Holian and Justin M. Ross, "Managing the Internal Organization of Colleges and Universities," in *Doing More with Less: Making Colleges Work Better,* ed. Joshua C. Hall (New York: Springer, 2010).

11. Respectively, John Woods, "A Market-Funded College's Approach to Student Learning and Job Placement: An Insider's View"; and G. Dirk Mateer, "A Tale of Two Partners: How Specialization and Division of Labor Are Reshaping the Academy," in *Doing More with Less: Making Colleges Work Better,* ed. Joshua C. Hall (New York: Springer, 2010).

12. Richard K. Vedder, "Thirty-Six Steps: The Path to Reforming American Education," *The Insider,* Center for College Affordability and Productivity, Heritage Foundation, Washington, December 2014.

13. Derek Bok, *Higher Education in America* (Princeton, NJ: Princeton University Press, 2015); Richard A. DeMillo, *Abelard to Apple: The Fate of American Colleges and Universities* (Cambridge, MA: MIT Press, 2011); Mitchell Stevens and Michael Kirst, *Remaking College: The Changing Ecology of Higher Education* (Palo Alto: Stanford University Press, 2015); Robert Zemsky, *Checklist for Change: Making American Higher Education a Sustainable Enterprise* (New Brunswick, NJ: Rutgers University Press, 2013).

14. Vedder, "Thirty-Six Steps."

15. George C. Leef and Roxana D. Burris, *Can Accreditation Live Up to Its Promise?* (Washington: American Council of Trustees and Alumni, 2002).

16. American Council of Trustees and Alumni (ACTA), "Why Accreditation Won't Work and What Policymakers Can Do about It," ACTA policy paper, Washington, July 2007.

17. Andrew Gillen et al., "The Inmates Running the Asylum? An Analysis of Higher Education Accreditation," Center for College Affordability and Productivity policy paper, Washington, October 2010.

18. Lindsey Burke and Stuart M. Butler, "Accreditation: Removing the Barrier to Higher Education Reform," Heritage Foundation report, Washington, September 21, 2012.

19. Margaret Spellings, "A Test of Leadership: Charting the Future of U.S. Higher Education," U.S. Department of Education report, Washington, September 2006.

20. Judith S. Eaton, "An Overview of U.S. Accreditation," Council for Higher Education Accreditation, Washington, 2011.

21. West Virginia Junior College primarily provides associate degrees in business, computer science, network administration, and so forth.

22. Association to Advance Collegiate Schools of Business (AACSB), "AACSB Business and Accounting Accreditation," http://www.aacsb.edu/accreditation.

23. The Council for Higher Education Accreditation is the advocacy voice for voluntary higher education accreditation in the United States. As part of its mission, CHEA recognizes accrediting organizations that meet their eligibility standards. CHEA's President, Judith Eaton, has been a forceful advocate for self-regulation and assessment. See, for instance, "Accreditation: What It Does and What It Should Do," *Change: The Magazine of Higher Learning*, January/February 2015, pp. 24–26.

24. Harold Demsetz, "Information and Efficiency: Another Viewpoint," *Journal of Law and Economics* 12 (1969): 1–22.

25. A non–higher education example would be those that call for regulation of bank overdraft protection without realizing that many individuals use overdraft protection to provide short-term liquidity instead of high-interest check-cashing stores or pawn shops. See Todd J. Zywicki, "The Economics and Regulation of Bank Overdraft Protections," *Washington and Lee Law Review* 69 (2012): 1141–97.

26. For example, consider the high-stakes testing that came about as a result of the publication of David P. Gardner et al., *A Nation at Risk* (Washington: U.S. Department of Education, 1983). Sharon L. Nichols and David C. Berliner detail the unintended consequences of high-stakes testing on American schools in *Collateral Damage: How High-Stakes Testing Corrupts America's Schools* (Cambridge, MA: Harvard Education Press, 2007). See also Justin M. Ross, "A Theoretical Model of the Distribution of Teacher Attention under Benchmark Testing," *Economics Bulletin* 9 (2008): 1–8.

27. Joshua C. Hall, "Higher-Education Accreditation: Market Regulation or Government Regulation?" *The Independent Review* 17 (2012): 237.

28. Randall G. Holcombe and Lora P. Holcombe, "The Market for Regulation," *Journal of Institutional and Theoretical Economics* 142 (1986): 684–96.

29. Daniel Bennett, "Myth Busting: The Laissez Faire Origins of American Higher Education," *The Independent Review* 18 (2014): 503–25.

30. Timur Kuran, *The Long Divergence: How Islamic Law Held Back the Middle East* (Princeton, NJ: Princeton University Press, 2012). Kuran's work shows how the institutions of Islamic Law were efficient for centuries in achieving relatively high living standards but, over time, those same institutions prevented political change that was necessary for economic advance.

31. Beverly McAnear, "College Founding in the American Colonies, 1745–1775," *Mississippi Valley Historical Review* 42 (1955): 24–44.

32. Martin Trow, "American Higher Education: Past, Present, and Future," *Educational Researcher* 17 (1988): 13–23.

33. McAnear, "College Founding in the American Colonies, 1745–1775."

34. Gillen et al., "The Inmates Running the Asylum?"

35. Judith S. Eaton, "Accreditation, Professional Interest and the Public Interest," *Inside Accreditation* 2 (2006): 1–3.

36. Elaine El-Khawas, *Accreditation in the USA: Origins, Developments and Future Prospects* (Paris: International Institute for Educational Planning, 2012).

37. For example, Beloit College ran the Beloit Academy to prepare students through 1910.

38. William K. Selden, *Accreditation: A Struggle over Standards in Higher Education* (New York: Harper and Brothers, 1960).

39. El-Khawas, *Accreditation in the USA.*

40. El-Khawas, *Accreditation in the USA.*

41. Leef and Burris, *Can Accreditation Live Up to Its Promise?*

42. Leef and Burris, *Can Accreditation Live Up to Its Promise?*

43. Judith Areen, "Accreditation Reconsidered," *Iona Law Review* 96 (2011): 1471–94.

44. George F. Zook et al., *Principles of Accrediting Higher Institutions* (Chicago: University of Chicago Press, 1936).

45. Areen, "Accreditation Reconsidered," p. 1478.

46. Zook et al., *Principles of Accrediting Higher Institutions.*

47. Areen, "Accreditation Reconsidered."

48. Gillen et al., "The Inmates Running the Asylum?"

49. Leef and Burris, *Can Accreditation Live Up to Its Promise?*

50. On this point, generally, see Betty Hollow, *Ohio University: The Spirit of a Singular Place* (Athens, OH: Ohio University Press, 2003). See, especially, p. 99.

51. Peter T. Ewell, "Assessment and Accountability in America Today: Background and Context," *New Directions for Institutional Research* (Fall 2008): 7–17. For Taft, see David S. Webster, "The Bureau of Education's Suppressed Rating of Colleges, 1911–1912," *History of Education Quarterly* 24, no. 4 (1984): 499–511.

52. See, for example, the rise of the YMCA evening law schools in Steven C. Bahls and David S. Jackson, "Legacy of the YMCA Night Law Schools," *Capital University Laws Review* 26 (1997): 235–40; and in Dorothy E. Finnegan, "Raising and Leveling the Bar: Standards, Access, and the YMCA Evening Law Schools, 1890–1940," *Journal of Legal Education* 55 (2005): 208–33. See also the discussion on the rise in private commercial and business schools during this era in Elyce J. Rotella, "The Transformation of the American Office: Changes in Employment and Technology," *Journal of Economic History* 41 (1981): 51–57.

53. Claudia Goldin and Lawrence F. Katz, "The Shaping of Higher Education," *Journal of Economic Perspectives* 13 (1999): 37–62.

54. Gillen et al., "The Inmates Running the Asylum?" p. 13.

55. Mary Watson, "Misplaced Incentives: The Baptists and Bootleggers Story of Accreditation in Higher Education," unpublished manuscript, 2013.

56. And many of them thought it was worth the cost, as higher education enrollment tripled from 1910 to 1940. See Goldin and Katz, "The Shaping of Higher Education."

57. Julie M. Morgan, "Consumer-Driven Reform of Higher Education: A Critical Look at New Amendments to the Higher Education Act," *Journal of Law and Policy* 17 (2008): 531–78.

58. American Council of Trustees and Alumni, "Why Accreditation Won't Work," p. 12.

59. Beaver argues that during this period, low-quality, proprietary, for-profit schools experienced relative decline. Although he does not link that decline to the lack of third-party payers, it is certainly consistent with the data.

William Beaver, "Fraud in For-Profit Higher Education," *Social Science and Public Policy* 49 (2012): 274–8.

60. Richard L. Morrill et al., "In Loco Parentis Revisited?" *Change: The Magazine of Higher Learning* 18 (1986): 34–41.

61. Joseph Sipley, "For-Profit Education and Federal Funding: Bad Outcomes for Students and Taxpayers," *Rutgers Law Review* 64 (2011): 267.

62. Morgan, "Consumer-Driven Reform of Higher Education," p. 540.

63. John Bound and Sarah Turner, "Going to War and Going to College: Did World War II and the G.I. Bill Increase Educational Attainment for Returning Veterans?" *Journal of Labor Economics* 20 (2002): 784–815.

64. Beaver, "Fraud in For-Profit Higher Education."

65. Gillen et al., "The Inmates Running the Asylum?"

66. Beaver, "Fraud in For-Profit Higher Education," p. 275.

67. Beaver, "Fraud in For-Profit Higher Education."

68. For more on this point, see Chapter 6 of James D. Gwartney et al., *Economics: Private & Public Choice* (Mason, OH: Cengage Learning, 2014).

69. Gillen et al., "The Inmates Running the Asylum?"

70. Watson, "Misplaced Incentives."

71. Areen, on p. 1483 in "Accreditation Reconsidered," notes that "the most significant challenges to accreditation have come from the federal government." For McGrath, see Barbara Brittingham. "Accreditation in the United States: How Did We Get to Where We Are?" *New Directions for Higher Education* 145 (Spring 2009): 10–11.

72. Gillen et al., "The Inmates Running the Asylum?" p. 29.

73. Watson, "Misplaced Incentives."

74. Watson, "Misplaced Incentives."

75. Gillen et al., "The Inmates Running the Asylum?"

76. Sipley, "For-Profit Education and Federal Funding." Title IV of HEA provided federal grants for low-income students and federally subsidized loans for middle-class students.

77. Gillen et al., "The Inmates Running the Asylum?" p. 5.

78. Leef and Burris, *Can Accreditation Live Up to Its Promise?*

79. The two obvious exceptions of accredited institutions where students cannot receive federal funds are Hillsdale College and Grove City College, both of which have very distinctive identities.

80. Daniel Golden, "Your Taxes Support For-Profits as They Buy Colleges," *Bloomberg*, March 4, 2010.

81. It should also be noted that barriers to new entrants serve accreditors as well. Unlike in a competitive marketplace where more institutions accredited means more business, in the post-G.I. Bill era making a mistake by accrediting a new entrant is politically risky.

82. Leef and Burris, *Can Accreditation Live Up to Its Promise?*

83. Leef and Burris, *Can Accreditation Live Up to Its Promise?*

84. Areen, "Accreditation Reconsidered," p. 1484.

85. Gillen et al., "The Inmates Running the Asylum?"

86. A. Lee Fritschler, "Government Should Stay Out of Accreditation," *Chronicle of Higher Education*, May 18, 2007.

87. Areen, "Accreditation Reconsidered."

88. John W. Bardo, "The Impact of the Changing Climate for Accreditation on the Individual College or University: Five Trends and Their Implications," *New Directions for Higher Education* (Spring 2009): 49.

89. Judith S. Eaton, "Will Ratings Displace Accreditation?" *Inside Higher Ed,* March 31, 2015, https://www.insidehighered.com/views/2015/03/31/federal-rating-system-could-displace-accreditation-judge-higher-ed-quality-essay.

90. They are hesitant with good reason.

91. Watson, "Misplaced Incentives."

Chapter 4

1. Brent W. Ambrose, Larry Cordell, and Shuwei Ma, "Impact of Student Loan Debt on Small Business Formation," Federal Reserve Bank of Philadelphia, Working Paper No. 15-26, July 2015. From the unpaginated abstract: "We find a significant and economically meaningful negative correlation between changes in student loan debt and net business formation for the smallest group of businesses, those employing one to four employees. This is important since these small businesses depend heavily on personal debt to finance new business formation." The authors might have added that it's important for another reason, too: Small businesses of this kind have also been the source of most of the new job creation in the national economy. People who have, in the past, rolled the dice on a start-up of their own are now laden with nondischargeable liabilities, so they are slouching off to the cubicles of established businesses instead—if they're finding jobs at all.

2. Robert Aliber and Charles Kindleberger, *Manias, Panics and Crashes: A History of Financial Crises*, 7th ed. (New York: Palgrave MacMillan, 2015).

3. Glenn Reynolds' *Instapundit* blog regularly covers issues of higher education financing, and his spirited 2012 book *The Higher Education Bubble* (New York: Encounter Books, 2012) and more recent *The Education Apocalypse: How It Happened and How to Survive* (New York: Encounter Books, 2015) have completed the work of mainstreaming the idea.

4. Reynolds often repeats Herbert Stein's Law "A state of affairs that can't continue, won't." Herbert Stein, "Problems and Not-Problems for the American Economy," *The AEI Economist* (June 1989): 1.

5. "Educational experience" admittedly has a whiff of edu-crat jargon. Regrettably, no better term is at hand. "Education" itself is apt to be understood in a sense more narrow than I mean. By "educational experience" I intend to reference the fairly complex bundle of private goods typically bought with college tuition: human capital development opportunities; social capital development opportunities; assortative mating opportunities; other kinds of socialization, including parties, personal growth opportunities, employment counseling and placement services, and, no doubt, other things I've left things out.

6. Bradley Campbell and Jason Manning, "Microaggression and Moral Cultures," *Comparative Sociology* 13 (2014): 692–726.

7. José L. Duarte et al., "Political Diversity Will Improve Social Psychological Science," *Behavioral and Brain Sciences* 38 (January 2015): 1–13; Scott Jaschik, "Moving Further to the Left," *Inside Higher Ed*, October 24, 2012, https://www.insidehighered.com/news/2012/10/24/survey-finds-professors-already-liberal-have-moved-further-left; Daniel B. Klein and Charlotta Stern, "Professors and Their Politics: The Policy Views of Social Scientists," *Critical Review* 17, no. 3–4 (2005): 257–303, https://doi.org/10.1080/08913810508443640; Stanley Rothman, April Kelly-Woessner, and Matthew Woessner, *The Still Divided Academy: How Competing Visions of Power, Politics, and Diversity Complicate the Mission of Higher Education* (Lanham, MD: Rowman & Littlefield, 2011); George Yancey, *Compromising Scholarship: Political and Religious Bias in American Higher Education* (Waco, TX: Baylor University Press, 2011); James Lindgren, "Measuring Diversity: Law Faculties in 1997 and 2013," *Harvard Journal of Law & Public Policy* 39 (2016): 89–151, http://ssrn.com/abstract=2581675; *but see* Neil Gross and Solon Simmons, eds., *Professors and Their Politics* (Baltimore, MD: Johns Hopkins University Press, 2014).

8. Lucca, Nadauld, and Shen find that each dollar of Pell Grants (which are targeted to low-income students) is associated with a 55-cent increase in tuition. Federally subsidized student loans with dollar caps and income caps produce 70 cents of tuition increase for every dollar loaned. Unsubsidized loans, available to all income groups but with higher interest rates, produce 30 cents of tuition increase for every dollar loaned. The authors helpfully stress that this is tantamount to borrowing 70 cents and paying back a dollar, with interest. David O. Lucca, Taylor Nadauld, and Karen Shen, "Credit Supply and the Rise in College Tuition: Evidence from the Expansion in Federal Student Aid Programs," Federal Reserve Bank of New York Staff Report no. 733, July 2015. The Lucca, Nadauld, and Shen paper identifies a larger pass-through effect than Andrew Gillen found in his 2012 paper on the subject, "Introducing Bennett Hypothesis 2.0," Center for College Affordability and Productivity, February 2012 (Gillen's data do not invite an effort to solve the simultaneity problem; he approached the causation issue by showing that it was plausible to think that the

causal arrow runs from loans to tuition rather than from tuition to loans). Grey Gordon and Aaron Hedlund, "Accounting for the Rise in College Tuition," NBER Working Paper no. 21967, February 2016, http://www.nber.org/chapters/c13711.pdf, find that most of the blame for tuition increases can plausibly be laid at the door of subsidized student loans. Earlier work found Bennett-type tuition effects from Pell Grants in highly ranked college programs, although not elsewhere. Larry D. Singell and Joe A. Stone, "For Whom the Pell Tolls: The Response of University Tuition to Federal Grants-in-Aid," *Economics of Education Review* 26 (2007): 285–95. Virginia Postrell helpfully called attention (posting December 8, 2011) to the analogy between the loans-inflate-tuitions story and work by Austan Goolsby that shows that investment tax credits primarily enrich equipment manufacturers and not the businesses that were the intended target of the subsidies. She also mentions the observation that farm subsidies push up the price of farmland. It is interesting that although Robert B. Archibald and David H. Feldman do not dwell on the debt-to-tuition causal arrow in *Why Does College Cost So Much?* (New York: Oxford University Press, 2011), they seem to assume it. Andrew Gillen has now provided a penetrating analysis, "Why Does Tuition Keep Increasing?" September 2015, http://papers.ssrn.com/sol3/papers.cfm?abstract_id=2663073, which agrees with the analysis I offer in this paper on all essential points, documented with the latest Integrated Postsecondary Education Data System (IPEDS) data. Beyond all that evidence (and it is not slight), I have an additional reason to credit Bennett, arising from personal experience. It's impossible for me, as I think about this causation question, to blot out the memory of a number of conversations with other law deans on this subject, nor my service on an Association of American Law Schools committee a number of years ago. The question on everyone's mind has been how to keep the student loan pipeline flowing so as to allow us to bring tuitions into line with needed investments for the sake of education quality. This is a perfectly respectable way to talk about schools' hunger for cash; nor does the recapitulation of the problem in affective language alter its substance. That's how everybody talked about the problem; no one was under the illusion that the tuition subsidies were ultimately meant to subsidize anyone but *us*. I wouldn't expect others who haven't shared these experiences to be influenced in the same way as I am, or even to take my word for it, but connecting the loan-to-tuition phenomenon isn't rocket science. The big problem with making the connection out loud is that enormous rents are at risk if the wrong sort of people—people on the House Appropriations Committee especially—come to believe it. Under the circumstances, virtuosity is to be expected from educators in not seeing things or, at worst, obscuring them with nuance.

9. William J. Bennett, "Our Greedy Colleges," *New York Times*, February 18, 1987.

10. College enrollment totaled 11.4 million students in 1980 and 20.3 million in 2010. United States Census Bureau, "CPS Historical Time Series Tables on School Enrollment," Table A-6, https://www.census.gov/data/tables/time-series/demo/school-enrollment/cps-historical-time-series.html.

11. National Center for Education Statistics, *Digest of Education Statistics: 2015*, Table 317.10, https://nces.ed.gov/programs/digest/d15/tables/dt15_317.10.asp?current=yes.

12. Paul Taylor et al., "Is College Worth It?" Pew Research Center, May 16, 2011, surveying the views of the general public and college presidents on a number of college-pertinent matters, is generally informative on the subject, with graphs and tables. "Go to college" may be good advice or bad advice, depending on the individual in question. People are different, after all. My economics department colleague Alex Tabarrok has long held college-skeptical views, but even he doesn't dispute that going is a smart choice for some students. (See Alex Tabarrok, "College Has Been Oversold," *Marginal Revolution*, November 2, 2011, http://marginalrevolution.com/marginalrevolution/2011/11/college-has-been-oversold.html.) Everyone acknowledges that college graduates' earnings on average exceed those of college dropouts and nonattenders. Not everyone agrees about what causal stories should be read off those facts. Some widely reported studies about the labor market value of higher education fail to make clear the extent to which an individual's decision to attend college resembles a gamble. It isn't smart to gamble looking only at the size of the pot. The probability of winning that pot has to be weighed too, and also the extent of the bad consequences that would follow from making a losing bet.

College-bound students spend a lot of time, typically, thinking about where they should go and what they should do, but seldom do they do so in a detached, analytical manner. Nothing deserves to be called "college planning" that doesn't take into account how a potential applicant stacks up with some reference group on a number of key attributes that enable or hinder success. There's no basis I know of for the assumption that, in general, potentially college-bound students subject themselves to this process of self-examination (as distinct from just drifting along with life's currents and eddies, what most of us do most of the time). The implication is that there will inevitably be many unplanned matriculations every year, some of which will be unfruitful just because they were unplanned. By college age, people have plenty of highly germane predictive information about themselves (How smart/talented/magnetic am I, really? What do I really like doing?) to help them decide what, in all good sense, they ought to do. Do they use that information? "The contempt of risk, and the presumptuous hope of success, are in no period of life more active than at the age when young people choose their professions," Adam Smith, *An Inquiry into the Nature and Causes of the Wealth of Nations*

(Book I, Chapter 10, part 1; first published 1776), loc. 1679, Kindle. We should expect young people especially to downplay or ignore as much of that information as conflicts with the plans, hopes, and dreams they have for themselves, which may have reached them by a road that took little account of the probability of getting what they believe they want. They may thus lead themselves, or be led, to overvalue training and education unsuited to their particular temperaments or capacities and to point themselves down a path that leads away from the opportunities that would give their real talents greatest scope. If college is wrong for them, it obviously dampens their chances of getting the degree. Leaving a four-year college without a degree in hand, in general, kills the economics of the deal; students who borrow a lot of money and then don't get a degree will in most cases have made an expensive mistake. (It would, furthermore, be the same mistake even if it didn't involve borrowed money because of the opportunity costs, of savings and of time, that were "borrowed" from more valuable options.) Human autonomy and liberty are important enough values that we consider it right to let people make their own mistakes if they insist on doing so, and then they must live with the consequences.

13. Sales pitches that rely on some version of "eliminate the middle man" capitalize on this confusion. A good discussion about the fallacy of confusing "cost" and "price" is found in Archibald and Feldman (*Why Does College Cost So Much?*).

14. I mean the sort of problems discussed in Roger Kimball, *Tenured Radicals: How Politics Has Corrupted Our Higher Education* (Chicago: Ivan R. Dee, 1990). It is unwise to make light of such issues, but discussing them seriously, with a view of doing anything about the problem, is no small undertaking. For starters, we do not have a real inventory of how widespread the phenomenon we should want to fix really is. There is a good reason for this. Without defined terms it is impossible to pin down the problem well enough to analyze it. Except perhaps in the extreme tail of the distribution, tenured radicalism will be in the eye of the beholder, and *de gustibus non est disputandum*. One might narrow the field of inquiry to traditional arts and sciences college education, but then one would need to find common ground on what that sort of program must always, at a minimum, be expected to do. Enough generality would be required to embrace some legitimate differences of opinion on how broadly or narrowly the mission should be defined but specific enough to make it possible to pin the horsefeathers badge on an offending breast. Good luck to anybody who wants to tackle this project.

15. Over many years I have become acquainted with many faculty members in a number of different disciplines and institutions, and although they are unquestionably a mixed bag for talent, they're mostly serious people with

conventional work habits, who are seriously engaged in teaching and research about perfectly sensible subjects. Carrying forward the discussion begun in the immediately previous footnote, I wonder whether it might be possible to count at least the extreme tail dwellers without a full-on embrace of the problem mentioned there. Just how fat *is* that extreme pathological tail of the distribution? It should not be necessary to bring forward a full-blown Theory of Everything Higher Educational to identify instances of borderline fraud—courses (or professors) qualifying as horsefeathers with respect to anything that even a broad-minded person would wish to defend. I suspect—it's just a guess—that a careful national census of that sort of character would reveal that there weren't very many.

16. The argument, in brief, is that students consume the reputation value of the college they attend, a reputation made up of relentlessly enforced high standards and exacting demands that require students to learn more than they may have any desire to learn of the subjects being studied. It would be a good deal for the students if they had the opportunity to free-ride on all that by taking courses that would reward them with high grades in exchange for little or no effort. The limiting factor would be the eventual decay and ruin of the school's reputation. If it were gradual enough, it likely wouldn't be of great concern to a particular student, at least from a purely self-interested perspective. David D. Haddock and Daniel D. Polsby, "Family as a Rational Classification," *Washington University Law Review* 74 (1996): 25–28.

17. The best example of gold plating I have heard recently comes courtesy of a professor at another law school who had recently returned from a conference at Harvard. She mentioned she had been in a women's restroom whose walls were clad in Carrera marble. I'm still not sure what to make of the observation, but whatever the other implications might be, I wouldn't think it a good guess that a Carrera marble restroom would affect Harvard tuition. In business, gold plating can be described as noncash compensation for firm employees. It can also be an effective way of sending a message to customers about the organization's successfulness and high quality. Whether it is wise or unwise to spend money in that way, the price of the organization's deliverables will be determined in markets that are *completely indifferent* to whatever the production costs may have been.

18. Many universities (including George Mason), as a part of the "sustainability" efforts they have made so much of in recent years, now make a practice of constructing buildings to the Leadership in Energy and Environmental Design (LEED) standards established by the U.S. Green Building Council. I was told by a senior George Mason facilities planner that LEED certification adds approximately 15 percent to the capital cost of a building, but that there were understood to

be offsetting lower operating costs of LEED-certified structures. Let us hope so. Mason hasn't independently audited or otherwise substantiated those claims, and they may turn out to be hype. Time will tell. See Peter Sepp, "LEED-ing Taxpayers to Waste Money?" *U.S. News and World Report,* May 8, 2014, http://www.usnews.com/opinion/economic-intelligence/2014/05/08/leed-certification-doesnt-add-value-and-costs-taxpayers.

19. Donna Desrochers and Rita Kirshstein, "Labor Intensive or Labor Expensive? Changing Staffing and Compensation Patterns in Higher Education," Delta Cost Project issue brief, February 2014, p. 15.

20. Regulatory compliance is lexically prior to educational or any other institutional purposes. The situation is the same as the one every taxpayer knows: the government is a creditor like no other. It has first claim on a tax debtor's assets, and its claim has to be 100 percent satisfied before any other creditor sees a penny. Moreover, as Howard Bowen wrote in 1980, in the springtime of federal regulatory proliferation, nonmonetary compliance costs (the Occupational Safety and Health Administration was his example) may exceed their cash costs because of the resulting diffusion of institutional focus on the school's primary mission. Howard R. Bowen, *The Costs of Higher Education: How Much Do Colleges and Universities Spend Per Student and How Much Should They Spend?* (San Francisco: Jossey-Bass, 1980).

21. See Bowen, *Costs of Higher Education,* fn. 27.

22. Nelson W. Polsby, "The Contributions of President Richard F. Fenno, Jr.," *PS* 17, no. 4 (Autumn 1984): 778–81. Raymond Wolfinger's brilliant aphorism "The plural of anecdote is data" never inspired a better or more skilled researcher (p. 779).

23. I was right, and they were wrong; however, to be completely fair to all concerned, it's debatable whether following my advice could have made much difference. The labor market conniptions that followed on the heels of the subprime fiasco cratered not only our own enrollment performance but that of the entire industry, drowning out whatever blame might otherwise have been assigned to individual mistakes.

24. In our decentralized system, the deans of the dozen or so academic units are charged primarily with tending their respective gardens. Deans—to be understood as a synecdoche for the academic units—weren't formally a part of the central planning process. I hadn't had to develop a feel for how the whole story was unfolding.

25. Benjamin Ginsberg, *The Fall of the Faculty: The Rise of the All-Administrative University and Why It Matters* (New York: Oxford University Press, 2011), p. 71.

26. "Expenditures per FTE student" means tuition revenue plus revenue appropriated by the general assembly from the general fund, divided by the

number of FTE students, all in constant dollars. These numbers and the ones that follow (unless otherwise noted) are stated in CPI-adjusted 2011 dollars, using the conversion tables worked out by the Federal Reserve Bank of Minneapolis. These expenditure numbers refer only to draws against the university's "educational and general" budget and ignore the separate capital budget altogether. The "educational and general" budget (which in normal speech would just be called "the budget") answers for the operating costs of the university—payrolls, phone bills, lavatory supplies, travel expenses, grounds-keeping, heating, cooling, electric lights, the police department, and so on. It's important to notice that it covers debt service on the bonds that have to be issued to build buildings, and in this one (but important) way it is connected to and affected by the capital budget.

27. Nor, as it turns out, was the George Mason experience unique. Gillen (2015), using IPEDS data, shows that nationally, diminished state subsidies—even added together with other much-blamed budget factors, such as rising faculty compensation—are considerably more than offset by the increased revenues attributable to rising tuition (Gillen, "Why Does Tuition Keep Increasing?").

28. The most often-used workload metric for professors who are appointed on a tenure line is number of classroom hours teaching per week. If there is any expectation that professors will have out-of-class contact with students (true at virtually all law schools but not always the case in other fields), a more realistic metric would be student contact hours per week, as some courses will have 3 students in them and some others 100 or more. Measuring the volume of research throughput raises some of the same issues as measuring teaching productivity. Two factors of very different weight and consequence may both tally as "one unit produced." Interpretative human judgment is required to make such measurements meaningful. In the past decade, citation counting has become the most widely accepted way to measure a professor's "influence," but that is not quite the same as productivity. Coming to grips with the issue of productivity in the arts may be so tricky that it might seem best to hire a consultant to explain it, or possibly two. See, generally, William Baumol and William G. Bowen, *Performing Arts, The Economic Dilemma: A Study of Problems Common to Theater, Opera, Music, and Dance* (New York: Twentieth Century Fund, 1966).

I recently heard a speech by a man who had been president of two large and highly reputable research universities. Reminiscing, he said that in his own undergraduate days, every professor was expected to teach five courses per semester and then produce research in his spare time. One doubts it. But declining productivity by professors, as measured by assigned per-credit teaching loads, has been much discussed. It may, indeed, be a fair criticism. One thing about the university world, which the institution of tenure contributes to but does not solely cause, is that there is an option to shirk baked into the employment contract. It is exercised commonly enough that it has its own acronym, borrowed from the military: ROAD, meaning "retired on active duty." Exercising the ROAD option is not cost free to the employee—at a minimum it costs a loss of face among colleagues and students. Whether things on this front are getting worse, or are worse now than back in the years that professors taught 10 courses per year, is not, to my knowledge, a question that can be answered on the basis of currently existing data. The ROAD phenomenon may be connected to the trend toward lighter teaching loads, but it isn't necessarily. Good research and writing is hard work, as hard to do as good teaching and probably harder. Research typically isn't counted in productivity computations, but that doesn't mean it isn't a valuable kind of productivity.

29. Something is definitely wrong with the numbers I have for this, which show much smaller growth in faculty salary lines than Bureau of Labor Statistics or IPEDS national data do. I suspect that health insurance must have been left out of my numbers—a substantial item in the compensation package in any year. State employees' health insurance is very expensive. The package is nearly as good as the legendary coverage offered by the federal government. The rate of increase in our Blue Cross premiums over the past several decades has been astounding, actually, even in comparison to the dotted line. If dollar-equivalent numbers for Blue Cross are added into the faculty salary numbers I have, George Mason's faculty compensation increase eyeballs out to about the national data. Archibald and Feldman argue that national data depicting increases in faculty compensation are about what one would expect once cost disease is taken into consideration (*Why Does College Cost So Much?*).

30. The same terminological uncertainty likely comes up with respect to other universities' "administrators" census.

31. It seems impossible to give a useful answer to the question of what the ratio "should" be between faculty (or students) and administrators.

32. Gillen, "Why Does Tuition Keep Increasing?"

33. Gillen found it in the IPEDS data (which is national) as well (Gillen, "Why Does Tuition Keep Increasing?"). Tuition revenues increased faster than state subsidy reductions and increases in faculty compensation offset them.

34. Archibald and Feldman say that cost disease basically explains the increase in faculty compensation over the past 80 years (*Why Does College Cost So Much?*). They are persuasive. However, Gordon and Hedlund, who are also persuasive, find the contrary ("Accounting for the Rise in College Tuition").

35. Bowen, *Costs of Higher Education.*

36. Bowen, *Costs of Higher Education*, p. 17. See discussion in Archibald and Feldman (*Why Does College Cost So Much?*) and Gillen ("Why Does Tuition Keep Increasing?").

37. Bowen, *Costs of Higher Education*, p. 20.

38. The term "credence product" was coined by Michael Darby and Edi Karni, "Free Competition and the Optimal Amount of Fraud," *Journal of Law and Economics* 16 (1973): 67–88. The discussion in text leans on Uwe Dulleck and Rudolf Kerschbamer, "On Doctors, Mechanics, and Computer Specialists: The Economics of Credence Goods," *Journal of Economic Literature* 44 (2006): 5; Uwe Dulleck, Rudolph Kerschbamer, and Matthias Sutter, "The Economics of Credence Goods: On the Role of Liability, Verifiability, Reputation and Competition," IZA Discussion Paper no. 4030 (2009); Winand Emons, "Credence Goods and Fraudulent Experts," *RAND Journal of Economics* 28 (1997): 107; and Timothy Feddersen and Thomas W. Gilligan, "Saints and Markets: Activists and the Supply of Credence Goods," *Journal of Economics and Management Strategy* 10 (2001): 149.

39. Dulleck and Kerschmer, "On Doctors, Mechanics, and Computer Specialists."

40. Philip Nelson, "Information and Consumer Behavior," *Journal of Political Economy* 78 (1970), p. 311.

41. This issue is clearly explained in Hal R. Varian, "Markets for Information Goods," 1998, http://people.ischool.berkeley.edu/~hal/Papers/japan/index.html, later published in Kunio Okina and Tetsuya Inoue, eds., *Monetary Policy in a World of Knowledge-Based Growth, Quality Change, and Uncertain Measurement*, proceedings from the eighth international conference of the Institute for Monetary and Economic Studies, the Bank of Japan (New York: Palgrave, 2001).

42. It's debatable whether that effort works, but of course that's another story. The main point is that much toil and trouble goes into the effort.

43. Doctors, dentists, and other professionals whose services may also be hard to evaluate even after having been experienced and paid for do analogous things for analogous reasons. They do not make so much parade about all this as does the legal profession, but neither do they labor under anything like the same cloud of negative public perceptions as lawyers do. People may fear dentists, but they don't think that dentists are a bunch of crooks.

44. See, for example, Heb. 11:1–39.

45. Among these I count "diversity," "sustainability," "globalism," "inclusion," "entrepreneurship," "interdisciplinary," "innovation," a new George Mason entrant is "well-being" (which I understand is quite big in the corporate world)—and apologies for any omissions. These themes perfuse university websites, waxing and waning in emphasis, with "education"

surprisingly seldom featured—sometimes not even mentioned. To avoid misunderstanding, I'm a fan of all the things on the list (and many other good things that aren't on it), but none of them is the main thing, the organizing principle through which the whole higher education enterprise is supposed to be justified and sustained, to which other values are subordinate or from which they are derived.

46. John Gapper, "American Apparel's Resistance to Fast Fashion Is Futile," *Financial Times*, October 7, 2015, https://www.ft.com/content/458bd4c6-6b5a-11e5-aca9-d87542bf8673.

47. A "haircut" is the difference between the face value of a debt and the amount that a secured creditor receives in liquidation.

Chapter 5

1. American Association of University Professors, "1940 Statement of Principles on Academic Freedom and Tenure," http://www.aaup.org/report/1940-statement-principles-academic-freedom-and-tenure.

2. Schools of lesser renown love to crow about "luring away" a professor from Harvard, even if Harvard was happy to unload the person. For a discussion of the tenure process at Harvard, see Nicholas P. Fandos and Noah B. Pisner, "Joining the Ranks," *Harvard Crimson*, April 11, 2013, http://www.thecrimson.com/article/2013/4/11/scrutiny-tenure-harvard/.

3. About 70 percent of the junior faculty members who come up for tenure are granted tenure. See Marcella Bombardieri, "Harvard Professor Challenges School's Denial of Tenure," *Boston Globe*, June 13, 2014, https://www.bostonglobe.com/metro/2014/06/12/harvard-professor-challenges-tenure-denial/E64ruokHoD1WpokjwsbR3M/story.html. That means that 30 percent who come up for tenure are denied and dismissed. Likely, more leave before coming up for tenure because they know that the decision will be negative, so the effective dismissal rate during the tenure track may well be 50 percent. See Fandos and Pisner, "Joining the Ranks."

4. The AAUP would probably put George Mason University on its "Censure List." Most of the schools on that list are likely less celebrated in academic stature than George Mason. Louisiana State University is probably the most noteworthy school currently on the list. I have no idea whether that has affected its ability to attract faculty or students. See AAUP, "Academic Freedom: Censure List," http://www.aaup.org/our-programs/academic-freedom/censure-list.

5. That is an indication of the self-centeredness of academics. Professors rarely express concern about the thousands of mid-level managers whose jobs are swept away each year in corporate reorganizations or downturns. Professors

seem to believe that they would be sleeping under a bridge should tenure be removed because they would never find another job.

6. This section draws on Ryan Amacher and Roger Meiners, *Faulty Towers: Tenure and the Structure of Higher Education* (Oakland, CA: The Independent Institute, 2004).

7. Walter Metzger, "Academic Tenure in America: A Historical Essay," in *Faculty Tenure: A Report and Recommendations*, by the Commission on Academic Tenure in Higher Education (San Francisco: Jossey-Bass, 1973), p. 126.

8. Charles Van Hise, "The Appointment and Tenure of University Professors," *Journal of Proceedings and Addresses of the Association of American Universities* (1910): 58–59.

9. E. D. Sanderson, "Definiteness of Appointment and Tenure," *Science* 39 (1914): 892.

10. The 15 members of the founding committee show only senior scholars at top institutions, such as Richard T. Ely (economics) from the University of Wisconsin and Roscoe Pound (law) from Harvard.

11. Metzger, "Academic Tenure in America," pp. 135–36.

12. Metzger, "Academic Tenure in America," pp. 142–43.

13. Committee on Academic Freedom, "Report," *Bulletin of the American Association of University Professors* (December 1915): 34.

14. Robert C. Brooks, "Tenure in Colleges and Universities," *School and Society* 19 (1924): 498.

15. Brooks, "Tenure in Colleges and Universities."

16. "Study of Tenure of University and College Teachers," *Bulletin of the American Association of University Professors* (April 1932): 256.

17. Or at least, it was not clear from my reading of AAUP documents.

18. See AAUP, "1940 Statement of Principles on Academic Freedom and Tenure."

19. See AAUP, "1940 Statement of Principles on Academic Freedom and Tenure."

20. See AAUP, "1940 Statement of Principles on Academic Freedom and Tenure."

21. As will be discussed, conducting reviews seems to be legislative in origin, not a quality-enhancing feature requested by faculty so as to weed out the indolent.

22. Service is generally minor for professors in general; most schools avoid giving committee assignments and other service duties to assistant professors so that they can focus on publications.

23. Some critics of tenure seem to believe that tenured faculty members devote all their time to research at the expense of teaching. My unscientific observation is that the belief is not true. Most faculty at typical, non-top-tier

schools produce a small amount of meaningful scholarship. They may not do much teaching, but they do not do much scholarship either. For a detailed study of publications in the economics profession, showing that few graduates of highly ranked PhD programs publish articles in major academic journals, see John P. Conley and Ali Sina Önder, "The Research Productivity of New PhDs in Economics: The Surprisingly High Non-Success of the Successful," *Journal of Economic Perspectives* 28, 3 (2014): 205–16.

24. That judgment will be seen as a scientifically inadequate measure of competence, but subjective valuations of professional work are common in the professions. Pure metrics often do not work. Professionals tend to know ability when they see it. Some schools have formal requirements, such as a visit to a class of a tenure candidate by a colleague or administrator, although how a one-time, known-in-advance visit provides useful input is difficult to see.

25. Board of Regents of State Colleges v. Roth, 408 U.S. 564 (1972).

26. Perry v. Sindermann, 408 U.S. 593 (1972), 603.

27. A. P. Menard, "May Tenure Rights of Faculty Be Bargained Away?" *Journal of College and University Law* 2 (1975): 256.

28. "Developments in the Law: Academic Freedom," *Harvard Law Review* 81 (1967–68): 1094.

29. Recent appeals court cases include Laskar v. Board of Regents of University System of Georgia, 740 S.E.2d 179 (App. Div. 2013), in which the Georgia Court of Appeals held that a tenured professor who had been dismissed from Georgia Tech had no right to appeal the holding of the university committee by writ of certiorari because the university proceedings were not judicial—a breach of contract suit would likely be the only legal recourse; Haegert v. University of Evansville, 977 N.E.2d 924 (Ind. 2012), in which the Supreme Court of Indiana held that a tenured professor in Indiana who had been dismissed for sexual harassment was given proper due process and so had no claim for breach of employment contract; Churchill v. University of Colorado at Boulder, 285 P.3d 986 (Colo. 2012), in which the Colorado Supreme Court held that a tenured professor at the University of Colorado at Boulder's Ethnic Studies Department who had made news when he praised the attack of 9/11 and was then found to have a history of bogus "scholarship" and was fired, was not eligible for equitable relief or monetary damages; to add insult to nonlegal injury, in Sadid v. Idaho State University, 294 P.3d 1100 (Idaho 2013), the Idaho Supreme Court held that a dismissed tenured professor was not eligible for unemployment compensation because of his misconduct.

30. Texas Education Code Sec. 51.942, Performance Evaluation of Tenured Faculty, http://www.statutes.legis.state.tx.us/Docs/ED/htm/ED.51.htm#51.942. See an example of a university policy adopted pursuant to the legislation at http://policies.tamus.edu/12-06.pdf.

31. Texas Education Code Sec. 51.942, Performance Evaluation of Tenured Faculty, 51.942(c)(1).

32. Texas Education Code Sec. 51.942, Performance Evaluation of Tenured Faculty, 51.942(c)(5).

33. Texas Education Code Sec. 51.942, Performance Evaluation of Tenured Faculty, 51.942(a)(3).

34. The University of Texas System Rules and Regulations of the Board of Regents, "Evaluation of Tenured Faculty" (Rule 31102) at https://www.utsystem.edu/board-of-regents/rules/31102-evaluation-tenured-faculty.

35. See, for example, University of Texas, Arlington, "Policy 6-725: Annual Review and Comprehensive Periodic Evaluation of Tenured Faculty," https://www.uta.edu/policy/hop/6-725.

36. The University of Texas System, "Post-Tenure Review Report," http://www.utsystem.edu/offices/academic-affairs/post-tenure-review-report.

37. I am pleased to report that at my institution, the unsatisfactory rate was only 1 percent, whereas in Austin, the flagship, the unsatisfactory rate was 2.4 percent—higher than the rate for other schools in the system.

38. An administrator's salary does not rise for incurring such unpleasant and time-costly activities. That fact is a matter of possible importance, as will be discussed later in this chapter. Some of the details of the procedure are spelled out at The University of Texas System, "Regents' Rules and Regulations," https://www.utsystem.edu/offices/board-regents/regents-rules-and-regulations. To go through the process, an administrator must have an excellent paper trail showing the poor performance over time, details of complaints, comparisons with other faculty members, and so forth. Such recordkeeping is costly, and the lack of it is a common reason why some cases of possible dismissal for poor performance do not go forward. A case of sexual harassment or other bad behavior is much simpler but has less to do with incompetence as a professor, as it is more narrowly understood.

39. Salaries can be searched at The Texas Tribune, "Government Salaries Explorer," http://salaries.texastribune.org/.

40. Numerous articles and books have been written contending that tenure secures a public good because it protects free intellectual discourse or other putative public goods. Many of these works have titles such as the one by Charles Hohm and Herbert Shore, "The Academy under Siege: Informing the Public about the Merits of Academic Tenure," *Sociological Perspectives* 41 (1998): 827–31. Such views make for fine straw men, but I rise above the temptation to feast on easy fodder and simply dismiss the assertion that brave academicians must be left free to do what they please for the greater good of society. The focus here is on economic arguments.

41. Michael S. McPherson and Gordon C. Winston, "The Economics of Academic Tenure: A Relational Perspective," *Journal of Economic Behavior and Organization* 4, 2–3 (1983): 163–84.

42. McPherson and Winston, "The Economics of Academic Tenure," p. 179.

43. McPherson and Winston, "The Economics of Academic Tenure," p. 180.

44. Looking at teaching evaluations and counting the number of articles written is not a costly exercise and is done for all professors, permanent or contract.

45. H. Lorne Carmichael, "Incentives in Academics: Why Is There Tenure?" *Journal of Political Economy* 96, 3 (1988): 453–4.

46. Carmichael, "Incentives in Academics," 471.

47. The founders of the AAUP wanted to solve the problem of ignorant administrators hiring faculty in different disciplines by having members of those disciplines participate in the hiring process. The founders' belief was that members of a discipline could identify more promising candidates, and their departments would benefit intellectually.

48. When airlines in the United States faced financial ruin, unions were willing to sacrifice the salaries, benefits, and working conditions of junior pilots to help protect senior pilots and reduce the wage burden on the airlines. The junior pilots were not inept, just paid less.

49. Again, employers forced to deal with union workforces tolerate a certain amount of featherbedding and inefficient work rules, including slow adoption of new technology. Some of those features seem consistent with tenure, and none are economically efficient. The U.S. auto and steel industries were damaged by the requirement that management cater to union demands, which drove up costs and retarded innovation.

50. Richard B. McKenzie, "In Defense of Academic Tenure," *Journal of Institutional and Theoretical Economics* 152 (1996): 326.

51. The AAUP allows financial exigency as a reason for revoking tenure, but even when demand is nil and a college might exercise that rationale, it appears to be rarely employed.

52. Individual firms may have offered benefits similar to tenure, but the practice has not come to dominate in any industry.

53. William O. Brown Jr., "University Governance and Academic Tenure: A Property Rights Explanation," *Journal of Institutional and Theoretical Economics* 153 (1997): 441.

54. Brown, "University Governance and Academic Tenure," p. 459.

55. Aloysius Siow, "Tenure and Other Unusual Personnel Practices in Academia," *Journal of Law, Economics, and Organization* 14 (1998): 153. A related paper is Zhao Chen and Sang-Ho Lee, "Incentives in Academic Tenure under Asymmetric Information," *Economic Modelling* 26 (2009): 200–208. Their model shows the tenure track to be efficient because an employer cannot predict productivity before the employee demonstrates experience, but the authors admit that tenure does not deal with the deadwood problem.

56. This is not to imply that for-profit firms routinely pitch out senior employees for minor drops in productivity. Hiring and dismissing employees is costly, and firms wish to be known as good places to work to help attract high-quality people in a competitive labor market.

57. Pilots tend to not switch airlines, but that is because of unionization, not because they have tenure. FAA regulations enhance the union position by making switching airlines difficult for a pilot, even if the same aircraft is involved.

58. João Ricardo Faria and Gonçalo Monteiro, "The Tenure Game: Building up Academic Habits," *Japanese Economic Review* 59, 3 (2008): 371. The authors employ a Stackelberg differential game to provide a mathematical proof.

59. This argument is based on the assumption that the primary objective of faculty is to produce academic research, not teach. Teaching quality is rarely mentioned as a concern of academic institutions.

60. Ronald G. Ehrenberg, Paul J. Pieper, and Rachel A. Willis, "Do Economics Departments with Lower Tenure Probabilities Pay Higher Faculty Salaries?" *Review of Economics and Statistics* 80 (1998): 503–12.

61. There are about 3,000 colleges. A relatively small percentage have faculty members who produce scholarship published in major journals. Most are teaching schools that grant tenure largely for adequate teaching ability and congeniality.

62. Thomas W. H. Ng and Daniel C. Feldman, "Organizational Tenure and Job Performance," *Journal of Management* 36 (2010): 1220.

63. Ng and Feldman, "Organizational Tenure and Job Performance," p. 1223. Average organizational tenure is 5.4 years. Why some firms average such long employee terms, given the negative relationship to productivity, was unclear.

64. The matter has worsened since the Age Discrimination in Employment Act was applied to academic institutions. Teaching, say, 9 hours per week for 30 weeks a year is not the burdensome task faced by most employees in private-sector jobs, so universities have become clogged with aging professors who see little reason to decamp. Many universities previously had mandatory retirement ages to help replace the old guard.

65. Dismissing such employees likely could be done more than it is, but, as discussed later, administrators have little incentive to take such steps.

66. Experience in the United States with proprietary higher education is so limited that it is likely a mistake to presume that the University of Phoenix is what college would look like in the absence of state-operated schools. Proprietary colleges only fill a niche in the higher-education market.

67. Armen Alchian, *Economic Forces at Work* (Indianapolis: Liberty Fund, 1977): 177–202.

68. Alchian explained why nonprofit administrators would not be as likely as for-profit administrators to fire people. "Firing a person is an unpleasant task, but in a profit-seeking business it is even more unpleasant not to fire them." The organization, not the administrator, bears the cost of keeping the inept employee. Armen A. Alchian, "Private Property and the Cost of Tenure," in *The Collected Works of Armen A. Alchian, Vol. 2* (Indianapolis: Liberty Fund, 2006), p. 381.

69. In 2003, state governments terminated "less than 2% of their employees annually." Sally Coleman Selden, "The Impact of Discipline on the Use and Rapidity of Dismissal in State Governments," *Review of Public Personnel Administration* 26 (2006): 335. Given the fairly high rate of dismissal of assistant professors before being granted tenure, faculty members likely face a dismissal rate higher as that of other public-sector employees before granting of tenure.

70. William O. Brown Jr., "Alchian on Tenure: Some Long Awaited Empirical Evidence," *Journal of Corporate Finance* 44(C) (2017): 487–505.

71. Armen A. Alchian and Harold Demsetz, "Production, Information Costs, and Economic Organization," *American Economic Review* 62 (1972): 778.

72. That buyers of existing firms are often willing to pay a huge premium to gain control indicates that the buyers (capital owners) must believe that the target organization is either quite inefficient or missing significant opportunities, a clear indication that not all firms are highly efficient machines. Further, many industries, such as banking, are subject to a host of federal rules concerning governance structure that move them away from a model of focusing first on return on equity.

73. In most of those markets, the state and charitable organizations intervene, but they tend not to do the actual production; rather, they subsidize acquisitions for certain beneficiaries. Direct subsidies for higher education, such as the GI Bill, allow the student to choose the college and direct resources to it.

74. Henry Manne outlined the weakness of the view that nonprofit organizations (private colleges and state colleges) and their employees are more saintly than those of for-profit colleges. He noted that all higher education is really for profit, it is just a question of who captures the net revenue. See "All Education Is For-Profit Education," James G. Martin Center for Academic Renewal, June 25, 2014, https://www.jamesgmartin.center/2014/06/all-education-is-for-profit-education/. Also reprinted as chapter 8 of this book.

75. The counterfactual is greatly complicated by the existence of huge federal intervention in nonprofit schools. They face a host of regulations—some imposed directly, others indirectly via accrediting bodies—and they receive massive federal dollars. They participate actively in managing relations with the federal government because of the aid. See, for instance, Tracy Jan, "Research

Giants Win on Federal Funding," *Boston Globe*, March 18, 2013, http://www.bostonglobe.com/news/nation/2013/03/17/harvard-mit-and-other-research-schools-thwart-obama-administration-effort-cap-overhead-payments/Nk5PT0Mc8MQZihFVNs5gNK/story.html. For our discussion, we must assume that the federal government would remain neutral about tenure.

76. Many states also have higher-education commissions empowered to constrain decisions made by assorted colleges—one group of bureaucrats monitors another group of bureaucrats. My impression is that the central planning bureaucrats justify their positions by requiring the production of lots of documentation to give the illusion of conscientious decisions. They may, in fact, be conscientious, but central planning is deeply flawed whether in higher education in the United States or in steel production in the Soviet Union.

77. The lack of remuneration does not mean that the positions may not be seen as valuable. Appointments to many boards are prestigious and highly coveted. Perks include increased connections with others in positions of consequence, first-class football tickets, assistance in admission for children of board members and their friends, and other benefits. Governors think carefully about board appointments. At private schools, there may be intense lobbying for positions on a board.

78. Louis de Alessi, "Managerial Tenure under Private and Government Ownership in the Electric Power Industry," *Journal of Political Economy* 82 (1974): 645–53. De Alessi found that managers of government-owned power companies, which have no clear residual claimants, enjoy greater job security. In "Implications of Property Rights for Government Investment Choices," *American Economic Review* 59 (1969): 13–24, he also explained that attempts to overcome the lack-of-residual-claimant problem by using cost-benefit analysis to justify expenditures by agencies does not work well because of basic flaws in cost-benefit analysis. Another, more important failure of that method is the incentives that decisionmakers have to shift expenditures in directions they personally prefer and then justify their decisions by cost-benefit analysis.

79. Whereas most Virginia residents probably know of George Mason, many fewer likely know of Strayer, and it probably has little effect on surrounding property values. Strayer only runs classes for paying customers; it offers no basketball games, rock concerts, or interesting speakers.

80. Although noteworthy personalities in the corporate world receive great attention, its success does not depend on a few celebrities such as Warren Buffett or Mark Cuban but on the incentives created by the corporate form of organization. See Raghuram G. Rajan and Luigi Zingales, *Saving Capitalism from the Capitalists: Unleashing the Power of Financial Markets to Create Wealth and Spread Opportunity* (Princeton, NJ: Princeton University Press, 2003).

81. A firm may be well managed yet still be subject to takeover because current managers fail to see, or cannot take advantage of, opportunities that would increase return on equity. The leadership of firms often is portrayed as cruel to employees, but managers know that employees are key to the success of any organization. Firms that treat employees well are less likely to be subject to acquisition. See Antonio Macias and Christo Pirinsky, "Employees and the Market for Corporate Control," *Journal of Corporate Finance* 31 (2015): 33–53.

82. This is a significant problem. College education is planned by academics who likely think less about what their "customers" need for a successful college experience than is true of corporations, for example, that produce cars. That reality may be reflected in the claim that many recent graduates believe that college was not worth the cost. See, for example, "Top Gallup-Purdue Index Findings of 2015," at http://news.gallup.com/opinion/gallup/187970/top-gallup-purdue-index-findings-2015.aspx?.

83. A few disciplines, such as accounting, have national exams that give evidence of quality of instruction, but value added might be difficult to discern—brilliant Berkeley students will likely have high pass rates regardless of instructional quality compared with Cal State-Fullerton students. Most fields offer even fewer measures.

84. Except for audited financial information, which is foolish to fiddle with, other measures can be adjusted to tell a good story. When schools come under fire for having too many administrators, they can reclassify administrators as professors, as most were at one point.

85. See Alan Finder, Patrick D. Healy, and Kate Zernike, "President of Harvard Resigns, Ending Stormy 5-Year Tenure," *New York Times*, February 22, 2006, http://www.nytimes.com/2006/02/22/education/22harvard.html?pagewanted=all&_r=0. Doctrinal purity was an issue at Harvard centuries ago; in Summers' case, the matter was one of political correctness; see Daniel Golden and Steve Stecklow, "Facing War with His Faculty, Harvard's Summers Resigns," *Wall Street Journal*, February 22, 2006, http://www.wsj.com/articles/SB114054545222679220.

86. In the business world, many companies have shuttered; there is no reason the same should not happen across colleges or to departments within colleges. Many colleges have French departments; few have Hindi departments, despite that language being much more commonly spoken than French, which is as common as Marathi.

87. One of the few moves is a merger of Hamline and William Mitchell law schools in St. Paul, Minnesota. They are across town from two other law schools, University of Minnesota and St. Thomas, which are both ranked higher. The result of the merger is, of course, litigation claiming that tenure

had been violated. For a copy of the complaint, see http://blurblawg.typepad.com/files/260810564-tenure-change-complaint.pdf. I'll wager that neither dean of the merging schools will ever be hired as dean of another school.

88. State legislatures, even in "conservative" places such as Texas, abet that process because they are never willing to pull the plug on a losing school. Members of the legislature always protect their local state school, regardless of the demand for it, and they always lobby for more unneeded programs to be funded at their schools.

89. When universities enjoyed seemingly unending increases in support from legislatures, the cost of deadwood faculty was less apparent than when budgets became more binding and growth would not solve all problems.

90. As Alchian noted, "The first theorem [in economics] says individuals act so as to further their own interest, even when acting as members of a group" (*supra* n. 68, p. 377). Even if universities are "special," no one has demonstrated that basic economic interests are not at work in them.

91. Pay was $800, $1,000, or $1,200, depending on qualifications. It may have risen since then but likely not significantly.

92. John W. Curtis and Saranna Thornton, *Losing Focus: The Annual Report on the Economic Status of the Profession, 2013–14*, Figure 1, http://www.aaup.org/our-work/research/annual-report-economic-status-profession.

93. The president of Princeton noted the high expense of dealing with accreditation that is justified "in the name of progress and accountability" as part of the "culture of assessment." Shirley M. Tilghman, "The Uses and Misuses of Accreditation," November 9, 2012, http://www.princeton.edu/president/tilghman/speeches/20121109/.

94. The University of Phoenix has the structure of each course set by experts. Instructors deliver the packages rather than design each course according to personal interests. As such, Phoenix employs efficiencies that do not exist in the traditional model, whereby every instructor crafts each course individually.

95. Google, which can pick among mass numbers of applicants for any job, focuses more on work tests than lists of academic accomplishments. The Google process is described by the company's head of People Operations, Laszlo Bock, in *Work Rules!: Insights from Inside Google That Will Transform How You Live and Lead* (New York: Twelve, 2015). Of course, Google gets applications from huge numbers of high academic achievers anyway, but Bock asserts that academic achievement is not their primary metric.

96. State schools could simply be declared on their own—hand the title to the board of trustees. That will not happen because legislators love the political benefits that come with control of the schools, including influence on admission to the most worthy schools and sweetheart construction deals.

97. Private schools tend to have missions more narrow than do state schools, which tend to offer any and every kind of degree program they can. Many private schools focus on undergraduate teaching and do not produce PhDs. They have little reason to care about significant scholarship by their faculty.

Chapter 6

1. Douglas Belkin and Scott Thurm, "Deans List: Hiring Spree Fattens College Bureaucracy—And Tuition," *Wall Street Journal,* December 28, 2012, https://www.wsj.com/articles/SB10001424127887323316804578161490716042814.

2. Benjamin Ginsberg, *The Fall of The Faculty* (Oxford, UK: Oxford University Press, 2011).

3. Ginsberg, *The Fall of The Faculty*, p. 2.

4. Ginsberg, *The Fall of The Faculty*, p. 2.

5. Jay P. Greene, Brian Kisida, and Jonathan Mills, *Administrative Bloat at American Universities: The Real Reason for High Costs in Higher Education* (Phoenix: Goldwater Institute, 2010).

6. Data on spending in higher education are available through the Integrated Postsecondary Education Data System (IPEDS) of the National Center for Education Statistics, http://nces.ed.gov/ipeds/. Two of the more comprehensive studies that have been done in the past few years include Greene, Kisida, and Mills, *Administrative Bloat at American Universities*, as well as Donna M. Desrochers and Jane Wellman, *Trends in College Spending 1999–2009: Where Does the Money Come From? Where Does It Go? What Does It Buy?* (Washington: Delta Cost Project at American Institutes for Research, 2009).

7. Henry G. Manne, "The Political Economy of Modern Universities," in *Education in a Free Society*, ed. Anne Husted Burleigh (Carmel, IN: Liberty Fund, 1973): pp. 165–206.

8. Henry G. Manne, "The Political Economy of Modern Universities."

9. Todd J. Zywicki, "Meet the Mid-Level Bureaucrats Who Impose Speech Codes on America's Universities," James G. Martin Center for Academic Renewal, Raleigh, NC, February 4, 2015, http://www.popecenter.org/2015/02/meet-the-mid-level-bureaucrats-who-impose-speech-codes-on-americas-universities/.

10. Todd J. Zywicki, "Institutional Review Boards as Academic Bureaucracies: An Economic and Experiential Analysis," George Mason Law and Economics Research Paper No. 07-20, May 2, 2007, https://papers.ssrn.com/sol3/papers.cfm?abstract_id=983649.

11. Robert E. Martin and R. Carter Hill, "Baumol and Bowen Cost Effects in Research Universities," working paper, March 2014, https://papers.ssrn

.com/sol3/papers.cfm?abstract_id=2153122; David O. Lucca, Taylor Nadauld, and Karen Shen, "Credit Supply and the Rise in College Tuition: Evidence from the Expansion in Federal Student Aid Programs," Federal Reserve Bank of New York, Staff Report no. 733, July 2015.

12. Desrochers and Wellman, *Trends in College Spending 1999–2009*, p. 12.

13. Desrochers and Wellman, *Trends in College Spending 1999–2009*, p. 13. Net tuition revenue is moneys received from tuition and fees, including grant and loan aid used by students to pay tuition.

14. Desrochers and Wellman, *Trends in College Spending 1999–2009*, p. 13. State and local appropriations include moneys received through state or local legislative organizations.

15. Desrochers and Wellman, *Trends in College Spending 1999–2009*, p. 13. Private gifts are moneys received from private donors or from private contracts for specific goods or services provided by the institution that are directly related to instruction, research, public service, or other institutional purposes. Investment revenues are from interest income, dividend income, rental income, or royalty income. Endowment income is generally income from trusts held by others and income from endowments and similar funds.

16. Desrochers and Wellman, *Trends in College Spending 1999–2009*, p. 13. These revenues are those received from state or local government agencies.

17. Desrochers and Wellman, *Trends in College Spending 1999–2009*, p. 13. These moneys are revenues generated by or collected from auxiliary enterprise operations of the institution that furnish a service to students, faculty, or staff and that charge a fee related to the cost of service.

18. Desrochers and Wellman, *Trends in College Spending 1999–2009*, p. 13. These moneys are those received from the operation of hospitals by the university and other operations that are independent or unrelated to instruction, research, or public services.

19. Roger L. Geiger and Donald E. Heller, "Financial Trends in Higher Education: The United States," Pennsylvania State University, Center for the Study of Higher Education Working Paper no. 6, January 2011, https://ed.psu.edu/cshe/working-papers/wp-6.

20. Geiger and Heller, "Financial Trends in Higher Education: The United States," p. 4.

21. Greene, Kisida, and Mills, *Administrative Bloat at American Universities.*

22. Authors' calculations based on the underlying data from the reports listed in the remainder of the endnotes. For data, see Donna M. Desrochers and Steven Hurlburt, *Trends in College Spending: 2001–2011: A Delta Data Update* (Washington: Delta Cost Project at American Institutes for Research, 2014): Figure S1.

23. Preston Cooper, "Pennies on the Dollar: The Surprisingly Weak Relationship between State Subsidies and College Tuition," Washington: American Enterprise Institute, June 7, 2017, http://www.aei.org/wp-content/uploads/2017/06/Pennies-on-the-Dollar.pdf.

24. Greene, Kisida, and Mills, *Administrative Bloat at American Universities.*

25. Lucca, Nadauld, and Shen, "Credit Supply and the Rise in College Tuition."

26. Martin and Hill, "Baumol and Bowen Cost Effects in Research Universities"; Lucca, Nadauld, and Shen, "Credit Supply and the Rise in College Tuition."

27. Desrochers and Wellman, *Trends in College Spending 1999–2009*, p. 24.

28. Desrochers and Wellman, *Trends in College Spending 1999–2009.*

29. Desrochers and Wellman, *Trends in College Spending 1999–2009*, p. 26–7.

30. Geiger and Heller, "Financial Trends in Higher Education: The United States." The authors found that expenditures increased in both public and private universities, with spending increasing as follows: instruction (19 percent in public, 57 percent in private), student services (45 percent, 106 percent), academic support (33 percent, 93 percent), and institutional supports (34 percent, 66 percent)

31. Greene, Kisida, and Mills, *Administrative Bloat at American Universities.*

32. Desrochers and Hurlburt, *Trends in College Spending: 2001–2011.*

33. Greene, Kisida, and Mills, *Administrative Bloat at American Universities*, p. 5. Their list of leading universities is taken from the Integrated Postsecondary Education Data System (IPEDS) list of four-year universities that grant doctoral degrees and engage in a high or very high level of research activity.

34. Greene, Kisida, and Mills, *Administrative Bloat at American Universities*, p. 5. Public institutions employed, on average, 28.3 employees, and private institutions employed 44.9 employees.

35. Greene, Kisida, and Mills, *Administrative Bloat at American Universities*, p. 5. Public institutions employed, on average, 21.3 employees, and private institutions employed 53.6 employees.

36. Greene, Kisida, and Mills, *Administrative Bloat at American Universities*, pp. 6–7.

37. Greene, Kisida, and Mills, *Administrative Bloat at American Universities*, pp. 7–8.

38. Greene, Kisida, and Mills, *Administrative Bloat at American Universities*, pp. 8–9.

39. Donna M. Desrochers and Rita Kirshstein, "Labor Intensive or Labor Extensive? Changing Staffing and Compensation Patterns in Higher Education," Issue Brief, Delta Cost Project at American Institutes for Research, Washington, February 2014.

40. Desrochers and Kirshstein, "Labor Intensive or Labor Extensive?"

41. National Center for Education Statistics, Institute for Education Sciences, "Percentage of Full-Time Instructional Staff with Tenure for

Degree-Granting Institutions with a Tenure System, by Academic Rank, Sex, and Control and Level of Institution: Selected Years, 1993–94 through 2011–12" (Table 305), https://nces.ed.gov/programs/digest/d12/tables/dt12_305.asp.

42. Greene, Kisida, and Mills, *Administrative Bloat at American Universities*, p. 7; see also Desrochers and Wellman, *Trends in College Spending 1999–2009*, Table A1.

43. Greene, Kisida, and Mills, *Administrative Bloat at American Universities*, p. 7; see also Desrochers and Wellman, *Trends in College Spending 1999–2009*, Table A1.

44. Greene, Kisida, and Mills, *Administrative Bloat at American Universities*, p. 7; see also Desrochers and Wellman, *Trends in College Spending 1999–2009*, Table A1.

45. Greene, Kisida, and Mills, *Administrative Bloat at American Universities*, Figure 6; see also Desrochers and Wellman, *Trends in College Spending 1999–2009*, Table A1.

46. Greene, Kisida, and Mills, *Administrative Bloat at American Universities*, p. 8; see also Desrochers and Wellman, *Trends in College Spending 1999–2009*, Table A1.

47. Greene, Kisida, and Mills, *Administrative Bloat at American Universities*, p. 8; see also Desrochers and Wellman, *Trends in College Spending 1999–2009*, Table A1.

48. Greene, Kisida, and Mills, *Administrative Bloat at American Universities.*

49. Greene, Kisida, and Mills, *Administrative Bloat at American Universities.*

50. Greene, Kisida, and Mills, *Administrative Bloat at American Universities*, p. 15.

51. Larry L. Leslie and Gary Rhoades, "Rising Administrative Costs: Seeking Explanations," *Journal of Higher Education* 66, no. 2 (1995): 187–212.

52. Leslie and Rhoades, "Rising Administrative Costs," p. 194.

53. Leslie and Rhoades, "Rising Administrative Costs," p. 193.

54. Greene, Kisida, and Mills, *Administrative Bloat at American Universities*, p. 15.

55. Brian Jacob, Brian McCall, and Kevin M. Stange, "College as Country Club: Do Colleges Cater to Students' Preferences for Consumption?" National Bureau of Educational Research (NBER) Working Paper no. 18745, NBER, Cambridge, MA, January 2013, http://www.nber.org/papers/w18745.

56. Jacob, McCall, and Stange, "College as Country Club," pp. 3–4.

57. Jacob, McCall, and Stange, "College as Country Club," p. 34.

58. Robert Morse, "Methodology: Undergraduate Ranking Criteria and Weights," *U.S. News & World Report*, September 11, 2012, http://www.usnews.com/education/best-colleges/articles/2012/09/11/methodology-undergraduate-ranking-criteria-and-weights-2.

59. Zywicki, "Institutional Review Boards as Academic Bureaucracies."

60. William A. Niskanen Jr., *Bureaucracy and Representative Government* (Rutger's Livingston Campus, NJ: Aldine Transaction, 2007).

61. Martin and Hill, "Baumol and Bowen Cost Effects in Research Universities"; Lucca, Nadauld, and Shen, "Credit Supply and the Rise in College Tuition."

62. Andreas Ortmann and Richard Squire, "A Game-Theoretic Explanation of the Administrative Lattice in Institutions of Higher Learning," *Journal of Economic Behavior and Organization* 43, no. 3 (2000): 377–91.

63. Ortmann and Squire, "A Game-Theoretic Explanation."

64. Ortmann and Squire, "A Game-Theoretic Explanation."

65. Ortmann and Squire, "A Game-Theoretic Explanation."

66. Ortmann and Squire, "A Game-Theoretic Explanation."

67. Ortmann and Squire, "A Game-Theoretic Explanation," p. 381.

68. Ortmann and Squire also argue that as with faculty members, academic administrators might also be seeking to expand their free time and opportunities for outside income. Although that assumption is valid for many professors (at least those who have valuable private-sector expertise), it does not seem valid for administrators, who work standard workweeks and have no obvious demand for their services outside the university.

69. This paragraph is based on the personal experiences of one of the authors (Zywicki), who served for four years on the board of trustees of an Ivy League university from which he had graduated.

70. William F. Buckley, *God and Man at Yale,* (Washington: Gateway Editions, 1986; originally published 1951).

71. Ginsberg, *The Fall of The Faculty.*

72. Zywicki, "Institutional Review Boards as Academic Bureaucracies."

Chapter 7

1. William G. Bowen and Eugene M. Tobin, *Locus of Authority: The Evolution of Faculty Roles in the Governance of Higher Education* (Princeton, NJ: Princeton University Press, 2015), p. 1.

2. Richard C. Blum, "We Need to Be Strategically Dynamic," open letter to the University of California Regents, August, 2007, https://www.scribd.com/document/34048298/Strategically-Dynamic-Blum.

3. Commission on the Academic Presidency, *Renewing the Academic Presidency: Stronger Leadership for Tougher Times* (Washington: Association of Governing Boards of Universities and Colleges, 1996), p. 8.

4. Candace de Russy, "Public Universities Need Rigorous Oversight by Trustees," *Chronicle of Higher Education,* October 11, 1996.

5. José A. Cabranes, "Myth and Reality of University Trusteeship in the Post-Enron Era," *Fordham Law Review* 76 (2007): 960.

6. Benjamin Ginsberg, *The Fall of the Faculty and the Rise of the All-Administrative University and Why It Matters* (New York: Oxford University Press, 2011), pp. 15–16.

7. Gary C. Fethke and Andrew J. Policano, *Public No More: A New Path to Excellence for America's Public Universities* (Stanford, CA: Stanford University Press, 2012), p. 172.

8. Jon Marcus, "Polls: Americans Increasingly Mistrustful of College Costs, Leadership, and Value," *The Hechinger Report,* November 7, 2016.

9. Philip G. Altbach, "The American Model in Comparative Perspective," in *In Defense of American Higher Education,* ed. Philip G. Altbach, Patricia J. Gumport, and D. Bruce Johnstone (Baltimore, MD: Johns Hopkins University Press, 2001), p. 11.

10. Adam Smith, *An Inquiry into the Nature and Causes of the Wealth of Nations* (New York: Modern Library College Editions, 1985; first published 1776), p. 427.

11. Smith, *The Wealth of Nations,* p. 427.

12. Thomas Sowell, *Inside American Education: The Decline, the Deception, the Dogmas* (New York: Free Press, 1993), p. 294.

13. Fritz Machlup, *Knowledge—Its Creation, Distribution and Economic Significance, Vol II: The Branches of Learning* (Princeton, NJ: Princeton University Press, 1982), p. 132.

14. In this respect, American colleges more closely resembled late medieval universities than English colleges: "In place of immediate control of the colleges by teachers or professors, the practice evolved [in colonial America] of granting complete corporate power to governing boards composed of external members," the origins of which "lie in the medieval universities of northern Italy" (E. D. Duryea, "Evolution of University Organization," in *The University as an Organization,* ed. James A. Perkins [New York: McGraw Hill, 1973], p. 18). The *universitas,* or "free corporation," of the 13th century was itself an organizational response to the deficiencies of earlier student control, municipalities' growing interests in protecting their investments, and the desire of the Church to limit local power and influence over those increasingly important institutions. (Hastings Rashdall, *The Universities of Europe in the Middle Ages, Volume 2,* ed. F. M. Powicke and A. B. Emden [London: Oxford University Press, 1936], pp. 59–62; Alan B. Cobban, "Medieval Student Power," *Past & Present* 53 [1971]: 28–66).

15. Machlup, *Knowledge—Its Creation, Distribution and Economic Significance, Vol II,* pp. 132–35.

16. Laurence R. Veysey, *The Emergence of the American University* (Chicago: University of Chicago Press, 1965), p. 142.

17. Louis Agassiz, as quoted in Larry G. Gerber, *The Rise and Decline of Faculty Governance: Professionalization and the Modern American University* (Baltimore, MD: John Hopkins University Press, 2014), p. 25.

18. See Veysey, *The Emergence of the American University,* pp. 303–305; Duryea, "Evolution of University Organization," p. 23; Bowen and Tobin, *Locus of Authority,* pp. 29, 39; Gerber, *The Rise and Decline of Faculty Governance,* pp. 48–49. At the close of the first decade of the 20th century, "the greatest concern among [the nation's leading scientists] was not direct interference by trustees but autocratic rule by presidents" (Gerber, 48–49).

19. Duryea, "Evolution of University Organization," p. 31.

20. Veysey, *The Emergence of the American University,* p. 322.

21. Duryea, "Evolution of University Organization," p. 21.

22. Veysey, *The Emergence of the American University,* p. 393. "Faculty government, where it existed, served much the same function as student government. It was a useful device whereby administrative leaders could sound out opinion, detect discontent so as better to cope with it, and further the posture of official solidarity by giving everyone parliamentary 'rights'" (Veysey, p. 305).

23. Duryea, "Evolution of University Organization," p. 21; Paul Westmeyer, *A History of American Higher Education* (Springfield: Charles C. Thomas, 1985), p. 95.

24. Gerber, *The Rise and Decline of Faculty Governance,* p. 48.

25. Gerber, *The Rise and Decline of Faculty Governance,* pp. 63–64.

26. Duryea, "Evolution of University Organization," p. 23.

27. Bowen and Tobin, *Locus of Authority,* p. 33.

28. James M. Cattell, *University Control* (New York: Science Press, 1913), pp. 23–24.

29. Report of Committee T (1924), as reported in Gerber, *The Rise and Decline of Faculty Governance,* appendix.

30. Gerber, *The Rise and Decline of Faculty Governance,* pp. 75–79.

31. John R. Thelin, *A History of American Higher Education* (Baltimore, MD: John Hopkins University Press, 2004), p. 310.

32. The "Administrator Determination" category was further divided into "Consultation," "Discussion," or "None," depending on the nature and form of communication between faculty and administrators to be undertaken before a decision. For a breakdown of responses for these three subcategories, see Scott E. Masten, "Authority and Commitment: Why Universities, Like Legislatures, Are Not Organized as Firms," *Journal of Economics and Management Strategy* 15 (2006): 649–84. Note that faculty lack the ability to block actions by administrators under these three subcategories, unlike under "Faculty Determination" and "Joint Action."

33. Surveys were completed jointly by administrators and faculty representatives in two-thirds of the institutions (542), by administrators alone at 169 institutions, and by faculty representatives at 45 institutions. Faculty and administrators submitted separate survey responses at 70 institutions (Masten, "Authority and Commitment").

34. The survey allowed for variation in governance arrangements within an institution and asked respondents to report the percentage of faculty governed by each arrangement. The vast majority of responses indicated that the governance mode applied uniformly within the institution, implying that most of the observed variation in governance arrangements resulted from differences between rather than within institutions (Masten, "Authority and Commitment").

35. Comparisons in Figure 7.2 are for the 527 institutions that participated in both surveys. The 2001 survey obtained responses from 882 institutions (Gabriel E. Kaplan, "Preliminary Results from the 2001 Survey on Higher Education Governance," 2002; Unpublished report presented to Committee T of the American Association of University Professors, Washington, February 15–16). Kaplan compares average responses for all respondents in the 1970 and 2001 surveys (Gabriel E. Kaplan, "How Academic Ships Actually Navigate: A Report from the 2001 Survey on Higher Education Governance," in *Governing Academia: Who Is in Charge at the Modern University?,* ed. Ronald G. Ehrenberg [Ithaca, NY: Cornell University Press, 2004], pp. 165–208).

36. Henry G. Manne, "How the Structure of Universities Determined the Fate of American Legal Education—A Tribute to Larry Ribstein," *International Review of Law and Economics* 38 (2014): 116.

37. Manne, "How the Structure of Universities Determined the Fate of American Legal Education," p. 113. The predominance of nonprofit and state institutions in higher education is likely not an accident but rather an endogenous institutional response to problems of contracting for education services. See, among others, Henry Hansmann, "The Role of Nonprofit Enterprise," *Yale Law Journal* 89 (1980): 835–901; Henry Hansmann, "The Evolving Economic Structure of Higher Education," *University of Chicago Law Review* 79 (2012): 159–83; Scott E. Masten, "Old School Ties: Financial Aid Coordination and the Governance of Higher Education," *Journal of Economic Behavior and Organization* 28 (1995): 23–47; Tyler Cowen and Sam Papenfuss, "The Economics of For-Profit Education," in *Doing More with Less: Making Colleges Work Better,* ed. Joshua C. Hall (New York: Springer Publishing, 2010).

38. Bowen and Tobin, *Locus of Authority,* pp. 29, 39; Veysey, *The Emergence of the American University,* pp. 303–5.

39. Cowen and Papenfuss, "Economics of For-Profit Education," p. 18.

40. Bowen and Tobin, *Locus of Authority,* pp. 31, 40.

41. Thelin, *A History of American Higher Education*, p. 310.

42. Gerber, *The Rise and Decline of Faculty Governance,* p. 81.

43. Rosen similarly attributes the introduction of tenure to faculty monopoly power. Sherwin Rosen, "Some Economics of Teaching," *Journal of Labor Economics,* 5 (1987): 561–75. Glaeser offers a model in which faculty authority, along with tenure and the emphasis on research, is an outgrowth of rent seeking motivated and enabled by the increasing wealth of universities (Edward L. Glaeser, ed., *The Governance of Not-for-Profit Firms* [Chicago: University of Chicago Press, 2003], pp. 1–44).

44. Changing definitions and survey methods complicate comparisons over time. More recent estimates using a narrower definition (excluding research assistants) put the number of full-time faculty at 369,000 and of all faculty at 474,000 in 1970. The corresponding figures for 2001 (using yet another methodology) were 618,000 full-time and 1.113 million total faculty (Thomas D. Snyder, Cristobal de Brey, and Sally A. Dillow, *Digest of Education Statistics 2015* [NCES 2016-014], [Washington: U.S. Department of Education, 2016], Table 315.10).

45. Thomas D. Snyder, *120 Years of American Education: A Statistical Portrait,* (Washington: U.S. Dept. of Education, 1993), Table 26; U.S. Census Bureau, *Decennial Census of Population*, 1900 to 2000. Available statistics did not begin to distinguish two- and four-year institutions until 1917, at which time 46 of the 980 total were two-year colleges; two-year colleges accounted for 52 of the 1,041 institutions in 1920 (Snyder, *120 Years of American Education*, Table 26). The number of pre–Civil War colleges is a matter of speculation but probably numbered between 400 and 500, many of which did not survive the century. The 1860 census reported 467 colleges (including two-year institutions), whereas a 1980 study by the Department of Education identified 381 surviving institutions founded before 1860 (Snyder, *120 Years of American Education*, p. 105). This contrasts with findings by Westmeyer, who reports that, of the more than 800 colleges founded in the United States between 1776 and 1860, only 180 survived until 1900 (Paul Westmeyer, *A History of American Higher Education* [Springfield, IL: Thomas], p. 24).

46. Veysey, *The Emergence of the American University,* p. 330; John R. Thelin, *A History of American Higher Education*, pp. 110–13. In an essay devoted to debunking the "myth" of the laissez-faire origins of American higher education, Bennett nevertheless devotes several pages to describing the general ease of entry, proliferation of new institutions, high level of experimentation, significant failure rate, and generally overall competitiveness of higher education in 19th-century America. Daniel L. Bennett, "Myth Busting the

Laissez-Faire Origins of American Higher Education," *Independent Review* 18 (2014): 513–17.

47. Thelin, *A History of American Higher Education,* pp. 153–4.

48. Thelin, *A History of American Higher Education,* p. 151.

49. Veysey, *The Emergence of the American University,* p. 339.

50. Bowen and Tobin, *The Locus of Authority,* pp. 37–38.

51. Gerber, *The Rise and Decline of Faculty Governance,* p. 68.

52. Gerber, *The Rise and Decline of Faculty Governance,* p. 34.

53. Veysey, *The Emergence of the American University,* p. 340.

54. Veysey, *The Emergence of the American University,* pp. 174–5, 177.

55. Lori Thurgood et al., "U.S. Doctorates in the 20th Century," NSF Division of Science Resources Statistics, NSF 06-319, Arlington, VA, p. 5. American institutions began offering PhDs before becoming research universities. The first PhD awarded at an American institution occurred at Yale in 1861 (Veysey, *The Emergence of the American University*, p. 50). According to Westmeyer, 44 PhDs were awarded by 25 universities in the United States in 1876, the year Johns Hopkins was founded (Westmeyer, *A History of American Higher Education,* pp. 95–96).

56. Although the number of doctorate-granting institutions continued to grow thereafter, reaching 409 in 2000 and 432 in 2015, the proportion of all institutions offering doctorates leveled off in the range of 15 percent and 17 percent (Thurgood et al., "U.S. Doctorates in the 20th Century," p. 5; National Science Foundation, National Center for Science and Engineering Statistics, *Doctorate Recipients from U.S. Universities: 2015. Special Report NSF 17-306* (Arlington, VA, 2017), www.nsf.gov/statistics/2017/nsf17306/.

57. National Academy of Sciences, A *Century of Doctorates: Data Analyses of Growth and Change* (Washington: National Academies Press, 1978; distributed by ERIC Clearinghouse); National Science Foundation, *Doctorate Recipients from U.S. Universities: 2015.*

58. Thurgood et al., "U.S. Doctorates in the 20th Century," p. 9.

59. Michael Billig, *Learn to Write Badly: How to Succeed in the Social Sciences* (Cambridge, UK: Cambridge University Press, 2013). See also Kyle V. Sweitzer, "The Increase in Research Output among Liberal Arts Colleges: Exploring the Data and the Rationale," unpublished paper presented at the American Educational Research Association Annual Meeting, Washington, D.C. April 11, 2016.

60. Scott E. Masten, "The Enterprise as Community: Firms, Towns, and Universities," in *Handbook of Economic Organization: Integrating Economic and Organization Theory,* ed. Anna Grandori (Cheltenham, UK: Edward Elgar Publishing, 2013), pp. 105–6.

61. Gerber, *The Rise and Decline of Faculty Governance,* pp. 6, 81.

62. Veysey, *The Emergence of the American University,* p. 388; Thelin, *A History of American Higher Education,* pp. 127–8, 154. According to Gerber, "The increasing professionalization of the faculty . . . was an essential factor in the development of the principles and practices of shared governance," support for which is "the definite correlation between the reputation of an institution and the extent to which its faculty enjoyed a measure of self-government" (Gerber, *The Rise and Decline of Faculty Governance,* pp. 78, 146).

63. James P. Munroe, "Closer Relations between Trustees and Faculty," *Science* 22 (1905): 850, 852.

64. Duryea, "Evolution of University Organization," p. 23.

65. Gerber, *The Rise and Decline of Faculty Governance,* p. 78.

66. Duryea, "Evolution of University Organization," p. 30.

67. Duryea, "Evolution of University Organization," p. 25. McCormick and Meiners argue that the difficulty of assessing faculty performance creates an agency problem to which tenure and faculty governance are a response but consider the drawbacks of making decisions collectively to outweigh the benefits, resulting in inferior outcomes at universities with more faculty governance. They raise, but do not attempt to answer, the question of why universities adopt inefficient governance arrangements (Robert E. McCormick and Roger E. Meiners, "University Governance: A Property Rights Perspective," *Journal of Law & Economics* 31, no. 2 [1988]: 423–42). Brown, like McCormick and Meiners, argues that tenure makes faculty partial residual claimants in the organization but serves also to "provide faculty members with the freedom to participate openly and honestly in the monitoring and evaluation" of administrators and trustees (1997). Faculty authority, the merits of which vary with the type of decision, meanwhile affords faculty the effective power to constrain administrators (2001) (William O. Brown Jr., "University Governance and Academic Tenure: A Property Rights Explanation," *Journal of Institutional and Theoretical Economics* 153 [1997]: 459; William O. Brown Jr., "Faculty Participation in University Governance and the Effects on University Performance," *Journal of Economic Behavior & Organization* 44 [2001]: 129–43. See also Cowen and Papenfuss, "The Economics of For-Profit Education," pp. 185–8).

68. Veysey, *The Emergence of the American University,* pp. 304–5.

69. Veysey, *The Emergence of the American University,* pp. 391–4. A preference for control tied to professional status also fails to account for the greater incidence of "Joint Action" relative to "Faculty Determination" in more prestigious research institutions universities compared with other institutions (Masten, "Authority and Commitment," p. 677).

70. Kaplan, "How Academic Ships Actually Navigate"; Masten, "Authority and Commitment," pp. 649–84.

71. Although loss of priority is costly mainly to an individual scholar, interruptions in research may also harm society by delaying advances in knowledge and slowing the rate of scientific progress—again, particularly if advances are cumulative in nature.

72. For discussions of the difficulty of contracting for academic services, see, among others, Richard B. McKenzie, "In Defense of Academic Tenure," *Journal of Institutional and Theoretical Economics* 152 (1996): 325–41; Paul Milgrom and John Roberts, *Economics, Organization & Management* (New Jersey: Prentice Hall, 1992), pp. 127–9; and Douglas B. Bernheim and Michael D. Whinston, "Incomplete Contracts and Strategic Ambiguity," *American Economic Review* 88 (1998): 902–4.

73. Compare Duryea, "Evolution of University Organization," p. 28: "Diversity became the pervasive quality of the new era—diversity among institutions and within the major universities."

74. Democratic governments are less likely than autocratic ones to infringe on individual property and political interests to the extent that those interests are represented in legislatures (Martin C. McGuire and Mancur Olson Jr., "The Economics of Autocracy and Majority Rule: The Invisible Hand and the Use of Force," *Journal of Economic Literature* 34 [1996]: 72–96; Douglass C. North and Barry R. Weingast, "Constitutions and Credible Commitments: The Evolution of the Institutions of Public Choice in 17th Century England," *Journal of Economic History* 49 [1989]: 803–32).

75. See, for example, Russell Hardin et al., *The Federalist Papers and the New Institutionalism* (New York: Agathon Press, 1989), pp. 100–120; and Barry R. Weingast, "Constitutions as Governance Structures: The Political Foundations of Secure Markets," *Journal of Institutional and Theoretical Economics* 149 (1993): 286–311.

76. The argument that heterogeneity favors democratic governance contrasts with Hansmann's positon that "strong homogeneity . . . seems essential to effective self-governance" and that increasing heterogeneity will lead to "less discretion we can expect to be delegated to university faculties to choose their own colleagues (Hansmann, "The Evolving Economic Structure of Higher Education," p. 180). Hansmann predicts, "As a consequence of increasing faculty heterogeneity, we can reasonably expect that faculty self-governance in all respects—not just with respect to hiring but also with respect to setting the curriculum and allocating teaching responsibilities and research opportunities among the faculty—will decline. . . . In general, then, the future is likely to bring greater centralization of authority within American universities, which means an administrative model much closer to that found in conventional proprietary firms" ("The Evolving Economic Structure of Higher Education," p. 180).

77. Masten, "Authority and Commitment," pp. 649–84.

78. Masten, "The Enterprise as Community," pp. 105–6.

79. Adam Smith, *An Inquiry into the Nature and Causes of the Wealth of Nations* (New York: Modern Library College Editions, 1985; first published 1776), p. 428.

80. Smith, *The Wealth of Nations*, p. 428.

81. Smith, *The Wealth of Nations*, p. 427.

82. Cobban, "Medieval Student Power"; Rashdall, *The Universities of Europe in the Middle Ages, Volume 2.*

83. Rosen, "Some Economics of Teaching," pp. 561–75.

84. "The Trends Report," *Chronicle of Higher Education,* March 4, 2016.

Chapter 8

1. This essay originally appeared on the website of the James G. Martin Center for Academic Renewal on June 25, 2014, https://www.jamesgmartin.center/2014/06/all-education-is-for-profit-education/. We are grateful to them for allowing us to reprint it.

2. Robert Shireman, "Perils in the Provision of Trust Goods: Consumer Protection and the Public Interest in Higher Education," Center for American Progress, May 2014, https://cdn.americanprogress.org/wp-content/uploads/2014/05/ConsumerProtection.pdf.

3. Henry B. Hansmann, "The Role of Nonprofit Enterprise," *Yale Law Journal* 89 (1980): 835–901.

Chapter 9

1. Danielle Kurtzleben, "Just How Fast Has College Tuition Grown?" *U.S. News & World Report*, October 23, 2013, http://www.usnews.com/news/articles/2013/10/23/charts-just-how-fast-has-college-tuition-grown.

2. John Cassidy, "College Calculus: What's the Real Value of Higher Education?," *New Yorker*, September 7, 2015, http://www.newyorker.com/magazine/2015/09/07/college-calculus.

3. Robert Shireman, "The Important Difference between For-Profit and Nonprofit Colleges," *Huffington Post*, July 17, 2014, http://www.huffingtonpost.com/robert-shireman/the-important-difference-_b_5595903.html.

4. It is worth noting at the outset that the modern institution of higher learning, in actual fact a scholastic guild, is distinctly medieval "as much so as constitutional Kingship, or Parliaments, or Trial by Jury," emerging then in two separate archetypes: (a) the "customer"-centric *studium* originating in Bologna, Italy, and (b) the faculty-centric *universitas* founded in Paris. See Hastings Rashdall, *The Universities of Europe in the Middle Ages*, 3 vols. (Originally published in 1895), Reprint (New York: Cambridge University Press, 2010).

Especially see Volume 1, of which no one interested in the historical roots of today's colleges and universities should be ignorant. We thank Erik Lidström for bringing Rashdall's monumental work to our attention.

5. United States Senate Health, Education, Labor and Pensions Committee, "Emerging Risk? An Overview of Growth, Spending, Student Debt and Unanswered Questions in For-Profit Higher Education," June 24, 2010, p. 2.

6. Vicente M. Lechuga, "Who Are They? And What Do They Do?" in *For-Profit Colleges and Universities: Their Markets, Regulation, Performance, and Place in Higher Education*, eds. Guilbert C. Hentschke et al. (Sterling, VA: Stylus, 2010), pp. 51–52.

7. Eric Lichtblau, "Romney Offers Praise for a Donor's Business," *New York Times*, January 14, 2012, http://www.nytimes.com/2012/01/15/us/politics/mitt-romney-offers-praise-for-a-donors-business.html.

8. Stephanie Riegg Cellini and Rajeev Darolia, "Different Degrees of Debt: Student Borrowing in the For-Profit, Nonprofit, and Public Sectors," Brown Center on Education Policy at Brookings, June 2016, https://www.brookings.edu/wp-content/uploads/2016/07/cellini.pdf.

9. Mark L. Pelesh, "Markets, Regulation, and Performance in Higher Education," in *For-Profit Colleges and Universities: Their Markets, Regulation, Performance, and Place in Higher Education,* eds. Guilbert C. Hentschke et al. (Sterling, VA: Stylus, 2010), p. 92.

10. Pelesh, "Markets, Regulation, and Performance in Higher Education."

11. Pelesh, "Markets, Regulation, and Performance in Higher Education," p. 93.

12. Pelesh, "Markets, Regulation, and Performance in Higher Education," p. 95.

13. Eric Kelderman, "For-Profit Colleges Find Few Reasons to Lobby a Friendlier Education Dept," *Chronicle of Higher Education*, August 28, 2017, http://www.chronicle.com/article/For-Profit-Colleges-Find-Few/241024.

14. National Center for Education Statistics, "Table 301.10: Enrollment, Staff, and Degrees/Certificates Conferred in Degree-Granting and Non-Degree-Granting Postsecondary Institutions, by Control and Level of Institution, Sex of Student, Type of Staff, and Level of Degree: Fall 2010, Fall 2011, and 2011–12," *Digest of Education Statistics: 2013*, July 2013, https://nces.ed.gov/programs/digest/d13/tables/dt13_301.10.asp.

15. The discrepancy between these two figures is in large part explained by the fact that for-profit colleges award many degrees and certificates that take two years or less to complete. Consequently, for-profits award large numbers of degrees and certificates relative to enrollment; fewer students enter, but they finish faster.

16. National Center for Education Statistics: "Table 303.10: Total Fall Enrollment in Degree-Granting Postsecondary Institutions, by Attendance Status, Sex of Student, and Control of Institution: Selected Years, 1947 through 2023," July 2014, https://nces.ed.gov/programs/digest/d13/tables/dt13_303.10.asp.

17. United States Senate Health, Education, Labor and Pensions Committee, "Emerging Risk?," p. 1.

18. Michael Stratford, "Cash Monitoring List Unveiled," *Inside Higher Ed*, March 31, 2015, https://www.insidehighered.com/news/2015/03/31/education-department-names-most-colleges-facing-heightened-scrutiny-federal.

19. Gregory D. Kutz, "For-Profit Colleges: Undercover Testing Finds Colleges Encouraged Fraud and Engaged in Deceptive and Questionable Marketing Practices," Testimony GAO-10-948T before the Committee on Health, Education, Labor, and Pensions, U.S. Senate, 2010, p. 7, http://www.gao.gov/assets/130/125197.pdf.

20. United States Senate Health, Education, Labor and Pensions Committee, "Emerging Risk?," p. 6.

21. Richard Vedder, *Going Broke by Degree: Why College Costs Too Much* (Washington: AEI Press, 2004), pp. 43–46.

22. Ronald G. Ehrenberg, "American Higher Education in Transition," *Journal of Economic Perspectives* 26 (2012): 196.

23. Christopher Avery and Sarah Turner, "Student Loans: Do College Students Borrow Too Much—Or Not Enough?," *Journal of Economic Perspectives* 26 (2012): 165–92.

24. Avery and Turner, "Student Loans: Do College Students Borrow Too Much—Or Not Enough?" p. 186.

25. United States Senate Health, Education, Labor and Pensions Committee, "Emerging Risk?," p. 9.

26. See National Center for Education Statistics, Table 326.10: "Graduation Rates of First-Time, Full-Time Bachelor's Degree-Seeking Students at 4-Year Postsecondary Institutions, by Race/Ethnicity, Time to Completion, Sex, and Control of Institution: Selected Cohort Entry Years, 1996 through 2006," *Digest of Education Statistics*, January 2014, https://nces.ed.gov/programs/digest/d13/tables/dt13_326.10.asp.

27. Tyler Cowen and Sam Papenfuss, "The Economics of For-Profit Higher Education." Working paper, Center for Study of Public Choice, George Mason University, Fairfax, VA, July 2009, pp. 6–7, https://d101vc9winf8ln.cloudfront.net/documents/28239/original/Cowen-Papenfuss-revisedagain.pdf?1527191628.

28. Government Accountability Office, "Proprietary Schools: Stronger Department of Education Oversight Needed to Help Ensure Only Eligible

Students Receive Federal Student Aid," Report GAO-09-600 to the Chairman, Subcommittee on Higher Education, Lifelong Learning and Competitiveness, Committee on Education and Labor, U.S. House of Representatives, 2009, http://www.gao.gov/new.items/d09600.pdf.

29. Constance Iloh and William G. Tierney, "A Comparison of For-Profit and Community Colleges' Admissions Practices," *College and University* 88 (2013): 5.

30. Anthony J. Guida Jr., and David Figuli, "Higher Education's Gainful Employment and 90/10 Rules: Unintended 'Scarlet Letters' for Minority, Low-Income, and Other At-Risk Students," *University of Chicago Law Review* 79 (2012): 131–58.

31. Ellen Frishberg, John B. Lee, Carla Fletcher, and Jeff Webster, "How to Graduate High-Risk Students: Lessons from Successful For-Profit Colleges and Schools in Texas," *TG*, 2010, pp. 10–14, https://files.eric.ed.gov/fulltext/ED542509.pdf.

32. Carolyn Arcand, "How Can Community Colleges Better Serve Low-Income Single-Mother Students? Lessons from the For-Profit Sector," *Community College Journal of Research and Practice* 39 (2015): 1188.

33. Watson Scott Swail, "Graduating At-Risk Students: A Cross-Sector Analysis," Imagine America Foundation, 2009, http://www.educationalpolicy.org/pdf/GraduatingAtRiskStudents.pdf.

34. Swail, "Graduating At-Risk Students," p. 15.

35. Swail, "Graduating At-Risk Students," p. 23.

36. National Center for Education Statistics, "Institutional Retention and Graduation Rates for Undergraduate Students," May 2015, https://nces.ed.gov/programs/coe/pdf/Indicator_CTR/coe_ctr_2015_05.pdf. Graduation rates for private nonprofit institutions are similar to those at for-profit colleges.

37. Swail, "Graduating At-Risk Students," pp. 13–19.

38. Thomas Bailey, Norena Badway, and Patricia J. Gumport, "For-Profit Higher Education and Community Colleges," p. 23, National Center for Postsecondary Improvement, Stanford University, 2001, http://web.stanford.edu/group/ncpi/documents/pdfs/forprofitandcc.pdf.

39. Neal McCluskey, "Even For-Profit Universities Are Better than America's Terrible Community Colleges," *Washington Post*, January 13, 2015, https://www.washingtonpost.com/posteverything/wp/2015/01/13/even-for-profit-universities-are-better-than-americas-terrible-community-colleges/.

40. Quoted in Constance Iloh and William G. Tierney, "Understanding For-Profit College and Community College Choice through Rational Choice," *Teachers College Record* 116 (2014): 17.

41. Iloh and Tierney, "Understanding For-Profit College and Community College Choice."

42. Iloh and Tierney, "Understanding For-Profit College and Community College Choice," pp. 16–17.

43. Frishberg et al., "How to Graduate High-Risk Students."

44. Frishberg et al., "How to Graduate High-Risk Students."

45. Arcand, "How Can Community Colleges Better Serve Low-Income Single-Mother Students?" p. 1188.

46. Bailey, Badway, and Gumport, "For-Profit Higher Education and Community Colleges," pp. 33–34.

47. JoAnna Schilling, "What's Money Got to Do with It? The Appeal of the For-Profit Education Model," *Community College Journal of Research and Practice* 37 (2013): 155.

48. McCluskey, "Even For-Profit Universities Are Better than America's Terrible Community Colleges."

49. Iloh and Tierney, "Understanding For-Profit College and Community College Choice."

50. Iloh and Tierney, "Understanding For-Profit College and Community College Choice," p. 11.

51. Quoted in Iloh and Tierney, "Understanding For-Profit College and Community College Choice," p. 19.

52. Schilling, "What's Money Got to Do with It?" p. 155.

53. Schilling, "What's Money Got to Do with It?" p. 155.

54. Bailey, Badway, and Gumport, "For-Profit Higher Education and Community Colleges," pp. 43–44.

55. Bailey, Badway, and Gumport, "For-Profit Higher Education and Community Colleges," pp. 25–26.

56. Bailey, Badway, and Gumport, "For-Profit Higher Education and Community Colleges," pp. 27–28.

57. Iloh and Tierney, "Understanding For-Profit College and Community College Choice," pp. 20–21.

58. Of course, the listed tuition rates of community colleges and for-profit colleges are not indicative of the true social costs of the two options. The funding that community colleges receive from taxpayers through state and federal subsidies represents a social cost that would have to be incorporated to make a true comparison. Nevertheless, the individual student at the moment of choice will perceive community college to involve a lesser financial outlay.

59. Kutz, "For-Profit Colleges: Undercover Testing."

60. Iloh and Tierney, "Understanding For-Profit College and Community College Choice."

61. Iloh and Tierney, "Understanding For-Profit College and Community College Choice," pp. 8–10.

62. Bailey, Badway, and Gumport, "For-Profit Higher Education and Community Colleges," p. 32.

63. Some of this revenue is received in the form of federally subsidized loans, in which case the student must eventually repay the federal loan.

64. United States Senate Health, Education, Labor and Pensions Committee Report, "For Profit Higher Education: The Failure to Safeguard the Federal Investment and Ensure Student Success," July 30, 2012, p. A9-5.

65. United States Senate Health, Education, Labor and Pensions Committee, "Emerging Risk?," pp. 3–4.

66. Specifically, those 20 for-profit colleges had received $66.6 million in 2006 and were projected to receive $521.2 million in 2010. United States Senate Health, Education, Labor and Pensions Committee, "Benefitting Whom? For-Profit Education Companies and the Growth of Military Educational Benefits," December 8, 2010, p. 9.

67. United States Senate Health, Education, Labor and Pensions Committee, "Benefitting Whom?" p. 5.

68. United States Senate Health, Education, Labor and Pensions Committee, "Benefitting Whom?" p. 8.

69. David O. Lucca, Taylor Nadauld, and Karen Shen, "Credit Supply and the Rise in College Tuition: Evidence from the Expansion in Federal Student Aid Programs," Staff Report no. 733, Federal Reserve Bank of New York, 2015, http://www.newyorkfed.org/research/staff_reports/sr733.html.

70. Stephanie Riegg Cellini and Claudia Goldin, "Does Federal Student Aid Raise Tuition? New Evidence on For-Profit Colleges," *American Economic Journal: Economic Policy* 6 (2014): 174–206.

71. For example, Larry D. Singell and Joe A. Stone, "For Whom the Pell Tolls: The Response of University Tuition to Federal Grants-in-Aid," *Economics of Education Review* 26 (2007): 285–95; and Grey Gordon and Aaron Hedlund, "Accounting for the Rise in College Tuition," Working Paper 21967, National Bureau of Economic Research, Cambridge, MA, 2016, http://www.nber.org/papers/w21967. For a comprehensive list of such studies, see Neal McCluskey, "The Newly Updated Help-That-Hurts List," *See Thru Edu*, January 7, 2016, http://www.seethruedu.com/the-newly-updated-help-that-hurts-list/.

72. Securities and Exchange Commission (SEC), 102 [20 U.S.C. 1002] (b)(1)(A). "Definition of Institution of Higher Education for Purposes of Title IV Programs: Proprietary Institutions of Higher Education."

73. Questions here worth pondering here are whether the goals of public, private, and for-profit institutions really are systematically different and consequently whether it makes sense to hold different institutions to different standards.

74. U.S. Department of Education, "Fact Sheet on Final Gainful Employment Regulations: Details of the Final Regulations and [their] Impact," October 30, 2014, http://www2.ed.gov/policy/highered/reg/hearulemaking/2012/gainful-employment-fact-sheet-10302014.pdf.

75. U.S. Department of Education, "Five Percent of Career Training Programs Risk Losing Access to Federal Funds; 35 Percent Meet All Three Standards under Gainful Employment Regulation," news release, June 26, 2012, http://www.ed.gov/news/press-releases/five-percent-career-training-programs-risk-losing-access-federal-funds-35-percent-meet-all-three-standards-under-gainful-employment-regulation.

76. U.S. Department of Education, "Obama Administration Announces Final Rules to Protect Students from Poor-Performing Career College Programs," news release, October 30, 2014, http://www.ed.gov/news/press-releases/obama-administration-announces-final-rules-protect-students-poor-performing-care.

77. Kelderman, "For-Profit Colleges Find Few Reasons to Lobby a Friendlier Education Dept."

78. Ali Elkin, "Bernie Sanders to Introduce Bill to Make College Tuition-Free," Bloomberg Politics, May 17, 2015, http://www.bloomberg.com/politics/articles/2015-05-17/bernie-sanders-to-introduce-bill-to-make-college-tuition-free.

79. Elkin, "Bernie Sanders to Introduce Bill"; Julie Bosman and Tamar Lewin, "With $350 Billion Plan, Hillary Clinton Prods Rivals on Student Debt," *New York Times*, August 13, 2015, http://www.nytimes.com/2015/08/14/us/with-350-billion-plan-hillary-clinton-prods-rivals-on-student-debt.html.

80. Pelesh, "Markets, Regulation, and Performance in Higher Education," p. 94.

81. Pelesh, "Markets, Regulation, and Performance in Higher Education," pp. 95–97.

82. Gordon Tullock, "The Politics of Bureaucracy," in *The Selected Works of Gordon Tullock: Vol. 6. Bureaucracy,* ed. Charles K. Rowley, (Indianapolis, IN: Liberty Fund), pp. 23–24.

83. Pelesh, "Markets, Regulation, and Performance in Higher Education," p. 103.

84. George Stigler, "The Theory of Economic Regulation," *Bell Journal of Economics and Management Science* 2 (1971): 3–21.

85. Ernesto Dal Bó, "Regulatory Capture: A Review," *Oxford Review of Economic Policy* 22 (2006): 203–25.

86. United States Senate Health, Education, Labor and Pensions Committee, "Emerging Risk?" p. 2.

87. Pelesh, "Markets, Regulation, and Performance in Higher Education," pp. 103–4.

88. Alec MacGillis, "Higher Ed Lobby Quietly Joins For-Profit Schools to Roll Back Tighter Rules," ProPublica, May 5, 2015, https://www.propublica.org/article/higher-ed-lobby-quietly-joins-for-profit-schools-to-roll-back-tighter-rules.

89. Molly Corbett Broad, letter to Chairman Kline, Chairwoman Foxx, Representative Hastings, and Representative Salmon, American Council on Education, February 23, 2015, http://www.acenet.edu/news-room/Documents/Letter-Congress-SAFRRA.pdf.

90. Vedder, *Going Broke by Degree.*

91. Daniel L. Bennett, Adam R. Lucchesi, and Richard K. Vedder, "For-Profit Higher Education: Growth, Innovation and Regulation," Center for College Affordability and Productivity Policy Paper, July 2010, https://eric.ed.gov/?id=ED536282.

92. John Cassidy, "College Calculus: What's the Real Value of Higher Education?," *New Yorker,* September 7, 2015, http://www.newyorker.com/magazine/2015/09/07/college-calculus.

93. Quoted in Cassidy, "College Calculus."

Chapter 10

1. U.S. Department of Education, "Important Information on the Derecognition of ACICS," April 3, 2018, https://www.ed.gov/acics.

2. Accrediting Council for Independent Colleges and Schools v. DeVos, U.S.D.C. for the District of Columbia, Civ. Action No. 16-2448 (RBW); "Briefing Complete on ACICS Motion for Summary Judgment in U.S. District Court," June 22, 2017, http://www.acics.org/news/content.aspx?id=6958.

3. White House, "Remarks by the President on America's College Promise," news release, January 9, 2015, https://obamawhitehouse.archives.gov/the-press-office/2015/01/09/remarks-president-americas-college-promise.

4. For details, see the website for Tennessee Promise, http://tennesseepromise.gov/.

5. Katie Lobosco, "Tuition-Free College Is Getting Bigger. Here's Where It's Offered," *CNN Money,* August 4, 2017; Editorial Board, "Hillary's For-Profit Education," *Wall Street Journal,* September 15, 2015.

6. Katie Lobosco, "New York Just OK'd Tuition-Free College for Middle Class," *CNN Money,* April 10, 2017, http://money.cnn.com/2017/04/08/pf/college/new-york-free-tuition/index.html. For details, see Tuition-Free Degree Program: The Excelsior Scholarship, https://www.ny.gov/programs/tuition-free-degree-program-excelsior-scholarship.

7. Lobosco, "Tuition-Free College Is Getting Bigger."

8. National Conference of State Legislatures, "Free Community College," April 25, 2016, http://www.ncsl.org/research/education/free-community-college.aspx.

9. In making this case, I will not address two logically prior questions: (a) whether it is true that literally everyone should attend college and (b) whether the public should pay higher taxes to subsidize that goal. Rather, we will take the goals of increasing the percentage of American high school graduates who go to college and increasing the public subsidy to college attendance as givens. Put another way, if we assume that policymakers will continue to seek ever-larger enrollments in postsecondary education, then taxpayers should want the for-profits to remain in the picture, given their superior performance in tailoring their programs to the needs and desires of their predominantly nontraditional students.

10. Negotiated Rulemaking Committee; Public Hearings, 82 Fed. Reg. 27640, June 16, 2017, https://www.federalregister.gov/documents/2017/06/16/2017-12555/negotiated-rulemaking-committee-public-hearings. For the reaction from the nonprofit side of higher education, see Adam Harris, "DeVos Will Roll Back 2 Obama Regulations, a Blow to Consumer Advocates," *Chronicle of Higher Education*, June 14, 2017, http://www.chronicle.com/article/DeVos-Will-Roll-Back-2-Obama/240337; and Adam Harris, "What DeVos's 'Reset' on 2 Major Consumer Rules Means for Colleges," *Chronicle of Higher Education*, June 14, 2017, http://www.chronicle.com/article/What-DeVos-s-Reset-on/240348.

11. In fiscal year 2014, the U.S. Department of Education disbursed $133.8 billion in federal student aid—low-interest loans, grants, and work-study funds—to 12.9 million students (U.S. Department of Education, *Federal Student Aid Annual Report FY 2014*, November 14, 2014), http://www2.ed.gov/about/reports/annual/2014report/fsa-report.pdf. Spending on those programs has grown rapidly; the total spent in 1986–87 (in constant dollars) was only $30 billion. Daniel L. Bennett, Adam R. Lucchesi, and Richard K. Vedder, "For-Profit Higher Education in the United States," in *The Profit Motive in Education: Continuing the Revolution,* ed. James B. Stanfield, (London: Institute of Economic Affairs, 2012), pp. 120, 123, http://www.iea.org.uk/sites/default/files/publications/files/The%20Profit%20Motive%20in%20Education%20-%20Continuing%20the%20Revolution.pdf.

12. Daniel L. Bennett, Adam R. Lucchesi, and Richard K. Vedder, "For-Profit Higher Education: Growth, Innovation and Regulation," evaluative report, Center for College Affordability and Productivity, Washington, July 2010, https://eric.ed.gov/?id=ED536282.

13. James Coleman and Richard Vedder, "For-Profit Education in the United States: A Primer," policy paper, Center for College Affordability and Productivity, Washington, May 2008, http://files.eric.ed.gov/fulltext/ED536281.pdf.

14. Definition of Institution of Higher Education for Purposes of Student Assistance Programs, 20 U.S.C. § 1002 (2012).

15. David J. Deming, Claudia Goldin, and Lawrence F. Katz, "The For-Profit Postsecondary School Sector: Nimble Critters or Agile Predators?" *Journal of Economic Perspectives* 26, no. 1 (Winter 2012): 139–64, http://scholar.harvard.edu/files/lkatz/files/dgk.pdf.

16. Rebecca R. Skinner, "Institutional Eligibility and the Higher Education Act: Legislative History of the 90/10 Rule and Its Current Status," Congressional Research Service, 2005, http://www.policyarchive.org/handle/10207/1904.

17. Coleman and Vedder, "For-Profit Education in the United States."

18. U.S. Department of Education, National Center for Education Statistics, *Digest of Education Statistics,* February 2017, Table 303.10, https://nces.ed.gov/programs/digest/d16/tables/dt16_303.10.asp?current=yes.

19. Apollo Education Group, SEC Form 10K for fiscal year ended August 31, 2010, p. 14, http://investors.apollo.edu/phoenix.zhtml?c=79624&p=irol-reportsannual.

20. U.S. Department of Education, *Digest of Education Statistics,* Table 303.10. Because total enrollment in higher education fell by more than a million students—or 4.95 percent—from 2010 to 2015, focusing on the for-profits' loss of market share is more appropriate than focusing on their absolute losses in enrollment.

21. Compare Apollo Education Group, SEC Form 10K for fiscal year ended August 31, 2015, pp. 5 and 10 with Apollo Education Group, SEC Form 10K for fiscal year ended August 31, 2016, pp. 6 and 10, http://investors.apollo.edu/phoenix.zhtml?c=79624&p=irol-reportsannual.

22. Shares of the common stock of Apollo Education Group opened at $34.16 on January 2, 2015, and closed on February 5, 2016, at $6.95. That decline in share price of 80 percent translates to a loss of more than $2.9 billion in market value in just 13 months. On February 8, 2016, Apollo announced that it had agreed to be purchased for $9.50 per share in cash—or $1.1 billion—by a group of investors that included the Vistria Group, a Chicago private equity firm "with close ties to the Obama administration." Patricia Cohen and Chad Bray, "University of Phoenix Owner, Apollo Education Group, Will Be Taken Private," *New York Times*, February 8, 2016, https://www.nytimes.com/2016/02/09/business/dealbook/apollo-education-group-university-of-phoenix-owner-to-be-taken-private.html. Tony Miller, Vistria's chief operating officer, was deputy secretary of education from 2009 to 2013. He became chairman of the board of Apollo after the transaction closed. Vistria's founder, Marty Nesbitt, is described in the *New York Times* article as "one of President Obama's closest friends and the chairman of the Obama Foundation." The article also notes that "The new owners . . . are promising to lead a clean-up of the for-profit education industry."

23. Danielle Douglas-Gabriel, "For-Profit Corinthian Colleges Files for Bankruptcy," *Washington Post*, May 4, 2015, http://www.washingtonpost.com/news/business/wp/2015/05/04/for-profit-corinthian-colleges-files-for-bankruptcy/.

24. Jillian Berman, "ITT Is the Second Major For-Profit College to Declare Bankruptcy Since Last Year," *MarketWatch*, September 18, 2016, http://www.marketwatch.com/story/itt-is-second-major-for-profit-college-to-declare-bankruptcy-since-last-year-2016-09-16.

25. The Art Institutes, "Education Management Corporation Announces Execution of a Definitive Agreement for the Sale to the Dream Center Foundation," news release, March 3, 2017, https://www.artinstitutes.edu/about/blog/dream-center-foundation.

26. Goldie Blumenstyk, "Purdue's Purchase of Kaplan Is a Big Bet—and a Sign of the Times," Chronicle of Higher Education, April 28, 2017, http://www.chronicle.com/article/Purdue-s-Purchase-of-Kaplan/239931. For the official version of this transaction, visit https://www.purdue.edu/newsroom/releases/2017/Q2/purdue-to-acquire-kaplan-university,-increase-access-for-millions.html.

27. The Federal Trade Commission (FTC) is investigating whether the University of Phoenix's recruitment of military veterans amounts to "unfair or deceptive acts or practices" under the FTC Act. The California attorney general is conducting an investigation along parallel lines. Anne Flaherty, Associated Press, "FTC Investigating Online College University of Phoenix," *San Diego Union Tribune,* July 29, 2015, http://www.sandiegouniontribune.com/sdut-ftc-investigating-online-college-university-of-2015jul29-story.html. In January 2014 the *Wall Street Journal* reported that 32 attorneys general had active investigations under way and had begun to cooperate with the federal Consumer Financial Protection Bureau. Stephanie Armour and Alan Zibel, "For-Profit College Probe Expands," *Wall Street Journal*, January 13, 2014, https://www.wsj.com/articles/forprofit-college-probe-expands-1389647449. In February 2014 the *Chronicle of Higher Education* reported that 22 state attorneys general were conducting 82 investigations of 10 large for-profits. Goldie Blumenstyk, "Government Investigations and Suits against For-Profit Colleges: The Grid," *Chronicle of Higher Education*, February 28, 2014, http://www.chronicle.com/blogs/bottomline/government-investigations-and-suits-against-for-profit-colleges-the-grid/. Numerous state investigations of smaller, non-national for-profit firms are under way. Many of the state investigations proceed under the authority of state "little FTC acts," which publish "unfair or deceptive" actions or practices. The website "Republic Report" maintains an updated list of "pending and recent federal and state government investigations and actions regarding for-profit colleges." David Halperin, "Law Enforcement

Investigations and Actions Regarding For-Profit Colleges," April 9, 2014, http://www.republicreport.org/2014/law-enforcement-for-profit-colleges/.

28. Warren quoted in Danielle Douglas-Gabriel, "What Staggering Loan Defaults at For-Profit Schools Say about Accreditors," *Washington Post*, September 8, 2015, http://www.washingtonpost.com/business/economy/what-staggering-loan-defaults-at-for-profit-schools-say-about-accreditors/2015/09/07/f9b6f47c-4cf5-11e5-bfb9-9736d04fc8e4_story.html.

29. U.S. Department of Education, "Statement from U.S. Secretary of Education Arne Duncan on House Republicans Proposing to Block Gainful Employment Regulations," news release, June 16, 2015, http://www.ed.gov/news/press-releases/statement-us-secretary-education-arne-duncan-house-republicans-proposing-block-gainful-employment-regulations; Duncan quoted in Editorial Board, "Help for Victims of College Fraud," *New York Times*, June 10, 2015, https://www.nytimes.com/2015/06/10/opinion/help-for-victims-of-college-fraud.html.

30. Letter to Secretary of Education Arne Duncan from the attorneys general of Massachusetts, California, Connecticut, Illinois, Kentucky, New Mexico, New York, Oregon, and Washington State, April 9, 2015, https://oag.ca.gov/sites/all/files/agweb/pdfs/letter-asg-arne-duncan-04-09-2015.pdf.

31. See Craig Eyermann, "The U.S. Department of Education's $1 Trillion Debt Milestone," MyGovCost.org, July 6, 2017, http://www.mygovcost.org/2017/07/06/the-u-s-department-of-educations-1-trillion-debt-milestone/.

32. Matthew A. McGuire, "Subprime Education: For-Profit Colleges and the Problem with Title IV Federal Student Aid," *Duke Law Journal* 62 (2012): 120, http://dlj.law.duke.edu/article/subprime-education-for-profit-colleges-and-the-problem-with-title-iv-federal-student-aid/.

33. U.S. Department of Education, *Digest of Education Statistics*, Table 303.10.

34. Kelly Field, "Senators Mull Changes in 90/10 Rule to Rein In For-Profits," *Chronicle of Higher Education*, March 2, 2011, http://www.chronicle.com/article/Senators-Mull-Changes-in-90-10/126564/; "90-10 Rule," *Wikipedia*, https://en.wikipedia.org/wiki/90-10_rule.

35. Deming, Goldin, and Katz, "The For-Profit Postsecondary School Sector, p. 152.

36. The Association for Private Sector Colleges and Universities ("APSCU") successfully challenged the first version of the GE rule in federal district court in Washington, D.C. (Association of Private Sector Colleges and Universities v. Duncan, 870 F.Supp.2d 133 [D.D.C. 2012]). However, the court refused to strike down a revised version of the rule on June 23, 2015, and APSCU lost its appeal. Association of Private Sector Colleges and Universities v. Duncan, 110 F.Supp.3d 176 (D.D.C. 2015), *affirmed* 640 Fed. Appx. 5 (D.C. Cir. 2016). The APSCU has since reconstituted itself as Career Education Colleges and Universities.

37. Program Integrity: Gainful Employment, 79 Fed. Reg. 64890-01 (Oct. 31, 2014) (final rule, eff. July 1, 2015), https://www.federalregister.gov/documents/2014/10/31/2014-25594/program-integrity-gainful-employment.

38. Department of Education, "Fact Sheet: Obama Administration Increases Accountability for Low-Performing For-Profit Institutions," July 1, 2015, https://www.ed.gov/news/press-releases/fact-sheet-obama-administration-increases-accountability-low-performing-profit-institutions. Headline writers had a field day. See, for example, Allie Grasgreen, "Obama Pushes For-Profit Colleges to the Brink," *Politico*, July 1, 2015, http://www.politico.com/story/2015/07/barack-obama-pushes-for-profit-colleges-to-the-brink-119613.

39. Fernanda Zamudio-Suaréz, "Education Dept. Delays Compliance Deadline for Gainful-Employment Rules," *Chronicle of Higher Education*, June 30, 2017, http://www.chronicle.com/blogs/ticker/education-dept-delays-compliance-deadline-for-gainful-employment-rules/119203.

40. Adam Harris, "DeVos Will Roll Back 2 Obama Regulations, a Blow to Consumer Advocates," *Chronicle of Higher Education*, June 14, 2017, http://www.chronicle.com/article/DeVos-Will-Roll-Back-2-Obama/240337.

41. U.S. Department of Justice, "U.S. Files Complaint against Education Management Corp. Alleging False Claims Act Violations," news release, August 8, 2011, https://www.justice.gov/opa/pr/us-files-complaint-against-education-management-corp-alleging-false-claims-act-violations. The Department of Justice provided support for, but did not intervene in, an earlier False Claims Act suit brought against the University of Phoenix by former employees and settled in 2009. See U.S. Department of Justice, "University of Phoenix Settles False Claims Act Lawsuit for $67.5 Million," news release, December 15, 2009, https://www.justice.gov/opa/pr/university-phoenix-settles-false-claims-act-lawsuit-675-million.

42. Quoted in U.S. Department of Justice, "U.S. Files Complaint Against Education Management Corp."

43. Goldie Blumenstyk, "Little for Students in 'Historic' Settlement of Education Management Case," *Chronicle of Higher Education*, November 17, 2015, http://www.chronicle.com/article/Little-for-Students-in/234229.

44. The Art Institutes, "Education Management Corporation Announces Execution of a Definitive Agreement for the Sale to the Dream Center Foundation," https://www.artinstitutes.edu/about/blog/dream-center-foundation.

45. The SEC sued ITT Educational Services in the U.S. District Court for the Southern District of Indiana on May 12, 2015. The complaint is available on the SEC's website, http://www.sec.gov/litigation/complaints/2015/comp-pr2015-86.pdf.

46. Bennett, Lucchesi, and Vedder, "For-Profit Higher Education," Table 1 (based on 2008–2009 enrollment data), July 2010.

47. Federal Trade Commission, "FTC Brings Enforcement Action Against DeVry University," news release, January 27, 2016, https://www.ftc.gov/news-events/press-releases/2016/01/ftc-brings-enforcement-action-against-devry-university.

48. Shannon Najmabadi, "DeVry Settles Federal Lawsuit for $100 Million," *Chronicle of Higher Education*, December 15, 2016, http://www.chronicle.com/blogs/ticker/devry-settles-federal-lawsuit-for-100-million/116150.

49. U.S. Department of Education, "U.S. Department of Education Heightens Oversight of Corinthian Colleges," news release, June 19, 2014, http://www.ed.gov/news/press-releases/us-department-education-heightens-oversight-corinthian-colleges.

50. U.S. Department of Education, "U.S. Department of Education Accepts Operating Plan from Corinthian Colleges Inc.," news release, July 3, 2014, http://www.ed.gov/news/press-releases/us-department-education-accepts-operating-plan-corinthian-colleges-inc.

51. See the case here, http://files.consumerfinance.gov/f/201409_cfpb_complaint_corinthian.pdf.

52. From 12 U.S.C. 5536(a)(1)(B).

53. From 12 U.S.C. 5531(c)(1).

54. John Tumilty and Katherine Guarino, "The CFPB's Confusing Definitions of Unfair, Deceptive or Abusive Acts and Practices," *Inside Counsel*, September 30, 2012.

55. Consumer Financial Protection Bureau, "CFPB Sues For-Profit Corinthian Colleges for Predatory Lending Scheme," news release, September 16, 2014, http://www.consumerfinance.gov/newsroom/cfpb-sues-for-profit-corinthian-colleges-for-predatory-lending-scheme/.

56. U.S. Department of Education, "Notice of Intent to Fine Heald College," letter to Jack D. Massimino, April 14, 2015, http://www2.ed.gov/documents/press-releases/heald-fine-action-placement-rate.pdf.

57. There were 10 of 28 graduates reported as placed by the IT-Network Systems Administration program at Heald College–Fresno that were hired by a temporary agency for work in "brief, temporary positions at its Fresno campus."

58. U.S. Department of Education, "Notice of Intent to Fine Heald College."

59. Duncan quoted in Andy Thomason and Goldie Blumenstyk, "$30-Million Fine for Corinthian May Portend Tougher Scrutiny of For-Profits," *Chronicle of Higher Education*, April 15, 2015, http://chronicle.com/article/30-Million-Fine-for/229355/.

60. Business Wire, "Corinthian Announces Cessation of Effectively All Operations," news release, April 26, 2015, https://www.businesswire.com/news/home/20150426005017/en/Corinthian-Announces-Cessation-Effectively-Operations.

61. Business Wire, "Corinthian Announces Cessation."

62. Douglas-Gabriel, "For-Profit Corinthian Colleges Files for Bankruptcy."

63. U.S. Department of Education, "Statement from Education Under Secretary Ted Mitchell on the Closure Announcement from Corinthian Colleges, Inc.," news release, April 27, 2015, http://www.ed.gov/news/press-releases/statement-education-under-secretary-ted-mitchell-closure-announcement-corinthian-colleges-inc.

64. Durbin quoted in Grasgreen, "Obama Pushes For-Profit Colleges to the Brink."

65. Duncan quoted in Michael Stratford, "Debt Relief Unveiled," *Inside Higher Ed*, June 9, 2015, https://www.insidehighered.com/news/2015/06/09/us-will-erase-debt-corinthian-students-create-new-loan-forgiveness-process.

66. Mark Schneider and Jorge Klor de Alva, "Real Cost of Obama's War against For-Profit Colleges," *The Hill*, September 22, 2014, http://thehill.com/blogs/congress-blog/education/218374-real-cost-of-obamas-war-against-for-profit-colleges.

67. Kelly Field, "Plan to Forgive Corinthian Students' Loans Offers Hope to Other Borrowers," *Chronicle of Higher Education*, June 9, 2015, http://chronicle.com/article/Plan-to-Forgive-Corinthian/230761/.

68. Field, "Plan to Forgive Corinthian Students' Loans."

69. U.S. Department of Education, *Fact Sheet: Protecting Students from Abusive Career Colleges*, http://www.ed.gov/news/press-releases/fact-sheet-protecting-students-abusive-career-colleges. Useful surveys on the subject of common law fraud and for-profit colleges include Charlie Shelton, *Private Actions Against Proprietary Schools*, 40 Rutgers L. Rec. 81 (2012–13), and Blake Shinoda, Note, *Enabling Class Litigation as an Approach to Regulating For-Profit Colleges*, 87 S. Cal. L. Rev. 1085, 1108-12 (2014).

70. U.S. Department of Education, "First Report of the Special Master for Borrower Defense to the Under Secretary," news release, September 3, 2015, http://www2.ed.gov/documents/press-releases/report-special-master-borrower-defense-1.pdf.

71. Christine DiGangi, "Students Will Have $3.5 Billion of Student Loan Debt Wiped Out and They Are Not Happy about It," *Credit.com*, June 11, 2015, https://blog.credit.com/2015/06/students-will-have-3-5-billion-of-student-loan-debt-wiped-out-they-are-not-happy-about-it-118442/.

72. Andy Thomason, "In Shift, Education Dept. Will Automatically Forgive Student Loans Incurred at Defunct For-Profit," *Chronicle of Higher Education*, January 13, 2017 (discussing the case of American Career Institute), http://www.chronicle.com/blogs/ticker/in-shift-education-dept-will-automatically-forgive-loans-held-by-students-of-defunct-for-profit/116452.

73. Andrea Fuller and Douglas Belkin, "The Watchdogs of College Education Rarely Bite," *Wall Street Journal*, June 17, 2015.

74. U.S. Department of Education, "Student Assistance General Provisions, Federal Perkins Loan Program, Federal Family Education Loan Program, William D. Ford Federal Direct Loan Program, and Teacher Education Assistance for College and Higher Education Grant Program," 81 Fed. Reg. 75926 (November 1, 2016), https://www.gpo.gov/fdsys/pkg/FR-2016-11-01/pdf/2016-25448.pdf.

75. U.S. Department of Education, "Borrower Defense Final Regulations: Summary of Major Provisions," https://www2.ed.gov/documents/press-releases/borrower-defense-final-regulations.pdf.

76. U.S. Department of Education, "Secretary DeVos Announces Regulatory Reset to Protect Students, Taxpayers, Higher Ed Institutions," news release, June 14, 2017, https://www.ed.gov/news/press-releases/secretary-devos-announces-regulatory-reset-protect-students-taxpayers-higher-ed-institutions.

77. Adam Harris, "18 States Sue Education Dept. over Rollback of Borrower-Defense Rule," *Chronicle of Higher Education*, July 6, 2017, http://www.chronicle.com/blogs/ticker/18-states-sue-education-dept-over-rollback-of-borrower-defense-rule/119245; New York State Office of the Attorney General, "A. G. Schneiderman—Part of Coalition of 19 Attorneys General—Sues U.S. Department of Education for Abandoning Critical Student Protections," news release, July 6, 2017, https://ag.ny.gov/press-release/ag-schneiderman-part-coalition-19-attorneys-general-sues-us-department-education.

78. William L. Megginson and Jeffry M. Netter, "From State to Market: A Survey of Empirical Studies on Privatization," *Journal of Economic Literature* 39 (2001): 321, http://media.terry.uga.edu/socrates/publications/2011/07/stateToMarket_1.pdf?_ga=2.106802883.1904815168.1498751807-816517644.1498500332; Andrei Shleifer, "State versus Private Ownership," *Journal of Economic Perspectives* 12, no. 4 (Fall 1998): 133, https://scholar.harvard.edu/shleifer/publications/state-versus-private-ownership; Aidan R. Vining and Anthony E. Boardman, "Ownership Versus Competition: Efficiency in Public Enterprise," *Public Choice* 73 (1992): 205; Anthony E. Boardman and Aidan R. Vining, "Ownership and Performance in Competitive Environments: A Comparison of the Performance of Private, Mixed, and State-Owned Enterprises," *Journal of Law and Economics* 32 (1989): 1.

79. Robin Wilson, "For-Profit Colleges Change Higher Education's Landscape," *Chronicle of Higher Education*, February 7, 2010, http://chronicle.com/article/For-Profit-Colleges-Change-/64012/.

80. Bennett, Lucchesi, and Vedder, "For-Profit Higher Education: Growth, Innovation and Regulation," pp. 29–30.

81. Deming, Goldin, and Katz, "The For-Profit Postsecondary School Sector," pp. 159, 161. The authors did note that the students at nonprofit colleges reported higher satisfaction with their institutions. For more on student satisfaction, see Judah Bellin, "The Unacknowledged Value of For-Profit Education," Manhattan Institute Issue Brief no. 20, April 2013, http://www.manhattan-institute.org/pdf/ib_20.pdf.

82. Deming, Goldin, and Katz, "The For-Profit Postsecondary School Sector," p. 149.

83. Deming, Goldin, and Katz, "The For-Profit Postsecondary School Sector," p. 150.

84. Bennett, Lucchesi, and Vedder, "For-Profit Higher Education: Growth, Innovation and Regulation," p. 25.

85. Office of Senator Sherrod Brown, "Sen. Brown Introduces Bill to Ban Colleges from Spending Federal Financial Aid Dollars on Marketing and Recruiting," news release, July 30, 2015, http://www.brown.senate.gov/newsroom/press/release/sen-brown-introduces-bill-to-ban-colleges-from-spending-federal-financial-aid-dollars-on-marketing-and-recruiting.

86. American Private Sector Colleges and Universities, "Letter to U.S. Under Secretary of Education Ted Mitchell," June 11, 2015. The text of this letter was made public on the APSCU website. However, when APSCU reconstituted itself as Career Education Colleges and Universities, it did not include the letter in the publicly accessible areas of the successor organization's website, http://www.career.org/.

87. Deming, Goldin, and Katz, "The For-Profit Postsecondary School Sector: Nimble Critters or Agile Predators?" p. 146.

88. Jorge Klor de Alva and Mark Schneider, "Do Proprietary Institutions of Higher Education Generate Savings for States? The Case of California, New York, Ohio, and Texas," Nexus Research and Policy Center, March 2014, https://www.insidehighered.com/sites/default/server_files/files/How%20Much%20Does%20Prop%20Ed%20Save%20States%20v9.pdf

89. Importantly, both authors have been associated with the University of Phoenix. In addition, Schneider was U.S. Commissioner of Education Statistics from 2005 to 2008, and Klor de Alva was the Class of 1940 Professor at the University of California, Berkeley.

90. Schneider and Klor de Alva, "Real Cost of Obama's War against For-Profit Colleges."

91. White House, "Remarks by the President on America's College Promise."

92. Amanda Stone, "Follow Along: Our 2015 Back-to-School Tour," White House, September 9, 2015, https://www.whitehouse.gov/blog/2015/09/09/heads-find-out-how-you-can-join-movement-make-community-college-free.

93. National Public Radio, "Tennessee Promise Lets Kids Start College for Free," *NPR Weekend Edition*, September 12, 2015, http://www.npr.org/2015/09/12/439727383/tennessee-promise-lets-kids-start-college-for-free.

94. This statistic, along with the tax payments number in the next sentence in the text, was displayed on ASPCU's website. However, when APSCU reconstituted itself as Career Education Colleges and Universities, it did not include those numbers on the publicly accessible areas of the successor organization's website, http://www.career.org/. In 2015 APSCU estimated the total cost per full-time student at a four-year public institution at $29,464, compared with $16,999 at a for-profit institution, and that 45 percent of the costs of a public institution (apparently including both two- and four-year colleges) are paid for by taxpayer-funded operating subsidies. American Private Sector Colleges and Universities, "Letter to U.S. Under Secretary of Education Ted Mitchell" (noted at footnote 86). Because four-year colleges are more complex institutions, arguably generating positive externalities through research or medical education (for example) that do not apply to the two-year college market, this chapter will focus on the comparison of community colleges and for-profit colleges.

95. White House, "FACT SHEET: Providing More Americans with Affordable Access to Education and Job Training Opportunities to Help Grow the Middle Class," news release, September 9, 2015, https://www.whitehouse.gov/the-press-office/2015/09/09/fact-sheet-providing-more-americans-affordable-access-education-and-job.

96. Richard Arum and Josipa Roksa, *Academically Adrift: Limited Learning on College Campuses* (Chicago: University of Chicago Press, 2011), p. 36. See also American Council of Trustees and Alumni, "What Will They Learn 2016-17 Executive Summary," September 2016, https://www.goacta.org/executivesummary/what_will_they_learn_2016_17_executive_summary (critique of general education curricula at nonprofit colleges and universities).

97. See, for example, Jay Stooksberry, "Selling Higher Education Is Sleazier Than Selling a Used Car," Foundation for Economic Education, February 28, 2017, https://fee.org/articles/selling-higher-education-is-sleazier-than-selling-a-used-car/. Although the author does not identify his former employer as a nonprofit college, he describes employer's charges for undergraduate room and board—not a part of the for-profit world.

98. David O. Lucca, Taylor Nadauld, and Karen Shen, "Credit Supply and the Rise in College Tuition: Evidence from the Expansion in Federal Student

Aid Programs," Federal Reserve Bank of New York, July 2015, http://www.newyorkfed.org/research/staff_reports/sr733.html.

99. Kevin Carey, "Gaps in Earnings Stand Out in Release of College Data," *New York Times*, September 13, 2015, http://www.nytimes.com/2015/09/14/upshot/gaps-in-alumni-earnings-stand-out-in-release-of-college-data.html?_r=1. The 2015–16 tuition at Bennington was $47,590; at Bard it was $49,226.

100. Modern Language Association (MLA), "Report of the MLA Task Force on Doctoral Study in Modern Language and Literature," May 2014, http://www.mla.org/pdf/taskforcedocstudy2014.pdf.

101. Abram Brown, "Why Forbes Removed 4 Schools from Its America's Best Colleges Rankings," Forbes, August 12, 2013, https://www.forbes.com/sites/abrambrown/2013/07/24/why-forbes-removed-4-schools-from-its-americas-best-colleges-rankings.

102. See Joel F. Murray, "Professional Dishonesty: Do U.S. Law Schools That Report False or Misleading Employment Statistics Violate Consumer Protection Laws?," *Journal of Consumer and Commercial Law* 15, no. 3 (2012): 97–108, http://www.jtexconsumerlaw.com/V15N3/V15N3_Professional.pdf.

103. WSJ News Graphics, "How Accredited Colleges Stack Up," *Wall Street Journal*, June 17, 2015, http://graphics.wsj.com/accredit-2015/.

104. Robert Maranto, Richard E. Redding, and Frederick M. Hess, eds., *The Politically Correct University: Problems, Scope, and Reforms* (Washington: AEI Press, 2009); Christopher E. Cardiff and Daniel B. Klein, "Faculty Partisan Affiliations in All Disciplines: A Voter-Registration Study," *Critical Review* (2005) 17: 237–55 (11 California universities); John O. McGinnis, Matthew A. Schwartz, and Benjamin Tisdell, "The Patterns and Implications of Political Contributions by Elite Law School Faculty," *Georgetown Law Journal* 93 (2005): 1167; James Lindgren, "Measuring Diversity: Law Faculties in 1997 and 2013," *Harvard Journal of Law and Public Policy* 39 (2016): 89, http://harvardjlpp.wpengine.com/wp-content/uploads/2010/01/39_1_Lindgren_F.pdf.

The Center for Responsive Politics compiled a list of institutions that were the top 20 contributors to the 2012 Obama campaign. Its website, OpenSecrets.org, explained that the institutions themselves did not make donations, "rather the donations came from the organizations' PACs, their individual members, or employees or owners, and those individuals' immediate families." The largest contributor was the University of California, which contributed $1,350,139. Six other universities were in the top 20: Harvard (#5, $680,918), Stanford (#8, $532,246), Columbia (#9, $478,123), New York University (#18, $357,822), the University of Chicago (#19, $354,282), and the University of Michigan (#20, $351,118). If the four federal agencies whose employees were contributors are combined into one "federal government" entry, then those universities represent 7 of the top 17 sources of funds for the Obama campaign, and the higher-education sector is by far the largest industry in the top 20. OpenSecrets .org, "Barack Obama (D), Top Contributors, 2012 Cycle," https://www.opensecrets.org/pres12/contrib.php?id=N00009638.

105. Editorial Board, "Hillary's For-Profit Education."

106. Robert Shireman, "Perils in the Provision of Trust Goods: Consumer Protection and the Public Interest in Higher Education," Center for American Progress, May 2014, https://cdn.americanprogress.org/wp-content/uploads/2014/05/ConsumerProtection.pdf.

107. Henry B. Hansmann, "The Role of Nonprofit Enterprise," *Yale Law Journal* 89 (1980): 835–901.

108. Shireman, "Perils in the Provision of Trust Goods."

109. Shireman, "Perils in the Provision of Trust Goods," p. 8.

110. An earlier Manne essay on university governance is Henry G. Manne, "The Political Economy of Modern Universities," Association of Governing Boards of Universities and Colleges (AGB) Reports, October 1972, http://files.eric.ed.gov/fulltext/ED098834.pdf.

111. Richard K. Vedder, "Time to Make Professors Teach," *Wall Street Journal,* June 8, 2011, https://www.wsj.com/articles/SB10001424052702304432304576369840105112326.

112. Quoted in Vance H. Fried, "Federal Higher Education Policy and the Profitable Nonprofits," Cato Policy Analysis no. 678, June 15, 2011, https://object.cato.org/sites/cato.org/files/pubs/pdf/PA678.pdf.

113. Similarly, a Senate committee staff report critical of for-profits spoke in terms of "ensur[ing] student success." See Staff of Senate Committee on Health, Education, Labor and Pensions, "For Profit Higher Education: The Failure to Safeguard the Federal Investment and Ensure Student Success," Majority Final Report on For-Profit Higher Education, 2012, http://www.help.senate.gov/imo/media/for_profit_report/Contents.pdf.

Chapter 11

1. Talmud, Baba Metzia 5b.

2. Kenneth J. Arrow, "Uncertainty and the Welfare Economics of Health Care," *American Economic Review* 53 (1963): 965.

3. U.S. Senate Committee on Health, Education, Labor and Pensions, "For Profit Higher Education: The Failure to Safeguard the Federal Investment and Ensure Student Success," 2012, http://www.gpo.gov/fdsys/pkg/CPRT-112SPRT74931/pdf/CPRT-112SPRT74931.pdf .

4. American Hospital Association, "Fast Facts on U.S. Hospitals: Fast Facts 2018," http://www.aha.org/research/rc/stat-studies/fast-facts.shtml.

5. David A. Hyman and William M. Sage, "Subsidizing Health Care Providers through the Tax Code: Status or Conduct?" *Health Affairs* 25 (2006): W312.

6. Jill Horwitz, "Nonprofit Healthcare Organizations and the Law," in *The Oxford Handbook of US Health Law*, eds. I. Glenn Cohen, Allison K. Hoffman, and William M. Sage (New York: Oxford University Press, 2016).

7. Sara Rosenbaum et al., "The Value of the Nonprofit Hospital Tax Exemption Was $24.6 Billion in 2011," *Health Affairs* 34 (2015): 1–9.

8. Internal Revenue Service, Revenue Ruling 56-185, 1956-1 C.B. 202.

9. Internal Revenue Service, Revenue Ruling 69-545, 1969-2 C.B. 117.

10. Internal Revenue Service, Additional Requirements for Charitable Hospitals, Final Rule, 79 Fed. Reg. 78954-79016 (December 31, 2014).

11. Adam H. Langley, Daphne A. Kenyon, and Patricia C. Bailin, "Payments in Lieu of Taxes by Nonprofits: Which Nonprofits Make PILOTs and Which Localities Receive Them," working paper, Lincoln Institute of Land Policy, Cambridge, MA, September 2012.

12. Horwitz, "Nonprofit Healthcare Organizations and the Law."

13. The two literature reviews are Frank A. Sloan, "Not-for-Profit Ownership and Hospital Behavior," in *Handbook of Health Economics*, eds. Anthony J. Culyer and Joseph P. Newhouse (Amsterdam: Elsevier Science Publisher B.V., 2000), pp. 1141–74; and Horwitz, "Nonprofit Healthcare Organizations and the Law." The pieces examining variability in results are Yu-Chu Shen et al., "Hospital Ownership and Financial Performance: What Explains the Different Findings in the Empirical Literature?" *Inquiry* 44 (2007): 41–68; and Karen Eggleston et al., "Hospital Ownership and Quality of Care: What Explains the Different Results in the Literature?" *Health Economics* 17 (2008): 1345–62.

14. Sloan, "Not-for-Profit Ownership and Hospital Behavior," p. 1168.

15. Shen et al., "Hospital Ownership and Financial Performance," p. 41.

16. Eggleston et al., "Hospital Ownership and Quality of Care," p. 1345.

17. Jill Horwitz, "Nonprofit Healthcare Organizations and the Law," in *The Oxford Handbook of U.S. Health Law*, eds. I. Glenn Cohen, Allison K. Hoffman, and William M. Sage (New York: Oxford University Press, 2016), pp. 537–38.

18. Congressional Budget Office, "Nonprofit Hospitals and the Provision of Community Benefits," Pub no. 2707, December 2006, p. 2, https://www.cbo.gov/sites/default/files/109th-congress-2005-2006/reports/12-06-nonprofit.pdf.

19. Erica Valdovinos, Sidney Le, and Renee Y. Hsia, "In California, Not-For-Profit Hospitals Spent More Operating Expenses on Charity Care than For-Profit Hospitals Spent," *Health Affairs* 34 (2015): 1296–303.

20. Valdovinos, Le, and Hsia, "In California, Not-For-Profit Hospitals Spent More," p. 1299.

21. Ge Bai and Gerard F. Anderson, "Extreme Markup: The Fifty US Hospitals with the Highest Charge-To-Cost Ratios," *Health Affairs* 34 (2015): 922–7; G. J. Young and K. R. Desai, "Nonprofit Hospital Conversions and Community Benefits: New Evidence from Three States," *Health Affairs* 18 (September/October 1999): 146–55.

22. David M. Studdert et al., "Regulatory and Judicial Oversight of Nonprofit Hospitals," *New England Journal of Medicine* 356, no. 6 (2007): 625–31.

23. Lucette Lagnado, "Call It Yale v. Yale," *Wall Street Journal,* November 14, 2003.

24. Jonathan Cohn, "Uncharitable?" *New York Times Magazine*, December 19, 2004.

25. Chris Arnold, "When Nonprofit Hospitals Sue Their Poorest Patients," National Public Radio, December 19, 2014, http://www.npr.org/2014/12/19/371202059/when-a-hospital-bill-becomes-a-decade-long-pay-cut.

26. Cohn, "Uncharitable?" 2014.

27. David A. Hyman, "Hospital Conversions: Fact, Fantasy, and Regulatory Follies," *Journal of Corporation Law* 23 (1998): 741–78.

28. Hyman, "Hospital Conversions," p. 754.

29. Gary J. Young, Kamal R. Desai, and Carol VanDeusen Lukas, "Does the Sale of Nonprofit Hospitals Threaten Health Care for the Poor?" *Health Affairs* 16 (January/February 1997): 137–41; and Gary J. Young and Kamal R. Desai, "Nonprofit Hospital Conversions and Community Benefits: New Evidence from Three States," *Health Affairs* 18 (September/October 1999): 146–55.

30. Jack Needleman, JoAnn Lamphere, and Deborah Chollet, "Uncompensated Care and Hospital Conversions in Florida," *Health Affairs* 18 (1999): 125–33.

31. Kenneth E. Thorpe, Curtis S. Florence, and Eric E. Seiber, "Hospital Conversions, Margins, and the Provision of Uncompensated Care," *Health Affairs* 19 (2000): 187–94.

32. Jill R. Horwitz and Austin Nichols, "Hospital Ownership and Medical Services: Market Mix, Spillover Effects, and Nonprofit Objectives," *Journal of Health Economics* 28 (2009): 924–37.

33. Daniel Kessler and Mark McClellan, "The Effects of Hospital Ownership on Medical Productivity," *RAND Journal of Economics* 33 (2002): 488–506; Jack Hadley, Bradford. H. Gray, and Sara R. Collins, "A Statistical Analysis of the Impact of Nonprofit Hospital Conversions on Hospitals and Communities, 1985–1996," report, The Commonwealth Fund,

New York, May 2001, http://citeseerx.ist.psu.edu/viewdoc/download;jsessionid=5B5A737D9863300AF60AD937A0C1F96D?doi=10.1.1.493.9533&rep=rep1&type=pdf; Mark Schlesinger et al., "Competition, Ownership, and Access to Hospital Services: Evidence from Psychiatric Hospitals," *Medical Care* 35, no. 9 (1997): 974–92; Susan L. Ettner and Richard C. Hermann, "The Role of Profit Status under Imperfect Information: Evidence from the Treatment Patterns of Elderly Medicare Beneficiaries Hospitalized for Psychiatric Diagnoses," *Journal of Health Economics* 20 (2001): 23–49; Robert G. Hughes and Harold S. Luft, "Keeping Up with the Joneses: The Influence of Public and Proprietary Neighbors on Voluntary Hospitals," *Health Services Management Research* 3 (1990): 173–81.

34. John Braithwaite, *Corporate Crime in the Pharmaceutical Industry* (New York: Routledge, 1984).

35. Joe Stephens and Mary Pat Flaherty, "Inside the Hidden World of Thefts, Scams and Phantom Purchases at the Nation's Nonprofits," *Washington Post*, October 26, 2013.

36. Paul Yingling, "A Failure in Generalship," *Armed Forces Journal*, May 1, 2007.

37. John M. Darley and Joel Cooper, eds., *Attribution and Social Interaction: The Legacy of Edward E. Jones* (Washington: American Psychological Association, 1998).

38. David M. Cutler, *The Changing Hospital Industry: Comparing Not-for-Profit and For-Profit Institutions* (Chicago: University of Chicago Press, 2000); Bradford H. Gray, ed., *For-Profit Enterprise in Health Care* (Washington: National Academy Press, 1986).

39. Bradford H. Gray and Walter J. McNerney, "For Profit Enterprise in Health Care: The Institute of Medicine Study," *New England Journal of Medicine* 314 (1986): 1523–4.

40. Hyman and Sage "Subsidizing Health Care Providers."

41. Henry Manne, "All Education Is For-Profit Education," James G. Martin Center for Academic Renewal, June 25, 2014, https://www.jamesgmartin.center/2014/06/all-education-is-for-profit-education/.

42. George Orwell, *Animal Farm* (New York, NY: Signet Classics, 1996), p. 11.

INDEX

Note: Information in figures and tables is denoted by *f* and *t;* n designates a numbered note.

ABOUT THE CONTRIBUTORS

Michael E. DeBow is the Stephen E. Wells Professor of Municipal Law at Samford University, where he teaches property, business organizations, administrative law, and local government law. He is a coauthor of *Conservative and Libertarian Legal Scholarship: An Annotated Bibliography* (Federalist Society, 2d ed., 2011). From 2014 to 2016, DeBow was associate director of the Center for College Affordability and Productivity. He holds a BA and an MA in economics from the University of Alabama and a JD from Yale.

Joshua C. Hall is an associate professor of economics and director of the Center for Free Enterprise in the College of Business and Economics at West Virginia University. He earned BA and MA degrees in economics from Ohio University and a PhD from West Virginia University in 2007. Before returning to his alma mater, he was the Elbert H. Neese, Jr., Professor of Economics at Beloit College. Hall is a past president of the Association of Private Enterprise Education and is also a senior fellow at the Fraser Institute. A coauthor of the widely cited *Economic Freedom of the World* annual report, he is also author or coauthor of more than 100 articles in peer-reviewed journals such as *Public Choice*, *Contemporary Economic Policy*, *Journal of Economic Behavior and Organization*, *Urban Studies*, *Southern Economic Journal*, *Public Finance Review*, and *Journal of Public Administration Research and Theory*.

David A. Hyman is a professor at Georgetown University Law Center. He focuses his research and writing on the regulation and financing of health care and on empirical law and economics. He teaches or has taught health care regulation, civil procedure, insurance, medical malpractice, law and economics, professional responsibility, consumer protection, and tax policy. While serving as special counsel to the Federal Trade Commission, Hyman was principal author and project leader for the first joint report ever issued by the Federal Trade Commission and the Department of Justice, "Improving Health Care: A Dose of Competition" (2004). He is also the author of *Medicare Meets Mephistopheles* (Cato Institute, 2006), which was selected by the National Chamber Foundation (now the U.S. Chamber of Commerce Foundation) as one of the top 10 books of 2007. He has published widely in student-edited law reviews and peer-reviewed medical, health policy, law, and economics journals.

Christopher Koopman is the senior director of strategy and research at the Center for Growth and Opportunity at Utah State University. He is also a senior affiliated scholar at the Mercatus Center at George Mason University. Koopman earned his JD from Ave Maria University and his LLM in law and economics at George Mason University.

Jayme S. Lemke is a senior research fellow and associate director of academic and student programs at the Mercatus Center at George Mason University. She is also a senior fellow in the F. A. Hayek Program for Advanced Study in Philosophy, Politics, and Economics at the Mercatus Center. Her research on public choice economics, constitutional political economy, and the political economy of women's rights has appeared in outlets such as the *Journal of Institutional Economics*, *Public Choice*, and *Studies in Emergent Order.* She was recently awarded the 2016 Gordon Tullock Prize for best article published in *Public Choice* by a junior scholar. In addition, she is coeditor, with Virgil H. Storr, of *Economy, Polity, and Society*, an interdisciplinary book series in political economy published by Rowman & Littlefield International.

Henry G. Manne was dean of the George Mason University School of Law from 1986 to 1996 and professor there from 1986 to 1999. He also taught at St. Louis University, the University of Wisconsin, the George Washington University, the University of Rochester, the University of Miami, and Emory University. Manne received a BA in economics at Vanderbilt University, a JD at the University of Chicago Law School, and an SJD at Yale Law School. He was a member of numerous professional organizations and boards and is an honorary life member of the American Law and Economics Association, which honored him as one of the four founders of the field of law and economics. Among his notable educational innovations at George Mason University School of Law were the Law and Economics Center, the Economics Institute for Law Professors, the Law Institute for Economists, the Economics Institute for Federal Judges, the first specialized law degree program for PhDs in economics, and the first law school whose curriculum was built around the use of economics in law.

Scott E. Masten is professor of business economics and public policy in the University of Michigan Stephen M. Ross School of Business. In addition to his primary appointment, he has held appointments as the Louis and Myrtle Moskowitz Research Professor in Business and Law at the University of Michigan, the John M. Olin Faculty Research Fellow at Yale Law School, and the John M. Olin Distinguished Visiting Professor of Law at the University of Virginia Law School. He was also a visiting professor in the University of Michigan Law School. His research focuses on issues at the intersection of law, economics, and organization, and his work has made him a leading scholar in the area of transaction cost economics. Masten was a founding board member and is a past president of the Society for Institutional & Organizational Economics (formerly, the International Society for New Institutional Economics). In 2014–15, he chaired the University of Michigan faculty Senate and Senate Advisory Committee on University Affairs, the Senate's executive committee.

Roger E. Meiners is the Goolsby-Rosenthal Chair of Economics and Law at the University of Texas–Arlington, where he is also chair of the Department of Economics. A lawyer-economist by training, Meiners held previous faculty appointments at Texas A&M University, Emory University, and the University of Miami. He served as the director of the Atlanta office of the Federal Trade Commission. His research has focused on the economic structure of universities and on common-law solutions to environmental problems. Publications include *Faulty Towers: Tenure and the Structure of Higher Education* (Independent Institute, 2004).

Daniel D. Polsby is professor of law at the George Mason University Antonin Scalia Law School. He joined the faculty in 1999 after serving 23 years on the Northwestern University law faculty, where he had been the Kirkland & Ellis Professor of Law since 1990. He has held visiting appointments at the University of Southern California, the University of Michigan, and Cornell University. He was appointed acting dean of the George Mason University School of Law in 2004, was named dean in 2005, and served until he stepped down in June 2015. Polsby has published dozens of articles on such diverse subjects as voting rights, family law, employment rights, and spectrum utilization. Polsby received his BA from Oakland University and earned his JD magna cum laude from the University of Minnesota. He teaches criminal law, family law, constitutional law, and other subjects.

Jane Shaw Stroup is board chairman of the James G. Martin Center for Academic Renewal (previously the Pope Center for Higher Education Policy). She was president of the center from 2008 to 2015 and spent 22 years with PERC, the Property and Environment Research Center in Bozeman, Montana, where she was a senior fellow. Before joining PERC, she was an associate economics editor of *Business Week* in New York City and previously worked as a correspondent for McGraw-Hill Publications in Washington, D.C., and Chicago. Stroup received her BA in English literature from Wellesley College. Stroup is a former trustee of the Philadelphia Society and a past president of the Association of Private Enterprise Education.

William F. Shughart II is research director and senior fellow at The Independent Institute, the J. Fish Smith Professor in Public Choice at Utah State University, and past president of the Southern Economic Association. Shughart is also editor-in-chief of the journal *Public Choice* and the author of several books. A former economist at the Federal Trade Commission, Shughart received his PhD in economics from Texas A&M University, and he has taught at George Mason University, Clemson University, the University of Mississippi, and the University of Arizona.

Richard K. Vedder is Distinguished Professor of Economics Emeritus at Ohio University and an adjunct scholar at the American Enterprise Institute. A graduate of Northwestern University and the University of Illinois, Vedder has published more than 200 papers and several books, including *Going Broke by Degree: Why College Costs Too Much* (American Enterprise Institute, 2004). He also writes extensively in the popular press, including the *Wall Street Journal*, the *Washington Post*, the *New York Times*, *Forbes*, and *Investor's Business Daily*. For years, he directed the Center for College Affordability and Productivity and also the Best College rankings of *Forbes* magazine. An economic historian, Vedder has written several books related to historical themes, including *The American Economy in Historical Perspective* (Wadsworth, 1976) and, with Lowell Gallaway, *Out of Work: Unemployment and Government in Twentieth-Century America* (New York University Press, 1993).

ABOUT THE EDITORS

Neal P. McCluskey is director of the Cato Institute's Center for Educational Freedom. He is the author of the book *The Feds in the Classroom: How Big Government Corrupts, Cripples, and Compromises American Education* (Rowman & Littlefield, 2007) and is coeditor of *Educational Freedom: Remembering Andrew Coulson, Debating His Ideas* (Cato Institute, 2017). He also maintains Cato's Public Schooling Battle Map, an interactive database of values- and identity-based conflicts in public schools. His writings have appeared in such publications as the *Wall Street Journal*, the *Washington Post*, and *Forbes*. McCluskey holds a BA from Georgetown University, where he double majored in government and English; has an MA in political science from Rutgers University, Newark; and holds a PhD in public policy from George Mason University.

Todd J. Zywicki is George Mason University Foundation Professor of Law at the Antonin Scalia Law School at George Mason University and former executive director of the George Mason Law and Economics Center. He is also a senior fellow at the Cato Institute, a senior scholar of the Mercatus Center at George Mason University, and a senior fellow of the F. A. Hayek Program for the Advanced Study of Politics, Philosophy, and Economics. He received his JD from the University of Virginia, where he was executive editor of the *Virginia Tax Review* and the John M. Olin Scholar in Law and Economics. Zywicki also received an MA in economics from Clemson University and a BA cum laude, with high honors in his major, from Dartmouth College. He currently serves on the Board of Trustees of the Center for Excellence in Higher Education, is Trustee Emeritus of Dartmouth College, and is a former trustee of Yorktown University.

Founded in 1977, the Cato Institute is a public policy research foundation dedicated to broadening the parameters of policy debate to allow consideration of more options that are consistent with the principles of limited government, individual liberty, and peace. To that end, the Institute strives to achieve greater involvement of the intelligent, concerned lay public in questions of policy and the proper role of government.

The Institute is named for *Cato's Letters*, libertarian pamphlets that were widely read in the American Colonies in the early 18th century and played a major role in laying the philosophical foundation for the American Revolution.

Despite the achievement of the nation's Founders, today virtually no aspect of life is free from government encroachment. A pervasive intolerance for individual rights is shown by government's arbitrary intrusions into private economic transactions and its disregard for civil liberties. And while freedom around the globe has notably increased in the past several decades, many countries have moved in the opposite direction, and most governments still do not respect or safeguard the wide range of civil and economic liberties.

To address those issues, the Cato Institute undertakes an extensive publications program on the complete spectrum of policy issues. Books, monographs, and shorter studies are commissioned to examine the federal budget, Social Security, regulation, military spending, international trade, and myriad other issues. Major policy conferences are held throughout the year, from which papers are published thrice yearly in the *Cato Journal.* The Institute also publishes the quarterly magazine *Regulation.*

In order to maintain its independence, the Cato Institute accepts no government funding. Contributions are received from foundations, corporations, and individuals, and other revenue is generated from the sale of publications. The Institute is a nonprofit, tax-exempt, educational foundation under Section 501(c)3 of the Internal Revenue Code.

CATO INSTITUTE
1000 Massachusetts Ave., N.W.
Washington, D.C. 20001
www.cato.org